China's Financial Markets

An Insider's Guide to How the Markets Work

Editors
Salih N. Neftci
Michelle Yuan Ménager-Xu

AMSTERDAM • BOSTON • HEIDELBERG • LONDON
NEW YORK • OXFORD • PARIS • SAN DIEGO
SAN FRANCISCO • SINGAPORE • SYDNEY • TOKYO

Academic Press is an imprint of Elsevier

Acquisitions Editor: Karen Maloney
Assistant Editor: Dennis McGonagle
Publisher: Duncan Enright
Project Manager: Sarah Hajduk
Marketing Manager: Christian Nolin
Cover Design: Maria Ilardi Design
Composition: Cepha Imaging Pvt. Ltd.
Cover Printer: Phoenix Color
Interior Printer: Sheridan Books

Elsevier Academic Press
30 Corporate Drive, Suite 400, Burlington, MA 01803, USA
525 B Street, Suite 1900, San Diego, California 92101-4495, USA
84 Theobald's Road, London WC1X 8RR, UK

This book is printed on acid-free paper. ♾

The CD-ROM accompanying this book contains English translations of Chinese financial
rules and regulations. Neither the authors nor the Publisher shall be responsible for any
error or variances in the translations. Furthermore, as regulations are always subject to
change, neither the authors nor the Publisher warrant that they are either current or complete.
The materials in the accompanying CD-ROM should not be used as the basis for any decisions
or analysis.

Library of Congress Cataloging-in-Publication Data
APPLICATION SUBMITTED

British Library Cataloguing in Publication Data
A catalogue record for this book is available from the British Library

ISBN 13: 978-0-12-088580-0
ISBN 10: 0-12-088580-8

For all information on all Elsevier Academic Press Publications
visit our Web site at www.books.elsevier.com

Printed in the United States of America
06 07 08 09 10 9 8 7 6 5 4 3 2 1

Working together to grow
libraries in developing countries

www.elsevier.com | www.bookaid.org | www.sabre.org

ELSEVIER   BOOK AID
            International   Sabre Foundation

DEDICATION

To Philippe, for his kind support and understanding over these years.

— Yuan

CONTENTS

PART I
China's Money and Foreign Exchange Markets

Contents

On enclosed CD-ROM: Chinese Financial Regulations (see inside back cover)

Regulation 1—Access of Banking Institutions to National Interbank Lending Market

Regulation 2—Bond Forward Trading on the National Interbank Bond Market

Regulation 3—Financial Bonds on the National Interbank Bond Market

Regulation 4—The Bankcard Industry

Regulation 5—Short-term Financing Bills

Regulation 6—Administration of the Issuance of RMB Bonds

Regulation 7—Administration Rules for Pilot Securitization of Credit Assets

Regulation 8—Lending Interest Rates of Financial Institutions

Regulation 9—Management Guidance for Commercial Bank Mortgages

For updates on regulations and statistical data on the Chinese financial markets, please go to the site: www.ruiji-regis.com

PREFACE

This book on China's financial markets is intended as a manual for market professionals, academics, and researchers. It will be revised and new editions will be published hopefully, every two years.

The book has few, very clear aims. Essentially we wanted to collect in the same source "current" market practices, regulations, and the conventions in major financial markets in China. We did this by asking market professionals to write separate chapters on their market of expertise. The same chapters also give a brief description of the history of how each market has evolved during the last twenty-five years.

The book does not contain much in terms of analysis. We completely left out any statistical work that researchers may attempt on the existing data from Chinese markets. On the other hand, readers may have access to financial time series from China and to the recent regulatory changes in our Web site, www.ruiji-regis.com.

The chapters are written almost in entirety by Chinese market professionals who have worked in that particular sector for significant amounts of time. The contributors are not academics, and their approach is not in the format of an academic journal article. Rather, all chapters describe the players, instruments, and the market conventions. The role of the regulators is introduced and a brief history of each market is included. Chapters generally end with a section on the existing problems and future prospects.

There are several caveats. First, Chinese markets have their own ways of developing and it is not always easy to give the correct perspective. We think that our contributors have done an excellent job on this. Still, the reader should be aware of this issue. Second, China and Chinese markets are in continuous transformation. Some of the practices discussed in this book will quickly, and inevitably, become obsolete as reforms continue. Finally, the data on Chinese markets is not easy to obtain. Most of our tables would stop at annual data for 2005. Some earlier. On the other hand, in terms of market practices and organization, we tried to update the chapters through July 2006.

After the publication we will keep revising many of the tables, figures and the data used in this book. Important reforms and regulatory changes will also be followed closely. These will be incorporated in further editions of this book. However, in the meantime, some of this information can be obtained from our Web site www.ruiji-regis.com.

Salih N. Neftci
Michelle Yuan Ménager-Xu

October 2006

ABOUT THE CONTRIBUTORS

Guan Lin
Mr. Guan joined the life insurance department Charima at the China Insurance Regulation Commission (CIRC) in 2000. He currently focuses on the regulation and development of life and health insurance. He has worked in the actuarial division, product division and the health and pension division of the personal insurance department of CIRC. He has a Master's degree from Peking University and is a Fellow in the Society of Actuaries.

Le Jiachun
Le Jiachun is Senior Editor and Reporter, Shanghai Securities News. As one of the first Chinese financial reporters, Mr. Le has personally witnessed and followed the history of Chinese stock and bond market since their inception in 1991, and so has a deep knowledge of these markets. Mr. Le has published numerous economics papers and news articles. Mr. Le has a PhD in Economics from Fudan University in Shanghai, China.

Le Yan
Le Yan is Deputy General Manager, Bank of China Trading Centre, Shanghai. Mr. Le heads the Bank of China's RMB bond and money market trading and is also in charge of the bank's trading activity in China's domestic precious metal market. Prior to this role, Mr. Le was the head of the Bank of China's treasury business, Shanghai Branch. Before joining the Bank of China in 1990, Mr. Le worked as a foreign exchange dealer in Shanghai and Hong Kong for almost a decade. Mr. Le has a Bachelor of Economics degree from Fudan University and an IMBA from the University of Hong Kong.

Lisheng Liu
Lisheng Liu is Professor and Researcher of Economics and Management at Renmin University of China, Beijing, and Wuhan University, Wuhan. He is

also Officer of the International Cooperative Department in the China Securities Regulatory Commission (CSRC). Well known as a Chinese economist and management specialist, Mr. Liu's work integrates the domains of finance, management, policy, and practice. He has authored more than twenty books, such as New Methods of Utilizing Foreign Capital, Mutual Funds, and Financial Analysis for Listed Companies. Mr. Liu is also a Registered Financial Planner in Hong Kong. He has a PhD from the Ministry of Personnel of the People's Republic of China.

Liu Qiang

Liu Qiang is Professor of Finance, School of Management, University of Electronic Science and Technology of China, Chengdu, China. From 1997 to 2004 Mr. Liu worked in New York at Credit Suisse First Boston and then at Highbridge Capital Management. He is a graduate of the University of Science and Technology of China and has a PhD in Quantum Chemistry from Cornell University.

Mu Xianjie

Mu Xianjie is Director, Golden China Asset Management Co, Ltd, Shanghai. He is also Manager, Shipping Department, China Ocean Shipping Company Group and Commodity Trading Advisor to COFCO Futures Company Ltd and China Nanhua Futures. He holds a bachelor's of science in Economics degree from Shanghai Maritime University, a Master's of Arts degree in International Economic Law, and a Master's of Science degree in Finance from University of Essex, UK.

Tan Wentao

Tan Wentao is a Treasury Dealer in Malayan Banking Berhad, Shanghai Branch. Since 1994, Mr. Tan has worked with Futures Co. Ltd, Shanghai, the largest player in China's futures market. Previously, he spent nine years as Chief Futures Dealer and Investment Manager for a private investment fund deeply involved in China's futures and equities markets. Mr. Tan has a Master's Degree in International Security Investment and Banking from the University of Reading, UK.

Thom Thurston

Thom Thurston is professor of economics at Queens College of the City University of New York (CUNY) and the CUNY Ph.D. Program in Economics, where he is currently Executive Officer. He has published many articles ranging from applied monetary/macroeconomic theory to finance. Mr. Thurston has been an economist at the Federal Reserve Bank of New York, and visiting professor at the Catholic University of Louvain (Belgium) and the University of

Tunis (Tunisia). He has been a frequent speaker at the Zhejiang Conference on WTO and Financial Engineering. He is an honorary professor at the University of Shanghai for Science and Technology — Shanghai Li Gong Da Xue.

Wu Xuchuan

Wu Xuchuan is a researcher and assistant professor at the PBC research center. He obtained his PhD and Master's degrees in Finance from the China Academy of Social Sciences (CASS). He has worked at CBRC since 2003, and is responsible for risk management. Previously, he worked in the real estate research division, at Construction Bank, Beijing.

Zheng Xu

Zheng Xu is the Fund Manager for Yin Hua Fund Management Company, Beijing. She possesses rich experience in the Chinese security industry, with working experience in investment banking, and fixed income analysis. She is also one of the first group of QFII sales traders in China, providing research and trading services for their investments in China's capital markets to QFIIs including Citigroup Global Markets Inc., Goldman Sachs Asset Management, and Nikko Asset Management. Zheng Xu graduated from Renmin University of China, Beijing, and holds a Master's degree in Economics.

ABOUT THE EDITORS

Salih N. Neftci

Professor Neftci completed his PhD at the University of Minnesota. Currently he teaches at the Graduate School, City University of New York, ICMA Centre, University of Reading, UK, and at the University of Lausanne, Switzerland. He is also a Visiting Professor in the Finance Department at Hong Kong University of Science and Technology. He is the head of the FAME Certificate program in Switzerland.

Professor Neftci is known for his books and articles. His books, *An Introduction to the Mathematics of Financial Derivatives* and *Principles of Financial Engineering*, are standard texts in most university derivatives courses. The more recent book, *Principles of Financial Engineering*, was selected as the runner-up for The Book of the Year award by Risk magazine during 2004. His current research deals with pricing of contingent credit lines, the relationship between yield curve curvature and volatility. He is also working on using the Credit Default Swap prices to predict financial crises. Overall, Professor Neftci's research and teaching is in the areas of financial engineering, risk management of extreme events and in emerging market asset trading strategies. His latest papers deal with risk measurement using extreme value theory and volatility dynamics.

Professor Neftci is a consultant to various financial institutions and teaches high-level courses on cutting-edge issues to advanced financial market professionals. He was recently a consultant with the World Bank and with the IFC. He regularly holds highly visible workshops for market professionals on Financial Engineering, Mathematics for Financial Derivatives, and Calibration Methods. Currently he is a Risk Management Advisor to IMF. Professor Neftci is also a regular columnist for CBN daily, a financial daily in Shanghai, the most influential financial newspaper in China. His columns dealing with current financial market activity are regularly quoted on sina.com and on sohu.com.

Michelle Yuan Ménager-Xu

Michelle Yuan Ménager-Xu graduated from the School of Business, University of Lausanne, Switzerland. She holds Master's degrees in both Actuarial Science and in Banking & Finance. Michelle is an associate of the Swiss Actuarial Society, and has worked at various consulting firms and in insurance and reinsurance companies in both Switzerland and China. Previously, she worked at Swiss Reinsurance Company in Zurich, Switzerland, and was in charge of business in the China Region (Mainland, Hong Kong, Taiwan and Macao), including risk management, reserve issues, and various insurance and bank-insurance product pricing. Currently she is writing her Doctoral Thesis at the Institute of Actuarial Science, Lausanne University. Her research focuses on applications of swaption pricing theory to surrender options found in insurance contracts. Her research areas are: risk management, FX market, fixed income, financial engineering and tourism economics. She is a lecturer in finance at GHIE in Switzerland. Meanwhile, she is also Senior Consultant at Ruiji–Regis Consulting, Shanghai.

CHAPTER 1

An Overview of China's Financial Markets

Liu Lisheng
International Cooperation Department, China Securities Regulatory Commission

1.1 OVERVIEW OF CHINA'S FINANCIAL MARKETS

China's securities and futures markets have been developing since the late 1980s, in tandem with market reforms and the liberalization of the national economy. Sizable markets have taken shape with enhanced market infrastructures, a better legal framework, and a unified regulatory system. They have been playing an increasingly important role in the allocation of resources and facilitating economic structuring and growth.

By the end of February 2006, a total of 1,381 companies had been listed on the Shanghai and Shenzhen stock exchanges. The proceeds for both A and B share offerings in the preceding years totaled 912.7 billion yuan. Total market capitalization was 3.3367 trillion yuan, among which 1.0692 trillion yuan were tradable shares. The monthly turnover was 412.9 billion yuan, with an average daily turnover of 214.9 billion yuan.

As of the end of February 2006, there were 114 securities companies and 183 futures brokerage firms in China. The number of securities investment accounts reached 73.61 million, including 36.89 million institutional accounts. The assets managed by institutional investors accounted for 70% of the total market capitalization. There were also 54 fund management companies managing 223 funds with total assets of 474.7 billion yuan. The Social Security Fund can entrust qualified asset management institutions for securities investments on its behalf as well as invest in the securities market on its own.

Insurance funds and corporate annuities are also permitted to invest in the securities market.

A variety of financial products are available in the market, including A shares (common shares denominated in RMB), B shares (domestically listed shares traded in U.S. dollars or H.K. dollars), securities investment funds, treasury bonds, corporate bonds, convertible bonds, commodity futures, ETF, LOF, and warrants. Great importance has been attached to the development of new financial products, and financial innovation has been encouraged.

China now has three commodity futures exchanges, 183 futures brokerage companies, and 12 types of transactions, which include agricultural products such as beans, wheat, and cotton and industrial products such as copper, aluminum, and fuel. In 2005, the trading volume of the futures market amounted to 323 million units, equal to US$13.45 trillion. Currently, the country is preparing to construct a financial futures exchange, and research is also being conducted on financial derivatives, including index futures, bond futures, and the like.

The system of relevant laws and regulations for the Chinese securities and futures markets has basically been established and has been improving gradually. In October of 2005, the National People's Congress approved revisions to the Securities Law and the Corporate Law. Those laws, initially put into effect on January 1, 2006, laid a solid legal foundation for the long-term development of the Chinese securities and futures market and indicate that a new step forward in the construction of a legally based securities market, has been taken.

The first decade of the 21st century is a crucial period for the development of China's securities market. In recent years, the securities market in China has been undergoing adjustments and transformation. On February 1, 2004, China's State Council issued guidelines on promoting reform, opening up, and steady development of China's capital market. The guidelines sum up China's experiences in the capital market and point out the direction for future growth. As a blueprint and a principal document, it is of far-reaching historical significance in ensuring the harmonious, sound, and steady development of China's capital market. The Chinese government has doubled its reform efforts to adopt a series of policies and measures for promoting the reform, opening up, and stable development of the securities market. China's securities market is showing a better situation.

1.2   THE STOCK MARKET

Given the current state of Chinese financial markets, a discussion of equity markets needs to begin with the reform of nontradable shares, which have represented a crucial turning point in Chinese financial markets and equity markets in particular.[1] This has been a major factor behind equity market movements in China since 1999. The problem of nontradable shares in China's securities market is a major historical artefact. Here is how the issue developed.

1.2.1 REFORM OF NONTRADABLE SHARES

Initially, there was neither an explicit ban nor a specific floating arrangement for state-owned shares. A hands-off approach was adopted. Consequently, state-owned shares became nontradable when state-owned enterprises were restructured into joint-stock companies and got listed on stock exchanges. As a result, pre-IPO non-state-owned shares held by legal persons and natural persons also became nontradable. By the end of 2004, nontradable shares of listed companies accounted for 64% of total share capital in the domestic market, with the state owning 74% of all nontradable shares. The negative effect of nontradable shares is obvious.

The CSRC set out a series of basic principles and strategies in order to reform nontradable shares:

1. Relevant government authorities only prescribe basic rules, while the solution for each company is left to itself, assisted by intermediaries and approved via classified voting by its shareholders.
2. Companies with nontradable shares are required to disclose their commitments to the public. In due course, the intensity of reform, the speed of market growth, and the resilience of the market should all be taken into account and be well balanced to achieve the good timing and steady pace of reform.
3. The legitimate interests of investors, especially public investors, should be protected.

On April 29, 2005, a pilot reform program for nontradable shares was launched. Significant progress has been made since. As of May 15, 2006, 919 companies had completed or were engaged in reform, accounting for 68% of 1,344 listed companies, 71% of total market capitalization, and 69% of all share capital. The program gained popularity and received a positive response from investors and listed companies. It appears that when the reform of nontradable shares has progressed sufficiently, there will be no division

---

[1] The problems caused by nontradable shares is considered further in Chapters 7 and 8.

between tradable shares and nontradable shares for new companies seeking IPOs; i.e., all shares can be freely traded in the market.

1.2.2   RESTRUCTURING AND RECAPITALIZATION OF SECURITIES COMPANIES

During the course of developments in China's securities market, securities firms have been playing an important role. Over time they started having problems, such as heavy historical burdens, high liquidity risks, and rigid operational models. Unbalanced corporate governance and the absence of adequate internal control started to drive the securities firms into severe stress.

During 2005, the CSRC started a new campaign to implement a comprehensive program for restructuring securities companies and consolidating the securities industry. The principles governing the restructuring and recapitalizing securities companies were as follows. The CSRC should use favorable conditions in the macro economy and the steady development of the securities market, with the goals of strengthening risk prevention, improving relevant systems, and cracking down on violations and crime. Within two years, the CSRC is expected to make concerted efforts in risk disposition, daily supervision, and the advancement of the securities industry in order to resolve the current risks, prevent new risks, and lay the foundation for the normal, sustainable, and steady development of securities companies.

1.3   THE OPENING UP OF THE SECURITIES INDUSTRY

The opening up of China's securities industry and capital market is consistent with the general trend of economic globalization. Significant effort is being made to open up the securities industry. Toward that end, the following three principles were adopted.

1. The securities industry should be opened in an active, cautious, and progressive manner. This means that the opening up of China's securities markets should be done in line with the pace of China's overall reform.
2. China must take a comprehensive approach and combine opening up with domestic liberalization. This means that the authorities will try to learn from the practices of developed markets but act based on the special features of the Chinese markets.
3. Authorities should try to promote competition and mutual benefits. According to this, the opening up should be reciprocal and mutually beneficial to both overseas and domestic securities institutions.

1.3.1 WTO COMMITMENTS

When China entered into the World Trade Organization (WTO) in December 2001, its commitments on the securities sector were as follows.

- Foreign securities firms may engage directly in B share business (without Chinese intermediaries).
- Representative offices in China of foreign securities firms may become Special Members of Chinese stock exchanges.
- Foreign service suppliers will be permitted to establish joint-venture securities companies and fund management companies.

China made good progress along these lines. As of September 2005, the Shanghai Stock Exchange had 4 special members and 39 foreign firms authorized to trade B shares directly. The corresponding figures for the Shenzhen Stock Exchange were 4 and 19. The China Securities Regulatory Commission (CSRC) has licensed 4 securities companies and 20 fund management companies for foreign shareholding. Before accession to the WTO, there were three joint-venture securities firms in China: China International Capital Co., BOC International Co., and Ever-bright Securities Co.

More importantly, given the nonconvertibility of Chinese currency under capital accounts, China began to implement the qualified foreign institutional investor (QFII) scheme in December 2002 as a transitional measure to attract foreign portfolio investment and partly open up China's capital markets. As of the summer of 2006, 40 foreign institutions had been licensed as QFIIs, with a total investment quota of USD 69 billion, their invested securities assets had reached 48.2 billion yuan, and four foreign banks had been licensed as custodian banks.

The last two additions to the QFII scheme were made on June 18, 2006. China's foreign exchange regulator gave permission for two more foreign institutions to invest a total of up to $250 million in the Chinese securities markets.[2] This means that as of June 2006, foreign institutions had permission to invest a total of up to $7.145 billion in China's securities markets under the qualified foreign institutional investor scheme.

The operation of the QFII pilot program has been quite successful in helping to improve the structure of securities investors. It appears that authorities will continue to increase the quota gradually to attract more long-term foreign funds into China's securities market. The operation of the QFII scheme has gone beyond WTO commitments.

---

[2] Canada's Bank of Nova Scotia obtained an investment quota of $150 million and KBC Financial Products UK Ltd. secured a quota of $100 million.

1.3.2 OVERSEAS LISTINGS

The Chinese government supported eligible enterprises to list overseas to better support their participating in international competition. As of the end of February 2006, a total of 125 Chinese companies had listed H shares on the Hong Kong and overseas stock exchanges, raising US$55.907 billion.[3] Among the 123 Hong Kong–listed shares, 10 were listed in both Hong Kong and New York, four were listed in both Hong Kong and London, and one was listed in Hong Kong, New York, and London. Two were listed solely in Singapore. At the time of this writing, 31 of these H share companies had also issued and listed A shares domestically.

The "Opinions on Issues Concerning Foreign Investment in Listed Companies" specifies that eligible foreign-invested enterprises can issue and list A shares in China. As of the summer of 2006, a number of foreign-invested enterprises have done so.

In November 2002, the CSRC promulgated the "Notice" on Issues Concerning the Transfer of State-Owned Shares and Legal-Entity Shares in Listed Companies to Foreign Investors, which sets forth the policies and procedures on the transfer of state-owned shares and legal-entity shares in listed companies to foreign investors. By the end of 2005 there had been 26 such transfers.

On December 31, 2005, the "Administrative Measures on Foreign Investors' Strategic Investments in Listed Companies" was jointly issued by the Chinese Ministry of Commerce, the CSRC, the State Tax Administration, the State Administration for Industry and Commerce, and the State Administration for Foreign Exchange. Accordingly, foreign investors can now hold strategic M&A investments in either listed companies that have finalized nontradable share reform or newly listed postreform companies. Through medium- and long-term investments, they can hold a significant stake in A share companies, which can be no less than 10% of the listed company shares and which cannot be transferred for 3 years. The explosion of M&A activity in Asia during 2006 was to a large extent due to these measures.

Provided that domestic enterprises can get a license for overseas futures business issued by the Chinese State Council, they can trade futures in overseas markets for hedging risk. As of June 2006, 31 domestic enterprises had qualified for this license. These enterprises can choose overseas brokerage companies and exchanges according to certain regulated conditions, but the trading variety must be approved by the Chinese Commerce Department.

---

[3]For further details on H shares, see Section III.

1.4 SECURITIES OFFERINGS

Chinese IPO activity dramatically increased during 2006 after a dormant period of two years. The nontradable-share reform played a role in this. But just as important were reforms introduced concerning share offerings.

Before the Security Law was promulgated in 1999, the system for review and approval was the required process for public offering. On December 28, 2003, the CSRC issued the "Interim Measures on the System Sponsoring for Public Securities Offerings," which defines the sponsors' responsibilities in the course of public offerings. These rules also provide details on registering the sponsoring institutions and on their representatives, the working procedures, and the coordination, regulation, and legal liabilities of sponsors.

The following procedures for review and approval were adopted by the CSRC:

- The issuers are required to make public their application documents after being accepted by the CSRC.
- The CSRC's Department for Supervising Public Offerings will conduct preliminary reviews of the application documents.
- The application documents are subject to the review and examination of the Public Offering Review Committee,[4] which comprises both the CSRC staff and external experts. The Review Committee members vote by majority when recommending to the CSRC for a public offering.
- Taking into consideration the recommendation of the Review Committee, the CSRC finally decides whether or not to approve a public offering.

The current pricing mechanism for a public offering is market oriented. Developed from fixed pricing, P/E ratio–based pricing, and controlled P/E ratio–based pricing, the Inquiry Pricing System was introduced on a trial basis on January 1, 2005. This is in essence a book-building pricing system, which generally involves two stages. In the first stage, the issuer and its sponsor propose an initial price range to solicit offers from institutional investors.[5] After receiving first-round feedback, the issuer and the lead underwriter adjust the price range and offer it to the institutional investors for a second round of feedback, which sets the final price of the offering.

---

[4] The Public Offering Review Committee is composed of 25 members. Five of them are the CSRC staff, and the rest are non-CSRC experts. The tenure of a committee member is one year, and consecutive tenures shall be no more than three terms. Some of them are full-time members.

[5] This comprises the securities investment fund management companies, securities firms, trust and investment firms, financial companies, insurance companies, and QFIIs.

1.4.1 THE A SHARE MARKET

A shares are the common shares issued by incorporated companies and registered in Mainland China and traded by domestic entities or retail investors (excluding investors from Taiwan, Hong Kong, and Macau) in Chinese currency. A company applying for a public offering of A shares has to submit its application to the CSRC and meet the requirements stipulated in the Company Law, the Securities Law, the Provisional Regulations on the Issuing and Trading of Stocks, and other relevant laws and regulations.

To this end the following objectives were adopted:

- Introduce stricter standards in corporate governance and financing. High-quality companies are given priority to finance in the A share market.
- Support the development of growing and innovative enterprises. This promotes the construction of a multilayered capital market.
- Increase the responsibilities of recommenders, and ask the agencies to take responsibility for the authenticity, accuracy, and integrity of all documents they issue.
- Increase the transparency of listed companies.

Along these lines, as of January 1, 2007, listed companies will begin to implement new accounting standards in accordance with the international accounting standard.

Public issuance will happen in three situations. The first is to *initiate* a joint-stock limited company via public issuance of stocks for financing. The promoter holds a significant portion of the shares, while the rest are offered to the public. Such a public offering has to meet a number of requirements as prescribed in the Company Law. There shall be no less than 2 but no more than 200 promoters. Of these, half or more should have offices in China. And the shares held by the promoters should be no less than 35% of the total shares.

The second situation is to conduct an IPO *after* the establishment of the company. According to Article 13 of the Securities Law, an IPO of a company should meet a number of requirements, including the following:

- Have a complete and well-functioning organizational structure.
- Be capable of making profits continuously in sound financial conditions.
- Have no record of false financial statements for the previous 3 years and no record of other wrongdoings.

By the end of 2005, listed companies in China had issued a total of 596.6 billion A shares, raising a total of RMB858.9 billion. Figure 1.1 summarizes the capital raised from the A share market in 1991–2005. In fact, since April 2005, IPOs and other offerings for listed companies have been suspended. As a result, only 15 companies went through IPO during 2005, raising about

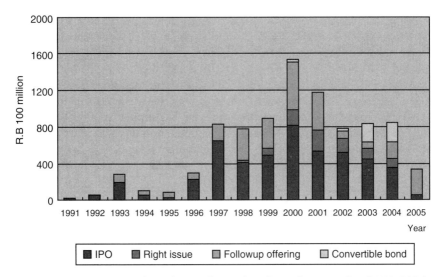

FIGURE 1.1 Summary of Total Capital Raised in the A Shares Market (1991–2005). *Source: "China's Securities and Futures Markets,"* the CSRC.

RMB5.7 billion yuan. In addition, two companies made rights issue, raising RMB260 million yuan, and another five companies made follow-on offerings, raising RMB27.9 billion yuan.

1.4.2 THE B SHARE MARKET

B shares are denominated in renminbi, but they are offered and traded in foreign currencies. The inception of B shares marks the first step in the internationalization of China's capital markets. Before February 2001, investors in B shares were limited to foreign natural persons, juridical persons, other foreign institutions, and Chinese citizens residing in foreign countries. On February 19, 2001, the government opened the B share market to domestic citizens and allowed domestic citizens to open B share accounts, using their own foreign currencies, and to trade B shares.

At the end of 1999, the first B stock, issued by the Shanghai Vacuum Electron Devices Co., went public. Since 1992, B shares have been issued and traded on both the Shanghai (in U.S. dollars) and Shenzhen (in H.K. dollars) stock exchanges. At the end of 2005, there were 109 B stocks and the total number of B stocks issued amounted to 19.701 billion shares, with a total market value of 7.4622 trillion yuan. China has also explored equity-linked structures for B shares. For example, Shenzhen Southern Glass Co. issued B share convertible bonds in 1995. Four companies in Shanghai or Shenzhen have converted their B stocks to Level I ADR to be traded in the U.S. over-the-counter market.

According to the Company Law, the Securities Law, the Provisional Regulations on Issuing and Trading of Stocks, and the State Council Rules Regarding the Domestic Listing of Foreign-Owned Shares, B share issuers should meet the following requirements:

- The capital raised by issuing B shares shall be used in a manner consistent with state industrial policy.
- They must comply with regulations regarding fixed-asset investments.
- They must comply with regulations on foreign investments.
- The promoters must hold at least 35% of the issued shares at the time the company is set up.
- The capital contributions should be no less than RMB150 million.
- The company must float at least 25% of the company's total shares.
- Should a company's total share capital exceed RMB400 million yuan, the public floating requirement may be reduced to no less than 15% of its total shares.
- Neither (a) any predecessor entity (entities) of which the joint-stock company is a part nor (b) any major promoter that is a state-owned enterprise should have committed any significant violations of the law over the preceding three years.

At the end of 2005, 109 companies had issued a total of 19.466 billion B shares, raising RMB38.1 billion yuan. Additional data are shown in Table 1.1.

TABLE 1.1   Summary of the B Share Market (2000–2005)

	2000	2001	2002	2003	2004	2005
Number of B share companies	114	112	111	111	110	109
Market cap. of B share companies (RMB100 million yuan)	635.19	1,276.65	802.57	937.23	746.22	619.73
Market cap. of tradable B shares (RMB100 million yuan)	563.31	1,118.28	765.81	872.60	690.17	602.08
Trading volume of B shares (100 million shares)	200.36	688.88	156.70	170.80	154.82	152.86
Turnover of B shares (RMB100 million yuan)	547.97	5,063.13	848.42	845.30	642.64	564.94

Source: Shanghai and Shenzhen Stock Exchanges.

1.5   THE BOND MARKET

A multitier trading market for bonds has taken shape in China. This includes the exchange bond market, the interbank bond market, and the OTC market. On July 1981, the issuance of *treasury bonds* (T-bonds) resumed in China; six years later, a secondary market for T-bonds was established. The bond market grew rapidly thereafter. In 1984, corporate bonds were issued.

In 2005, the total issuance of bonds reached RMB704.2 billion yuan, a significant increase over the RMB4.9 billion yuan in 1981. Apart from T-bonds, there are also *corporate bonds*, *financing bonds*, *convertible bonds*, and *short-term corporate notes*. In 2005, the turnover of exchange-traded bonds reached RMB2.8367 trillion yuan.[6]

Treasury bonds and Central Bank bills are discussed in detail in Chapters 5 and 6. Next we give some comments concerning convertible bonds and bonds issued by securities companies.

1.5.1   CONVERTIBLE BONDS

Convertible bonds refer to corporate bonds that can be converted into common stock under certain preagreed conditions. The issuance of convertible bonds should meet the requirements for a new public offering as prescribed in Article 13 of the Securities Law, plus the following requirements regarding corporate bonds in Article 16:

- The net assets of a joint-stock limited company should be no less than RMB30 million yuan, and the net assets of a limited-liability company should be no less than RMB60 million yuan.
- The accumulated outstanding bonds should constitute no more than 40% of the net assets of a company.
- The average annual distributable profits for the previous 3 years should be sufficient to pay 1 year of interest on the bonds.
- The funds raised should be invested in a manner consistent with state industrial policies.
- The coupon of the bonds should not exceed the interest rate range set by the State Council.

---

[6] As of June 2006, the issuance of bonds such as T-bonds, financial bonds, and corporate bonds is subject to the approval of government authorities other than the CSRC. The issuance of convertible bonds and bonds of securities companies is subject to the approval of the CSRC and shall meet certain requirements.

1.5.2   BONDS ISSUED BY SECURITIES COMPANIES

This type of bond is issued by securities companies that agree to redeem both principal and interest within a certain period of time. Such bonds can be issued to the public or to qualified investors via private placement. The issuance of bonds by securities companies is subject to CSRC review and approval. Securities companies can also issue short-term financial notes, which can be traded only on the interbank bond market.

1.6   SECURITIES EXCHANGES

Originally only the Shanghai and Shenzhen security exchanges were established. Subsequently, local governments also set up 29 securities exchange centers and 41 OTC markets. The ministries and commissions of the State Council established STAQ and NET systems for trading legal-person shares.

At the end of 1997, the government reformed the OTC markets and closed 29 security exchange markets and 41 illegal stock exchange locations. On September 27, 1999, the stocks listed on STAQ and NET ceased to trade. Since then, a new pattern has emerged. The Shanghai and Shenzhen exchanges coexist and develop together; stock trading is concentrated mainly in the stock exchanges.

To accommodate the variety of demands for investment and finance, the construction of the legal and multilayered securities market is being explored actively. On June 19, 2001, with the approval of the CSRC, the Securities Association of China (SAC) issued Provisional Measures on Agency Share Transfer Services (ASTS) for Securities. The ASTS is an independent system by which securities companies provide share transfer services for nonlisted joint-stock companies. At the beginning, the companies listed in the ASTS were those in NET and STAT. The first company in the ASTS was quoted on July 16, 2001, and share transfer for delisted companies was introduced into the ASTS on August 29, 2002.[7]

By the end of 2005, market capitalization of China's stock market had reached RMB3.243 trillion yuan, equivalent to 17.79% of China's GDP.

---

[7]On May 27, 2004, the Small and Medium Enterprises Segment was launched on the Shenzhen Securities Exchange with the approval of the State Council. This observes the same laws and regulations and IPO eligibility criteria as other segments of the main board. The SME Segment provides a direct financing platform for high-tech or rapidly growing small and medium enterprises with prominent competitive core businesses. The SME Segment implements comparative independent management, including independent operation, independent supervision, independent code, and independent index.

Market capitalization for tradable shares amounted to RMB1.0631 trillion yuan, roughly 5.83% of GDP. In 2005, the total trading volume of the stock secondary market reached 624 billion shares, worth 3.1663 trillion yuan.

The turnover of exchange-traded bonds was valued at RMB2.800 trillion yuan, of which the turnover of T-bonds, corporate bonds, and convertible bonds accounted for 94.1%, 4.3%, and 1.6%, respectively. The turnover of bond repos accounted for more than 88% of total bond turnover.[8]

1.6.1   LISTING OF SECURITIES

According to Article 39 of the Securities Law, publicly issued stocks, corporate bonds, or other securities shall be listed on a stock exchange or other securities marketplace as approved by the State Council. A listing application shall be filed with a stock exchange for its review and approval.

A joint stock limited company applying for a listing of securities shall meet the following requirements:

- The stocks have been publicly issued upon the approval of the CSRC.
- Its total share capital shall be no less than RMB30 million yuan.
- Publicly issued shares shall exceed 25% of the total shares; where total share capital exceeds RMB400 million yuan, the publicly issued shares shall be no less than 10% thereof.
- The company shall commit no material violations of law or issue false financial statements during the preceding three years.

A listing agreement shall be signed by an exchange and a listing applicant, to cover mainly the code of conduct for the listed company, listing fees, suspending or terminating the listing, services provided by the exchange, etc. In other words, such an agreement sets forth and governs the relations between the listed company and the exchange.

A company applying for a listing of corporate bonds shall meet the following requirements:

- The maturity of the corporate bonds shall be more than 1 year.
- The actual issuance shall be no less than RMB50 million yuan.
- Issuing requirements will be met.

The listing of convertible bonds, in addition to the foregoing requirements, shall also meet the requirements for the public offering of stocks.

---

[8]Bond repo markets are dealt with in Chapter 5.

1.6.2 TRADING OF SECURITIES

A centralized bidding method, block trading, and agreement transfer were adopted by the Chinese securities secondary market. The *centralized bidding method* refers to simultaneous offering of bid or ask prices. The minimum ask price and the maximum bid price are matched to make the deal. The orders are sent to the central electronic auction system through computer terminals. The opening price of the market is determined by the aggregate auction. The securities trading system is based on the principle of price and time precedence to match the biding and asking orders directly. The centralized bidding method is the main trading method in today's Chinese securities market.

Block trading is introduced for large-volume stock transactions. In China, large-volume transactions can include stocks, bonds, funds, and bond repurchase agreements listed on exchanges. After finishing the block trade, the trading volume will be included in the turnover of the corresponding stock.

Agreement transfer refers to one party's transferring his shares to another by agreement and not through auction or bidding. Agreement transfer is used in the acquisition of public companies and significant reconstruction. It is also a main exchange method in the reform of a split-share structure.

1.6.3 THE PARTICIPANTS

The participants in the secondary market consist mainly of securities companies, insurance companies, securities investment funds, trust companies, and other, nonfinancial institutional investors and individual investors.

Investors purchase or sell securities through the brokerage of securities companies. The commissions[9] paid to securities companies can be no higher than 0.3% of the trading value (but no lower than the total amount of the trading regulatory fee and the charges by the stock exchanges). Furthermore, according to the prevailing taxation law, both buyers and sellers are levied a stamp duty of 0.1% of the trading value.

As of June 2006, except for *specially treated shares*,[10] which are subject to the daily price limit of ±5%, all other shares are subject to the daily price limit of ±10%.

---

[9]For any trading value (of A shares or securities investment funds) less than RMB5 yuan, the minimum commission is RMB5 yuan. For a trading value of less than US$1 or HK$5 (of B shares), the minimum commission is US$1 or HK$5.

[10]These are shares of listed companies with poor financial or operating conditions that require special treatments.

1.6.4 REGISTRATION

The registration and clearing of securities is centralized through the China Securities Depository and Clearing Corporation Ltd. (CSDCC). Before trading on a stock exchange, an investor must place all the securities (fully dematerialized) into an account opened with the CSDCC.

Currently, the settlement for A shares is $T + 1$ and the settlement for B shares is $T + 3$.

1.7 LISTED COMPANIES

The number of domestically listed companies has been growing quite rapidly in China. In 1990 there were only 10 listed companies. By the end of 2005, the number had reached 1,381. Out of this total, 1,240 companies had issued A shares only, 23 companies had issued B shares only, 86 companies were issuing both A shares and B shares, and 32 companies were issuing both A and H shares (see Table 1.2 and Figure 1.2). The share capital of domestically listed companies is mostly between RMB100 million and RMB1 billion yuan, with only 108 listed companies owning more than RMB1 billion yuan of share capital.

Listed companies are located in different parts of China and across various industrial sectors, mainly machinery, metallurgy, chemicals, electronics, infrastructure, transportation, and energy.

By the end of 2005, the total number of shares of listed companies had reached 762.95 billion. The number of tradable shares was 291.5 billion, accounting for 38.2% of the total shares of listed companies.

TABLE 1.2 Number of Listed Companies (1998–2005)

	1998	1999	2000	2001	2002	2003	2004	2005
Issuing A shares only	727	822	955	1,025	1,085	1,146	1,237	1,240
Issuing A and H shares	18	19	19	23	28	30	30	32
Issuing A and B shares	80	82	86	88	87	87	86	86
Issuing B shares only	26	26	28	24	24	24	24	23
Total	851	949	1,088	1,160	1,224	1,287	1,377	1,381

Source: "China's Securities and Futures Markets," the CSRC.

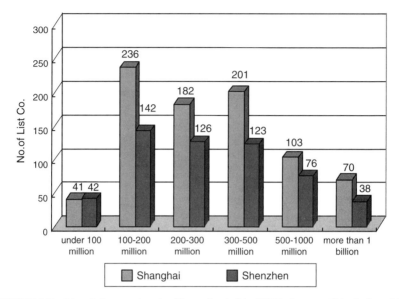

FIGURE 1.2   Listed Companies, by Share Capital in 2005. *Source: China's Securities and Futures Markets*, the CSRC.

1.7.1   OVERSEAS LISTED COMPANIES

In 1993, the Chinese government initiated a trial program that encouraged domestic companies to go public overseas. On July 15, 1993, Tsingtao Brewery Co. Ltd. was listed in Hong Kong, which marked the first overseas listing by a Chinese enterprise.

As of the end of 2005, a total of 122 domestic companies had issued shares overseas, raising a total of US$55.54 billion (see Figure 1.3). Of this total, 103 were listed only on the Hong Kong Exchanges and Clearing Ltd. (including 40 stocks at GEM); 12 were listed in both Hong Kong and New York; four were listed in both Hong Kong and London; one was listed in Hong Kong, New York, and London; and two were listed solely in Singapore. Figure 1.4 shows the equity structure of overseas listed companies as of the end of 2005. There were 83 red chip stock companies[11] listed on the Hong Kong Exchanges, and they have raised about 52.36 billion yuan in capital. Previously the overseas listed companies had been primarily large state enterprises that were critical to the national economy and attracted attention from foreign investors.

---

[11] These are Chinese-holding companies registering overseas, listing on Hong Kong, and operating business and managing assets in Mainland China.

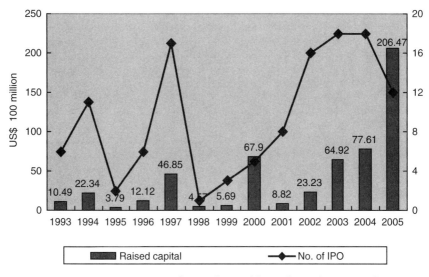

FIGURE 1.3 Summary of Capital Raised by H Shares (1993–2005).

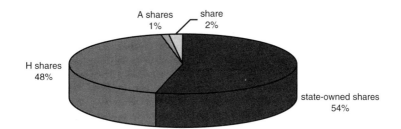

FIGURE 1.4 Equity Structure of Companies Issuing H Shares (as of December 2005).
Source: China's Securities and Futures Markets, the CSRC.

Where a domestic enterprise directly or indirectly issues or lists any securities abroad, it is subject to CSRC approval, according to Article 238 of the Securities Law. After restructuring into joint-stock companies, all state-owned companies, collectively owned companies, and enterprises of other ownership that have met the specific requirements are entitled to apply for overseas listing.

Recently, with the increasing overseas listing of small and medium-sized enterprises (SMEs), particularly privately owned enterprises, these companies have exhibited truly diversified ownership structures and industrial sectors with a higher degree of transparency and compliance. These companies have not only raised a significant amount of capital, but also optimized their capital structure and corporate governance.

1.8   SECURITIES COMPANIES

Securities companies are the leading intermediaries in China's capital market. By the end of 2005, there were 116 securities companies, with 3,090 retail branches nationwide, under the supervision of the CSRC.

A securities company applies to the CSRC for a license, provided it meets the following requirements:

- Its major shareholders have the ability to make profits continuously, have a good reputation, and have committed no major violation of laws or wrongdoings over the preceding 3 years, with a net asset of no less than RMB200 million yuan.
- Its registered capital satisfies the provisions of the Securities Law.
- It has a sound risk-control system as well as an internal control system.
- It meets all other requirements as prescribed by laws and regulations as well as by the CSRC.

A securities company may undertake some or all of the following businesses upon the approval of the CSRC:

1. Securities brokerage
2. Securities investment consultation
3. Financial advising relating to securities trading or securities investment
4. Underwriting and sponsorship of securities
5. Securities proprietary trading
6. Securities asset management

If a securities company engages in any of the business operations listed in item 1, 2, or 3, its registered capital cannot be less than RMB50 million yuan. Where a securities company engages in any of the business operations listed in item 4, 5, or 6, its bottom-line registered (paid-in) capital should be RMB100 million yuan. Where a securities company engages in two or more of the business operations listed in item 4, 5, or 6, its minimum registered (paid-in) capital should be RMB500 million yuan.

As prescribed by the Securities Law, the CSRC shall formulate provisions on the risk-control indicators of a securities company, such as net capital, the ratio between net capital and liabilities, the ratio between net capital and net assets, the ratio between net capital and proprietary trading, underwriting, and asset management, the ratio between liabilities and net assets, as well as the ratio between current assets and current liabilities. A securities company shall establish an internal control system and build up effective Chinese walls so as to prevent any conflict of interest between the company and its clients or between different clients. It shall segregate its securities operations on brokerage, underwriting, proprietary trading, and asset management.

The clients' trading settlement funds of a securities company shall be deposited in a commercial bank and managed through separate accounts under the clients' names. A securities company shall by no means commingle any settlement funds or securities of its clients with its own assets. Meanwhile, any entity or individual is prohibited from misusing the funds or securities of its/his clients in any form. Where a securities company is under bankruptcy or liquidation procedures, the settlement funds or securities of its client shall not be defined as its insolvent assets or liquidation assets. Unless for paying the liabilities of its clients or prescribed by law, the funds or securities of its clients shall not be sealed up, frozen, deducted, or enforced compulsorily. A securities company shall not provide any financing or guaranty for its shareholders or any related person.

During the second half of 2004, the CSRC launched an important reform to consolidate all securities companies for compliant operations. The campaign was estimated to last about 2 years. Its major tasks include conducting an in-depth evaluation of corporate risks and structural reforms, tightening supervision over senior management and shareholders, pressing forward with differentiated regulation over securities firms, and optimizing the industrial structure. As a result, the financial conditions of many securities companies have improved somewhat.

1.9   SECURITIES DEPOSITORIES AND CLEARING

The establishment of a securities depository and clearing institution is also subject to the approval of the CSRC. Prior to 2001, securities depository and clearing business were operated by the security exchanges themselves. The business scale of securities depositories and clearing has since been expanded. Such system functions as opening accounts on a real-time basis, electronic clearing for securities and cash, and electronic management for business documents have improved gradually.

In March 2001, the China Securities Depository and Clearing Corporation Ltd. (CSDCC), the only institution of its kind in China, was established. Starting on October 1, 2001, the CSDCC took charge of all the depositing and clearing of listed securities, which marked the establishment of a unified securities depository and clearing system, subject to the CSRC's supervision. The general manager, who reports to the board of directors, is responsible for corporate operations. Headquartered in Beijing, the CSDCC has two subsidiaries, in Shanghai and Shenzhen.

In addition, the CSDCC is responsible for the depositing and clearing of other exchange-listed instruments as well as open-ended funds. Its business scope covers the opening and managing of securities accounts and settlement fund accounts, securities registration and transfer, securities depository, securities/ payment clearing and delivery, acting as the agent for securities interests distribution, Internet information services, and any other businesses approved by the CSRC. At present, the settlement is $T + 1$ for A shares and $T + 3$ for B shares.

1.9.1   OTHER SECURITIES TRADING SERVICE INSTITUTIONS

Securities trading service institutions are the entities that provide services to issuers and investors. They can be divided into different groups based on the type of services they provide: securities depository and clearing, investment advice, credit ratings, financial advisory companies, accounting firms, asset appraisal agencies, and law firms. As of the end of 2005, there were 108 securities investment advisers and 70 accounting firms engaging in securities-related businesses. All of these institutions except law firms are licensed by the CSRC for securities-related businesses. Although a law firm does not have to obtain a license from the CSRC for securities services, it is still subject to the CSRC's ongoing supervision and sanctions.

The employees of an investment consulting institution, financial advisory institution, or credit rating agency who engage in securities trading services shall have securities expertise as well as at least 2 years of related work experiences.

An investment consulting institution as well as its practitioners shall be involved in none of the following:

1. Engaging in any securities investment on behalf of its entrusting party.
2. Signing any agreement with any entrusting party on sharing the gains or bearing the loss of securities investments.
3. Purchasing or selling any stock of a listed company for which the consulting institution provides services.
4. Providing or disseminating any false or misleading information to investors through the media or by any other means.
5. Any other act prohibited by any law or regulation.

1.9.2   INSTITUTIONAL INVESTORS

As of the end of 2005, a total of 73.66 million securities investment accounts (including A shares and B shares) had been opened. In recent years, because the number of individual investors in the Chinese securities market has increased greatly, the CSRC has made vigorous efforts to nurture the growth of institutional investors.

1.10 INVESTMENT FUNDS

In recent years, securities investment funds have developed significantly in China and become significant players.[12] At the end of 2005, there were 54 closed-ended and 154 open-ended securities investment funds under the management of 53 fund management companies (including 20 joint ventures). Statistics show that the total net assets of these funds were RMB469.1 billion yuan. The market value of securities they held accounted for 44% and 17%, respectively, of the total tradable share market capitalization in China.

A diversified pool of funds has been put forward over the past few years, covering most fund products available in developed markets. At present, besides equity funds, there are bond funds, index funds, money market funds, umbrella funds, principal-guaranteed funds, exchange-traded funds, and listed open-ended funds.

Fund managers must be approved by the CSRC. According to Article 13 of the Securities Investment Fund Law, the following conditions shall be met in order to establish a fund management company:

- Having a registered capital of no less than RMB100 million yuan.
- Principal shareholders demonstrating a good track record and public reputation in the securities business, securities investment consultation, trust assets management, or other financial assets management, committing no violation of law within the preceding 3 years, and having a registered capital of no less than RMB300 million yuan.
- The number of licensed fund professionals that meets the statutory requirement.

A fund manager will, before its fund placement, submit its application and relevant documents to the CSRC. The fund placement starts within 6 months from the date of receiving the ratification. According to Article 59 of the Securities Investment Fund Law, fund assets cannot be used in the following activities:

1. Underwriting of securities
2. Providing loans or guarantees to others
3. Engaging in investment with unlimited liability
4. Trading other fund units, unless otherwise approved by the State Council

---

[12]Chapter 13 deals with funds in China.

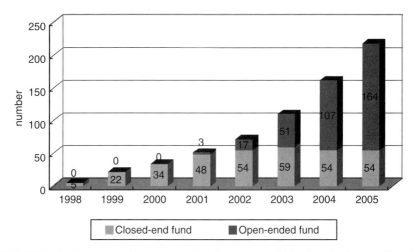

FIGURE 1.5 Summary of Investment Funds Issuance (1998–2005). *Source: China's Securities and Futures Markets*, the CSRC.

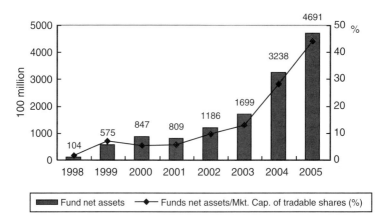

FIGURE 1.6 Net Asset Value and Ratio in Tradable Market Capitalization (1998–2005). *Source: China's Securities and Futures Markets*, the CSRC.

5. Making capital contribution to the fund manager and custodian or trading the stocks or bonds issued by the aforesaid manager and custodian.
6. Trading the securities issued or underwritten by the shareholders controlling the fund manager or custodian or by companies with other significant interests with the aforesaid manager or custodian
7. Insider dealing, market manipulation, or other wrongdoings
8. Other activities prohibited by the CSRC.

Fund custodians should be selected among qualified commercial banks. A custodian needs to be jointly licensed by the CSRC and the China Banking Regulatory Commission (CBRC). A fund custodian and a manager cannot be the same party or invest in each other or cross-hold shares.

1.11 QUALIFIED FOREIGN INSTITUTIONAL INVESTORS (QFIIs)

The QFII scheme introduces the investment strategies and philosophies of developed markets and leads to more effective allocation of resources and more competitiveness and attractiveness for the Chinese securities market.

At the end of 2005, 34 overseas financial institutions had been licensed as QFIIs, with a total investment quota of USD5.6 billion, and 11 banks (including four overseas banks) were licensed as the QFIIs' custodians. As mentioned earlier, the number of licensed QFIIs had risen to 40 by June 2006. The securities assets of the QFIIs amounted to RMB34.7 billion yuan, accounting for 90% of their investment quotas at the end of 2005. Of their investment portfolios, RMB22.3 billion yuan (64%) was invested in A shares, RMB6.0 billion (17%) in funds, RMB2.6 billion (7%) in convertible bonds, and RMB3.7 billion (11%) in treasury bonds.

In order to become a QFII, an applicant should be in sound financial and credit condition, meeting the requirements set by the CSRC on asset size and other indicators. In this respect, the criteria for the scale of assets and other factors are as follows.

1. *For fund management institutions*: having operated a fund business for over 5 years, with the most recent accounting year managing assets of no less than US$10 billion.
2. *For insurance companies*: having operated an insurance business for over 30 years, with paid-in capital of no less than US$1 billion and managing securities assets of no less than US$10 billion in the most recent accounting year.
3. *For securities companies*: having operated a securities business for over 30 years, with paid-in capital of no less than US$1 billion and managing securities assets of no less than US$10 billion in the most recent accounting year.
4. *For commercial banks*: ranking among the top 100 in the world in total assets for the most recent accounting year and managing securities assets of no less than US$10 billion.[13]

---

[13] The CSRC may adjust these requirements subject to developments in the securities market.

There are additional general requirements on QFIIs. Their risk-control indicators should meet the requirements of their home jurisdiction. Their employees should meet the professional qualification requirements of their home jurisdiction. With a sound management and internal control system, the applicants should have a good track record without any substantial penalties having been imposed by their home regulators over the three years prior to application. Finally, their home jurisdiction should have a sound legal and regulatory system, and the securities regulator must have signed a Memorandum of Understanding with the CSRC and maintained an efficient cooperative regulatory relationship.

Based on the approved investment quota, a QFII can invest in A shares, treasuries, convertible bonds, and corporate bonds listed in China's stock exchanges as well as other financial instruments approved by regulators.

1.12   OTHER MAJOR INSTITUTIONAL INVESTORS

1.12.1   NATIONAL SOCIAL SECURITY FUND

The National Social Security Fund (NSSF) is funded by reducing the state's stake in listed companies, by the transfer of capital from the central treasury, and by other capital collected by the central government and approved by the State Council.

The National Council for Social Security Fund (NCSSF), in charge of the NSSF, entrusts fund management companies to invest up to 40% of total assets in funds and stocks. At the end of December 2005, the total net assets of NSSF amounted to approximately RMB192.1 billion, of which the assets entrusted by clients for stock investment reached 20.5 billion yuan, accounting for 13% of foreign investment.

1.12.2   INSURANCE COMPANIES

Insurance assets can be invested in the capital market in two ways: (1) directly purchasing stocks up to 5% of total insurance assets; and (2) buying securities investment funds up to 15% of total insurance assets.

At the end of 2005, total insurance assets had reached approximately RMB1.500 trillion yuan, of which the assets invested in security markets amount to RMB109.9 billion yuan. Insurance funds account for 23.43% of total investment funds and have become the most important institutional investor in fund markets.

1.12.3   CORPORATE ANNUITY FUNDS

A corporate annuity is a type of pension plan voluntarily established by a corporation and its workers. It is an important part of the China Pension Security Scheme and a major legislative component of the "Multiparts" Pension Security Strategy. A Chinese corporate annuity fund is fully cumulative, managed through individual accounts. According to the Provisional Measures on the Administration of Corporate Annuity Funds, these funds may invest up to 30% of total assets in the capital market. At the end of 2005, these funds had approximately RMB50 billion yuan in assets, which is expected to increase rather quickly in the near future.

1.12.4   SECURITIES INVESTOR PROTECTION FUND

The purpose of the Securities Investor Protection Fund (SIPF) is to protect investors' interests and to create confidence among investors trading securities on the exchange. The SIPF was launched in the second half of 2005 with a paid-in capital of RMB6.3 billion yuan. Corporation Limited (SIPFC) was established to initiate, manage, and develop the SIPF. The board of the SIPFC consists of nine directors, and the chairman is recommended by the CSRC, subject to the approval of the State Council.

SIPF revenues come primarily from five sources: (1) 20% of the transaction fees submitted by the Shanghai and Shenzhen stock exchanges when their risk reserves reach the stipulated upper limits; (2) 0.5–5% of operating revenues of securities companies; (3) interest income from the "locked" funds offering stocks or convertible bonds; (4) proceeds from the compensation of liable parties and the liquidation of securities companies; (5) donations of domestic and foreign institutions, organizations, and individuals as well as other legitimate income.

When security companies are revoked, liquidated, and closed down or taken over administratively by the CSRC, the CSRC will work out risk-disposal plans based on the nature of the risk. Then the SIPFC formulates the implementation plan and executes it accordingly upon the approval of the State Council. After compensating the creditors of securities companies, the SIPFC obtains corresponding claims and the right to participate in the liquidation of the securities companies. The SIPF can only be invested on bank deposits, treasury bonds,

Central Bank bonds (including Central Bank notes), financial bonds issued by central financial institutions, and other means approved by the State Council.

1.13   STOCK EXCHANGES

At present, there are two stock exchanges in China—the Shanghai and Shenzhen stock exchanges—both under the supervision of the CSRC. Each stock exchange has a general assembly of members and a board of governors. The former is the highest authority, while the board of governors is the executive body, with a chairman and a vice chairman nominated by the CSRC subject to election by the board. In addition, the president of each exchange is appointed by the CSRC.

1.13.1   SHANGHAI STOCK EXCHANGE (ShSE)

The Shanghai Stock Exchange (ShSE) was founded on November 26, 1990. As of December 2005, a total of 834 companies with 878 equities were listed at the ShSE, and the total market capitalization amounted to RMB2.310 trillion. The ShSE had 156 members, including 137 domestic securities firms or their equivalent, 15 other domestic companies concurrently providing certain securities services, and 4 overseas special members. In addition, special B share trading seats had been granted to 39 overseas securities companies.

1.13.2   SHENZHEN STOCK EXCHANGE (SzSE)

The Shenzhen Stock Exchange (SzSE) was established on December 1, 1990, as a nonprofit membership institution. On May 27, 2004, the Small and Medium-sized Enterprises (SME) Segment was launched at the SzSE, which observes the same IPO criteria as other segments of the main board. The SME Segment provides a direct financing platform for high-tech or rapidly growing small and medium-sized enterprises with competitive core businesses.

As of the end of 2005, a total of 544 companies with 586 equities were listed on the SzSE, including 50 companies listed in the SME Segment; total market capitalization reached RMB933 billion. Among its 177 members were 141 domestic securities firms or equivalent, 32 domestic companies concurrently providing certain securities services, and 4 overseas special members. Additionally, 19 overseas securities companies had special B share trading seats at the SzSE.

1.14   FUTURES MARKETS

China's commodities futures market started almost simultaneously with the stock market. At the time, for lack of relevant laws and regulations and an administrative department, the commodities market experienced a phase of blind development. In 1994, the CSRC was mandated to consolidate the whole market. Today, the market has three exchanges (the Shanghai Futures Exchange, the Zhengzhou Commodity Exchange, and the Dalian Commodity Exchange) and 183 brokerage firms, compared with 50 exchanges and 1,000 brokerage firms at the peak period of 1994. The number of traded products has decreased from 35 to 12.

In 2001, the Chinese government decided to develop futures markets further. A recovering growth in turnover and trading volume was recorded. In 2005, total trading volume and turnover reached 323 million lots (a year-on-year increase of 5.63%) and RMB13.45 trillion (a decrease of 8.48%).

The variety of listed futures increased during 2004, which attracted attention from domestic and overseas markets. Both the Zhengzhou Commodity Exchange (ZCE) and the Dalian Commodity Exchange (DCE) trade contracts on agricultural products, such as wheat, cotton, corn, soybeans, mung beans, bean oil, and sugar, while the Shanghai Futures Exchange (SHFE) provides futures contracts on other commodities, such as copper, aluminum, rubber, and fuel oil.

The authorities are accelerating the construction of financial futures exchanges and are preparing to introduce financial derivatives such as stock index futures into the market as occasion offers. Figure 1.7 shows the trading statistics for futures products in 2005.

On August 18, 2006, China announced appointments for the financial derivatives exchange and securities watchdog, paving the way for the exchange's formal launch. This included the appointment of the new Shanghai Financial Derivatives Exchange. The derivatives exchange had not been formally launched as of August 2006. However, it will be located in Shanghai and owned by China's three futures exchanges and two stock exchanges. It was expected to offer its first product, stock index futures, during late 2006 or early 2007. Further financial derivative products, including bond index and currency futures, will be introduced later.

1.14.1   FUTURES BROKERAGE COMPANIES

By the end of 2005, 183 futures brokerage companies were operating in China. Futures brokerage companies are legal intermediaries in the futures market that

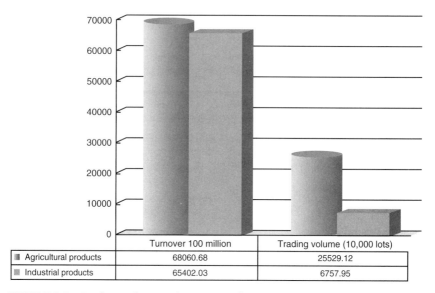

	Turnover 100 million	Trading volume (10,000 lots)
Agricultural products	68060.68	25529.12
Industrial products	65402.03	6757.95

FIGURE 1.7 Trading Volume and Turnover of Futures (1993–2005). *Source: China's Securities and Futures Markets*, the CSRC.

are entrusted by their clients with conducting futures trading in the name of the companies, for which they ask commissions from clients. Futures brokerage companies are intermediaries between investors and the futures exchange. Their functions include trading futures contracts for their clients, conducting the self-operating futures business, transacting the clearing procedure, providing futures market information for clients, and acting as trading advisors for customers.

According to regulations issued by the Chinese government, the CSRC implements a license system to manage futures brokerage companies. Besides the relevant provisions in the Company Law, an applicant must meet the following conditions: (1) registered capital of no less than RMB30 million; (2) senior executives and main employees who are qualified professionals in the futures business; (3) an immobile business venue and sufficient trading facilities; (4) a well-established management system; (5) any other conditions stipulated by the CSRC. Futures brokerage companies can, based on their business needs, apply to the CSRC to establish their branches/subsidiaries.

In China, the relevant provisions regarding the behavior of futures brokerage companies include mainly the following: (1) The futures brokerage companies shall, in accordance with the trading instructions of clients, conduct the futures trading. The futures brokerage companies shall not conduct the futures trading without the authorization of their clients or beyond the scope authorized by their clients. (2) The futures brokerage companies shall keep clients' commercial secrets. (3) The futures brokerage companies shall provide the true and precise status of the futures market and shall conceal no important issues or resort to any improper means to coax clients into issuing their trading instructions. (4) The futures brokerage companies shall make no profit-earning pledges for their clients, agree with their clients on the shared benefits or risks, conduct futures trading in the personal name when authorized by the companies, enterprises, or other economic organizations, and re-entrust the entrusted business or accept the re-entrusted business.

A futures broker shall set up a specific department or positions for risk control that monitor its own financial condition, business operation, and compliance as well as drafts risk-control reports. It shall also recruit qualified accounting firms to audit its financial and operating statements annually.

1.14.2 FUTURES EXCHANGES

According to the Provisional Regulations on the Administration of Futures Trading and the Measures on the Administration of Futures Exchanges, futures exchanges are self-regulating legal entities performing functions pursuant to their articles of association. All three futures exchanges (ShFE, ZCE, and DCE) are under the CSRC's supervision.

In a futures exchange, the general assembly of members is the highest authority, and the board of governors is the executive body, whose chairman and vice chairman are nominated by the CSRC and elected by the board. The CSRC is entitled to appoint and discharge the general manager of an exchange.

Future exchanges shall fulfill the following functions:

- Providing the venues, facilities, and services for futures transactions.
- Designing futures contracts and arranging the listing of futures contracts.
- Organizing and supervising futures transactions, settlement, and delivery.
- Ensuring the honoring of futures contracts.
- Establishing and running the risk-management system (e.g., regarding margins, daily debt-free netting, price fluctuation limit, position limit, large positions reporting, risk reserves).

According to the Measures on the Administration of Futures Exchanges, the supervision and administration of a futures exchange regarding its members include:

- Formulating the administrative rules of its members.
- Formulating the administrative rules on trading seats and prohibiting members from transferring the seats entirely or partly in the form of a lease or subcontract.

- Making selective or extensive inspections are the members' compliance with the exchange business rules and reporting the results to the CSRC. All members are compelled to cooperate.

According to the earlier-mentioned measures, the supervision and administration of a futures exchange regarding futures trading include:

- Implementing the system of margins, daily debt-free netting, investor trading coding, review of hedging positions and limits on speculative positions, reporting of arbitrage positions, limits on price fluctuations, etc.
- Promulgating market information on real-time quotations, ranking in terms of positions and trading volume, etc. in an appropriate manner.
- Compiling and publishing relevant trading statements in a timely manner.
- Taking the following provisional measures to prevent ongoing violations by a member or a client: (1) to limit the injection of margins; (2) to limit the withdrawal of margins; (3) to limit the opening of new positions; (4) to raise the margin ratio; (5) to close positions before a designated date; (6) to immediately close positions. When the exchanges do any of items (4), (5), and (6), they should report to the CSRC immediately.

1.14.3 SHANGHAI FUTURES EXCHANGE

The Shanghai Futures Exchange (SHFE), which originated from the merging of the Shanghai Metals Exchange, the Shanghai Cereal and Oils Exchange, and the Shanghai Commodity Exchange, started operation in December 1999. As of December 2005, the SHFE had a total of 215 members, of which 175 were brokerage firms (81%) and 34 were proprietary traders (15%). It had 248 remote trading terminals nationwide.

At present, copper, aluminum, rubber, and fuel oil contracts are traded on the SHFE. In 2005, trading volume hit 67.58 million lots, and the turnover registered RMB6.5402 trillion, 49% of the national total.

There are 17 departments under the SHFE, in charge of office administration, market surveillance, trading, settlement, delivery, legal affairs, information, enforcement, research, financial futures, and so on.

1.14.4 DALIAN COMMODITY EXCHANGE

The Dalian Commodity Exchange (DCE) was established on February 28, 1993. As of December 2005, it had a total of 195 members, among which 93%

are futures brokerages companies. The DCE had 163,837 registered investors, including 44,385 new investors in 2005.

Corn, soybeans, bean meal, and bean oil contracts are traded at the DCE. Among them, the soybean is the most actively traded product, and its price in the DCE has become an important indicator for China's soybean production and sales. In 2005, trading volume at the DCE amounted to 198.35 million lots (61% of the national total), with turnover at RMB4.7417 trillion (35% of the national total).

There are 14 departments under the DCE (including departments on trading, delivery, settlement, market surveillance, technology) and Beijing office.

1.14.5   ZHENGZHOU COMMODITY EXCHANGE

The Zhengzhou Commodity Exchange (ZCE) was established in October 1990. By the end of 2005, it had 223 members, including 179 futures brokers and 44 proprietary traders.

The products traded on the ZCE include wheat, cotton, mung beans, and sugar, with wheat and cotton being the most actively traded. In 2005, the ZCE registered a trading volume of 56.95 million lots (a 17.49% year-on-year increase), with a turnover at RMB2.165 trillion (a year-on-year increase of 86%).

The ZCE has 12 departments in charge of trading, delivery, settlement, options, market development, research and development, etc.

1.15   LEGAL FRAMEWORK

The legal framework of Chinese security markets has improved since 1990. By the end of 2005, a legal framework had taken shape focusing on three pieces of legislation: the Company Law, the Securities Law, and the Securities Investment Fund Law. These were supplemented by 13 regulations and administrative rules, such as Provisional Regulations on Public Offering and Trading and Provisional Regulations on Futures Trading, as well as over 300 departmental rules, guidelines, and codes.

Within this framework, there were regulations that govern:

- Securities offering, listing, and disclosure
- Securities and futures trading
- Corporate governance, mergers and acquisitions of listed companies
- Securities and futures intermediaries
- Supervision of securities investment funds
- Supervision of securities and futures markets, and legal liabilities.

1.16   REGULATORY SYSTEM AND ORGANIZATIONAL STRUCTURE

In October 1992, the State Council Securities Committee and its executive arm, the CSRC, were established, mandated to regulate China's securities and futures markets. In 1998, the State Council Securities Committee terminated operation and its functions were transferred to the CSRC, which became the sole regulator supervising nationwide securities and futures markets. The CSRC is now one of the 14 organizations directly under the State Council.

The top executive body of the CSRC comprises one chairman, five vice chairmen, and one assistant chairman. The commission consists of 16 functional departments and three affiliate centers. Headquartered in Beijing, the CSRC has 36 regulatory bureaus throughout China's provinces, municipalities, autonomous regions, and key cities, as well as two supervisory offices, in Shanghai and Shenzhen. At present, there are 1,905 on staff in the CSRC, with an average age of 35 years; 41% of the staff hold master degrees or above.

1.17   CONCLUSIONS

We close the chapter by providing a non-comprehensive list of the more significant reforms introduced by Chinese authorities since 2005. These data are prepared from Reuters news.

- March 1, 2005 – China announced it will let international development agencies issue yuan-denominated bonds for the first time. The Asian Development Bank and the International Finance Corporation (IFC) subsequently launched the first *panda bonds* in October.
- March 21 – China Construction Bank and the *policy bank* China Development Bank are selected to introduce asset-backed securities (ABS).
- April 30 – Stock regulators reintroduced the floating $250 billion in non-traded state holdings in listed firms.
- May 16 – The Peoples Bank of China (PBC) lets banks and other financial institutions trade bond forwards. The objective appears to introduce instruments to hedge interest rate risks.
- May 18 – Domestic trading begins in eight hard-currency pairs.
- May 24 – The Peoples Bank of China (PBC) lets domestic firms issue commercial paper (CP) of maturities one year or less. These are officially called *short-term corporate bills*.
- June 23 – Shares in Bank of Communications, the first domestic bank to list outside the mainland, debut in Hong Kong.

- July 21 – China revalues the yuan by 2.1 percent against the dollar. This is abandonment of an 11-year-old dollar-peg. China moves to a managed float linked to a basket of currencies that allows the yuan to rise or fall by 0.3 percent a day against the dollar.
- August 15 – Onshore foreign exchange forwards in the yuan are launched. Trade expands reasonably within a few months, but there are difficulties.
- October 27 – China Construction Bank lists in Hong Kong. This is the first of the country's *big-four* state-owned banks to do so.
- November 15 – Inter-dealer broker Tullett Prebon, sets up the country's first money-broking venture with a Shanghai trust firm.
- November 23 – China said it has launched a long-awaited market-making system for renminbi trading against foreign currencies in another crucial step toward greater flexibility for the currency. Any qualified foreign exchange bank is allowed to apply to SAFE with relevant documents for the status of market makers, and will be allowed to perform that duty once they get approval.
- November 25 – The Peoples Bank of China (PBC) launches its first domestic currency swaps market with a $6 billion deal.
- January 4, 2006 – China launches over-the-counter trading for the yuan and starts a market-making system.
- January – China decides to launch new Financial Derivatives Exchange, to be 20 percent owned by each of the five stock and futures exchanges.
- February 9 – The central bank publishes rules permitting interest rate swaps for the first time. China Everbright Bank and China Development Bank have conducted the first interest rate swap.
- February 21 – The Peoples Bank of China (PBC) says in a monetary policy report it will widen the channels for capital to leave China legally.
- February 22 – Hong Kong and Beijing are discussing allowing yuan-denominated debt to be issued in the Hong Kong and allow cross-border trade to be settled in the yuan.
- March 26 – China Banking Regulatory Commission (CBRC) announces that China may set up a postal service bank. China Post has accepted deposits since mid 1980s, and this is now being planned as a separate bank. This could potentially be the country's fifth largest bank.
- April 12 – China announces that it will launch the first bank-run insurance firm later in 2006. Under current rules the businesses of domestic banks and insurers are separated. Bank of China and China Construction Bank Corporation are seeking approval to this end.
- April 14 – China announces regulations that will permit Chinese institutional investors to invest abroad and at the same time make it easier for Chinese firms and individuals to buy foreign exchange.

- April 14 – State Administration of Foreign Exchange (SAFE) announced that it relaxes the controls on foreign exchange accounts, simplifies approval procedures for foreign exchange payments in the service trade and makes it easier for corporations and individuals to buy foreign currencies. The SAFE said it would raise the foreign exchange holding limit for domestic firms with experience in foreign exchange. It said it would raise to $500,000 from $200,000 the limit on FX accounts for firms new to the foreign exchange market, and that it would allow individuals to buy up to $20,000 in foreign exchange a year. The administration said the regulations on foreign exchange would take effect May 1, 2006.
- April 16 – China Banking Regulatory Commission (CBRC) announces that a new regulatory department will be set up to better manage the risks of policy banks.
- April 24 – China introduces a formal FX swap market.
- August 24, China appointed the Head for the new Shanghai Financial Derivatives Exchange.
- August 27, China passes bankruptcy law, effective June 2007.

APPENDIX: CONTACTS

CHINA SECURITIES REGULATION COMMITTEE

Telephone: 010-88061000
Fax: 010-66210119
Address: Fukai Building, No. 19 Finance Boulevard, Xicheng District, Beijing, 100032
E-mail: csrcbgt@csrc.gov.cn
Website: www.csrc.gov.cn

SHANGHAI STOCK EXCHANGES

Telephone: 021-68808888
Fax: 021-68804868
Address: Securities Building, No. 528 Pudong Road South, Shanghai, 200120
E-mail: webmaster@secure.sse.com.cn
Website: www.sse.com.cn

China Securities Depository and Clearing Corporation Limited

Telephone: 010-66210988
Fax: 010-66210938
Address: 22~23/F, Investment Square, No. 27 Finance Boulevard,
   Xicheng District, Beijing, 100032
E-mail: webmaster@chinaclear.com.cn
Website: www.chinaclear.com.cn

Shenzhen Stocks Exchange

Telephone: 0755-82083333
Fax: 0755-82083947
Address: No. 5045, Shennan Road East, Shenzhen, 518010
E-mail: cis@szse.cn
Website: www.szse.cn

China Securities Association

Telephone: 010-88087770
Fax: 010-88087084
Address: 2/F, Tower B, Fukai Building, No. 19 Finance Boulevard,
   Xicheng District, Beijing, 100032
E-mail: sac@public.bta.net.cn
Website: www.sac.net.cn

Shanghai Futures Exchanges

Telephone: 021-68400000
Fax: 021-68401198
Address: No. 500, Pudian Road, Pudong New Area, Shanghai, 200122
E-mail: info@shfe.com.cn
Website: www.shfe.com.cn

CHINA SECURITIES ASSOCIATION

Telephone: 010-68573109
Fax: 010-68571529
Address: 7/F, Taiyang Building, No. 34, Fuwai Street Jia, Xicheng District,
　Beijing, 100037
E-mail: cfa@cfachina.org
Website: www.cfachina.org

DALIAN COMMODITIES EXCHANGE

Telephone: 0411-84808888
Fax: 0411-84808880
Address: No. 18, Huizhan Road, Dalian, 116023
E-mail: dce@mail.dce.com.cn
Website: www.dce.com.cn

ZHENGZHOU COMMODITIES EXCHANGE

Telephone: 0371-5610069
Fax: 0371-5613068
Address: No. 69, Weilai Boulevard, Zhengzhou, 450008
E-mail: dce@mail.dce.com.cn
Website: www.czce.com.cn

CHINA SECURITIES INVESTORS PROTECTION FUND MANAGEMENT CORPORATION LIMITED

Telephone: 010-88060055
Fax: 010-88060107
Address: 4/F, Fukai Building, No. 19, Finance Boulevard, Xicheng District,
　Beijing, 100032
E-mail: tanyj@csrc.gov.cn
Website: N/A

China's Money and Foreign Exchange Markets

Chinese money and foreign exchange (FX) markets are in the middle of a major transformation, which may continue during the years to come. In this part, Chapters 2 and 3 deal with the money markets and the banking sector. Chapter 4 is on foreign exchange markets. These chapters review the history of the markets, present the existing framework as of mid-2006, and discuss some policies and the major reforms.

The main issues faced by China's money and foreign exchange markets are in the limelight practically every day in the world media. Here we provide a summary of these recent issues, with the hope that they may help put the ensuing discussion in the proper context.

The first issue is reform of the *exchange rate regime*. As a result of the FX reforms, the pace of appreciation quickened (somewhat) since China let 13 banks start to create a market in the renminbi on January 4, 2006. The new system of market makers, who must quote two-way prices, is an important step toward exchange rate flexibility. Dealers estimate that the daily turnover in the FX market exceeded $2 billion a day during the first half of 2006 and was rising. The same figure was $1.2 billion in the first half of 2005.[1]

Yet the FX market still operates very much under the control of the PBC. The PBC trades with the banks via two systems. One is the *anonymous order-matching system*; the other is the newly created *over-the-counter interbank market*. Within this setting the renminbi is mainly traded between the Central Bank as one party and all other participants as the counterparty. Thus, at the end it is the PBC that absorbs most of the foreign capital inflow. Market participants estimate that the PBC accounts for about 75% of daily trading.

The launch of onshore RMB forwards in August 2005 was aimed to help the turnover in the FX market, but the forward FX market has been slow to develop.[2] China's foreign exchange regulator recently approved a total of 19 banks,[3] as members of the interbank foreign exchange forward market. During the month following the revaluation there were only three forward FX transactions in the interbank market. The onshore forward FX rate is in general higher than the offshore USD/RMB nondeliverable forward (NDF), traded in the relatively liquid offshore Singapore market.

The second issue is the *money market reforms* that are required in order to support the new exchange rate system and, in their own right, make a more efficient working of the financial system.

According to the PBC, the first priority of the Central Bank is to maintain an appropriate rate of *monetary growth*, and the second priority is the *interest rate reform*. Concerning the latter, in the long run China aims to simplify the structure of deposit rates and to eliminate controls. To this end, the *one-year deposit rate* is selected as the single interest rate benchmark.[4]

One measure toward eliminating interest rate controls was announced on February 9, 2006, by the PBC. The Central Bank allowed *interest rate swaps* and then started publishing daily *reference rates* for one- and seven-day repos. These reference rates are intended to increase liquidity in the interest rate swaps market.

The FX system and interest rate reforms have led to the market *expectation that the RMB would appreciate in the coming years*. This created new problems for the authorities.

---

[1] Figures are from Reuters.

[2] A ban on overnight position keeping hinders the FX forward and swap markets.

[3] This includes seven Chinese and 12 foreign banks.

[4] At the beginning of 2006 there were about 20 official benchmarks, from 20-day Central Bank loans (at that time 3.33%), to banks' five-year deposits (at that time pegged at 3.6%). China's one-year RMB deposit rate was set at 2.25% in late 2004.

The expectation that renminbi would appreciate encourages a version of carry trade, where players borrow foreign currency and invest in RMB-denominated assets. This results in excess liquidity as the PBC buys the foreign exchange and creates new renminbi against it.

In order to control such flows, Chinese authorities have taken various steps during 2005–2006. One measure was to put upper limits on the short term borrowing for Chinese and foreign banks in 2006, similar to the limits in 2005. Short-term loans by foreign banks operating in China could not exceed $34.8 billion. The limit for Chinese banks and some nonbanking institutions is set at $24.4 billion.

Note one dilemma faced by the Central Bank: In the presence of heavy capital inflows, lending and borrowing interest rates would in all likelihood fall if the Central Bank freed them. This would make it less attractive to invest in RMB assets and discourage capital inflows, but at the same time the drop in interest rates would further increase the high growth rate of 9–10% that the Chinese economy is experiencing.

Finally we present a chronology of China's interest rate reforms. China started focusing on interest rate reforms because of its drive for a more flexible exchange rate system. The sequencing of reforms in this area have been well understood by the authorities. Authorities have made clear their preference for a more structured money market *before* selecting benchmark rates and first establishing a liquid market in foreign currency rates *before* RMB-based floating exchange rates. In terms of reforming the interest rate formation, establishing liquid lending rates *before* deposit rates was deemed more important. Finally, according to the authorities, reforms on large, long-term deposits should *precede* the reforms on small, shorter-term deposits.

Here is a chronological list of reforms concerning China's interest rate structure since 1986.

November 1986   China allows banks to borrow and lend short-term money to each other for the first time.

January 1996   China sets up the interbank lending market in Shanghai, giving birth to China interbank offering rates (CHIBOR).

June 1996   China lifts all restrictions on CHIBOR and lets the market decide the rates.

June 1997   China sets up an interbank bond market, allowing financial institutions to trade debt spot and via repurchase agreements, with rates being decided by the market.

October 1999   China allows domestic insurance companies to bargain with banks for rates on large deposits (above 30 million yuan ($3.7 million)) and of more than five years' duration. Pension funds are granted the same right in 2002.

September 2000   China frees interest rates on dollar deposits of $3 million and above.

November 2003   The floor on rates for smaller dollar deposits is lifted.

March 24, 2004   The Central Bank raises reserve requirements for less healthy banks.

October 29, 2004   The People's Bank of China raises bank interest rates for the first time in nine years. The benchmark one-year RMB lending rate goes up to 5.58% from 5.31%, and the one-year deposit rate rises to 2.25% from 1.98%. It lets banks charge borrowers what they like above the benchmark but says lending rates must be at least 90% of that rate. It also gives banks some leeway to cut deposit rates.

November 2004   The ceiling is lifted on dollar savings longer than 12 months.

July 21, 2005   China revalues the RMB by 2.1% and scraps an 11-year-old dollar peg for a managed float.

August 15, 2005   Onshore forex forwards are launched.

November 25, 2005   The Central Bank launches a domestic currency swaps market with a $6 billion deal.

January 4, 2006   China launches over-the-counter trading for the RMB and starts a market-making system.

February 9, 2006   The People's Bank of China allows interest rate swaps.

April 24, 2006   China establishes the FX swap market.

(*Source*: Reuters)

CHAPTER 2

China's Money Markets

Zheng Xu
Fund Manager, Yin Hua Fund Management Company

The People's Bank of China is the authority in charge of the Chinese money market. The development of the money market reflects the reform of China's financial system, the change of commercial bank operation, and the development of the Central Bank's monetary policy. After over 10 years of development, China's money market has achieved significant improvement in terms of the scale of trade. However, there are still some structural flaws, which has prevented it from performing its function fully.

2.1   STRUCTURE

China's money market consists of four submarkets: the renminbi (RMB) lending market, the repo (outright repo) market, the bond market, and the bills market.

2.1.1   RMB INTERBANK LENDING MARKET

The PBC is the authority in charge of the interbank lending market. The CFETS (China Foreign Exchange Trade System) organizes market operations and provides the computer trading system.

Operation Mode

The *interbank* lending market gives quotations, standardizes price inquiries, and confirms deals. As soon as quotations are confirmed by the participants, the transaction notice is automatically produced by the system as valid proof of the deal.

Trading Instruments

Trading parties can agree on any maturity of up to four months. The CFETS calculates and publishes the underlying weighted average interest rate, named CHIBOR, for overnight, 7-day, 14-day, 21-day, 1-month, 2-month, 3-month, 9-month, and 1-year terms.

Trading Hours

The system is open from 9:00 to 11:00 a.m. and from 2:00 to 4:30 p.m., Monday through Friday (holidays excluded).

Membership

Participants include all independent commercial banks and their authorized branches, rural credit cooperatives, insurance companies, fund management companies, and securities companies and those foreign financial institutions approved by the PBC to handle RMB business in China.

Clearing

The trading parties perform bilateral clearing according to the transaction notice. Book transfers go through the clearing system owned by the PBC. The clearing speed is $T + 0$ or $T + 1$.

2.1.2 OUTRIGHT REPO MARKET

The repo market has two parts, the interbank market and the organized exchange market. The latter includes the Shanghai and the Shenzhen exchanges. The CFETS organizes the *interbank* market operation and provides the computer trading system. The Shanghai and Shenzhen stock exchanges organize the *exchange* market operation and provide the computer trading system. Normally, the volume of repo in the interbank market is much higher than the volume in exchanges. Moreover, the volume of repo in the Shanghai Stock Exchange is much greater than that in the Shenzhen Stock Exchange.

Operation Mode

The operation mode of the interbank repo market is the same as that of the interbank lending market.

Market Infrastructure of the Shanghai Stock Exchange (SSE)

Upgraded a few times, the computer system of the SSE is now of world standard. The host computer is capable of executing 29 million orders and settling 60 million transactions at a speed of 8,000 transactions per second.

The SSE has established a nationwide satellite telecommunications network with the most sophisticated equipment, the most complete range of functions, the largest number of users, and the widest coverage. It consists of more than 3,000 one-way satellite substations and 1,800 two-way substations.

The SSE is now performing real-time monitoring of market activities under a sophisticated surveillance system that meets the demand of market operation.

Trading and Clearing

A modern trading system supports SSE's paperless trading at a highest speed of more than 8,000 transactions per second. The orders are matched automatically by computer according to the principle of "price and time priority."

Orders can be sent to the SSE's mainframe through terminals either on the floor or from member firms. The SSE owns a 3,600-square-meter trading floor, which is the largest in the Asia-Pacific area. In addition, the largest domestic satellite and optical communications network, which can disseminate the real-time transaction information all over the country and abroad, has connected the SSE with more than 5,000 trading terminals.

Trading Instruments

In the interbank market, the bonds for repo include T-bonds, Central Bank papers, and financial bonds. Grouped by maturity, there are 10 repo terms to be traded in the interbank market: 7-day, 14-day, 21-day, 1-month, 2-month, 3-month, 4-month, 6-month, 9-month, and 1-year terms.

Similarly, there are 12 repo terms (including nine T-bond repo, and three corporate bond repo terms) to trade in the Shanghai Stock Exchange market.

Trading Hours

The interbank system is open from 9:00 to 11:00 a.m. and from 2:00 to 4:30 p.m., Monday through Friday (holidays excluded). The exchange system is open from 9:30 to 11:30 a.m. and from 1:00 to 3:00 p.m., Monday through Friday (holidays excluded).

The trading hours of the SSE are Monday to Friday. The morning session is 9:15 to 9:25 a.m. (for centralized competitive pricing) and 9:30 to 11:30 a.m.

(for consecutive bidding). The afternoon session is 1:00 to 3:00 p.m. (for consecutive bidding). The market is closed on Saturdays and Sundays and other holidays announced by the SSE.

Membership

Since April 2002, all institutions qualified to trade bonds in the interbank market must be approved as participants in the interbank bond and repo markets. These institutions include independent commercial banks and their authorized branches, rural credit cooperatives, insurance companies, fund management companies, and securities companies and those foreign financial institutions approved by the PBC to handle RMB business in China.

Except for commercial banks and rural credit cooperatives, all types of investors (including institutional investors and personal investors) can participate in the exchange market.

Clearing

In the interbank market, the clearing speed is $T + 0$ or $T + 1$. In the organized exchanges, the China Securities Central Clearing and Registration Corporation (CSCCRC) is responsible for the central depository, registration, and clearing of securities. It carries out the $T + 1$ settlement for A shares, repo, and bonds.

2.1.3   BOND MARKET

The bond market is also made up of two parts, the interbank market, and the exchange market (including the Shanghai Exchange Market and the Shenzhen Exchange Market). The CFETS organizes the interbank market operation and provides the computer trading system. The Shanghai and Shenzhen stock exchanges organize the exchange market operation and provide the computer trading system.

The operation mode, trading hours, membership, and clearing are the same as those for the repo market.

2.1.4   BILLS MARKET

This market is essentially the same as the interbank lending market.

(Source: http//www.chinamoney.com.cn)

2.2 HISTORY AND STATISTICS

2.2.1 MARKET MEMBERS

By the end of December 2004, the national interbank funding market and bond market had 1,037 members, with 119 new entrants that year. Among the total membership, 882, including 97 newcomers in 2004, were connected to the interbank lending and bond trading systems; 451 institutions signed agreement that year with the CFETS for outright repo business.

2.2.2 HISTORY OF INTERBANK LENDING

The interbank lending market is the central part of the money market. Related data are supplied in Tables 2.1 and 2.2. China's interbank lending was born in the 1980s. However, in the early stages, due to a lack of other money markets and capital market instruments, interbank lending was not the main instrument for managing bank reserves, but usually the means to swap the chronic capital shortage among financial institutions. Thus, coastal areas borrowed capital from inland regions to make up the local capital shortage, and the maturity was generally long.

TABLE 2.1 Interbank Lending Market

Year	Turnover of credit lending	Turnover of repo	Turnover of outright repo	Turnover of bond trading	Turnover of bills trading
1996	5,871.58	N/A		N/A	
1997	4,149.24	309.87 (June–Dec.)		9.66 (June–Dec.)	
1998	989.48	1,021.48		33.19	7,691
1999	3,291.60	3,956.93		77.41	8,725
2000	6,728.07	15,781.24		682.68	16,559
2001	8,082.02	40,133.29		839.32	
2002	12,107.25	101,885.21		4,411.69	
2003	22,220.00	117,203.00		30,848.00	
2004	13,919.56	93,104.90	1,262.65	25,041.15	20,678
2005	12,327.68	156,784.34	2210.91	63,378.92	

Unit: 100 million yuan.

TABLE 2.2 Members of the National Interbank Funding Center

	Number		
Financia institution	End-2003	End-2004	End-2004
Solely state-owned bank	4	4	4
Joint stock commercial bank	11	12	12
Policy bank	2	3	3
Urban commercial bank	108	109	110
Authorized branch of commercial bank	125	130	131
Foreign-funded bank	53	67	88
Financial leasing company	3	3	3
Insurance company	22	29	49
Securities company	80	87	97
Investment fund	129	180	239
Financial company	41	43	51
Rural credit co-operative	268	278	298
Trust & investment company	25	29	32
Fund management company	18	29	37
Urban credit co-operative	27	31	36
Social security fund	1	1	1
Asset management company	0	1	1
Other	1	1	1
Total	918	1037	1193

Source: http//www.chinamoney.com.cn

Around 1993, interbank lending between financial institutions started to have problems. The major effect was that nonfinancial institutions such as trust and investment companies borrowed capital from commercial banks and invested the short-term capital in the securities and real estate markets. At that time, interbank lending became a major channel through which to break the loan management and helped nonfinancial institutions get a large amount of capital. However, it is generally believed that this led to inflationary pressures. Interbank lending became the natural target of monetary tightening.

2.2.3 DEVELOPMENT OF INTERBANK LENDING

In January 1996, the Central Bank again started reforming the interbank lending market and began to establish a unified interbank lending market in China.

In comparison with the pre-reform interbank lending market, the new market structure has two important characteristics.

First, the *qualification* of financial institutions that participate in the interbank lending market has been made clearer. In the new system, the financial institutions that participate in the interbank lending market are divided into two groups: members and common participants. Members include such financial institutions as commercial banks and their authorized branches, urban commercial banks, financial companies, and some securities companies. Other financial institutions are common participants. Members must conduct their deals through the computerized trading system provided by CFETS. Other financial institutions can conduct deals on their own, but their deals must be filed at the PBC local branches.

Second, the Central Bank has set *ceilings* of interbank lending maturities and *lines* for all the financial institutions. For commercial banks, the lending maturity is within 4 months and the line is calculated at a certain proportion of their deposit balance. For nonfinancial institutions, the maturity is within 7 days. The relevant line is checked and rectified according to the capital level. The purpose of setting the ceiling was to prevent financial institutions from excessive interbank lending and thus turning this instrument into a source of long-term capital.

It is worth noting that the requirement that all interbank lending market members conduct their deals through the computerized trading system is of great significance in terms of macro control. First, market members produce deal contracts through the computerized trading system. This can enhance efficiency and is conducive to establishing a unified market in China. Second, because the Central Bank can effectively set the maturity and line ceilings through the trading system, it can prevent financial institutions from offering excessive interbank loans and long-term use of short-term capital. Third, the Central Bank can find out the exact reasons behind the fluid fluctuation of the financial system. This function of the trading system will be even more important with the gradual opening up of the capital account. The reason is that when there is speculation in the financial market, this system will help the Central Bank to find out the source and scale of the speculation capital and implement the corresponding monetary policy operation in time.

The interbank offering rate was an important beginning to China's interest rate reform. On January 3, 1996, the National Interbank Funding Center, through the China Foreign Exchange Trade System, operated and produced a unified interbank offering rate in China (CHIBOR). In June 1996, the PBC stipulated that financial institutions can decide their own interbank offering rate according to the supply and demand in the capital market and started publishing the CHIBOR regularly. In an economy where interest rates are determined by the market, the interbank offered rates (IORs) are often taken as a base rate that determines the rates of other financial instruments. This is a step toward further interest rate reform, although CHIBOR is not fully indicative of market conditions.

2.2.4 STATISTICS FOR INTERBANK LENDING

Turnover

Table 2.3 shows interbank lending. In terms of turnover, the interbank lending market has grown larger and larger since 1999. In 2003, the total turnover reached 2.4113 trillion yuan, up 99.16% from the previous year. However, as the Central Bank gradually adopted a "strict" monetary policy in 2004 to cool down the credit overheating that had appeared since 2003, interest rate and liquidity risks became more significant, and therefore the turnover shrank.

In 2004, a total of 8,108 interbank lending deals were made, with a total turnover of 1.455,552 trillion yuan and a daily turnover of 5.776 billion yuan, down 39.88%, in all eight maturities. The worst hit were the maturities of 1 day, 14 days, and 1 month, down 56.03%, 69.33%, and 42.86%, respectively.

The turnover of maturities below 7 days accounted for over 90% of the market total. That means short-term deals still dominate the market. However, the trading scale is still low when taking into consideration the overall scale of China's financial system.

Interest Rates

Average interbank lending rates are displayed in Table 2.4. In terms of the inter-bank offered rates of all varieties, the average rates of all maturities gradually

TABLE 2.3   Lending Turnover of the National Interbank Market, by Maturity

Maturity	1999	2000	2001	2002	2003	2004	2005
IBO001		28,733.00	102,275.50	199,598.40	641,524.00	283,336.52	223,030
IBO007	94,252.37	420,240.50	558,450.00	824,975.10	1,453,290.60	1,041,146.72	896,260
IBO021	24,339.00	79,817.00	91,415.00	99,695.00	56,503.40	30,151.00	60,420
IBO1M	69,761.00	33,401.50	33,823.70	28,068.60	44,104.70	18,920.81	29,910
IBO2M	91,896.00	58,867.00	9,370.00	10,566.40	10,094.60	9,194.90	7,510
IBO3M	10,876.00	15,230.70	4,726.40	4,628.00	10,183.97	5,841.94	14,090
IBO4M	2,160.00	752.00	817.00	11,813.00	2,809.41	2,572.56	1,540

Unit: million yuan.

TABLE 2.4 Lending Weighted Average Interest Rate of the National
Interbank Market

Maturity	1999	2000	2001	2002	2003	2004
IBO001		2.46%	2.42%	2.09%	2.18%	2.09%
IBO007	2.90%	2.40%	2.47%	2.14%	2.24%	2.26%
IBO014					2.30%	2.34%
IBO021	2.93%	2.44%	2.46%	6.21%	2.33%	2.54%
IBO1M	3.16%	2.49%	2.69%	2.27%	2.44%	2.80%
IBO2M	3.21%	2.38%	2.87%	2.56%	2.68%	3.12%
IBO3M	3.33%	2.66%	2.91%	2.79%	2.87%	3.39%
IBO4M	5.72%	5.41%	4.12%	2.57%	3.68%	3.76%

dropped after 1999, reached their lowest point in 2002 and started to climb up
thereafter. One reason is that on February 21, 2002, the Central Bank adjusted
the reserve requirement ratio from 2.07% to 1.89% and lowered the interest
rate of loans at all maturities.

In the first quarter of 2004, the interbank offered rate declined, due to
liquidity in the money market as shown in Figure 2.1. In the second quarter,
because of macroeconomic controls, the rate bounced back to the highest point
of the year. In the second half of the year, capital oversupply steadily pushed
down the rate, which dropped back to the March level at the end of 2004.
During that year, the highest and lowest weighted average rates were 2.40%
and 2.07%, respectively. Compared with 2003, seven out of eight interbank
lending varieties went up and only one went down.

All the long-term varieties with maturities over 1 month rose, with the
3-month and 2-month varieties enjoying the biggest advances, up by 19.77%
and 16.58%, respectively. Due to the influence of comprehensive factors,

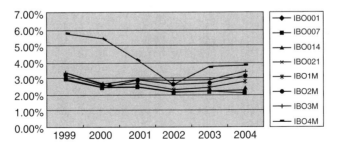

FIGURE 2.1 Lending Weighted Average Interest Rates in the Interbank Market

TABLE 2.5   Lending Term Structure of National Interbank Market, by Maturity

Year	Overnight	7 days	20 days	14 days	30 days	60 days	90 days	120 days
1997	6.5	26.15	10.63		13.74	23.14	12.91	6.93
1998	6.0	22.5	14.5		22.6	18.3	10.5	5.6
1999	10.9	28.6	7.4		21.2	27.9	3.3	0.7
2000	7.7	63.7	12.0		4.9	9.2	2.3	0.1
2001	12.85	69.38	11.55		4.37	1.16	0.58	0.11
2002	16.64	70.4	8.29		2.41	0.89	0.39	0.98
2003	26.65	60.38	7.83	2.35	1.83	0.42	0.42	0.12
2004	19.48	71.59	4.34	2.07	1.30	0.63	0.40	0.18

The figures represent the proportion of the turnover of each lending variety weighted by the total lending turnover.
Source: National Interbank Funding Center.

including macro control, an expectation of an interest rate rise and capital supply and demand, the interest rate in the money market yo-yoed more seriously.

The highest interbank offered rate with 7-day maturity reached 7.5%, while the lowest dropped to 1.62%. The range of 560 basis points was a rarity in recent years.

Term Structure

Table 2.5 shows a significant recent change in the term structure of interbank lending. In 1997, interbank lending with maturity of less than 7 days (including overnight) accounted for 32.5% of the market total. In 2000, the figure went up to 71.4%. In 2003 and 2004, the figure reached 87.03% and 91.08%, respectively. Accordingly, it appears that interbank lending is no longer a channel for some nonfinancial institutions to acquire capital from commercial banks to engage in long-term investment. Instead it became a way for financial institutions to adjust their short-term positions.

2.3   REPO (OUTRIGHT REPO) MARKET[1]

Before 1990, interbank lending dominated China's money market. Securities repo did not appear until 1991. In order to increase the liquidity of the securities, in July 1991 the Securities Trading Automated Quotation (STAQ) system

---

[1] Two excellent papers on repo and money markets are Fan and Zhang (2006) and Fan and Zhang (2006).

started the security outright repo[2] business on a trial basis. Then many securities exchange centers, e.g., the Wuhan Securities Exchange, started repo business. On December 19, 1993, the Shanghai Stock Exchange began to conduct securities repo business, taking five securities listed in the Shanghai Stock Exchange as their basis. From then on, securities repo, as a new instrument, officially entered China's financial system. At the very beginning, most repo business was concentrated in the stock exchanges: the Wuhan Securities Exchange, the Tianjin Securities Exchange, and the STAQ system.

2.3.1 ESTABLISHMENT OF EXCHANGE REPO MARKET

In 1994, the securities market developed swiftly. The turnover of the repo market increased dramatically, totaling over 300 billion yuan, and there were more and more participants. However, because it was a new financial instrument, many problems appeared shortly after repo's introduction: (1) the nonstandardized ways of trading, (2) the nonstandardized use of capital, (2) serious illegal charging and use of fees by financial institutions, and (4) the existence of on-floor and off-floor markets in both repo business and reverse repo business.[3]

Thus, in August 1995 China began the rectification of the securities repo market. Because there were serious financial risks in the repo business in the Wuhan Securities Exchange, the Tianjin Securities Exchange, and the STAQ system, they were shut down by the authorities. After the rectification and before June 1997, most of the securities repo business was conducted on the Shanghai Stock Exchange. Then a unified securities repo market began to take shape, and so did a unified repo price and rate. All this has created a basis for promoting China's interest rate reform.

In the early stages of China's repo market, repo business had become an important trading method for nonbank financial institutions to acquire capital from commercial banks. Repo business was closely related to the stock market. At present, the members of the Shanghai and Shenzhen stock exchanges can still engage in securities repo business, and a fairly large industry has already taken shape.

2.3.2 ESTABLISHMENT OF THE INTERBANK REPO MARKET

Although China's unified securities repo market was based on the exchanges, commercial banks also participated extensively in the business. Therefore, some

---

[2]Henceforth called *repo*.

[3]Off-floor, as an "underground business," is not allowed, by policy.

securities companies and institutional investors obtained large amounts of capital from commercial banks and invested this capital in the stock market. This was one of the reasons behind the great bull stock market between 1995 and 1998. These positions carried high risk for the banking system. Table 2.6 provides data on interbank bond repurchases by maturity.

In early 1997, to stop the flow of bank capital into the stock market, the PBC decided to prohibit commercial banks from the exchange repo business and start another repo business exclusively for banks. Then, an *interbank securities repo market* was established and China began to have *two* parallel repo markets: the exchange repo market and the interbank repo market.

The significance of building the interbank repo business is threefold. First, thanks to the interbank repo business, short-term financing between financial institutions can be more secure and interbank lending is no longer the only way to do it. Second, financial institutions can exercise liquidity management through securities, which has greatly promoted securities issuance. Third, the development of repo business made it possible for the Central Bank to implement various policies.

At the very beginning, the interbank securities market was open exclusively to commercial banks, and nonbank financial institutions, including securities companies, had no access to this market. Such an arrangement aroused great controversy as an artificial barrier to capital flow between money and capital markets. In 2000, the interbank repo market also began to include securities companies, fund management companies, and other financial institutions with a certain threshold. From then on, a regular channel was officially set up to facilitate capital flow between money and capital markets.

In the current interbank market, the number of repo members, which has exceeded the number of lending members, includes over 1,000 financial institutions, such as Chinese commercial banks and their authorized branches, foreign banks in China, insurance companies, securities companies, funds, trust investment companies, rural cooperatives, and Social Security funds.

Since October 2002, interbank repo business has further expanded because settlement agents could conduct reverse repo business with enterprises. In fact, 39 commercial banks were allowed to engage in settlement agent business for enterprise securities. At present, the members of the interbank repo market have covered almost the entire financial system and are extending to normal corporations.

2.3.3 REPO MARKET STATISTICS

Currently, all institutions and individuals can participate in the repo market in the Shanghai and Shenzhen stock exchanges except for commercial banks and

TABLE 2.6 Treasury Bonds Repurchase Turnover of Trading of the National Interbank Market, by Maturity

					Maturity						Total turnover of trading
	7 days	14 days	21 days	1 month	2 months	3 months	4 months	6 months	9 months	1 year	
Total in 2001	31,271.32	5,168.67	1,945.45	916.71	490.07	250.98	19.05	39.75	25.31	6.00	40,133.30
Total in 2002	84,487.53	12,257.42	2,166.35	1,335.37	797.78	439.55	215.85	107.88	22.99	54.50	101,885.21
Total in 2003	78,330.93	13,382.31	2,185.82	1,729.09	925.06	633.27	88.92	143.09	0.00	0.00	97,418.48
Total in 2004	54,208.63	10,700.87	2,866.30	2,331.55	903.78	696.07	145.29	131.78	36.40	34.00	72,054.67

Unit: 100 million yuan.

rural and urban credit cooperatives. Furthermore, the membership threshold of the interbank repo market is lower than that of interbank lending, and the risk is also lower. Therefore, in comparison with the interbank lending market, the repo market is more efficient, and its interest rate is stable enough to fully reflect the liquidity change of the financial market.

Turnover

Tables 2.1 and 2.7 show that since 1997, the turnover of interbank repo has increased rapidly, much faster than that of interbank lending. In 1997, the turnover of interbank lending was 414.924 billion yuan, 13 times the turnover of interbank repo of 30.987 billion yuan. In 2002, the lending turnover was 1,210.725 billion yuan, only one-eighth of the repo turnover, which stood at 10,188.5 billion yuan. In 2004, the repo turnover was also eight times that of lending.

Table 2.8 and Figure 2.2 show that since 2001, interbank repo has been dominating the overall repo business. Currently, exchange repo turnover is less than half of interbank repo's.

Since the launching of outright repo in May 2004, 911 deals have been sealed on the interbank market, with a trading value of 126.265 billion yuan. In terms of turnover, among the seven varieties, short terms remained the most popular modes of transaction. The 7-day was the most active, accounting for 65.65% of the total turnover and the 14-day ranked second, with its trading accounting for 12.82% of the grand total.

TABLE 2.7 Turnover of Lending and Repo of the National Interbank Market

Year	Turnover of lending	Turnover of repo
1996	5,871.58	
1997	4,149.24	
1998	989.48	1,021.48
1999	3,291.60	3,956.93
2000	6,728.07	15,781.20
2001	8,082.02	40,133.30
2002	12,107.25	101,885.00
2003	24,113.00	117,203.00
2004	14,555.00	117,203.00

Unit: 100 million yuan.
Source: National Interbank Funding Center.

TABLE 2.8   Comparison of Turnover of Interbank Repo and of Exchange Repo

Year	Turnover of exchange repo	Turnover of interbank repo	Ratio of turnover of exchange repo to turnover of interbank repo
1996	1602.91	N/A	N/A
1997	2216.41	309.87 (June–Dec.)	N/A
1998	4538.55	1021.48	444%
1999	12890.90	3956.93	326%
2000	14732.15	15781.24	93%
2001	15491.72	40133.29	39%
2002	24327.78	101885.21	24%
2003	55352.44	117203.00	47%
2004	46606.21	117203.00	40%

Unit: 100 million yuan.

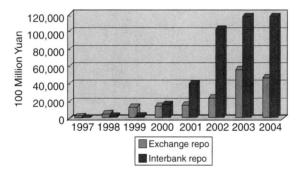

FIGURE 2.2   Comparison of Turnover of Interbank Repo and Exchange Repo

Repo Rate

Table 2.9 and Figure 2.3 show that from 2002 to 2004 the interbank weighted average repo rate fluctuated above the 1.89% legal reserve requirement ratio rate. By the end of August 2004, the repo rate had risen dramatically. The reason was that on August 2004, the PBC raised the reserve requirement ratio of the financial institutions from 6% to 7%, except for rural and urban credit cooperatives (for which it remains at 6%). This change led to a drastic drop of market liquidity in the short term.

TABLE 2.9 Average Interbank Repo Rates by Maturity (%)

	7 days	14 days	21 days	1 month	2 months	3 months	4 months	6 months	9 months	1 year	Weighted average interest rate
	Weighted average interest rate	Weighted average interest rate	Weighted average interest rate	Weighted average interest rate	Weighted average interest rate	Weighted average interest rate	Weighted average interest rate	Weighted average interest rate	Weighted average interest rate	Weighted average interest rate	
2002											
2002.01*	2.14	2.15	2.16	2.21	2.22	2.28	0	0	0	0	2.14
2002.02	2.05	2.12	2.14	2.18	2.11	2.16	2.15	0	0	0	2.08
2002.03	1.96	1.97	1.99	2.01	2.02	2.02	2.04	2.07	2.09	0	1.96
2002.04	1.95	1.95	1.97	1.98	2	1.99	1.94	2.04	0	0	1.95
2002.05	1.95	1.95	1.97	1.98	1.99	1.98	2.05	0	0	0	1.95
2002.06	1.95	1.95	1.97	1.98	1.99	1.97	0	2.08	0	2.2	1.95
2002.07	1.95	1.95	1.96	1.98	1.99	2.03	0	1.99	0	2.01	1.95
2002.08	1.96	1.97	1.98	2.02	2.02	2.12	2.04	2.14	0	0	1.97
2002.09	2.17	2.25	2.3	2.25	2.22	2.23	2.23	2.28	2.32	0	2.2
2002.1	2.24	2.26	2.28	2.31	2.34	2.34	2.3	2.35	2.4	0	2.25
2002.11	2.23	2.25	2.27	2.25	2.29	2.33	2.31	0	2.4	0	2.23
2002.12	2.29	2.35	2.41	2.39	2.47	2.37	2.38	2.54	2.55	0	2.31
2003											
2003.01	2.27	2.3	2.29	2.31	2.38	2.39	2.41	0	0	0	2.28
2003.02	2.24	2.26	2.28	2.29	2.3	2.31	2.31	0	0	0	2.25
2003.03	2.03	2.08	2.11	2.17	2.23	2.24	2.3	2.29	0	0	2.04
2003.04	1.96	1.98	1.99	2.05	2.11	2.17	2.18	2.25	0	0	1.97

2003.05	2.03	2.04	2.1	2.13	2.14	2.16	0	2.25	0	0	2.04
2003.06	2.16	2.19	2.22	2.24	2.23	2.28	0	2.38	0	0	2.17
2003.07	2.2	2.22	2.3	2.34	2.29	2.34	0	2.48	0	0	2.2
2003.08	2.25	2.23	2.26	2.37	2.43	2.36	2.6	2.34	0	0	2.24
2003.09	2.86	3.14	3.08	3.08	3.25	3.68	3.76	3.05	0	0	2.93
2003.1	3.09	3.17	3.23	3.28	3.44	3.45	3.45	3.75	0	0	3.11
2003.11	2.7	2.85	2.83	3.23	3.23	3.1	3.48	3.51	0	0	2.66
2003.12	2.14	2.17	2.37	2.77	2.83	2.94	0	3.2	0	0	2.17
2004											
2004.01	2.29	2.74	2.66	2.78	2.59	2.84	2.96	3.25	0	0	2.43
2004.02	2.22	2.27	2.42	2.3	2.3	2.33	2.42	2.54	0	0	2.23
2004.03	1.91	1.96	2	2.17	2.2	2.27	2.27	2.48	2.75	2.93	1.93
2004.04	2.06	2.35	2.58	2.62	2.63	2.61	2.71	2.68	2.68	0	2.13
2004.05	2.18	2.25	2.36	2.66	2.71	2.81	0	2.55	0	2.66	2.17
2004.06	2.41	2.54	2.68	3.04	3.14	3.11	0	3.55	2.5	2.62	2.41
2004.07	2.33	2.4	2.47	2.84	2.92	3.03	2.91	3.6	0	0	2.34
2004.08	2.28	2.36	2.46	2.78	2.95	3	0	0	0	3.81	2.31
2004.09	2.12	2.35	2.55	2.72	2.83	2.93	2.72	3.1	0	0	2.2
2004.1	2.14	2.18	2.3	2.48	2.75	2.94	2.8	0	0	0	2.16
2004.11	2.09	2.22	2.31	2.44	2.68	2.91	3.33	0	2.9	0	2.11
2004.12	1.87	1.92	1.99	2.11	2.68	2.73	3.25	3.57	0	0	1.88

*Decimals following the year indicate month of the year. For example, 2002.01 equates to January 2002. Readers will find this style in many places in this book, as it is a Chinese style.

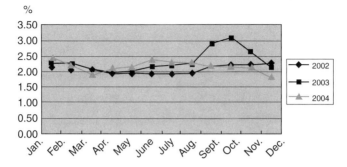

FIGURE 2.3   Weighted Average Interest Rate of Treasury Bonds Repurchase Trading of the Interbank Market (*Source:* National Interbank Funding Center)

In 2004, the movements of the outright repo rate and the repo rate basically kept in line with each other. The high and low of the weighted rate were 2.58% and 2.12%, respectively, with a range of 46 basis points.

Term Structure

Table 2.10 and Figure 2.4 show that the short-term financing function of securities repo has become more and more effective. The turnover of securities repo with a maturity of 7 days accounted for 8.40% of total repo business in 1997 but 67.9% in 2000, up by 26 percentage points in comparison with the same period of 1999. Since 2000, the proportion of the turnover of 7-day maturity securities repo has always exceeded 60%. According to transaction rules, the longest maturity for interbank repo is 1 year. However, most interbank repo business is of 7-day maturity. That means the major purpose of financial institutions in doing repo business is short-term capital management.

2.4   BOND MARKET[4]

The development of China's interbank repo business is also based on the development of the interbank bond market. The development of China's money market in recent years demonstrates that the activities in the bond market will greatly promote the development of the overall money market. Hence we now look at the bond market.

[4]The bond market is discussed in more detail in Chapter 5.

TABLE 2.10 Repo Term Structure of Interbank Market

Year	7 days	14 days	21 days	1 month	2 months	3 months	4 months	6 months	9 months	1 year
1997	8.40%	17.70%	8.20%	17.00%	19.30%	12.50%	16.90%	N/A	N/A	N/A
1998	37.00%	17.80%	6.50%	16.90%	9.90%	7.00%	3.80%	N/A	N/A	N/A
1999	41.40%	23.60%	6.80%	11.90%	8.00%	6.70%	1.00%	N/A	N/A	N/A
2000	67.90%	15.40%	6.80%	3.30%	4.20%	2.10%	0.30%	N/A	N/A	N/A
2001	77.92%	12.88%	4.85%	2.28%	1.22%	0.63%	0.05%	0.10%	0.06%	0.01%
2002	82.92%	12.03%	2.13%	1.31%	0.78%	0.43%	0.21%	0.11%	0.02%	0.05%
2003	80.41%	13.74%	2.24%	1.77%	0.95%	0.65%	0.09%	0.15%	0.00%	0.00%
2004	75.23%	14.85%	3.98%	3.24%	1.25%	0.97%	0.20%	0.18%	0.05%	0.05%

Maturity

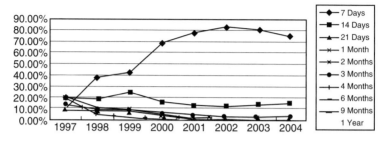

FIGURE 2.4   Repo Term Structure of the Interbank Market

2.4.1 HISTORY OF THE INTERBANK BOND MARKET

In the first half of 1997, the overheated stock market attracted a large amount of bank capital via various channels. One of the important channels was the exchange bond repo business. In June 1997, the PBC demanded that all commercial banks withdraw from the Shanghai and Shenzhen securities exchanges and that the government securities trusted in the exchanges be transferred to the China Government Securities Depository Trust and Clearing Co. At the same time, the PBC stipulated that commercial banks can use the proprietary bonds trusted in the China Government Securities Depository Trust and Clearing Co.[5] to engage in repo business and cash business through the computerized trading system provided by the National Interbank Funding Center (NIFC).

At the moment, the interbank bond market has become an important part of China's bond market. Over 50% of government securities, 100% of financing bonds and subordinated bonds of commercial banks are issued via the interbank bond market. In 2003, the turnover of the bond market (including cash and repo) reached nearly 1.5 trillion yuan.

2.4.2 ORGANIZATIONAL STRUCTURE

The PBC performs the functions of supervising and managing the interbank bond market. The PBC is in charge of regulating the market, exercising comprehensive supervision and management over the market, making market development plans, and promoting innovation via new instruments.

According to the regulation and authorization of the PBC, the China Government Securities Depository Trust and Clearing Co. and the China Foreign Exchange Trade System are in charge of providing securities trust,

---

[5]For example, the government securities, Central Bank financing bills, and financing bonds.

clearing, trade intermediary, and information services for market participants and exercising real-time supervision and monitoring over securities trade and clearing.

Currently, the participants of the interbank bond market are financial institutions and their authorized branches, nonfinancial institutions, and contractual-type capital investors. The Ministry of Finance, policy banks, and China International Trust and Investment Corporation (CITIC) issue the securities and raise capital via the interbank bond market. The PBC conducts open market operation in the interbank bond market to adjust the currency supply and achieve the goal of regulating the economy through monetary policy.

2.4.3   FRAMEWORK OF THE INTERBANK BOND MARKET

Transaction Varieties and Transaction Method

Currently, the transaction varieties in the interbank bond market include Treasury bonds, Central Bank bills, financing bonds, and corporate bonds of the CITIC group. Transaction methods include cash purchase and sale, repo, and outright repo.

Bond Transaction

Transactions in the interbank bond market are made through price inquiry, with the two parties negotiating on their own and sealing the transactions deal by deal. That is to say, the two parties negotiate over transaction factors through a transaction system, telephone, fax, or e-mail and sign the contracts deal by deal after reaching consensus. Currently, most transactions are made through the domestic transaction system provided by NIFC.

Bond Trust and Settlement

The interbank bond market applies the real-name primary account trust system. The trust is based on the bond booking system provided by the China Government Securities Depository Trust and Clearing Co.

Bond settlement includes two parts: bond transaction and capital payment. The real-time, full-volume, and deal-by-deal settlement method is applied. Bond transaction is conducted through the bond booking system provided by the China Government Securities Depository Trust and Clearing Co., and capital payment is conducted through accounts transfer.

2.4.4   DEVELOPMENT OF THE INTERBANK BOND MARKET

Since 1997, the interbank bond market has gone through reforms. Market rules and regulations have been improved. Market infrastructure development has been strengthened. The market has developed rapidly both in extent and in depth. To strengthen information services and improve market transparency, the China Government Securities Depository Trust and Clearing Co. and the China Foreign Exchange Trade System have improved information system building and introduced specialized websites like www.chinabond.com.cn and www.chinamoney.com.cn.

We can make the following points about the market's position.

1. The mechanics of bond issuance has been completed smoothly, and a modern bond market structure has basically been established. In August 1998, the State Development Bank issued financing bonds for the first time in the interbank bond market. Up until 2000, the State Development Bank and Export Import Bank of China issued all financing bonds via auction in the interbank bond market. Later, the Ministry of Finance started to issue Treasury bonds via auction in the interbank bond market. It did so for the first time on October 1999. Since 2000, all Treasury bonds issued by the Ministry of Finance in the interbank bond market have been through market-based auctions. At present, bond prices are set by the market. Primary bond market reform has also created conditions for secondary bond market reform. Underwriters have formed the core membership of the interbank market. Bond underwriters start to fulfill responsibilities in two-way quotations of bond purchase and bond sale in the interbank market to improve bond liquidity. A unified bond trust and paperless trading have been achieved in the interbank bond market.

2. Market membership has grown substantially and has gradually diversified in type. Beginning in April 2002, examination and approval replaced registration and recording for market access. After October 2002, the bond settlement agent business was expanded. Since then, the interbank bond market has included all financial institutions and legal persons of nonfinancial institutions. By the end of 2004, the number of members increased from 16 commercial bank head offices at the beginning to 1,037 institutional investors. There were 3,983 market participants, including banks, securities companies, fund and insurance institutions, other nonbank financial institutions, as well as enterprises and public service units. In addition, 50,000 private investors have indirectly participated in the interbank bond market through the over-the-counter bond business of four state-owned commercial banks.

3. The number of tradable bonds has increased substantially, with continual innovation in instruments and increasing diversity of trading. As the interbank

bond market expanded, tradable bond stocks have rocketed up rapidly. Bond varieties have increased dramatically as well. Currently, the major bonds issued in the interbank market are Treasury bonds and financing bonds. Only a small percentage of bonds are issued by corporations. At market launch, tradable bond stocks were valued at only 72.3 billion yuan. By the end of 2003, it had increased by 38 times to 2.855 trillion yuan. Meanwhile, bond types have also increased from the initial single category of more than 10 small and four major categories. These latter are Treasury bonds, Central Bank bills, financing bonds, and corporate bonds.

4. Trading is active and liquidity has been gradually enhanced. Settlement agents, two-way quotations, net price transactions, and other measures introduced by the PBC have played an important role in improving market liquidity. In 2003, repo transactions of the interbank bond market reached 11.7203 trillion yuan, up by 380 times that of 1997, while cash transactions reached 3.0848 trillion yuan, up by over 3,100 times that of 1997. With the rapid increase in market transactions, bond liquidity has become stronger. In 2003, bond turnover of the interbank bond market (year turnover/total tradable bond stock × 100%) hit 607%, 46 times that of 1997 (13%).

2.4.5   SIGNIFICANCE OF THE INTERBANK BOND MARKET

The development of the interbank bond market has had a great influence on the operation of commercial banks and the implementation of monetary policies.

First of all, the development of the interbank bond market has offered commercial banks the chance for timely adjustment of asset composition and reducing excess reserves in the Central Bank. In 1997, bonds accounted for 5% of total assets of commercial banks. By the end of 2000, this proportion had risen to 12.5%. This increase has reduced the excessively high loan–deposit ratio of commercial banks and improved the quality of bank assets. It has also created conditions for commercial banks to reduce the excessively high level of excess reserves and to exercise liquidity management through such transactions as bond repo under changed market conditions.

Second, because bond issuance and liquidity of the interbank bond market have become more and more market based, a reliable yield has basically been established.

Third, with the rising proportion of bonds in their assets, commercial banks have become more responsive to Central Bank policies, which create conditions for the Central Bank to expand open market business operation.

2.4.6 STATISTICS IN THE INTERBANK BOND MARKET

Bond Issuance

Table 2.11 shows that among the newly issued Treasury bonds and financing bonds of 2004, more than 65% were issued through the interbank bond market. In terms of bond issuance, the interbank bond market has become the main body of the China bond market, and financial institutions such as commercial banks have become the main investors in Treasury bonds and policy financial bonds.

In 2004, 153 bonds were issued in the interbank bond market, including 11 Treasury bonds, 32 financing bonds, 105 Central Bank bills, 1 corporate bond, and 4 subordinated bonds of banks. Among these, corporate bonds and subordinated bonds of banks got access to the interbank market for the first time. The number of floating-rate bonds and bonds with options was increasing.

Bond Stock

By the end of April 2005, bonds listed on the national interbank bond market included Treasury bonds, Central Bank papers, financing bonds, corporate bonds, and subordinated bonds, with a total value of 4.7855 trillion yuan. In addition, bonds with maturities shorter than one year were valued at 1.6259 trillion yuan (Table 2.12).

2004 Market Performance

Short-term bond trading was active and the composite index moved up, with some fluctuations.

TABLE 2.11   Bonds Issued in 2004

Issue	Size (100 million)
Book-entry T-bond	4,413.9
CDB financing bond	3,600.0
EIBC financing bond	340.0
ACBD financing bond	408.0
BOC subordinated bond	260.7
CCB subordinated bond	400.0
Total	9,422.6

TABLE 2.12   Value of Within-One-Year
Bonds and Papers of the National Interbank
Bond Market (as of the End of April 2005)

Issue	Value (100 million yuan)
T-bond	1,993.00
Central Bank paper	2,057.63
Financing bond	12,208.00
Total	16,258.63

In 2004, 21,972 transactions were made in the spot market, with a total turnover of 2504.115 billion yuan and a daily turnover of 9.977 billion yuan, down by 19.15% on a year-over-year basis. Most of the transactions were in short-term maturities. The within-one-year bonds were the most active; their turnover accounted for 45.84% of the total, up by one-third on a year-over-year basis. Three- to five-year bonds came in second, accounting for 21.87% of the total. However, the turnover of the over-7-years bonds accounted for only 10%. The composite bond index kept moving up as the yield on the short-term bond kept declining. The highest and lowest monthly composite indexes were 1175.96 and 1150.61, respectively, with a difference of 25 points.

In 2004, 292 bonds were transacted, including 60 government bonds with a turnover of 473.974 billion yuan; 103 financing bonds, 1008.071 billion yuan; 122 Central Bank bills, 1011.987 billion yuan; four corporate bonds, 64.56 billion yuan; and three bank subordinate bonds, 3.625 billion yuan. Compared with the previous year, the turnover of Central Bank bills increased very fast, while all the others more or less dropped.

2.5   BILLS MARKET

According to current regulations, China's current commercial bills[6] are bills of transactions; they are by no means ordinary financing bills. Therefore, China's bills market plays an important role in solving the arrears among enterprises in industries that are closely related.

---

[6]We use this term instead of *commercial paper*.

2.5.1 DEVELOPMENT OF THE BILLS MARKET

In recent years, pushed by Central Bank policies, the commercial bills business, with the *bank acceptance bill* as the core, has developed rapidly. Commercial bills, discounts, and rediscounts all grew substantially.

Table 2.13 shows that commercial bill transactions have increased rapidly and that the total discount of commercial banks has also grown in recent years. This shows that China's commercial banks currently play a very important role in the market for commercial bills. By the end of 2000, the added discount value accounted for 30% of the added loan value of that year, and the added discount value accounted for 23% of the added relending value of the Central Bank. The rapid development of bills business plays a positive role in expanding the channels of funding for enterprises, easing debt arrears among enterprises, improving the credit asset quality of commercial banks, and strengthening indirect regulation of the Central Bank.

Compared with corporate bonds, the rapid development of China's commercial bills is related to the current arrangement of the system. Under the current system, bonds issued by enterprises need examination and approval. Also, there is a limit, while no such limit exists for commercial bills. Though commercial bills have short terms, they can be issued by enterprises repeatedly. Therefore, bills can become a good financing method for enterprises.

Recently, the rediscount interest rate has gradually become an important base interest rate of the Central Bank. Since March 1998, there have been no links to other interest rates. The rediscount interest rate is decided by the Central Bank alone.

China's bills market is only in its initial stages of development. There are still some problems in market member composition and the transaction mechanism. This is mostly true in the secondary market. The issues include the following: (1) Market membership is small and without diversification. The parties have almost the same capital demand, which is not good for liquidity.

TABLE 2.13   1998–2000 Bills Market

Year	Commercial bill transaction	Total discount of commercial banks	Total rediscount of PBC
1998	3,841	2,650	1,200
1999	5,076	2,499	1,150
2000	7,445	6,447	2,667

Unit: billion yuan.
Source: China Money Market Annual Report (2000) and *China Financial Market Monthly.*

(2) The transaction mechanism is not conducive to the purchase and sale of big lots of bills. Quotations and the real bill transfer method are inefficient and complicated and lead to high transaction costs in the case of frequent purchases and sales. (3) The market price fluctuates dramatically. Due to the lack of bilateral quotation transaction agencies in the market, bill supply and demand may be imbalanced during certain time periods, leading to high volatility.

Statistics

In recent years, there have been more and more participants in this market as shown in Table 2.14. Besides state-owned commercial banks and joint stock commercial banks, local commercial banks, cooperatives, policy banks, foreign-funded banks, financial companies, and even fund management companies have all become members of this market. By the end of 2004, there were 1,027 members in the interbank bill market.

Since 1996, China's bank acceptances market has developed quite fast. From 1997 to the end of 2003, the volume of commercial bills increased from 460 billion yuan to 2,077 trillion yuan. The total bill discount increased from 274 billion yuan to 4.34 trillion yuan, with an annual growth rate of over 60%. Development of the bills business has played a positive role in accelerating the capital turnover of enterprises and improving the asset structure of commercial banks as well as many other fields. At the same time, bills crime has already become the third major financial crime, right after securities crime and

TABLE 2.14   Members of www.chinacp.com.cn

Financial institution	Number		
	End of 2003	End of 2004	End of 2005
Solely state-owned bank	4	4	4
Joint stock commercial bank	11	12	12
Urban commercial bank	93	97	101
Urban credit cooperative	29	35	38
Financial company	36	37	39
Rural credit cooperative	285	307	323
Authorized branch of commercial bank	419	517	600
Foreign-funded bank	14	18	19
Total	891	1,027	1,136

(*Source*: http://www.chinamoney.com.cn)

counterfeit currency crime. Therefore, standardizing commercial bill business development is still an important task.

In 2003, total commercial bills issued by enterprises reached 2.77 trillion yuan, up 72.2% and an increase of 1.16 trillion yuan over the same period the previous year. Total discount and rediscount reached 4.44 trillion yuan, up 91% and an increase of 2.12 trillion yuan over the same period the previous year. By the end of December, the balance of signed undue commercial bills was 1.28 trillion yuan, up 73.5% and an increase of 0.54 trillion yuan over the same period the previous year. The balance of bills discount and rediscount was 893.4 billion yuan, up 69.7% and an increase of 366.9 billion yuan over the same period the previous year.

Each month of 2003, in spite of small fluctuations of volume of commercial bills in some individual months, total transactions kept growing. In the first eight months, the balance of discounts maintained strong growth momentum, with an average monthly increase of 50.8 billion yuan. At the end of August, the discount balance was 926.6 billion yuan, and later the balance dropped markedly. At the end of December, it declined to 816.8 billion yuan.

In the first 11 months of 2003, acceptance bills signed by enterprises totaled 3.0847 trillion yuan, an increase of 625.1 billion yuan from the same period the previous year. Discounts totaled 4.1982 trillion yuan, an increase of 80.1 billion yuan over the same period the previous year. Rediscounts totaled 21.7 billion yuan, a decrease of 52.8 billion yuan. By the end of November, the balance of undue acceptance bills was 1.4179 trillion yuan, an increase of 177.2 billion yuan over that at the end of November of the previous year. The balance of discounts was 961.4 billion yuan, an increase of 78.2 billion yuan over that at the end of November of the previous year.

2.6   REGULATION AND SUPERVISION

In this section we consider the major regulatory authorities and the structure of supervision of Chinese money markets.

2.7   THE PEOPLE'S BANK OF CHINA

The PBC[7] was established on December 1, 1948, a consolidation of the former Huabei Bank, Beihai Bank, and Xibei Farmer Bank. In September 1983, the State Council decided to have the PBC function as a Central Bank.

---

[7]Website: http://www.pbc.gov.cn.

The Law of the People's Republic of China on the People's Bank of China passed by the Third Plenum of the Eighth National People's Congress on March 18, 1995, legally confirmed the PBC's Central Bank status. In March 2003, the First Plenum of the Tenth National People's Congress approved the Decision on Reform of the Organizational Structure of the State Council, separating the supervisory responsibilities of the PBC over banking institutions, asset management companies, trust and investment companies, and other depository financial institutions. Instead, the China Banking Regulatory Commission was established to supervise the financial industry.

On December 27, 2003, the Standing Committee of the Tenth National People's Congress approved at its Sixth Meeting the amendment to the Law of the People's Republic of China on the People's Bank of China, which has strengthened the role of the PBC in the making and implementation of monetary policy, in safeguarding overall financial stability, and in the provision of financial services.

2.7.1 MAJOR RESPONSIBILITIES

Under the guidance of the State Council, the PBC formulates and implements monetary policy, prevents and resolves financial risks, and safeguards financial stability.

The Law of the People's Republic of China on the People's Bank of China provides that the PBC perform the following major functions: issuing and enforcing relevant orders and regulations; formulating and implementing monetary policy; issuing renminbi and administering its circulation; regulating the interbank lending market and the interbank bond market; administering foreign exchange and regulating the interbank foreign exchange market; regulating the gold market; holding and managing official foreign exchange and gold reserves; managing the State treasury; maintaining normal operation of the payment and settlement system; guiding and organizing the anti-money-laundering work of the financial sector, and monitoring relevant fund flows; conducting financial statistics, surveys, analysis, and forecasts; participating in international financial activities in its capacity as the Central Bank; performing other functions specified by the State Council.

2.7.2 INSTITUTIONAL ARRANGEMENT

Under the leadership of the State Council, the PBC implements monetary policy, performs its functions, and carries out business operations independently according to laws and free from intervention by local governments, government departments at various levels, public organizations, or any individuals.

The PBC needs to report to the State Council (China's Cabinet) its decisions concerning the annual money supply, interest rates, exchange rates, and other important issues specified by the State Council for approval before they are put into effect. The PBC is also obliged to submit work reports to the Standing Committee of the National People's Congress on the conduct of monetary policy and the performance of the financial industry.

All capital of the PBC is invested and owned by the State.

2.7.3   THE CHINA FOREIGN EXCHANGE TRADING SYSTEM

As an outcome of foreign currency system reform, the CFETS was founded in April 1994 and has since then witnessed vigorous development. In accordance with the market development strategies of the PBC and the State Administration for Foreign Exchange (SAFE), the CFETS introduced the forex trading system in April 1994, the RMB credit lending system in January 1996, interbank bond trading in June 1997, and the trading information system in September 1999. The trial operation of RMB voice brokering began in July 2001, and the monthly periodical *China Money* went into publication in October 2002.[8] Forex deposit brokering debuted in June 2002, and the gold trading system was put into operation in October 2002.

Three service platforms covering the whole country were set up to provide trade and information services for the forex market and money market, and they function as supervisory facilities for the PBC and the SAFE. The CFETS network system is continually improving. Concurrently, the number of members is increasing and the trade of RMB and forex is steadily increasing. The RMB exchange rate is stable, and the interest rate exactly transmits the intention of monetary policies.

Internal Structure

The CFETS has one president and several vice presidents. Including its head office in Shanghai and its backup center in Beijing, the CFETS has 18 branches, with offices in Guangzhou, Shenzhen, Tianjin, Dalian, Nanjing, Xiamen, Jinan, Qingdao, Wuhan, Chengdu, Zhuhai, Shantou, Fuzhou, Ningbo, Xi'an, and Shenyang.

[8]Website: http://www.chinamoney.com.cn.

General Office: in charge of summarization and coordination of general business, secretarial work, foreign affairs, publicity and education, personnel affairs, wages and salaries, welfare management, and employee training.

Market Department I: in charge of forex market trading and member management. Responsibilities also include providing foreign currency deposit brokering service and developing new business for the forex market.

Market Department II: in charge of market trading and member management for the RMB funding market. Responsibilities also include RMB voice brokering services and developing new business for the funding market.

Clearing Department: The clearing of forex trading is the key task of the department; it includes the management and supervision of each member's clearance of RMB.

Engineering Department: responsible for the management of the computerized trading system, the maintenance of electronic equipment and the telecommunications network of the CFETS, and the coordination and supervision of technical affairs for subcenters.

Technical Development Department: responsible for developing software for new businesses and providing training to technical staff.

Research Department: responsible for statistics on and investigation and analysis of markets; also conducts new product research and development.

Information Department: in charge of building and managing the information system of the CFETS and for providing information services on the forex market, the funding market, the bond market, and other relative markets.

Finance Department: responsible for the overall financial management of the CFETS and the test key management of clearing funds involved in forex trading.

Administrative Department: in charge of the logistics of the CFETS and the management of the office building.

Shanghai Head Office: The CFETS includes 9 departments: General Office, Marketing Department, Clearing Department, Engineering Department, Technical Development Department, Research Department, Information Department, Finance Department, and Administrative Department.

Beijing Backup Center: The Beijing backup center is an integral part of the CFETS. With the same network and equipment as the Shanghai head office, it operates as the backup for the forex, RMB lending, and bond trading systems. It also organizes members in the Beijing area to trade in the network and provides technical support for spot and remote services. The backup center has a director, who is concurrently the vice president of the CFETS, and a vice director. Under the backup center are four departments: the General Office, the Marketing Department, the Clearing Department, and the Engineering Department.

2.7.4   RMB VOICE BROKERING

In order to satisfy the multiple demands of various financial institutions, the CFETS introduced voice brokering in the money market. The CFETS, endorsed by financial institutions, seeks potential counterparties, provides market analysis, and facilitates the transaction of two parties through telephone, fax, and the Internet.

Target Customer: those legal entity financial institutions qualified for market financing and their authorized branches that have signed the Agreement of Money Market Voice Brokering Service with the CFETS.

Service: to describe the financial market situation and provide relevant information; when endorsed, to give quotations, seek counterparts, conduct transactions and make inquiries, analyze credit worthiness, and create a financing plan.

Brokering Scope: RMB interbank lending, bond repo, spot bond, bond distribution, paper business, and other businesses permitted by the development of the market and relative policies.

Service Hours: the same as in the funding and bond markets.

2.8   MONETARY POLICY

The objective of monetary policy is to maintain the stability of the renminbi and thereby promote economic growth.

2.8.1   MONETARY POLICY INSTRUMENTS

The monetary policy instruments applied by the PBC include the reserve requirement ratio, Central Bank base interest rate, rediscounting, Central Bank lending, open market operation, and other policy instruments specified by the State Council.

2.8.2   MONETARY POLICY COMMITTEE

Article 12 of the Law of the People's Republic of China on the People's Bank of China provides:

> The People's Bank of China is to establish a monetary policy committee, whose responsibilities, composition, and working procedures shall be prescribed by the

State Council and shall be filed with the Standing Committee of the National People's Congress. The Monetary Policy Committee shall play an important role in macroeconomic management and in the making and adjustment of monetary policy.[9]

2.8.3 RULES ON MONETARY POLICY COMMITTEE OF THE PEOPLE'S BANK OF CHINA

Rules on Monetary Policy Committee of the People's Bank of China stipulate that the Monetary Policy Committee is a consultative body for the making of monetary policy by the PBC, whose responsibility is to advise on the formulation and adjustment of monetary policy and policy targets for a certain period, application of monetary policy instruments, major monetary policy measures, and the coordination of monetary policy and other macroeconomic policies. The committee plays its advisory role on the basis of comprehensive macroeconomic research and the macro targets set by the government.

The Monetary Policy Committee is composed of the PBC's governor and two deputy governors, a deputy secretary general of the State Council, a vice minister of the State Development and Reform Commission, a vice finance minister, the administrator of the State Administration for Foreign Exchange, the chairman of the China Banking Regulatory Commission, the chairman of the China Securities Regulatory Commission, the chairman of the China Insurance Regulatory Commission, the commissioner of the National Bureau of Statistics, the president of the China Association of Banks, and an expert from academia.

---

[9] The Monetary Policy Committee is composed of 13 members, as of August 2006 they were:

Chairperson: Zhou xiaochuan (governor of the People's Bank of China)
Commissioner: You quan (deputy general secretary of the State Council)
Zhu zhixin (deputy director of the State Development Planning Commission)
Li yong (vice minister of the Ministry of Finance)
Wu xiaoling (deputy governor of the PBC)
Su ning (deputy governor of the PBC)
Qiu xiaohue (head of the Chinese National Bureau of Statistics)
Hu xiaolian (head of the State Administration for Foreign Exchange)
Liu mingkang (chairperson of the China Banks Regulatory Commission)
Shang fulin (chairperson of the China Securities Regulatory Commission)
Wu dingfu (chairperson of the China Insurance Regulatory Commission)
Guo shuqing (governor of the Bank of China and head of the China Banks Association)
Yu yongding (head of the Institute of World Economics and Politics Chinese Academy of Social Sciences)

The Monetary Policy Committee performs its functions through its regular quarterly meeting. An ad hoc meeting may be held if it is proposed by the chairman or endorsed by more than one-third of the members of the Monetary Policy Committee.

The opinions expressed in the meeting of the Monetary Policy Committee are recorded in the form of "meeting minutes." Such minutes or any resulting policy advice, if approved by more than two-thirds of the members of the Monetary Policy Committee, should be attached as an annex to the proposed decisions of the PBC on the annual money supply, interest rates, exchange rates, or other important monetary policy issues to be reported to the State Council for approval. Should the PBC file its decisions on other monetary policy–related issues with the State Council, it must enclose the meeting minutes or policy advice of the Monetary Policy Committee at the same time.

2.9   MARKET PRACTICE

In 2004, against the background of macro control and serious fluctuation in financial markets, there was continuous innovation and strengthened efforts to build infrastructure and systems in the money market. The reform and innovation of the interbank market has accelerated its development.

First of all, there have been more and more market makers with a gradually established market maker system and an improved bond settlement agent system. On July 22, 2004, the PBC started to use the name of *market maker* to replace the original *bilateral quotation maker* in the interbank market. It was the first time the PBC officially used the name of market maker, which meant the market maker system was officially established in the bond market, and the liquidity problem that had troubled the market chronically began to be eased. Three years earlier, a similar system had been introduced. In August 2001, the central bank approved nine commercial banks to be bilateral quotation maker and designated 20 bond varieties open to quotation; then the market maker system in China's bond market in the preliminary sense was established. As a transitional system, the bilateral quotation maker system helped accumulate a great deal of experience for the formal introduction of the market maker system.

At the same time, the Central Bank approved six financial institutions, including China Merchants Bank, Minsheng Bank, Bank of Shanghai, Hangzhou City Commercial Bank, Guotai Junan Securities, and Zhongxin Securities, to be market makers in the interbank market. Then the number of market makers increased to 15. More importantly, this was the first time the Central Bank had granted market maker status to securities companies; previously market makers in the interbank market had always been the same type and with similar demand.

In addition, in 2004, the PBC approved Harbin Commercial Bank and six other financial institutions to launch the bond settlement agent business to facilitate the entrance of medium and small investors into the market. Therefore, the number of bond settlement agent institutions in the interbank bond market reached 43.

Second, there has been innovation in the transaction method, with the introduction of outright repo. On April 12, 2004, the PBC published the Management Regulation on Bond Outright Business in the National Interbank Bond Market. On May 20, the long-expected outright repo business was launched in the interbank bond market. The short-selling mechanism of the outright repo gave birth to the new transaction model and the short-selling profit model, increased the possibility of financial business innovation, and enhanced the functions of the repo market in terms of price discovery and risk evasion. In spite of initial difficulties, outright repo has gradually entered investor's portfolios.

Third, there has been a continual introduction of new bond varieties with the improved interbank market system. In July 2004, the Agricultural Development Bank of China was permitted to issue financing bonds in the interbank market for the first time. On 23 June, the PBC and the China Banking Regulatory Commission published *Management on Issuing Subordinate Bond by Commercial Banks*, stipulating that subordinate bonds could be issued in the national interbank bond market. Then the Bank of China and the Construction Bank publicly issued two batches of subordinate bonds in the market, with total volumes amounting to 26.07 billion yuan and 223.3 billion yuan, respectively.

On August 25, the PBC allowed the entrance of railway bonds into the interbank bond market. The appearance of the first corporate bond in the market changed the usual practice by which corporate bonds can only go public in the stock exchange.

On November 1, securities companies were allowed to issue and transact short-term bills in the interbank market.

On December 15, the Rules on Examining and Approving the Circulation of Bond Exchange of Nationwide Interbank Bond Market came into force, promoting the standardized and healthy development of the interbank bond market.

Fourth, there has been explosive growth of funds in the money market. In August 2004, the Transitional Rules on the Management of the Money Market Fund were issued, promoting the smooth introduction and standardized development of money market funds. On this basis, there has been explosive growth in money market capital, with eight funds launched that year. By the end of 2004, there were nine funds in the money market, with a total volume of 63.327 billion units accounting for 25.4% of the total fund, whereas by the end of 2003 there was only one fund in the market and the volume was only 4.255 billion units. Thus, in only one year, growth was 15 times. The rapid development of money market funds means more new and active market traders, more market investment instruments, more financial market layers, and more liquidity in the money market.

Finally, a reference index of the money market base rate has been introduced.

The interest rate market reform needs a market base rate. For a long time, China had been taking the one-year deposit interest rate of the banks with low market degree as the base rate, so the conflict between the low market of the base interest and the rapid development of the financial market has become more and more serious. On October 12, 2004, NIFC officially declared taking the 7-day maturity repo interest rate as the reference index of the base rate of the money market. That was China's first marketized reference index for the base rate, which has provided the issuers with a reference rate to issue floating-rate debt. The introduction of a reference index met the requirement of financial market development, conformed to the direction of interest rate market reform, created conditions for financial instrument innovation, provided an important reference for financial institutions to price their products, and also provided a market base for the Central Bank to engage in open market operation.

On November 17 and December 8, 2004, the China Development Bank issued the 17th and 20th batches of floating-rate finance bonds, with the 7-day maturity repo rate as the reference rate. This received great praise from the market.

2.9.1 The Central Bank's Open Market Activities

The Central Bank's open market operations have become more and more mature, and the interbank market has become an important place to exert indirect regulation through monetary policy.

At the beginning of 2004, in the rapid development of China's economy, the problems of excessive investment and continual price hikes stood out. The Central Bank released a series of financial regulations to step up the intensity, flexibility, and pertinence of its open market operations, so these moves gradually became the vane for the financial institutions to judge the possible adjustment of monetary policies and influenced the practice of credit issuance and debt market operations.

As traders become more and more sensitive to the signals of monetary policy, the transmission channel of monetary policy becomes progressively smoother, and the transmission chain continually extended. The flexibility and effectiveness of monetary policy keep improving and financial regulation plays a more important role in overall macro-control work. The open market operations have become the most important tool of the Central Bank's monetary policy; they promoted the further coordination of the interest rate market and the Central Bank's interest rate regulation capacity, and also exerted a more and more profound impact on the development of the interbank market. FX swaps introduced late in 2005 added further flexibility here [see Chapter 4]. They guide and stabilize the basic development of the money market interest rate, diversifies the market transaction varieties, and optimizes the yield curve formation.

In 2004, the PBC's open market operations developed significantly. In particular, the flexibility and intensity of the open market operations have improved. (1) Operational frequency has increased. To make the open market operation more efficient, since July 27, 2004, every Tuesday morning another short-term sale of repo business has been added; since August 5, every Thursday morning another Central Bank bill issuance has been added. Then the weekly operation frequency increased from once every Tuesday to twice a week, that is, once for Central Bank bill issuance and once for sale repo. Every Tuesday, the Central Bank issues the bills and also performs sale repo operation according to the requirements of monetary policy regulation. (2) The central bank's bill transaction time has been adjusted. To further improve the liquidity of the Central Bank's bills, since August 5, 2004, the settlement procedures changed from $T + 2$ to $T + 1$; and the transaction closure time before bill cashing has changed from $T + 10$ to $T + 3$. (3) New operation varieties have been introduced. According to the requirements of monetary policy regulation, the Central Bank began to issue 3-year bills (since December 2004) and 1-year bills (since the end of 2004).

The Central Bank's bills come in more and more varieties, and according to circulation and turnover records they have become the mainstream short-term bills in the interbank market. The turnover of the Central Bank's bills in 2004 reached 1507.15 billion yuan. The bills with 3-month, 6-month, and 1-year maturities kept being issued in order, forming one of the reference short-term interest rates in the money market. At the same time, new instruments kept being launched. After the 3-year time bill, the Central Bank introduced the preissuance of bills, an innovation that adds new vitality to the market. Since the second half of 2004, the Central Bank's bills have replaced financing bonds, becoming the most active instrument in the interbank bond market and taking nearly 40% of the market's overall turnover.

The goal of open market operations has begun to move toward interest rate formation in the money market. Since 2004, in response to ever-increasing forex reserves and in accordance with market interest rate changes and monetary policy requirements, the Central Bank flexibly applied the qualitative and interest rate bidding in issuing the bills and used more auctioning to issue the bills at discount, to discover the market rate level, and to find out the expectations of commercial banks as to the interest rate movements. By issuing bills via auction, the yield of the Central Bank's bills and the interest rate in the money market is getting increasingly closer.

All these efforts have created conditions for forming a reference rate, establishing the Central Bank's indirect regulatory mechanism, and deepening the market reform of the interest rate formation.

2.10   SOME CURRENT PROBLEMS

After more than 10 years, China's money market has developed significantly and improved in terms of transaction scale and transaction structure. However, some structural flaws still exist, slowing the money market in effectively performing its function.

2.10.1   ONE-WAY FLOW OF CAPITAL

A key issue in China's money markets is the one-way flow of the capital, which has not yet been altered. That is to say, in the interbank money market, which boasts the largest transaction scale, capital flow is always from state-owned banks and national joint-share banks to other institutions. If this one-way capital flow remains unchanged, China's money market will be fragile in the face of an external shock (e.g., the Central Bank's monetary policy regulation) and it will be seriously restricted in performing its functions.

Solely state-owned commercial banks are the capital net exporter. In both the interbank lending and repo markets, state-owned banks are the capital net exporter, and the scale of export is getting larger. For example, the total capital exported from state-owned banks in the two markets in 2003 reached nearly 8 trillion yuan. This has two indicators. First, in the context of segregated operation and commercial banks holding monopoly status, the deposited capital of the whole society is concentrated mainly in the state-owned commercial banks. Second, commercial banks have the tendency to be cautious in granting loans, so they tend to dispose of the ever-enlarging depositing capital in the money market, which is relatively safe. Therefore, on the one hand, state-owned commercial banks absorb a large amount of depositing capital; on the other hand, they are not willing to dispose of it as loans. This is the major reason why the difference between savings and loans is getting bigger and bigger in China's financial system in recent years.

Urban commercial banks are the most important capital importers. The major capital resource of urban commercial banks is the interbank repo market, while most of the capital in urban commercial banks will be disposed of as loans. Historical statistics show that the transaction behavior of the urban commercial banks is typically in line with the economic cycle. In 1998, when the economy plummeted to low ebb, their net position every month was basically capital net exports, and the total net exports that year exceeded 1.8 trillion yuan. However, in 2003, when there was local economic overheating, urban commercial banks every month enjoyed capital net imports, which reached a peak in July, August, and October, when net imports exceeded 560 billion yuan, 570 billion yuan, and 480 billion yuan, respectively. Although the scale of net capital imports declined after September, the ratio of repo turnover to reverse ratio turnover was still as high as 630%. That means urban commercial banks are the most serious capital demanders. When taking into consideration the problem of inadequate assets and debt term structure, granting loans with the capital acquired from the repo market will be riskier than granting loans with deposited capital.

Securities and fund companies are capital demanders second only to urban commercial banks. The major capital resource of securities and fund companies is the interbank lending market, and their capital is disposed mainly in the capital market, especially the stock market. In 2000, the securities and fund companies were permitted into the interbank market; then the interest rates of the interbank market and the exchange market became more and more correlated. Because the exchange repo market is naturally related to the stock market, the gap between China's money market and capital market has been leveled to some degree.

Securities and fund companies absorb capital from both the interbank lending and repo markets, but they are much more in favor in the lending market than in the repo market, for two reasons. First, commercial banks usually absorb capital from nonbank financial institutions, including securities companies, in the form of agreement deposits. As competition between commercial banks increases, they often offer a rate which is usually higher than the rate of the interbank lending and repo markets. This rate difference is a very good profit-taking opportunity for nonbank financial institutions. They will absorb capital from the interbank lending market and then deposit it in commercial banks in the form of deposits to generate the high profit from the interest rate differential. Second, the securities and fund companies are capital demanders. If they want to absorb capital from the commercial banks in the repo market, they need to possess a large number of bonds in advance. That means they need a great deal of investment capital.

Because the securities and fund companies are in favor of interbank lending, it is the interbank lending business, instead of the repo, that reflects the relationship between the interbank market and the exchanges repo market. Statistical analysis shows the following.

1. There is a close relationship between the interbank market and the exchanges repo market, and the two markets influence the stock market through the relationship.
2. The major factor between the two markets is the lending position of the securities and fund companies.
3. Because the lending position of securities and fund companies is under control of the state-owned banks, the exchanges market has little influence on the interbank market in terms of turnover and interest rate, while the latter's impact on the former is huge. The one-way influence means that the relation between the money market and the capital market is still pretty fragile.

Foreign-invested financial institutions have changed from net lending in to net lending out. Foreign-invested financial institutions started to enter China's interbank lending market in 1997, when the Asian financial crisis was at its peak and the domestic economy was at a low ebb. So they did not require renminbi funds at that time. In 1998, as the expansionary macroeconomic policies were implemented and took effect, China's economy resumed its rapid development, and foreign-invested companies and financial institutions that serve them began to demand more and more renminbi capital. The consequence in the interbank lending market is that foreign-invested financial institutions have changed from net lending out to net lending in, with the latter going to as high as 43.1 billion yuan in 2003.

2.10.2   IMPERFECT INTEREST-RATE-FORMING MECHANISM

In the interbank market with the largest transaction scale, the major transaction parties are state-owned banks, other banks, and bank institutions (mostly credit cooperatives). In addition, as mentioned earlier, capital flow is one-way, from the four state-owned banks and some state joint-stock banks to other institutions. Therefore, the interest-rate-formation mechanism in the interbank market is highly imperfect.

First, under the current system, the Central Bank allows the banks to maintain excess reserve ratios (see Table 2.15).[10] Therefore, if the market rate is lower than the excess reserve ratio granted by the Central Bank, the commercial banks, as major capital suppliers, would rather put the money in the Central Bank. So the bottom line of a zero rate in the interbank market is in fact the

---

[10] On March 17, 2005, the PBC reduced the interest rate on excess reserves of financial institutions to 0.99%, from 1.62%, while the interest rate on required reserves remained unchanged at 1.89%.

TABLE 2.15 Benchmark Interest Rates of the Central Bank

| Adjusted date | Reserve requirements[a] | Excess reserves[b] | Loans to financial institution | | | | Rediscount |
			1 year	6 months or less	3 months or less	Less than 20 days	
May 1, 1996	8.82	8.82	10.98	10.17	10.08	9.00	[b]
Aug. 23, 1996	8.28	7.92	10.62	10.17	9.72	9.00	
Oct. 10, 1997	7.56	7.02	9.36	9.09	8.82	8.55	
Mar. 21, 1998	5.22		7.92	7.02	6.84	6.39	6.03
July 1, 1998	3.51		5.67	5.58	5.49	5.22	4.32
Dec. 12, 1998	3.24		5.13	5.04	4.86	4.59	3.96
June 10, 1999	2.07		3.78	3.69	3.51	3.24	2.16
Sept. 11, 2001							2.97
Feb. 21, 2002	1.89		3.24	3.15	2.97	2.70	2.97
Dec. 20, 2003		1.62					
Mar. 25, 2004			3.87	3.78	3.60	3.33	3.24

[a]As of March 1998, reserve requirements and excess reserves were combined into the reserve requirements.
[b]Floating 5–10% lower than the Central Bank lending rates of corresponding maturity.
Unit: percent per annum.

excess reserve ratio. The artificial elevation of the lower bound on the interest rates has distorted the interest rate of the money market rates and the whole interest rate system.

Second, because banks, especially the state-owned banks, are the monopolistic capital suppliers, the basis of forming the market interest rate is weak. Position analysis shows that the net lending and net financing of other banks and financial institutions are positively related to the net lending out and net financing out of the state-owned banks. In other words, although other banks and financial institutions are much more active than state-owned banks, the amount of money that state-owned banks put into the market is crucial to the change in the interest rates. At the same time, the financial institutions, excluding state-owned banks, especially the urban commercial banks and rural credit cooperatives that imported several hundred billion yuan every month in 2003, are overdependent on the market, so any slight change will cause drastic rate fluctuations. For example, on August 23, 2003, the Central Bank announced an adjustment of the reserve ratio from 6% to 7% starting from September 1; the market interest rate suffered sharp fluctuations from September to November.

Third, the inefficiency of the market interest rate mechanism is also reflected by its seasonality. Since 1998, due to the impact of the banks' position change (which is reflected in the change of a bank's excess reserve ratio), the turnover of the interbank lending market always dropped drastically in January and increased greatly in December. If the Central Bank hadn't adjusted the reserve ratio several times during the interval, the lending rate would have demonstrated the same seasonality. In January 2004, the seasonality of the interbank lending market was shown again when the interest rate rocketed and turnover plummeted at the same time. Because the change of interest rates in both the interbank lending and repo markets basically are synchronized, the repo rate shows similar fluctuations. It is well known that in an efficient market the cyclical change caused by the seasonality factor should be offset by arbitrage. But in a market with banks as its major trading parties and capital flowing always in one way, arbitrage by other institutions cannot produce the offsetting effect.

Fourth, because China's financial system is dominated by banks and all the nonbank financial institutions have to depend on the capital support from the banks, especially the state-owned banks, the inefficiency of the interest rate in the interbank market will naturally impact the exchange market. For example, on certain trading days, the repo interest rate of the exchange market will be lower than the excess reserve ratio rate. But on most trading days, the zero-rate bottom line of the interbank market is also effective in the exchange market. At the same time, the fluctuation in the interbank market will cause even more drastic fluctuation of the repo rate in the exchange market. In addition, because the exchange market is closely related to the unstable stock market and is different from the interbank market in terms of its transaction model and clearing system, the exchange market will suffer more fluctuations than the interbank market.

2.10.3 INFLUENCE OF THE CENTRAL BANK

Since 2000, open market operations have become a more and more important way for the Central Bank to implement monetary policy. But with one-way capital flow and an imperfect interest-rate-forming mechanism, open market operation, which is very popular in other countries, seems unable to affect the interest rate in the money market. For example, statistics comparing 1999 and 2002 show the net turnover of the open market didn't have a serious influence on the money market. In other words, the interest rate transmission channel in countries with an advanced market economy is limited in China. The key reason is clear: In the Central Bank's effort to adjust interest rates through open market operation, the core mechanism is to influence the reserve position of commercial banks. However, due to the existence of the excess reserves, the commercial banks, especially the four state-owned banks and the state joint-stock banks, possess too much "cash." Therefore, just through open market business, the Central Bank doesn't necessarily have a stronger influence than the four commercial banks that put several hundred billion yuan of capital every month into the interbank market.

To solve some problems encountered during open market operations, especially the lack of short-term government bond varieties that open market operation depends on, at the end of 2002 the Central Bank began to issue Central Bank bills in the interbank market to strengthen market liquidity. Such an operation can yield partial results in terms of the market interest rate, let alone the high cost it has caused. The reason is that when there is big difference between the interest rate prescribed by the Central Bank and the market rate, issuing Central Bank bills via auction may have limited effects. This phenomenon happened several times in 2004. Since open market operation and Central Bank bill issuance cannot produce the expected results, the Central Bank during "special periods" utilizes nonmarket ways, such as adjusting the legal reserve requirement ratio or even applying a differentiated reserve ratio.

In comparison with open market operations and Central Bank bill issuance, the change in the excess reserve requirements will produce a more obvious influence on the interest rates in financial markets. The change in the excess reserve ratio influences the money market and bond market through influencing the excess reserve ratio of the banks. For example, analysis of monthly statistics in the interbank lending market from 1997 to 2003 shows that the excess reserve ratios of the state-owned banks and other banks have obvious positive relationships with the excess reserve ratio, with state-owned banks having the closer ties. In other words, a drop in the excess reserve ratio will reduce the excess reserve ratio of the banking system, with the state-owned banks' ratio dropping more seriously. At the same time, the turnover and interest rate of the interbank lending market are, respectively, negatively and positively related to the excess reserve rate. That is, the drop in the excess reserve ratio will result in a turnover hike and a price drop in the market.

Because the change in the legal reserve requirement ratio will influence the bank's excess reserve ratio, the reserve requirement ratio should also have a similar impact on the turnover and price in the money market. But the impact is pretty small because the incentive of the banks to maintain the excess reserve remains untouched under the condition of unchanged excess reserve ratio. Analysis shows that after 2000, the change in the excess reserve ratio will have a much stronger influence than the change in the excess reserve ratio. In fact, according to the turnover analysis, from August to December 2003 the fluctuations that took place after the Central Bank raised the legal reserve requirement ratio had a more profound reason—the "reaction" of the market players over the uncertainty regarding the future market. So when the excess reserve ratio remains at a high level, the market interest rate will stabilize sooner or later. This is a sure thing for a financial system dominated by banks. For example, in 2004 the Central Bank adjusted the legal reserve requirement ratio again and implemented the differentiated reserve ratio policy, but loan issuance of the commercial banks didn't change because of it.

2.11   CONCLUSIONS

In recent years, China's money market has developed rapidly, with increased transaction varieties, expanded transaction scale, and enlarged market membership. On this basis, the Central Bank has been more and more effective in indirectly regulating the market through monetary policy. However, China's money market is still in its initial stage. The market instruments available for transaction are still limited. To some degree, the market is segmented, with a small transaction scale and inefficient liquidity. Because the interest rates of deposits and loans are still subject to control, the influence of interest rate movements in the money market on other financial markets is still limited.

The main issue in China's money market is that the inefficient state-owned commercial banks absorb the overwhelming majority of the deposits. Therefore, comprehensive measures could be applied from the perspective of the whole financial system to promote the development of the money market, satisfy the needs of development of the financial market, and enhance the efficiency of monetary policy operation on this basis. Generally speaking, efforts are being made in the following areas:

1. Product innovation should be further accelerated. When the spot market has developed to a certain stage, the interest rate derivative transaction, such as the forward bonds, should be introduced to provide market members with convenient and flexible risk-offsetting instruments. This is being implemented in 2006.
2. Diversified market players could be fostered, to create market demand with several layers to enhance market liquidity.
3. Interest rate reform is being further promoted gradually.
4. The corporate bonds and commercial bills market could be further developed to change the current situation of overconcentration of deposit funds in limited financial institutions.
5. The development of money market funds could be further promoted to alter the one-way capital flow in the money market.
6. The money market investment products could be enriched to smooth the transmission between the money market and the capital market, especially through reforming the check management system and strengthening the issuance and circulation of short-term state Treasury bonds; the transmission mechanism between the money market and the capital market should be improved to make the money market a real place for the whole financial system to form a base rate and for institutional investors to manage liquidity, a place that serves as a key link in the monetary policy transmission mechanism.

REFERENCES

Fan, L. and Zhang, C. Beyond Segmentation: The Case of China's Repo Markets. Manuscript, 2006.

Fan, L. and Zhang, C. The Chinese interbank repo market: An analysis of term premiums. *The Journal of Futures Markets*, 2006.

Xie duo. Open market business practice and the change of monetary policy operation method. *Economic Study*, May 2000.

Xie duo. *The Development of China's Money Market and the Open Market Business*. http://www.unirule.org.cn/Forum/forum.html.2001.

Xie duo. Analysis of the development of China's money market. *Economic Study*, September 2001.

Dai guoqiang. On the goal and channel of the development of China's money market. *Economic Study*, 2001.

Financial and Securities Institute (FSI) of Renmin University of China (RUC). On the relationship between the money market and the capital market—Analysis report on the management policy of the credit capital flow into the stock market.

Chen wei. Comprehensive report on the transaction in the interbank lending and securities system in 2004. *China Money Market*, February 2005.

Xu lin and Wu fengdan. Actively developing and fostering the interbank market. *China Money Market*, February 2005.

Changjiang Securities and Finance Institute of CASS. Instrument innovation is needed to change the "one-way disintermediation" of the money market. *Shanghai Securities*, December 28, 2004.

Peng xingyun repo market is gradually showing its true color. *Shanghai Securities*, November 25, 2004.

Xu zhen. Solid development, new record and excellent performance—the summary of good performance of the interbank bond market in 2004 and the prediction of its development direction in 2005. *Government Securities Depository Trust and Clearing Co. Training Department.*

Zhang jingguo. Developing money market fund and strengthening the interest rate transmission effect. *Shanghai Securities*, April 22, 2004.

Guan Shengyi, An analysis of the effects of monetary policies changes on the bond market, Chinamoney, April 2005.

China International Capital Limited, Prospect into 2006 China's Bond Market.

SYWG Research & Consulting, China Bond Market Strategy in 2006.

CHAPTER 3

China's Money Markets: Policies and the Banks

Thom Thurston

Queens College and The Graduate Center, City University of New York

3.1 INTRODUCTION

Until recently it has been difficult to speak of a Chinese money "market" except in a very limited sense. The financial markets have been repressed, and there has been limited choice as to transactions, trading partners, and financial terms. Even today and despite impressive strides toward liberalization, the money market in China still lacks standard money market features such as an active CD market and Treasury bill sector. Interest rates on most securities and loans available to local depositors and borrowers are fixed or capped by the government. The financial markets are tightly controlled, so any gaps in development reflect a policy choice.

The Chinese government has chosen to liberalize its money market more slowly than other markets, for several reasons. First is a fear of speculative bubbles in commodities and financial instruments and associated funds flows within the domestic economy and with external markets. Second, the banking system is widely regarded as fragile; speculative flows might destabilize it. In addition, the lifting of deposit interest rate ceilings and of restrictions preventing ownership of other liquid assets, domestic and external, would almost certainly deprive banks of the captive deposit base on which they have depended for decades. The loss of this base could be seriously destabilizing for the banking system. Third, the banking system has acted, and with modifications continues to act, as a massive income-transfer facility. "Policy lending"—government-directed lending at more-favorable-than-market conditions, in some cases with small probability of amortization—still requires large "seigniorage" revenue collection on captive deposits. It also of course leads to loans on the books of banks that eventually appear as nonperforming. Fourth, China's exchange rate policy has involved an informal peg to the U.S. dollar since 1994.[1] The argument for keeping the yuan–dollar exchange rate pegged has centered on avoiding speculative capital flows and destabilization of the fragile banking system. Holding down the yuan relative to the dollar also has helped sustain export growth, which probably accounts for the greater share of China's high real growth.

Another factor is that the process of holding down the yuan has involved massive sales of yuan deposits in exchange for dollar foreign exchange reserves. This dollar accumulation, which exceeded $600 billion in 2004, has turned out to represent a new device for collecting seigniorage revenue.[2]

3.1.1 PRESSURE TO LIBERALIZE

Increasingly, the disadvantages of this system have begun to outweigh the perceived advantages. China's accession to the WTO and its requirement that China meet liberalization by early 2007 has led to a flurry of liberalization measures.[3] Inefficiencies of the system invite evasion and forms of perverse financial market behavior that increase risk. A number of observers have argued that a better-developed securities market with wider choice and flexible pricing would help avoid future Asian crisis–like destabilizing capital movements. The authorities lament the fact that commercial banks still handle the bulk of credit in China, and they look forward to a system that would emphasize "direct finance" through the securities industry. It will be difficult to create such a transformation in the next few years. The social infrastructure problems include incomplete resolution of basic issues of property rights and the notion of bankruptcy.

---

[1] In July 2005, the peg was changed to a "basket," which included the U.S. dollar and 10 other currencies. The immediate effect was to increase the dollar price of the China yuan by about 2%.

[2] In other countries, seigniorage is mainly collected via interest on assets that the Central Bank purchases with money that it has created. They of course could just spend the money, but that is frowned on. China in fact formally outlawed Central Bank lending to the central government in 1994. Apart from the issue of inflation control, there is a desire to have the credit markets work efficiently, thus a movement to reduce the amount of policy lending. An alternative, for the short run at least, is to collect seigniorage by means of buying foreign exchange with RMB. The foreign exchange can be an earning asset (although the return may be regarded as low by some). There is also some liquidity and political bargaining power that can result from holdings of foreign assets. The funds can then be used for bailing out banks, which has been done once, in the amount of $45 billion in 2003.

[3] The PBC posts data, regulatory information, and other information on its Website, www.pbc.com.

At least as serious in the short run, the very idea of liberalizing the money market conflicts with the authorities' control of the yuan value, dampening destabilizing expectations, and the transfer of seigniorage revenues. These considerations have led the authorities to limit liberalization largely to the interbank markets.

3.1.2   THE MONEY MARKET: INSTRUMENTS AND DEVELOPMENT

The money market consists of (1) an interbank market somewhat akin to the U.S. federal funds market or the LIBOR interbank placement market; (2) a bond market, which takes place both on the stock exchanges (which were established in 1990) and interbank with both outrights and (3) repo; and (4) a burgeoning commercial paper market. Deposit markets are still relatively nascent. The commercial banking sector, while still carrying the bulk of credit, suffers several handicaps: nonperforming loans (NPLs), reluctance to free the deposit market, need for seigniorage income.

In the mid-1990s, the money market grew rapidly in volume. By the early 2000s, trading in interbank loans, bonds, and bond repo had substantially surpassed the trading volume in the stock markets (Table 3.1). The dominant player is the Chinese government rather than private parties.

3.1.3   INTERBANK LENDING AND BORROWING[4]

Interbank borrowing seems to have originated in about 1981 in an "underground" and probably illegal market linking banks in Jiangsu and Zhejiang provinces with banks elsewhere. Demands for funds had become particularly strong on the part of the more developed township and village enterprises (TVEs), prompting inflows of funds from outside provinces and with interbank loans as the vehicle of intermediation (see Table 3.2).

In 1985, the People's Bank of China (PBC) officially allowed lending and borrowing among state-owned specialized banks. The specialized banks promptly exploited their officially sanctioned status to undertake a number of illegal transactions, including violating interest ceilings on lending as well as making forbidden loans to certain nonbanks. Since excess demand for funds tended to be in the medium- to long-term maturities, net fund flows coming from the

---

[4]Most of the information in this section is from Yang and Peng (2002), pp. 4–5; Iman (2004), pp. 19–20.

TABLE 3.1   Interbank Trading (100 million yuan)

Year	Interbank, bonds (repo and spot, exchange, and interbank)	Stocks
2001	68,519	38,305
2002	147,121	27,990
2003	198,180	40,258

Source: People's Bank of China, Website http://www.pbc.gov.cn/english/diaochatongji.

TABLE 3.2   Interbank Lending (in yuan)

Year	Total	7 days and under
2001	8,082	6,646
2002	12,107	10,539
2003	22,220	20,982

Source: People's Bank of China, statistical Website: http://www.pbc.gov.cn/english/diao.

hinterlands to the coastal areas, the bulk of interbank lending was also in these maturities.

The situation worsened in the 1990s, at least from the point of view of the authorities. Nonfinancial firms borrowed from commercial banks in order to invest in securities and real estate. Little discipline was exerted at the local branch level of the People's Bank of China, contributing to a spurt in money and credit, inflation, and "bubble sectors," particularly real estate in Shanghai and Beijing.

In 1995, the PBC tightened credit by raising interest rate ceilings and developed a reform program that was in place by early 1996. The new rules clarified which institutions could trade on the interbank market and, to monitor compliance, required all trading (from June 1996) to be executed through the electronic trading system provided in Shanghai (China Foreign Exchange Trading System). Maximum maturities (4 months for commercial banks, 7 days for nonbanks) were established, and limits on lending based on deposit levels and reserve levels were established. Commercial banks were explicitly forbidden to use interbank loans for purposes of acquiring fixed assets or making investments. The regulations limited interbank loans to be used for settling temporary discrepancies in accounts or temporary working capital loans. Interest rate ceilings on interbank lending, however, were eliminated.[5]

These regulations resulted in two rather obvious aggregate impacts. First, the interbank market changed after 1996 from a medium- to long-term market to a short-term market, predominantly with maturities of less than 1 week. For example, by 2003 less than 6% of interbank transactions took place at maturities of greater than 7 days; slightly over 3% at maturities of greater than 14 days. Second, while continuing to grow, the interbank lending market fell behind in size relative to other money market sectors, in particular the interbank bond trading market. The interbank market has become something closer to interbank lending markets in Western countries: primarily short-term and used to settle temporary discrepancies in balances.

State and joint stock banks (see later) are the major lenders in this market, for they tend to have ample deposits at centrally controlled rates. Interbank lending tends to be a safer outlet for funds than commercial loans to the state banks, which are already plagued by problem-loan portfolios. Joint stock banks, which fund themselves largely from the bond repo market (see later), also have been opting for lower-risk loans to financial firms.

3.2 BONDS: SPOT AND REPO

3.2.1 BONDS

The government of the People's Republic issued bonds for the first time in 1981. "Local governments," in the form of township and village enterprises (TVEs), began to issue securities in the early 1980s as well, though most of these securities took the form of stocks.[6] Capital market development in the 1980s was rather disorganized and inefficient.

The opening of the Shanghai Securities Exchange in late 1990 and the Shenzhen Stock Exchange in spring 1991 effectively opened the modern financial markets in China. These exchanges were particularly important for the development of the bond market because until 1997 both primary issue, secondary trading, and bond repo trading took place mainly on these exchanges.

---

[5]Other relevant details from Imam (2004): CHIBOR was for the first time open to negotiation between lenders and borrowers. Later, in May 1998, foreign banks were licensed to obtain RMB funding through interbank borrowing. Also, foreign-funded companies were permitted to borrow RMB from Chinese banks for a maximum term of 1 year.

[6]Shi Jianhuai, "Financial Innovations in China, 1990–2000," Working Paper No. E2001006, *China Center for Economic Research*, 2001, p. 13. The first stock with characteristics of Western shares was issued in Shanghai in 1984.

3.2.2 BOND TRADING IN THE INTERBANK MARKET

In early 1997, the interbank government bond market was created. The episode of "disorder" discussed earlier in connection with the interbank market included many instances of banks' funneling funds through trust and investment companies (TICs), many of which where owned by or affiliated with banks, directly into an apparent stock market bubble. In addition, some banks were using their own and affiliated TICs to fund themselves from the stock markets.[7] The 1997 measure permitting interbank trading in bonds was accompanied by restrictions on bank participation in the stock market, directly and indirectly through TICs. Effectively, the interbank bond market was being offered as an alternative to direct participation on the part of banks in the stock markets.

Since 2000, bond trading in the interbank market has far exceeded bond trading in the exchanges (Table 3.3). Trading in the interbank market is quote driven and is executed case by case at a negotiated price.[8] This is the most important market for block trading of bonds among financial institutions. The principal players are the PBC, commercial banks, securities companies, insurance companies, securities investment funds, and credit cooperatives. Nonfinancial institutions may use commercial banks as agents to trade in the interbank bond market.[9] The major instruments traded are Treasury bonds, financial bonds (see later), and a small number of PBC bills (see later). Banks conduct transactions in the securities at the behest of the China Government

TABLE 3.3 Treasury Bond Trading Volumes, 2001–2004 (unit: 100 million yuan)

Year	Interbank repo trading	Shanghai stock exchange trading		Shenzhen stock exchange trading	
		Spot	Repo	Spot	Repo
2001	40,133	4,383	15,343	433	145
2002	101,885	6,381	24,419	2,328	0
2003	117,203	5,500	52,982	256	18
2004	N.A.	2,962	44,086	5	0

Source: People's Bank of China, statistical Website: http://www.pbc.gov.cn/english/diao.

---

[7] Ibid, p. 15.

[8] Chapter 2 discusses these figures further.

[9] According to the CSRC, April 2004, certain commercial banks have been authorized to set up counters at their branches that are permitted to buy and sell bonds of individual customers.

Securities Depository Trust and Clearing Co. (CGSDTC). Especially important has been the development of an interbank "repo" market in these bonds, which has essentially swamped the spot market (see Table 3.3). Custody of the securities is also maintained at the CGSDTC. The repo market is discussed in more detail later.

Bonds are also still traded on the Shanghai and Shenzhen stock exchanges, with Shanghai dominating (see Table 3.3). The major players there are securities companies, insurance companies, securities investment funds, trusts, and individual investors. The PBC does not trade in this market, and commercial banks are not allowed access to it. Trading on the exchanges is order driven and is executed at a matched price.

The market for bonds, especially under repo, has been growing rapidly (Tables 3.3, 3.4, and 3.5) and is responsible for most of the recent growth in the money market. There are four major reasons for this. (1) The government has increasingly been financing its critical long-term projects, such as electricity projects and roads to depressed hinterlands, by borrowing in the securities markets. The government formally stopped borrowing from the PBC in 1994 and has reduced its borrowing from state banks as it has transformed them into (true) commercial banks. (2) There is a need to sterilize PBC purchases of foreign exchange (mainly U.S. dollars) with RMB; to prevent excessive RMB growth, the government has issued securities. (3) There is also a need for a large securities market in order for the PBC to be able to use open market operations as a primary monetary policy. In part, the recent need to issue bonds to dampen inflationary pressure has more or less automatically led to increased bond issuance; more generally, though, a large and liquid market in securities is necessary for efficient open market operations involving securities purchases as well. (4) There is a deliberate policy of the authorities to

TABLE 3.4   Bond Market Summary Data

	Year		
	2001	2002	2003
T-bonds issued (RMB 100 million yuan)	4,884	5,934.3	6,280.1
Corporate bonds issued (RMB 100 million yuan)	147	325	358
Bonds trading volume (1 million lots)	2,047.07	3,292.52	6,201.94
Bonds turnover (RMB 100 million yuan)	20,417.76	33,249.53	62,136.36
T-bond spot turnover (RMB 100 million yuan)	4,815.59	8,708.68	5,756.11
T-bond repurchase turnover (RMB 100 million yuan)	15,487.63	24,419.64	52,999.85

Source: China Securities Regulatory Commission, *China's Securities and Futures Markets*, April 2004.

TABLE 3.5   Exchange-Traded Bond Market Summary (2000–2003)

	2000	2001	2002	2003
Trading volume (10,000 lots)	197,979.00	204,707.68	329,480.25	620,194.41
Corporate bonds				
spot	906.15	672.13	639.81	26,973.40
repo	906.15	672.13	639.81	3,439.33
				23,534.07
Convertible bonds	11,717.48	3,684.55	688.29	5,830.70
T-bonds	185,355.37	200,351.00	328,152.15	587,390.31
T-bond spot	38,018.57	45,474.64	83,955.76	57,391.85
T-bond repurchase	147,336.80	154,876.36	244,196.39	529,998.46
Turnover (100 million yuan)	19,119.16	20,417.76	33,272.35	62,136.36
Corporate bonds				
spot	92.92	68.84	70.33	2,717.02
repo	92.92	68.84	70.33	363.61
				2,353.41
Convertible bonds	135.07	45.68	73.70	663.39
T-bond spot	4,157.49	4,815.60	8,708.68	5,756.11
T-bond repurchase	14,733.68	15,487.64	24,419.64	52,999.85

Source: Adapted from China Securities Regulatory Commission, China's Securities and Futures Markets, April 2004, Table 7.1, p. 31.

redress the perceived "imbalance" in the financial system reflected in a securities market that is too small, too backward, and insufficiently privately oriented. The authorities have made considerable efforts to improve the securities market infrastructure since 2002, with partial success.

3.2.3   EXCHANGE RATE POLICY AND THE DEVELOPMENT OF THE GOVERNMENT SECURITIES MARKET

The RMB has been informally pegged to the U.S. dollar since 1994.[10] Keeping the RMB low requires purchasing foreign exchange (mainly U.S. Treasuries) with RMB created for the purpose. The fact that the purchase of dollars is required suggests that controls on capital market transactions are porous.

[10] The exchange rate in 1994 started at 8.7 (RMB/$). In more recent years it has been 8.27.

In 2004 and 2005, large amounts of these increases in the monetary base were sterilized by means of the issuance of bonds (see Section 3.4.6 on financial bills). This has expanded the market for government securities. Since these are used as the basis for repo, that market has expanded as well. In this way the exchange market has proved to be a method by which China can exploit its seigniorage-gathering power. Foreign exchange assets by the end of 2004 had mounted to $609.9 billion.

"Cashing in" on the accumulated dollar wealth, of course, conflicts with the objectives of keeping RMB low. Gradual drawdown has, however, already taken place to help take nonperforming loans off bank balance sheets. In 2003, about $45 billion of these funds were used to inject capital into the China Construction Bank and the Bank of China. This provides a motive for keeping capital controls tight for some time, together with eventual gradual appreciation of the yuan, or a dramatic abandonment of the peg. Some writers have expressed fear that China (and other countries) will see the potential losses from dollar depreciation and thus feel compelled to dump their dollar assets suddenly.

3.3 CENTRAL BANK BILLS

The sterilization process has induced the PBC to introduce its own bills. The Central Bank bills were issued via auction and were highly liquid. Typically, interest rates on Central Bank bills have turned out to be lower than repurchase rates. This borrowing cost has proved in many instances to be lower than the return from holding foreign exchange reserves. The bills have been popular investments for banks because, under the 8% Basle II risk-weighted capital requirements required by January 2007, these bills have no capital requirement. Loans, in contrast, require a full weight in calculating capital requirements. Also, as suasion has been applied to banks to lend less, these bills have proved to be an attractive option. Earlier labeled "financing certificates," these bills had already been issued in 1993, 1995, and 1997. In September 2002, the PBC converted some outstanding repurchase contracts into Central Bank bill obligations. In April 2003, the PBC began to issue Central Bank bills outright. The total outstanding issues had reached 240 billion yuan.

The PBC's bills offer qualified investors a short-term security, which the Treasury does not offer. However, these bills are not completely integrated into the Treasury market. Wu Xiaoling, vice governor of the PBC, complained in a speech on March 2005 that the yield curve was still incomplete at the short end.

3.3.1   DEVELOPMENTS IN REPOS

Repos were traded on the exchanges through the 1990s, then primarily on the Shanghai Exchange. They were extensively used by TICs during the bubble episodes of the 1990s to obtain funds for stock market and real estate speculation. When the unified interbank bond market opened in 1997, interbank repo trading was established as well. By 2000, interbank repo trading had outstripped trading on the stock exchange.

The repo market is supervised by the PBC. The underlying bonds are mainly long term, and they have no regular issuing cycles. One Treasury and four corporate bond repos are available on the Shanghai and Shenzhen stock exchanges. The China Security Regulatory Commission publishes monthly turnover statistics in repos. The short-term money market is largely taken care of by repos, since there is no bill market with regular issues as in the United States. The most popular maturity range is 1 week (around 60%). The yield curve looks normal. Fan and Zhang (2004) find modest-term premiums at the short end. They conclude that rates on repos traded on exchanges tend to be affected by stock issues.

The dominance of repo trading over outright securities trading can be explained by several factors. First, growth in the market for outright securities has been modest as compared with its long-run potential. Various capital controls have shut off foreign participation, which has further limited the market. Bonds have not been liquid in the absence of market makers. Second, repos provide collateral. With failures of information and lack of adequate credit ratings, this can be an important generator of credit. Third, the bonds are concentrated in the banks, so it is convenient for them to use it to acquire funds. It is a device that allows a very short-term credit market among financial institutions (which in this case are almost exclusively banks). Fourth, the PBC has, since the late 1990s, engaged in increasing use of repo in its open market operations. In part this reflects the limited availability of the outright market, but this also tends to deepen the market. Fifth, and probably not last in importance, the repo market has flexible rates and can respond to market forces.

3.4   BONDS AND MONETARY POLICY

The PBC policy instruments are reserve requirement ratios, a Central Bank base rate, rediscounting and Central Bank lending, and open market operations. In contrast with the United States and some other highly financially developed countries, open market operations is a relatively new instrument, and the other instruments are more active than in many of the financially developed countries.

3.4.1 RESERVE REQUIREMENTS

Variation in reserve requirements has been used actively as an instrument to control credit growth. Since 1998, China has had a system of reserve requirements differentiated by bank. In spring of 1998, for example, a common legal requirement of 13% was applied to commercial banks, and an additional or "excess" reserve requirement, which varied from 5% to 7%, was applied at the PBC's discretion. In April 2004, a different sort of "differentiated" reserve requirement took effect. Reserve requirements now vary systematically with parameters such as banks' capital adequacy ratios and those that measure asset quality. Certain state-owned banks that have not yet undertaken shareholder reforms as well as rural and urban credit cooperatives are exempt from the differentiated requirement. The PBC pays interest on reserves, at different levels for required and excess reserves. As of March 2005, the interest rate on excess reserves was 0.99%, while the required reserve interest rate was 1.89%.

3.4.2 CENTRAL BANK BASE RATE AND CENTRAL BANK LENDING

The traditional instrument for controlling money and credit is Central Bank lending. Over the years, less emphasis has been put on discretionary allocation and more on varying the PBC's base interest rate and various PBC lending rates that have been tied to the base rate.

A drawback of the Central Bank lending mechanism is that in practice by as late as 1998 it was difficult to retrain provincial-level branches from providing excessive accommodation to local borrowers. One means of centralizing control over the monetary base was to consolidate the 30 provincial branches into six regional branches. Another method has been used to increase reliance on open market operations, an instrument initiated in the late 1990s and increased greatly in importance since 2000.

3.4.3 OPEN MARKET OPERATIONS

As the money market has developed, the PBC has relied on it increasingly for open market operations. The principal use of open market operations in the 2000s has been to absorb (rather than expand) the monetary base. This has been both for the purpose of restraining the growth of credit as well as to sterilize PBC dollar purchases. An obstacle to the use of the instrument was that the stock of securities in the PBC's portfolio has traditionally been meager. The PBC has been expanding its issuance of Central Bank bills. The PBC is also a major transactor in bond repos. This activity has expanded and deepened the interbank repo market, which is being used as a monetary indicator.

3.4.4 PRIMARY DEALERS

China has a primary dealers list of banks and other financial institutions with which it conducts open market operations. In early 2005, the PBC assessed the quality of dealers and licensed 52 of them based on so-called "survival of the fittest" characteristics. The breakdown included 42 commercial banks, 14 securities firms, 4 insurance companies, and 2 rural credit cooperatives.[11]

3.4.5 CORPORATE BONDS

As indicated in Table 3.6, total government or "quasi-government" securities (policy financial bonds) outstanding comprised about 30% of GDP in 2003

TABLE 3.6   Domestic Securities Issued in 2003

	100 million yuan	% of GDP
Treasury and other fiscal bonds outstanding	22,604	19.3
Policy financial bonds	11,650	9.9
Corporate bonds	358	0.3
Shares (total market capitalization)	42,458	36.2
Total	77,069	65.7
Total government securities	34,612	29.5
Outstanding loans of domestic banks	96,401	82.2

Source: People's Bank of China.

---

[11] People's Bank of China, *Highlights of China's Monetary Policy in the First Quarter of 2005*, June 16, 2005.

and an amount at the current exchange rate (8.27 RMB = $1) roughly equal to $414 billion. Outstanding corporate bond issues were strikingly low, comprising only about 1% of total bonds outstanding, or about $4.3 billion. Corporate bond growth has lagged, for several reasons: (a) Access to the market is restricted by the government issue, as well as participation in the secondary market; (b) the government is extremely cautious, owing to experiences with default in the early 1990s; (c) corporate bond rates are still restricted, at present limited to 140% of the bank savings rate; (d) there is only one rating agency, which is state owned. On the positive side, some encouraging indications include the fact that local enterprises have been permitted to issue bonds, there is some easing of restrictions on the purpose for which the funds have been raised, and the issue process has become more streamlined, with features such as paperless issue, electronic settlement systems, and registration of custody.

3.4.6   FINANCING BONDS

Financing bonds are issued mainly by policy banks, but they can also be issued by commercial banks, finance companies, and other financial institutions. Financing bonds may be issued in the national interbank bond market or to targeted investors. Institutions may not issue financing bonds without approval of the PBC. They must submit annual application for approval by the PBC. The China Clearing Company provides registration and trust services.

Financing bonds are issued by three "policy banks" (China Development Bank, which accounts for the larger share, the Export-Import Bank of China, and the Agricultural Development Bank). Financing bonds recently have accounted for about a third of debt outstanding in China. These quasi-government bonds plus corporate bonds in 2003 comprised only about 12.5% of outstanding bank loans and 28.3% of stock market valuation. Statistics such as these—heavy dependence on loan finance as opposed to security finance, lack of securities ownership except for shares, miniscule share of private securities—are lamented in official publications as underscoring the underdevelopment of the country's financial system.

3.5   ACCEPTANCES AND COMMERCIAL PAPER

Commercial paper is a discount bill used as a short-term portfolio tool for investors and a source of short-term cash for companies. In China, the paper is discounted as collateral in order to provide discount facilities from commercial banks.[12] The PBC often accepts this paper as rediscounted collateral by banks when the PBC wants to expand the monetary base by means of open market operations.

Starting in the early 1990s[13] but progressing very slowly, the short-term paper market began to grow rapidly in the late 1990s with the progression of enterprise reform. Until 2005, the market consisted of a type of "bankers acceptance" market involving commercial bills of exchange. Under Central Bank regulation, a firm could issue a commercial bill only after a commercial bank had accepted or "guaranteed" the payment indicated on the paper. Commercial banks typically discounted a large share of the paper and resold the acceptances to qualified investors. Bills could be issued only to qualified investors, such as banks and securities firms, not to the general public. Financing this way is cheaper than through bank loans. The PBC became a major "rediscounter," because it used these bills in its open market operations. Moreover, the PBC permitted firms to issue these instruments without prior approval (provided they had been accepted by a commercial bank). They could also roll over maturing paper without approval.

In the early 1990s, lack of laws, regulations, and a system of credit evaluation in this market held back market growth. A 1995 Commercial Paper Law and, more importantly, a series of regulations improved the attractiveness of the instrument to commercial banks. Most commercial banks have opened discount, rediscount, and acceptances business; many have established special branches for acceptance business.

There are still some drawbacks to the market that are inhibiting the growth of commercial paper. The bank-acceptance precondition limited the development of a firm credit-based market; instead, the quality of the paper depended primarily on the credit of the bank that had accepted it. The market was primarily bearer paper in printed form, with weak authentication procedures. In 2004, the PBC (together with the China Securities Regulatory Commission and the China Banking Regulatory Commission) set out new rules allowing firms to issue paper directly to qualified institutional investors in the interbank bond market. The PBC regulates issues, and regular reports must be filed with the PBC. The bills are restricted in their maturity and outstanding balances, but their issuance rates will be market determined. Issuers are required to provide credit ratings and to submit to certified public accounting audits. The emphasis is on reducing administrative interference and promoting market-based approaches "like commission sale underwriting and public bidding." The resulting paper is closer to a form of "commercial paper" as in Western-style markets, with

---

[12]In the United States the main purchasers of commercial paper are nonbank nonfinancial firms.

[13]According to Shi (2001), the market began in 1982 but was inactive for a decade.

the important difference that trading is restricted to the interbank market and among banks and qualified investors.

3.6   FOREIGN PARTICIPATION IN SECURITIES

In 1997, foreign financial institutions were allowed to enter China's interbank market. Initially there was no demand for RMB funds by foreign institutions, so close was this to the Asian financial crisis. But soon foreign financial firms became substantial net borrowers. In August 2003, seven Western institutions were granted qualified financial institutional investor (QFII) status. This permitted greater access to the domestic market and to a flexible foreign exchange arrangement for capital flows. Qualified foreign institutions can trade A-shares as well as Treasury, corporate, and convertible bonds via special custodian banks. By October 2004, 35 institutions had received licenses for quotas from $50 million to $800 million. QFII applicants must meet credit and financial soundness standards to be approved. If the institution is a bank, it must be in the top 100 by asset size and manage no less than $10 billion in securities. There are seven Chinese custodian banks (four state banks, three joint stock banks) and four foreign banks (Standard Chartered Bank, HSBC, Citibank, Deutsche Bank).

Foreign participation augurs well because conditions necessary to sell securities to foreigners are those ultimately necessary for a broad market for local investors. An additional side benefit would be to put pressure on commercial banks for reform.

3.7   COMMERCIAL BANKING

Commercial banks, the large ones comprising nine joint-stock company banks and seven wholly state-owned banks, still are responsible for most of China's financial flows. The four largest state banks—the Industrial and Commercial Bank of China, the China Construction Bank, Bank of China, and the Agricultural Bank of China (Table 3.7)—account for about six-tenths of total loans in China. Some of these banks are quite large by international standards. For instance, the *Economist* ranking for 2003 places the China Construction Bank at 21st worldwide in terms of "Tier I" capital[14]; the Industrial and Commercial Bank at 25th. In total assets, the Industrial and Commercial Bank of China was in 20th place.

---

[14]Tier I capital is core capital, which includes equity capital and disclosed reserves.

TABLE 3.7   Major Banks in China, 2002

	Assets	Capital	Capital as % of assets
State banks			
Industrial and Commercial Bank of China	4,734,236	177,855	3.76
China Construction Bank	3,083,195	107,236	3.48
Agricultural Bank of China	2,976,566	13,604	0.46
Bank of China	2,905,707	219,660	7.56
China Development Bank	1,041,711	75,401	7.24
Agricultural Development Bank of China	764,472	19,091	2.50
Export-Import Bank of China	110,182	6,519	5.92
Joint-stock banks			
Bank of Communications	489,556	32,565	6.65
China Merchants Bank Co., Ltd.	263,849	16,032	6.08
Huaxia Bank Co., Ltd.	126,504	3,601	2.85
CITIC Industrial Bank	222,350	9,337	4.20
Minsheng Banking Corporation Limited	188,274	6,004	3.19
China Everbright Bank Co., Ltd.	222,163	12,812	5.77
Shenzhen Development Bank Co., Ltd.	122,171	3,768	3.08
Industrial Bank Co., Ltd.	138,164	6,344	4.59
Shanghai Pudong Development Bank	279,741	8,432	3.01

Source: Annual Reports, figures assembled by Li Qingliu (2005).

The dominance of bank loans in the financial system reflects history and the government policy to protect banks from market competition as well as the need to suppress the deposit market (for purposes of seigniorage and exchange rate control). Banks were used, in the mid-1980s reforms, as a vehicle for investment allocation. Prior to that, profits (which were more or less guaranteed by monopoly and administered prices) were either plowed back into firms or taxed and reallocated according to government plan. In the mid-1980s, state banks were used to allocate credit to priority sectors. The issuance of cheap deposits (the low rates that were set, and a lack of alternative liquid assets for households and businesses) provided revenues that could be effectively transferred by means of terms preferable to those the market would demand. As the 1980s continued, pressure mounted to convert the banking system into a true market allocation system. Unlike other banking systems, the structure did not arise as a response to market needs for finance. Rather, it was imposed as part of a socialist system and had to be converted to a market-oriented sector.

As a result, balance sheets and the obligations of banks suffer the carryover effects from the previous system—NPLs are the prime manifestation.

On the liabilities side, interest rates are fixed or capped based on PBC-posted base rates. Holdings of alternative assets besides Treasury bonds and equity on the stock exchanges are prohibited. Apparently, the authorities are not willing to free up the banking market and exchange markets anytime soon. A key problem in this regard is the legacy of decades of "policy lending," which has produced a high share of nonperforming loans (NPLs) on the banks' balance sheets.

Before the banks can operate as true credit intermediaries, a large component of the NPLs must be removed form the banks' balance sheets. However, the "bailout" process is fraught with moral hazard issues. On the positive side, the process of disposing of NPLs will require a liberalized securities market; to this extent, the pressure for banking reform will have the advantage of pushing securities market reform. Also, requirements under China's WTO accession help, which includes access to foreign bank ownership.

3.7.1 AMCs

Estimates by the late 1990s of the NPL problem suggested NPLs were at about 40% of total loans outstanding, due largely to 40 years of command economy "policy loans" but also to weak performance of SOEs and lax internal credit risk controls of the state-owned banks. Asset management corporations (AMCs) were sent to buy bad debts of the four major state-owned commercial banks (the big four banks) and dispose of them over 10 years. The big four banks average about 65% of Chinese banks' loan portfolio.

Four AMCs were created in 1999 and 2000 in order to dispose of about $170 billion in NPLs from major state banks. It is widely estimated that a greater amount of NPLs still remains on state bank balance sheets. The actual transfers of bad loans took place over 1999 and 2000.

The amounts transferred are estimated at about half the total estimated NPLs at the big four banks. The particular loans transferred were considered as "policy-based" due to four characteristics: They were on the books at book value; the government financed them (i.e., explicitly said where the funds would come from); transfers were mainly from the pre-1995 loans; and transfers were "substandard" or "doubtful" before the end of 1998 under the old Chinese loan classification system. The general impression has been that the government is taking responsibility for the pre-1996 loans but not for later loans.

Information revealed by the government allows one only to speculate as to the remaining transfers of non-policy-type loans and later bad loans. Ma and

Fung (2002) estimated that 83% of the financing of the AMCs was through the issuance of AMC bonds and that 14% of the financing of the transfers were paid for by the PBC and 3% by the Ministry of Finance. The key challenge in more recent years has been to increase the recovery on the AMCs' assets. The recovery rates on disposed assets has been low, and the process of disposal has been slow. Faster and more successful recovery is important in order to contain the fiscal costs of bank restructuring and to free up the AMCs for future rounds of NPL disposal. A more active market in asset securitization would increase the prospects for this.

3.7.2 ASSET SECURITIZATION

Asset securitization is just beginning in China. In March 2005 the PBC launched a pilot program on credit asset securitization. The China Development Bank and the China Construction Bank were selected as the pilot institutions to engage in securitization of credit assets and mortgage loans. The market is likely to grow slowly because government restrictions will likely stay in place. Local nonbank investors will still be prohibited for some time from holding asset-backed securities (ABS), although foreign banks have been buying a significant share of NPLs[15] (see Table 3.8). Foreign banks are currently prohibited from issuing ABS. The entrance of foreign banks would nonetheless provide an important underpinning of this market, owing to their process experience and strong credit ratings.

3.7.3 FOREIGN BANK OWNERSHIP IN CHINESE BANKS

Foreign banks are quickly acquiring direct stakes in state banks that have been plagued with problem loans. Bank of America was reported to be about to acquire a $3 billion stake in the China Construction Bank.[16] UBS was reported to be considering investing $500 million in the Bank of China.[17] Goldman Sachs and Alianz of Germany were in talks to acquire $1 billion in the Industrial and Commercial Bank of China.[18]

---

[15]Goldman Sachs and Morgan have purchased substantial amounts of bad loans, *New York Times*, "Another China Bank Is Courted by the West," July 11, 2005.

[16]Ibid.

[17]Ibid.

[18]Ibid.

TABLE 3.8   China's AMC "Policy-Based" NPL Transfers During 1999–2000

Asset management corp.	Commercial bank	Assets transferred, in RMB billions	Share of bank loans outstanding (% at end of 1998)
Orient Asset Management	Bank of Communications	267.4	20.4
Great Wall Asset Management	Agricultural Bank of China	345.8	24.6
Cinda Asset Management	China Construction Bank	373.0	21.7
Huarong Asset Management	Industrial and Commercial Bank of China	407.7	17.9
Total		1,393.9	20.7

Source: Ma, Guonan and Ben S.C. Fung, "China's Asset Management Corporations," BIS Working Papers No. 115, August 2002, p. 1. Original source: Zhu, Dengshan, Yang Kaisheng, Wang Xingyi, and Bai Shizhen (2001a): conference speeches at the Beijing 2001 NPL Forum, October, Beijing.

Also, joint-stock banks in relatively good health will likely soon be acquired. Minsheng Banking Corporation, an institution having the lowest share of NPLs, is considered a top choice of foreign institutions.[19]

3.8   CONCLUSIONS

China's money market has developed in a way that preserves, for the time being, the authorities' control over the exchange rate and restricts local wealth holders from holding assets that would compete with bank deposits. Liberalization is extensive but is concentrated primarily in the interbank markets—for instance, interbank lending rates and repo rates are unrestricted, while loan and deposit rates are set and corporate bond rates are capped relative to bank deposit rates. Certain qualified institutions, now including foreign institutions, are permitted to trade along with banks in the interbank market.

Control over the exchange rate and liquid asset markets is motivated by fear of speculative capital movement, its effects on a fragile financial system, and concerns that the Central Bank might be unable to contain unsustainable growth of credit. In addition, though not openly acknowledged, repression of

[19] According to *The Economist*, May 2, 2005, p. 19, Minsheng's NPLs comprised 1.31% of total loans at the end of 2004, as compared with an average of 5.01% for joint-stock banks.

liquid instruments that can be owned by local investors serves to maintain the banking system as a source of seigniorage revenue. Seigniorage income requires a "captive" stock of deposits earning less than their true market rate. There are of course other obstacles to the growth of private securities markets, which include an underdeveloped credit evaluation system and a legal system not yet adapted to the concepts of default and bankruptcy.

REFERENCES

Fan, L. and Zhang, C. "Beyond Segmentation: The Case of China's Repo Markets," Manuscript, 2006.

Fan, L. and Zhang, C. The Chinese interbank repo market: An analysis of term premiums. *The Journal of Futures Market*, 2006.

Liu Qingliu, Unpublished Research, Graduate School, CUNY, 2005.

Ma, Guonan and Ben S.C. Fung, "China's Asset Management Corporations," BIS Working Papers, No. 115, August 2002.

Shi Jianhuai, "Financial Innovations in China, 1990–2000." Working Paper No. E2001006, *China Center for Economic Research*, 2001, p. 13.

APPENDIX: AN OVERVIEW OF CHINA'S BANKS*

In this appendix we provide a brief summary of the major financial institutions in China and focus mainly on the types of banks that existed as of 2006.

A.1 TYPES OF BANKS

1. There are three state policy banks:

    (a) The Import-Export Bank of China
    (b) The Agriculture Development Bank of China
    (c) China National Development Bank

2. There are three types of Commercial banks:

    (a) Four big state-owned banks: The Industrial and Commercial Bank of China, the Bank of China, the China Construction Bank, and the Agricultural Bank of China
    (b) Private banks:

        • Citic Industrial Bank
        • Evergrowing Bank

*Prepared by Michelle Yuan Ménager-Xu.

- Guangdong Development Bank
- Shenzhen Development Bank Co., Ltd.
- China Everbright Bank
- Industrial Bank Co., Ltd.
- Bank of Communications
- China Minsheng Banking Corp., Ltd.
- Hua Xia Bank
- Shanghai Pudong Development Bank
- China Zheshang Bank

(c) There are 118 City commercial banks

3. There are 61 rural cooperative banks
4. There are 198 foreign banks and branches

A.2 POLICY BANKS

State policy banks are the banks that are established and guaranteed by the government. Their primary aim is not to make profits, but to implement the nation's industrial and development policies. The state policy banks in China are under the guidance and supervision of the People's Bank of China.

As policy-oriented financial institutions, they have some special properties: (1) The capital of policy banks is mostly provided in the government's fiscal plans. (2) The goal of the state policy banks is for the benefit of nation and society as a whole, instead of just making profits. However, they also try to make reasonable profits via good management. (3) State policy banks have their own sources of capital, mainly composed of *financing bonds*. No personal deposits are received. (4) State policy banks operate in their own fields of business which do not cover competition with commercial banks.

China established three state policy banks in 1994: the China Development Bank, the Export-Import Bank of China, and the Agricultural Development Bank of China. They are all directly led by the State Council.

The objectives of the China Development Bank are: (1) financing key construction products in China to ensure the successful construction of projects with significant importance to the national economy and to social development; (2) centralizing the management of the then-scattered national investment funds by establishing examination mechanisms for issuing investment loans.

The Export-Import Bank of China was established to promote the development of foreign trade and create the foreign trade environment of fairness, transparency, and stableness. By acting in accordance with international practices, such as export trust and guarantee, it would especially expand the export of high-tech, high-value-added products and large-series equipment such as electromechanical products. The State Council decided to set up the Agricultural Development Bank of China, which is financially viable for meeting the reasonable capital needs for economic development in agriculture and rural areas as advocated by policymakers. It would also promote the circulation of the funds that purchase primary agricultural products.

A.3   COMMERCIAL BANKS

Commercial banks are profit-seeking financial enterprises with primary businesses in deposit, loans, and settlement of transferring accounts. Chinese commercial banks have the following characteristics and requirements. First, from the viewpoint of ownership structure, Chinese commercial banks are mostly solely owned by the state, while some joint-stock commercial banks exist. Second, the Law of Commercial Banks of the People's Republic of China provides that commercial banks are not allowed to engage in trust investment and stock operations, nor are they allowed to invest in nonbanking financial institutions or enterprises or real estate other than those they already own.

In terms of the organization of commercial banks in China, the headquarters control branches. From a legal point of view, branches of a commercial bank are permitted to be set up in a certain area or within the whole county. Commercial banks organized this way are independent legal entities and are prohibited from setting up other branches with an independent legal identity.

The headquarters of the four state-owned commercial banks are all in Beijing, with first-tier branches in provincial administrative regions, second-tier branches in provincial capitals and other provincial cities, and third-tier branches in counties. Therefore, first-tier and second-tier branches may co-exist in the same city. In recent years, joint-stock commercial banks have been developing rapidly and expanding nationwide by setting up branches in many big cities. Merchant Bank, Shanghai Pudong Development Bank, and Shenzhen Development Bank are some good examples. Urban commercial banks are established in the administrative regions of their cities. They are prohibited from setting up branches other than in their cities.

According to the Law of Commercial Banks, the major scope of business of commercial banks in China can include public deposit services; loan issuance; domestic and foreign account settlement; discounting notes; issuance of bond; agency issuance; clearing, cashing, and transaction of marketable securities such as enterprise bonds, stocks, and treasury bills; interbank RMB lending; agency transaction of foreign funds; guarantee of letter of credit services; agency collection and payment services; and insurance agency.

Along with the development of a market economy in recent years, commercial banks have diversified their business into the popularization of bank cards; consumer loans (such as auto loan and residential housing mortgage loans); custody of securities; and investment funds.

A.4 STATE-OWNED COMMERCIAL BANKS

State-owned commercial banks evolved from national banks with specified functions, including the Industrial and Commercial Bank of China (ICBC), the Agricultural Bank of China (ABC), the Bank of China (BC), and the China Construction Bank (CCB). The four banks are resumed and developed after 1979.

In terms of their original respective functions: ICBC was responsible for urban industrial and commercial credit*; ABC was responsible for rural credit; BC was responsible for the operation of foreign currencies; CCB was responsible for investment credit in the middle and long run. As financial reform has deepened, the original distinct functions of those banks have become less clearcut. In 1994, the policy businesses of the four banks was handed over to the three state policy banks.

On December 30, 2003, the State Council decided to raise total capital of US$45 billion for BC and CCB from foreign reserves as a beginning of the reformed state-owned commercial banks.

A.5 JOINT STOCK COMMERCIAL BANKS

On July 24, 1986, the State Council reestablished the Bank of Communications because of the need for economic reform. After that, another 11 nationwide joint-stock commercial banks were established, including the CITIC Industrial Bank, Shenzhen Development Bank, and Guangdong Development Bank. They have broken the monopoly of the four state-owned commercial banks.

The establishment of Minsheng Bank in 1996 was a breakthrough in terms of the traditional shareholder structure in China, by becoming the first joint-stock commercial bank with major shareholders from non-state-owned enterprises.

A.6 URBAN COMMERCIAL BANKS

The predecessor of the urban commercial bank was the urban union bank. Although "union" is in their names, these banks are actually joint-stock commercial banks, subject to the Law of Commercial Banks. There are about 5,000 urban credit unions in China, most of which are no longer unions but small commercial banks instead. Their major scope of business is local economic development and they serve the development of small and medium businesses. In 1998, all urban union banks changed their names to urban commercial banks.

A.7 TRUST INSTITUTIONS

Trust, a property management system that accompanied the development of the market economy, that is a legal contract between the grantor (creator) and the trustee that gives ownership to a trustee to manage wealth and direct income for the benefit of another. A trust and investment company (TIC) in China is a nonbanking financial institution entrusted by and managing wealth for the beneficiary. It is multifunctional in the management and utilization of wealth, the activation of capital, the provision of information and consulting as well as social investment.

The modern trust industry was introduced into China from foreign private banks. In 1917, the Shanghai Commercial Deposit Bank established its custodial division (later changing its name to trust division), which commenced the era of independent Chinese trusts. In 1918, the Zhejiang Industrial Bank started the business of renting safety deposit boxes, which has some trust characteristics. In 1919, the Juchengxin Bank Shanghai Branch established its trust division, operating transportation, storage, custom services, and agency transactions of marketable securities. These were the first three financial institutions commencing trust services in China, symbolizing the beginning of China's modern trust industry.

In October 1979, the BC headquarters pioneered in establishing the trust consulting division. The same year, the China International Trust and Investment Corporation (CITIC) was established in Beijing. In June 1980, the People's Bank of China formerly opened a trust business under the guidance of the State Council. Other banks operated the business subsequently to support economic integration and to activate the national economy.

The number of TICs reached 745 in 1988, most of them established by local governments and central government departments. Trusts then played an active role in attracting foreign investment and in activating the local economy for China. However, TCIs were not really trusted-by-one-party-and-manage-wealth-for-him institutions, but merely banks that absorb deposits and issue loans. Furthermore, blind competition, overlapping institutions, inadequate capital, and poor management all emerged in the development of TCIs, leading to huge financial risks. Therefore, the government reformed TCIs in 1982, 1985, and 1988 by consolidating many overlapping institutions. The total number was thus reduced to 376 in 1991. Further reforms have been carried out since 1993. As of the end of 2003, there were 57 TICs nationwide with total assets of 257.9 billion RMB.

In March 1999, the People's Bank of China began to reform the TICs under the guidance of the State Council. TICs now have to separate their businesses from banking and securities. They are not allowed to accept deposits. They are also prohibited from issuing loans backed by debts or investing in industrial enterprises.

TICs are allowed to operate part or all of the following businesses authorized by the People's Bank of China: (1) capital trust, i.e., the beneficiary entrusts the capital that he himself could not manage or was prohibited from managing under the law to the management, utilization, and disposal of TCIs under the conditions and goals of the contract; (2) entrusted movable properties, real estate, and other properties, i.e., the beneficiary entrusts his or her own movable properties, real estate, copyrights, and intellectual property rights to the management, utilization, and disposal of TCIs under the condition and goal of the contract; (3) the investment fund businesses allowed by relevant law in China, and to participate in it in the capacity of the sponsor of the fund management company; (4) intermediary businesses, such as mergers, acquisitions, project financing, corporate wealth management, and financial consultancy; (5) the underwriting of treasury bonds and corporate bonds entrusted and authorized by the State Council and other departments; (6) the management, utilization, and disposal of agency wealth; (7) agency safeguarding; (8) credit witness, credit information, and economic consultancy; (9) guarantee for others by their own assets of TICs. On April 28, 2003, the China Banking Regulatory Commission (CBRC) began its duties. The regulation of the trust industry was handed over to the CBRC.

A.8 POSTAL SAVINGS INSTITUTIONS

Authorized by the State Council and the People's Bank of China, the Bureau of China Postal Savings and Exchanges (BCPSE) is a postal finance institution based on the Bureau of Postal Savings and Exchange of the Postal Ministry. It operates in the spirit of "finding a position in the market by balancing itself and taking responsibility for its own profits and losses, risks, and performance." The BCPSE receives administrative guidance from the Bureau of Postal Services and business regulation by the People's Bank of China.

The client of the China Postal Savings Bank is an individual. Its scope of business includes taking RMB and foreign currency deposits, personal remittance and exchange, agency business, and underwriting government bonds. The China Postal Savings Bank is not allowed to issue loans. The deposits it takes must be set aside for deposit reserves and allowances. The remaining part could be transferred to the People's Bank of China.

State-owned commercial banks, or state policy banks or could be used to purchase Treasury bonds and the financial bonds issued by state-owned commercial banks and state policy banks.

CHAPTER 4

China's Foreign Exchange Markets

Le Yan
Deputy General Manager, Bank of China Trading Centre (Shanghai)

Like many developing countries, the People's Republic of China (PRC) regards foreign exchange policies as a crucial element in economic development. China's official currency, yuan (also known as renminbi, RMB, or CNY), is not yet fully convertible, which means that the conversion of foreign exchange against RMB is under restriction.

On the other hand, transactions between foreign exchange pairs are unrestricted. There is no limit on trades for exchanging the U.S. dollar (USD) for the Japanese yen (JPY) or the pound sterling (GBP), etc. Actually this kind of trade has become very popular among individual citizens since the mid-1990s because of the dearth of investment products for domestic foreign exchange owners.

So there are two foreign exchange markets in China: RMB against foreign exchanges and foreign exchange pairs. The latter is almost the same as in the international market because almost no restrictions are set on it. We discuss this in Section 4.3. First, we consider the RMB–foreign exchange market in China.

The first part of this Chapter deals with the FX regime in place until July 2005. Section 4.3 discusses reforms and modifications made since then.

4.1   CHINA'S FOREIGN EXCHANGE CONTROLS

The authority in charge of China's foreign exchange control is the State Administration for Foreign Exchange (SAFE), which is also a subordinate institution of the People's Bank of China (PBC), China's Central Bank.

China's current foreign exchange control system was first introduced on January 29, 1996 but is modified intermittently. The People's Republic of

China's Regulation of Foreign Exchange Management, enacted on January 29, 1996, and then revised on January 14, 1997, classifies foreign exchange transactions into two categories: *current account* items and *capital account* items.

Current account items include trade in goods and services, net income from foreign investment, and labor remittances. The foreign exchange earnings of domestic institutions should be sold to authorized banks or kept in the approved foreign exchange accounts with the authorized banks (the amount below a preset limit), while their foreign exchange demand can be met through buying from those authorized banks after submitting required documents.

The foreign exchange income of individual residents can be kept as cash or deposits or sold to the authorized banks. They can also buy foreign exchange after the SAFE approves their applications. However, individual residents' foreign exchange–denominated assets are not allowed to be transferred or remitted overseas without the approval of the SAFE. Some of these restrictions are being relaxed.

Foreign-invested companies or joint ventures usually enjoy more freedom. They are allowed to keep their foreign exchange in their bank accounts under a limit set by the SAFE. Such a limit is based on a company's volume of current account income.

Capital account items include the movement of capital between domestic and foreign residents that affects the assets or liabilities of domestic residents. Foreign direct investment, loans, loan-related security transactions, and security investments are the major components of capital account items. Foreign exchange income of China's domestic institutions in capital accounts should be kept in the foreign accounts with the authorized banks. Only after the approval of the SAFE can this kind of foreign income be sold to banks.

According to this foreign exchange control system, most domestic institutions are subject to a compulsory foreign exchange selling mechanism, which means they cannot keep any foreign exchange above their limits. On the other hand, foreign exchange transactions under *current account* need not be approved, while all *capital account* transactions are subject to approval of the SAFE.

However, corporations still need to submit related documents on foreign exchange transactions under current account for review, such as commercial contracts, letters of credit, and payment notices.

4.2   A HISTORY OF CHINA'S FOREIGN EXCHANGE SYSTEM

The Chinese government adopted a centralized foreign exchange (FX) control system when it came to power in 1949. In 1953, China officially started its decades-long planned economy, in which only state-owned foreign trade companies could import or export and only the Bank of China was authorized to conduct foreign exchange business. Under such a system, all foreign exchange income must be sold to the government, while all foreign exchange demands needed the approval and allocation of the government.

The reforms that began in 1979 were accompanied by an "open door" policy, which brought inevitable changes to China's foreign exchange control. While the principle of centralized management remained, a new foreign exchange retention system was introduced. Some provinces or enterprises that had foreign exchange income were allowed to keep a certain portion of this foreign exchange. These institutions could even trade their foreign exchange or quotas in the local foreign exchange swap markets, just like domestic residents.

During this period, the government issued two important regulations: the PRC Provisional Regulations on Foreign Exchange Control, promulgated on December 18, 1980, by the State Council, which took effect on March 1, 1981; and the Detailed Rules on Penalties for infringement of Foreign Exchange Control, which were promulgated and took effect on April 5, 1985; and other laws and regulations. Major provisions still in effect include the following.

1. Foreign exchange dealings are centralized and administered by the State Administration for Foreign Exchange Control and its branches (SAEC). Foreign exchange transactions are to be approved by the SAEC and carried out in the PRC through the Bank of China and other financial institutions approved by the state, now to include designated foreign banks.
2. PRC residents and foreigners with foreign exchange income residing in the PRC may deposit the foreign exchange in banks or sell the foreign exchange to banks.
3. Foreign investors in overseas Chinese enterprises and foreign enterprises may, after paying tax on their profits and income, apply to the Bank of China or other authorized banks to remit their profits out of the PRC.

The existence of foreign exchange swap markets caused the emergence of two different exchange rates—the official rate and the swap market rate. This two-tiered or double-tracked exchange rate system was ended in 1994.

The People's Bank of China, on December 28, 1993, issued the Notice on the Further Reform of the Foreign Exchange Control Structure, which took effect on January 1, 1994. The notice unifies the official RMB exchange rate and the market rate for RMB established at the foreign exchange swap centers throughout the PRC. Under the notice, all foreign exchange income of PRC enterprises must be sold to designated banks authorized to deal in foreign exchange. However, enterprises with foreign equity interests and enterprises allowed to have foreign exchange bank accounts are allowed to retain their foreign exchange earnings.

Control on the purchase of foreign exchange is also relaxed. Enterprises that require foreign exchange for their ordinary trading activities may purchase foreign exchange from designated foreign exchange banks if the application is supported by proper import contracts and payment notices. For import activities that require quotas, import license, and registration, foreign exchange may be purchased from designated banks if the applications are supported by import contracts and the relevant required documents. For nontrading activities, any application for purchase of foreign exchange needs to be supported by payment contracts or payment notice from relevant overseas organizations.

4.3   THE EXCHANGE RATE REGIME

Between 1949 and 1953, the central government set up an exchange rate regime aimed to encourage exports and inflow of overseas Chinese remittance in foreign exchange. The exchange rate of one U.S. dollar against *old* RMB (10,000 old RMB = 1 RMB) dropped from 80 (January 18, 1949) to 42,000 (March 13, 1950). The rate was 26,170 in December 1952. Since the central planning economy began officially in 1953, the rate had been pegged at 2.4618 against one U.S. dollar for almost two decades.

The fixed-exchange-rate system was partly due to domestic near-zero inflation but also to the international fixed-exchange-rate environment arranged by the Bretton Woods System. And under the centralized foreign exchange control, almost every kind of foreign exchange transaction was banned. The government also decided not to incur any foreign debt. Therefore the exchange rate was set on the basis of the cost of trade and the purchasing power of overseas Chinese remittance. It was more an accounting instrument than a market indicator.

When the Bretton Woods System collapsed in 1973, China's exchange rate had to be adjusted often to respond to changes in the world economy. The government also changed the link with inflation to a link of a basket of trade currencies. During that period, China revalued its currency almost every year and lifted the exchange rate of RMB gradually to as high as 1.5 against one U.S. dollar in the late 1970s, trying to lower the cost of imports. The high exchange rate in turn caused the trade deficit to surge. When the average cost of earning one U.S. dollar reached 2.40 RMB in 1979, an exchange rate of 1.50 would cause a loss of 0.90 RMB for every U.S. dollar of exports.

In order to develop a better balance between exports and imports but at the same time keep the benefits of a strong currency in nontrade foreign exchange business, China began in 1981 to use a double-rate system. One was the *official* rate for the nontrade sector, including foreign tourists' expenditures, remittance, and foreign investment, which stood at RMB1.50 for one U.S. dollar.

The other was the *internal* merchandise trade settlement rate, which was set at 2.80. It might be inaccurate to call it a double-rate system, because from October 1980 the government authorized the Bank of China to operate a foreign exchange swap business that created a third rate, the swap market rate. Although the swap market rate could only fluctuate in a band of 5–10% with the internal trade settlement rate as the pivot, it was the first market exchange rate in China after almost 30 years.

However, this system did not last long. While the average cost of earning one U.S. dollar kept rising (reaching 3.03 RMB in 1983), the price level of imported goods remained unchanged, which resulted in losses in both exports and imports. The government was forced to lower the official exchange rate. The official exchange rate and the internal trade settlement exchange rate finally merged as one official rate at 2.80 RMB in 1985, slipping to 3.20 later on.

Starting in 1985, China adopted a managed floating-exchange-rate system.[1] The severe domestic inflation and current account deficits pressured the Chinese government to depreciate its currency continually during the latter half of the 1980s. By the end of 1993, the official rate had dropped to 5.70 RMB from 3.20 on July 5, 1986. But this rate was still far above the swap market rate, which was around 8.70.

In addition, the volume traded in the swap market far surpassed those through official channels. Within only five years, the volume rose from $4.2 billion in 1987 to $25.1 billion in 1992. It was estimated that 80% of total foreign exchange transactions were conducted in the swap market. The swap exchange rate market obviously had more indicative information than the official rate.

To implement the policy of "Establishing a Socialist Market Economic System" decided at an important Chinese Communist Party plenary meeting held in November 1993, the central government further reformed its foreign exchange control system and the exchange rate regime. The optimal target was to form a "market-based, manageable, single floating-exchange-rate regime." From the first day of 1994, China's two-tiered exchange-rate regime was replaced by single-rate regime with a merge of the official rate and the swap market rate. The official rate was set at 8.70 RMB against one U.S. dollar. Along with this reform, China started a policy of compulsory foreign exchange selling and settlement and set up a new interbank foreign exchange market. Exporters were required to sell all their foreign exchange earnings above the preset limits to authorized banks, while importers had looser restrictions to buy their foreign exchange. These authorized banks in turn squared their foreign exchange positions in the interbank China Foreign Exchange Trade System,

---

[1] Actually, even now the International Monetary Fund (IMF) regards China as having a managed floating exchange rate, although it might look more like a virtual peg to the U.S. dollar.

which is located on the Bund in Shanghai. The swap markets gradually faded out because only foreign-invested companies or joint ventures were allowed to continue their trading in the swap market, which finally was closed in 1996.

After this radical reform, China's trade deficits reverted to surpluses and the Central Bank started accumulating huge foreign exchange reserves. RMB appreciated against the U.S. dollar, with its exchange rate rising from 8.70 to 8.4462 at the end of 1994 and then further to 8.2796 at the end of 1997. However, the Asian financial crisis alarmed the Chinese government. The fluctuation band of the RMB exchange rate was then shrunk to a very narrow one. The rate was stuck at almost 8.2770 until the latest revaluation of RMB. That further intensified the view that China has a virtual peg to the U.S. dollar exchange-rate regime.

China has been under great international pressure to revalue its currency— renminbi—since 2004. The United States, China's largest trade partner, tends to regard an undervalued RMB as the leading factor behind its large trade deficit, although many statistics and much research prove it the other way around. However, even the Chinese government admits that in recent years, a persistent expansion of the dual surpluses under both the current and capital accounts has worsened the balance of payments disequilibrium. At the end of June 2005, China's foreign exchange reserves reached USD711 billion, thanks to a huge trade surplus, Foreign Direct Investment (FDI), and other kinds of foreign exchange inflows based on the expectation of RMB appreciation. Trade friction with major partners such as the United States and the European Union is also intensifying. In order to implement a sustainable economic development strategy focused on domestic demand, to improve resource allocation, to increase the independence of the monetary policy, and to enhance the preemptiveness and effectiveness of financial macro control, China decided to adjust the exchange rate and reform the RMB exchange rate system.

On July 21, 2005, after the domestic markets and commercial banks closed their operations, and with the authorization of the State Council, the People's Bank of China announced the following.

1. Starting on July 21, 2005, China will reform the exchange rate system by moving into a managed floating exchange rate system based on market supply and demand with reference to a basket of currencies. RMB will no longer be pegged to the U.S. dollar, and the RMB exchange rate system will be improved by achieving greater flexibility.
2. The People's Bank of China will announce the closing price of a foreign currency such as the U.S. dollar traded against the RMB in the interbank foreign exchange market after the closing of the market each workday and will make it the central parity for trading against the RMB on the following workday.

3. The exchange rate of the U.S. dollar against the RMB will be adjusted to 8.11 yuan per U.S. dollar at 7 p.m. on July 21, 2005. The foreign-exchange-designated banks may thereafter adjust quotations of foreign currencies to their customers.
4. The daily trading price of the U.S. dollar against the RMB in the interbank foreign exchange market will continue to be allowed to float within a band of ±0.3% around the central parity published by the People's Bank of China, while the trading prices of the non-U.S. dollar currencies against the RMB will be allowed to move within a certain band announced by the People's Bank of China.

The PBC retains the right to adjust the exchange rate band when necessary according to market development as well as the economic and financial situation. It also vows to maintain the RMB exchange rate basically stable at an adaptive and equilibrium level so as to promote the basic equilibrium of the balance of payments and safeguard macroeconomic and financial stability.

The most important changes in this reform are as follows:

1. There is to be a shift from single peg (to the U.S. dollar) to an exchange system based on market supply and demand with reference to a basket of currencies (but not pegged to a basket of currencies); after this adjustment, the exchange rate changes of major currencies in the international market will objectively reduce volatility of the RMB exchange rate. Because depreciation of the U.S. dollar means simultaneous appreciation of other major currencies, such as the euro and the Japanese yen, their movements will offset each other while they are in the same basket of currencies. However, reference to a basket of currencies does not mean that the movement of the RMB exchange rate will necessarily follow the movements of those currencies within the basket. Also, the PBC has so far never announced the actual combination of these currencies and their weights in the basket, although it is widely accepted that the basket might include the U.S. dollar, which still has the biggest weight, the euro, the Japanese yen, the Korean won, and other currencies of those countries with which China registers an annual bilateral trade in excess of USD10 billion, such as the Singapore dollar, the British pound, the Australian dollar, the Thai baht, the Russian rouble, the Malaysian ringgit, and the Canadian dollar. The lack of transparency of this new system makes it difficult for outsiders to evaluate the proper or "reasonable" level of the RMB exchange rate, which helps the PBC maintain the stability of RMB and implement the independent monetary policy.
2. An "initial" 2% appreciation of RMB before its exchange rate was allowed to float with reference to a basket of currencies. The immediate movement

had stimulated the market's expectation of further RMB appreciation. However, the PBC later stressed that "initial" does not mean that additional adjustment of exchange rate would follow. "Initial adjustment" itself means a modification of the benchmark in the first place, simply like moving the scale to the zero position before weighing an object, which does not imply successive modifications. The new mechanism allows the RMB exchange rate to float according to market principles in the future, and thus there will be no official adjustment of the exchange rate level.

4.4   CHINA'S FOREIGN EXCHANGE MARKET

No official foreign exchange market existed in China for a very long time. In 1980, the Bank of China was authorized by the government to operate a foreign exchange swap business for institutions. Domestic companies could buy or sell their foreign exchange or quotas at the Bank of China. The price could move within a 10% range above or below the official price (official rate = 2.80 against one U.S. dollar; the upper limit was 3.08, while the lower limit was 2.52). The Bank of China also issued Foreign Exchange Certificates (FECs, which ceased to circulate after July 1, 1995) to foreign travelers, overseas Chinese, foreign diplomats, etc. These people could change FECs back to foreign exchange at the Bank of China when they leave China. However, it was still hardly a meaningful foreign exchange market.

The price limits and other restrictions hindered the development of the foreign exchange swap business. On the base of adjustments in Shanghai and Shenzhen, which lifted the price upper limit, the government further reformed the foreign exchange business. The SAFE itself replaced the Bank of China as the main body of swap business, and more financial institutions were authorized to offer this service to their customers. More provinces and cities set up local foreign exchange swap centers. The upper limit of domestic companies' transactions was further lifted to 4.20, while no limits existed at all for foreign-invested companies.

In 1988, the first public foreign exchange swap market emerged in Shanghai. Market participants included both brokers and dealers. The price limits were removed, so the price was decided only by the supply and demand in the market—the daily price limit was 0.15 plus or minus the opening price before July 27, 1992, but was canceled later. More institutions, even individuals (since Dec. 1, 1991), were allowed to trade in the market. The market itself also evolved from a direct search market (Chinese people call it a "hand-in-hand transaction") to an auction market. And the swap market itself settled all transactions.

Most of the spot transactions were settled one working day after the deal day. Between June 1992 and July 1993, the Shanghai Swap Center even started foreign exchange futures trading, with one year forward being the longest maturity. (This kind of futures trade was stopped by the authorities after the forward outright price reached as high as 11 RMB against one U.S. dollar while the official rate stood still at 5.70.)

Other cities, such as Beijing, Nanjing, and Fuzhou, followed Shanghai to set up such swap centers. A national center was located in Beijing that linked business in different cities. In 1992, 26 local swap centers merged their quotations into one network.

These swap centers might be regarded as an embryonic form of foreign exchange market, but they definitely were not a real one. Whereas a real market includes more different levels, such as the interbank market and the open market, China's foreign exchange swap market was only for nonfinancial customers. Commercial banks acted only as the settlement intermediaries. As a by-product of foreign exchange control, quotas were also traded in the swap market, which is not seen in a real market. The most important negative result was the two-tiered exchange regime caused by the existence of both the official rate and the swap market rate.

China's foreign exchange control system changed dramatically in 1994, which also brought radical reform to China's foreign exchange market. The two-tiered exchange-rate system was unified as one official rate. The foreign exchange retention quota system was phased out. Domestic institutions were required to quit trading in the swap markets, and foreign-invested companies and joint ventures followed suit in 1996. These corporations have to sell their foreign exchange incomes above their preset limit to authorized foreign exchange banks under the new compulsory foreign exchange selling mechanism. A new unified national foreign exchange trading center, China Foreign Exchange Trade System (CFETS) was created in Shanghai based on the former swap centers. It started operation on April 4, 1994. The main structure of this foreign exchange market has not changed a lot since then.

4.4.1 THE RECENT SETUP

China's foreign exchange market can be divided into two levels: an interbank market of the Central Bank (represented by the SAFE) and authorized foreign exchange banks, an over-the-counter market between these authorized banks and their institutional or individual customers.

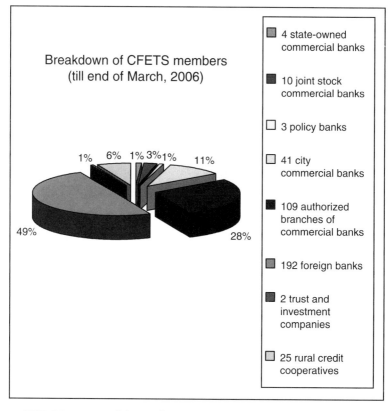

Breakdown of CFETS members (till end of March, 2006)

- 4 state-owned commercial banks
- 10 joint stock commercial banks
- 3 policy banks
- 41 city commercial banks
- 109 authorized branches of commercial banks
- 192 foreign banks
- 2 trust and investment companies
- 25 rural credit cooperatives

1% 6% 1% 3% 1% 11% 49% 28%

FIGURE 4.1   Breakdown of CFETS Membership as of the End of 2004

4.4.2   The Interbank Market: Spot Transactions

As mentioned earlier, China's interbank market, the China Foreign Exchange Trade System (CFETS), was formed in 1994. It is a mixture of visible and invisible markets. The CFETS has a trading floor in Shanghai and some subcenters in other cities. Its membership, including the SAFE and other authorized commercial banks (nonbanking financial institutions were no longer members under a regulation issued by the SAFE in 1998), could either send their traders to the trading floor or use a remote terminal linking to the CFETS network to conduct transactions. Since almost every institution chooses the computer network, there were hardly any traders sitting in the big trading hall. The CFETS recently transferred its trading floor to a newly set-up China Gold Exchange, which made it a completely invisible market. However, unlike the international foreign exchange market, which consists mainly of over-the-counter trading, China still keeps the market form of collective trading, to ensure that the government can closely watch the market.

By July 2005, 11 years after the CFETS was set up, the market had 366 members that can trade for their own interests or as a broker for their customers. Most of them are policy or commercial banks. However, in August 2005, non-banking financial institutions and even nonfinancial enterprises that met the criteria set by the PBC could enter the market on the basis of their true demand.

Before the quote system was introduced to the CFETS in August 2005, member banks relied on the central bidding system to conduct spot foreign exchange transactions. Like trading in a futures exchange, these members banks input their quotations, and these bids or offers will be matched automatically by the CFETS electronic system according to the principles of "first come, first done" and "best price, first done."

Example

1. Bank A bids for the USD1 million at a quotation of 8.2770. Bank B offers USD1 million at a quotation of 8.2770. After they input their quotations into the system, the system will automatically match the bid and the offer if Bank A's bid is the highest and Bank B's offer is the lowest.
2. Bank A bids for USD1 million at a quotation of 8.2770. Bank B offers USD0.5 million at a quotation of 8.2770. Then only 0.5 million is done. Bank A's bid for another 0.5 million USD at 8.2770 remains effective.
3. Bank A bids for USD1 million at a quotation of 8.2770. Bank B offers USD1 million at a quotation of 8.2760. 1 million USD is done at the rate of 8.2765 (the arithmetic average of 8.2770 and 8.2760).
4. Bank A bids for USD1 million at a quotation of 8.2770. Bank B offers USD1 million at a quotation of 8.2780. And they are the highest bid and lowest offer, respectively, at the time. Thus no deal is done yet.

Only spot foreign exchange deals were traded in the system before August 2005. Since that date CFETS members can also trade forward foreign exchange. These deals are settled one working day after the deal date (T + 1), and the settlement is centralized by the CFETS itself. In the early days of the CFETS, there were two currency pairs, the U.S. dollar against RMB, and the Hong Kong dollar against RMB. Contracts of the Japanese yen against RMB and Euro against RMB were added, respectively, on March 1, 1995, and April 1, 2002. These exchange rates are all shown in direct quotation, which is one unit of foreign currency equal to however many local currency (altogether five digits, with four digits after the decimal point).

Trading hours of the CFETS were from 9:30 a.m. to 3:30 p.m. every Chinese workday (usually from Monday to Friday every week). This was extended from 9:20 to 11:00 a.m. after February 8, 2003. The value date of its currency against

RMB will be postponed to the next workday if a workday happens to fall on a holiday in the United States, Japan, or Hong Kong.

Every workday morning, before trading hours begin, the PBC announces the day's mid-price of the U.S. dollar against RMB, based on the weighted average exchange rate of the previous day's transactions. Then the exchange rate of the U.S. dollar against RMB could only fluctuate within a band of 0.3% plus or minus the middle price.

The PBC also announced every workday's middle prices for the Hong Kong dollar, the Japanese yen, and euro against RMB. The fluctuation limits for these three currencies against RMB were 1%, 10%, 10% plus or minus the middle price, respectively, before July 2005. The fluctuation limits for all non-U.S. dollar currencies have changed to 1.5% on July 22, 2005. Then these limits were further widened to 3% on September 2005.[2] In addition, every quotation of U.S. dollars, Hong Kong dollars, and euro against RMB should be no more than 100 basis points away from the last deal price (1,000 basis points for Japanese yen against RMB). Recent behavior of USD/RMB rate is shown in Figure 4.2.

The members of the CFETS used to be forbidden to be both buyer and seller on a single trading day, which means that during the same day the member bank could not sell as long as it had a previous transaction of buying foreign exchange, or vice versa. This regulation was removed on October 1, 2003.

The CFETS charges its members a 0.03% settlement fee for every deal. The settlement fee is 0.15% for every broker deal, of which 0.10% goes to the CFETS and the remaining 0.05% to the broker bank.

Every member had a foreign exchange holding limit preset by the SAFE. This limit usually includes an upper limit and a lower limit. A commercial

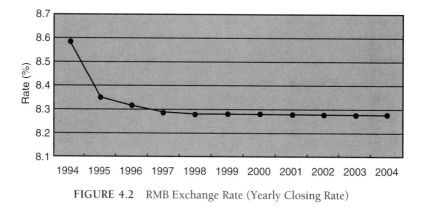

FIGURE 4.2   RMB Exchange Rate (Yearly Closing Rate)

---

[2]Forward FX market is discussed in Section 4.6.1, and later in Chapter 10.

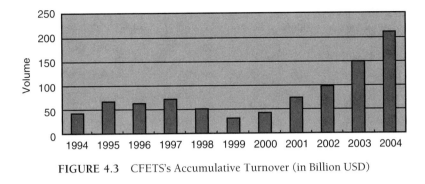

FIGURE 4.3 CFETS's Accumulative Turnover (in Billion USD)

bank cannot have a foreign exchange position more than the upper limit or less than the lower limit. The SAFE sets the limits based on the bank's size, capital amount, daily foreign exchange turnover, macroeconomic conditions, etc. Adjustment of this kind of limit helps the SAFE to control the volume of foreign exchange transactions in the CFETS, because the SAFE, on behalf of the government, which has to be the last liquidity provider of this market, needs some cushion against massive selling or buying of foreign exchange when the whole market is betting on the appreciation or depreciation of the domestic currency. Obviously the effect of this kind of help is also limited. Currently the lower limit is zero. CFETS accumulated turnover is shown in Figure 4.3.

Example

Suppose the SAFE assigns Bank A an upper foreign exchange holding limit of USD500 million and a lower limit of USD. On a particular workday, Bank A finds its foreign exchange holding balance (all other foreign exchange converted to U.S. dollars) to be $750 million. It has to sell at least $250 million to bring its foreign exchange holding position below the upper limit. On another day, Bank A finds its foreign exchange holding balance is minus $50 million. It needs to buy at least $50 million to keep its position above the down limit.

In this case, we can see that even if Bank A is betting on depreciation of RMB—in other words, it wishes to long more foreign exchange—it still could only hold no more than $500 million; on the other hand, it cannot sell short even if it is expecting RMB appreciation.

4.4.3 AUTHORIZED FOREIGN EXCHANGE BANKS AND THEIR CUSTOMERS

As mentioned earlier, the compulsory foreign exchange sale and settlement system forces most domestic companies to give up their foreign exchange.

Even those who get the approval of the SAFE have quantity limits on foreign exchange holdings, although these limits may change. Companies often need to sell or buy their foreign exchange income to or from those authorized banks.

Based on the middle prices of the SAFE, which include the U.S. dollar, the Hong Kong dollar, Japanese yen, and euro against RMB, every authorized bank will publish its own exchange rates. Usually the median price of the U.S. dollar against RMB published by authorized foreign exchange banks will be close to the median price announced by the PBC, while the median prices of other currencies against RMB are set more on the basis of the level of the international foreign exchange market, which means they need not follow the PBC's indicated median prices.

An Authorized FX Bank's Exchange Rate Quotation

Date: Thursday, October 27, 2005
Unit: RMB/100 Foreign Exchange

Currency	Mid-price	Bidding	Bank note's bidding	Offer	PBC's mid-price
USD	808.67	807.05	800.58	810.29	808.67
Hong Kong dollar	104.29	104.08	103.25	104 5	104.25
Japanese yen	6.9755	6.9476	6.7244	7.0034	7.0204
Euro	975.18	971.28	940.07	979.08	979.57
British pound	1,435.71	1,429.97	1,384.02	1,441.45	–
Swiss franc	630.3	627.78	607.61	632.82	–
Canadian dollar	690.7	687.94	665.83	693.46	–
Australian dollar	609.33	606.89	587.39	611.77	–
Singapore dollar	477.68	475.77	460.48	479.59	–
Danish krone	130.72	130.2	126.01	131.24	–
Norwegian krone	124.92	124.42	120.42	125.42	–
Swedish krona	102.44	102.03	98.75	102.85	–
Macao pataca	101.01	100.81	100.00	101.21	–
New Zealand dollar	566.64	564.37	546.24	568.91	–

The PBC established that the spread between authorized foreign exchange banks' bid and offer of the U.S. dollar against RMB could not exceed 0.4% of the PBC's middle price. This spread was expanded to 1% on September 14, 2005.

The limit of the spread between bank's bid price and offer price is set at 4%. However, most authorized banks still set their bid–offer spread at or less than 0.4% for the U.S. dollar against RMB.

As for non-U.S. dollar currencies, the PBC has no limit on the bid–offer spread. Most banks set the spread at or less than 0.8%.

4.4.4 THE INTERBANK MARKET—FORWARD OUTRIGHT TRANSACTIONS

China's movement to adopt a more flexible exchange rate system means greater risk to those institutions or individuals with foreign exchange exposure in daily life or operations. To help them hedge against such risk, a more deregulated domestic foreign exchange market and additional instruments are required.

On August 2, 2005, the PBC issued the "Notice of the People's Bank of China on Issues Regarding Expanding Designated Banks" Forward Sale and Purchase of Foreign Exchange Businesses to Customers and Launching RMB Swaps Against Foreign Currencies, which was followed on August 8 by the Notice of the People's Bank of China on Accelerating the Development of the Foreign Exchange Market.

A forward outright foreign exchange transaction is a binding contract to buy or sell a given amount of foreign currency against RMB for settlement at some future date and at an exchange rate agreed on by the counterparties at the time of dealing.

Such forward outright transactions have now been introduced to the CFETS system. The forward outright market operates from 9:30 a.m. untill 5:30 p.m. every workday. In less than two months, there were 19 banks, including Chinese and foreign banks' mainland branches that became members of the interbank forward outright market after their applications were approved by the authority. These members use a new system—a system to quote their bid or offer prices every day and have the transactions done through the electronic system as well. This system, different from the central bidding system used in spot transactions, is a single trading platform used by multiple entities and matching all entities' lowest offers and highest bids according to the rule of price priority and time priority and is believed to help price discovery and to improve fairness and transparency. This new quote system was later introduced into the spot market, by means of which interbank market participants can complete a transaction by negotiating the trading currency, amount, exchange rate, and date of delivery directly, on the base of mutual credit authorization.

The forward outright transactions can be settled at full amount or at the net amount between the forward price and the spot price at maturity. Banks can decide the maturity structures at their own discretion, which means these forward outright transactions can be odd dated. So far, most transactions have a maturity of less than one year.

The introduction of forward outright transactions into the interbank market obviously helps commercial banks to manage FX risk. In the past, these banks had no way to hedge their own exposure if their customers passed the exchange rate risk on to banks through the forward transaction.

Theoretically the pricing of RMB forward outright transactions is no different than for other forward deals of any foreign currency pairs. It follows the same formula:

R_s: the spot exchange rate of foreign currency against RMB
R_f: the forward exchange rate of foreign currency against RMB
I_f: the interest rate of foreign currency for a certain period
I_r: the interest rate of RMB for the same period

Then, we have

$$R_f = R_s * (1 + I_r)/(1 + I_f)$$

Example

Suppose that today the spot exchange rate of the U.S. dollar against RMB is 8.2770 and that one year interest rates for the U.S. dollar and RMB are 3.60% and 2%, respectively. Then the one-year RMB forward exchange rate should be around the level of 8.1492 ($8.2770 * (1 + 2\%)/(1 + 3.6\%)$). Based on this level, the bank will mark up its offer price and mark down its bid price. Because of the existence of the bid–offer spread in the interest rates, the spread between bid and offer of a forward quotation is usually bigger than that of a spot quotation.

When a customer closes a forward exchange transaction with one bank, the bank will immediately operate in the spot exchange market and money market to hedge the risk.

Example

Bank A today quotes the spot exchange rate at RMB8.2770 per U.S. dollar and the 1-year forward exchange rate at 8.1200/8.1800. A customer sells $1 million at the bank's bid price of 8.1200 for 1-year forward transaction. To hedge its future exchange rate risk, the bank will borrow $965,250.97 for 1 year from the money market at an interest rate of 3.60% and then sell this amount right away in the CFETS at the spot exchange rate of 8.2770, to get RMB7,989,382.28. Then it deposits this RMB for 1 year in the domestic money market at the interest rate of 2%. One year later, the customer comes to exercise this forward contract, so the bank has to get $1 million and pay out RMB8.12 million. On the same day, the money market deals also expire, so the bank needs to pay back $1 million ($965,250.97 plus its interest cost of $34,749.03) and get back RMB8,149,169.92 (RMB7,989,382.28 plus its interest income of RMB159,787.65). The bank will use the U.S. dollars that its customer pays to repay its lender and use the repaid RMB to deliver to its customer. Then all positions will be squared and the bank still makes a profit.

However, such perfect hedging exists only in theory. In practice, due to the upper limit and lower limit set by the SAFE on their foreign exchange holding position, the banks cannot sell or buy all that they might want. And, more importantly, the SAFE forbids banks to combine their spot and forward positions, which means banks cannot transfer their forward position to their spot holding position. So it is almost impossible for banks to disassemble one forward outright transaction into one spot and two money market transactions, which means banks still are unable to hedge any forward market risks. Several months after the CFETS started forward outright transactions, not too many activities had been seen in the market.

4.4.5   AUTHORIZED FOREIGN EXCHANGE BANKS AND THEIR CUSTOMERS—FORWARD OUTRIGHT TRANSACTIONS

Spot foreign exchange transactions can provide little help to hedge exchange rate risk. On April 1, 1997, the SAFE approved the Bank of China as the only provider of forward outright foreign exchange transactions for its institutional customers. Six more domestic commercial banks were later allowed to start such business. After China further reformed its foreign exchange system in July 2005, another six foreign banks were allowed to provide this instrument to their customers.[3]

This kind of service, which is called an *RMB forward exchange transaction*, is not only for those deals under current account but also partly for some deals under capital account, which include repayment of bank foreign exchange loan, repayment of foreign debt registered by the SAFE, or other foreign exchange cash flows approved the SAFE. Customers need to provide the bank those required documents related to the transaction in order to avoid noncommercial deals originating from speculation on the RMB exchange rate.

---

[3]Since July 2005 there have been several reforms in this respect. This is discussed in Section 4.6.

At present, most authorized banks will quote bid and offer prices for eight foreign currencies against RMB, which include the U.S. dollar, Hong Kong dollar, euro, Japanese yen, Australian dollar, Canadian dollar, Swiss franc, and pound sterling.

The terms are often 7 days, 1 month, 2 months, 3 months, etc. to as long as 1 year. Customers can choose the fixed-date forward transaction when they are certain of the actual delivery date of the contract or the optional-date forward transaction when they are not certain of the delivery date. For the latter, customers can select two different terms for the forward transaction if they predict the actual delivery date will fall in the time period between those two terms.

Example

Company A signs a contract with an overseas buyer in which it will buy foreign currency at a future date of delivery of its products. Company A believes that the delivery date will be between 3 and 4 months in the future but is not sure of the actual date. Then the company can choose to deal an optional date forward transaction with the bank, which sets the value date between 3 and 4 months forward. The company is entitled to exchange currencies with the bank on any workday during the 1-month period after 3 months.

Each transaction can be rolled over for a period within 12 months if delivery has to be delayed. That means the longest period a customer can hedge against the exchange rate risk will be 24 months. However, the customer still faces the risk of the change of premium or discount on the 1-year forward rate when he/she chooses to roll over at the end of the first 1-year forward contract.

We can also see that once the spot exchange rate is locked, the forward exchange rate is affected only by the interest rates of RMB and foreign currency or, to be more accurate, by the interest rate differential between them. So if we believe the change in interest rate differential will not be very big, a forward RMB transaction still can help a lot to hedge the exchange-rate risk even after a rollover.

Example

On March 1, 2005, Company ABC in China signs a contract to deliver a ship to its overseas buyer in two years. In return Company ABC will get 10 million USD when it makes the delivery. To hedge the exchange-rate risk within two years, Company ABC decides to sell its future foreign exchange income to protect itself against possible appreciation of RMB. The quotation of 12 months forward RMB transaction against the U.S. dollar at Bank A on that day is 8.1200/8.1800. Company ABC will sell $10 million at 8.1200, which means that on March 1, 2006, it needs to pay Bank A $10 million in exchange for RMB81.2 million. But obviously Company ABC will only get that $10 million one more year later; it will apply to the bank several workdays before March 1, 2006, for a rollover of another 12 months. Suppose the quotation of 12 months forward RMB transaction on March 1, 2006, is 8.1100/8.1700, while the spot rate is 8.2700. (These three rates would not have too big an effect on the effective 24 months forward price unless the interest rate differential between the United States and China changes a lot. We discuss this later.) Then on that day, Company ABC will first need to buy back $10 million at the spot exchange rate of 8.2600, which brings the loss of RMB0.14 per U.S. dollar, and sell the $10 million 12 months forward contract again at the new rate of 8.1100.

Company ABC's actual hedge cost for 24 months forward exchange rate now becomes RMB7.9700 per dollar. This actual 24 months forward exchange rate will not differ, even if the spot rate changes while the interest rates differential remains unchanged. Suppose that on March 1, 2006, the spot rate is 7.5000. Then the 12 months forward exchange rate at that time might be RMB7.3500/7.4100 per dollar, with the middle price around 7.3840 ($7.5000 * (1 + 2\%)/(1 + 3.6\%)$) if the interest rates of the U.S. dollar and RMB do not change. Company ABC will then buy $10 million at a spot rate 7.5000, which will earn the company a profit of RMB0.62 per dollar, and then sell again the 12 months forward contract at the new rate of 7.3500. However, the actual 24 months forward rate is still 7.9700.

The result will not change a great deal if the spot rate goes up as long as the interest rates of RMB and the U.S. dollar do not change too much. Even if the interest rates do change dramatically, the impact on the forward exchange rate is still limited—we can easily get this conclusion from the forward rate formula.

4.4.6 AUTHORIZED FOREIGN EXCHANGE BANKS AND THEIR CUSTOMER—FX SWAP TRANSACTIONS

An FX swap transaction regarding RMB and foreign exchange currency combines two transactions in opposite directions, featuring domestic currency against foreign currency between a domestic entity and a bank. In the first transaction, the domestic entity sells spot or forward outright foreign exchange for RMB at the contracted exchange rate from the bank; in the second transaction, the entity buys forward outright foreign exchange with RMB at the contracted exchange rate from the bank. The settlement of these two transactions should be dated differently, with the former always being earlier than the latter. These transactions can also be carried out in a reverse.

Example
Company A receives 10 million in U.S. dollars today for exporting goods overseas. It needs to sell the U.S. dollars for RMB to repay its supplier.

Meanwhile, it signs a contact to import raw materials and make a payment of 10 million U.S. dollars in 6 months. Thus Company A can enter into an FX swap transaction with a bank in which Company A sells 10 million U.S. dollars for RMB right now and purchases forward outright 10 million U.S. dollars with RMB delivered in 6 months. By means of this RMB swap transaction, Company A can square the positions of different currencies, there by avoiding the exchange rate risks.

To begin an RMB FX swap business, banks that have been approved to conduct the business of forward sale and purchase of foreign exchange longer than 6 months are allowed to register with SAFE. And the rules regulating RMB FX swap transactions are almost the same as those on forward sale and purchase of foreign exchange transactions.

4.4.7   THE INTERBANK MARKET—FOREIGN EXCHANGE CURRENCY PAIRS

The CFETS used to conduct only RMB-related business. On May 18, 2005, China's interbank foreign currency pairs system went live in the CFETS. By the end of July-2005, there were 34 banks that were members of the interbank foreign currency pairs system, within which 10 banks are the market makers.

These 10 market makers, most of them foreign banks, need to quote two-way prices in the system. Other non market-maker members can match the prices and make the deal. There are eight foreign exchange currency pairs traded in the system: euro vs. USD, Australian dollar vs. USD, British pound vs. USD, USD vs. Japanese yen, USD vs. Canadian dollar, USD vs. Swiss franc, USD vs. Hong Kong dollar, and euro vs. Japanese yen. However, since most members can also trade in the international foreign exchange market, they are not active in this system.

4.5   THE "OTHER" FOREIGN EXCHANGE MARKET

After domestic citizens were allowed to keep foreign exchange earnings, bank deposits used to be the only means of "foreign currency–denominated investment." In 1993, the Bank of China began to provide its individual customers in some coastal cities, like Shenzhen, Guangzhou, and Shanghai, a service of exchanging foreign currencies on the basis of international market rates. Some other banks followed suit later.

This business developed quite slowly due to investors' lack of knowledge of this new market, big spreads between bid and offer—300 basis points for banknotes and 100 basis points for foreign exchange bill, a relatively high interest rate in USD and a strong U.S. dollar.

Since then the competition has intensified between commercial banks, the spread between bid and offer shrank a lot to only 40 basis points, large-amount deals can even have the international interbank spread, which is usually less than 10 basis points. To customers, the narrowing spread means a lower service fee. The big slump in the U.S. dollar in the mid-1990s also reminded Chinese individuals that holding foreign currencies (mainly the U.S. dollar) is risky as well. These two factors, plus more knowledge of international financial markets, pushed investors to trade more actively in this business. The trading volume boomed since the mid-1990s. It is estimated to rise from almost zero to $1 billion a day. Many domestic banks have big incentives to develop this business, not only because of its bid–offer spread margin, but also because of the potential interest rate spread of keeping the foreign exchange deposits.

The most popular foreign exchange trading pairs are USD/JPY, because most Chinese citizens' foreign exchange deposits are in USD and in JPY. The trading volume of EURO/USD, AUD/USD, and GBP/USD also picked up recently.

During the last two to three years, some structured products that combine deposits and foreign exchange or interest rate derivatives were introduced to China's market. Some banks even provide foreign exchange option trading for their VIP customers. These kinds of products usually are packaged as "wealth management services," to attract individual customers, and become the new source of bank profits.

Long before commercial banks provided such foreign exchange trading products for their individual customers, institutional customers were being allowed to use these instruments to hedge foreign exchange and interest rate risk. Unlike individual clients who only trade based on deposits, companies need to hedge the risks in both asset and liability terms, which led to demand for swaps, swaptions, etc.

Generally speaking, this market is almost a subdivision market of the international foreign exchange market, which runs according to the world's rule of business.

4.6 CONCLUSIONS

A country that pegs its currency to a foreign currency will have some difficulties in practicing its own independent monetary policy, which is critical in managing the macroeconomy. When the macroeconomic environment changes, there will always be internal and external pressures on the fixed exchange rate. Since the late 1990s, China has been under the pressure first of currency depreciation and then of currency appreciation. A more flexible exchange-rate regime may be a "better" solution.

Since the Chinese government set up a goal of "forming a market-based, single, and manageable floating system" in 1994, the reform of the Chinese exchange-rate regime has been a hot issue in both domestic and international circles. The reform of China's foreign exchange market is one of the most important extensions of it.

APPENDIX: CURRENCY SWAPS

China launched currency (FX) swaps on April 24, 2006. This was a major step toward establishing the foundation of a forward FX market. China sees this as a precondition of a more freely floating exchange rate system.

The FX swap market may end up being a better tool than forwards in hedging FX risk. It is less risky and easier to transact. Swap rates are priced off interest rate differentials, which were about 3% between one-year dollar and RMB deposits as of mid-2006. Clearly it may take some time before the FX swap market becomes liquid.

Here are the details of the new market.

- *Currencies*: RMB against USD, euro, yen, and the Hong Kong dollar
- *Trading units*: RMB quoted up to 0.0001 against the USD, euro, and yen and up to 0.00001 to the Hong Kong dollar
- *Denomination*: Volumes quoted in terms of foreign exchange
- *Trading time*: Monday to Friday 9:30 a.m. to 5:30 p.m. (0130 to 0930 GMT), except public holidays
- *Delivery*: Full amounts, including principal, or just the difference between the first settlement and buy-back dates
- *First settlement*: Two days, unless otherwise agreed
- *Trading commission*: Ten yuan for each 1 million yuan charged on quarterly basis, adjustable with regulatory approval
- *Eligibility to trade*: Banks must have had approval to trade RMB forwards for at least six months
- *Initial members*: Fifty-four lenders including China's five biggest banks and the Shanghai branches of Citigroup Inc., HSBC Holdings Plc., Standard Chartered, Deutsche Bank, and Commerzbank AG.

(*Source:* Reuters)

PART II

China's Bond Markets

This Part deals with RMB-denominated bond markets in China.[1] China has very active local currency bond markets. The capital inflows experienced during the years 2003–2006 created excessive liquidity, which had to be mopped up by the PBC. The variety of instruments and the maturities grew as the Central Bank became more active in the bond and bills markets.

Also, the authorities have made an excellent effort in trying to build yield curves in RMB-denominated bonds and this helped the bond market significantly.

In this Part we provide two Chapters that deal with China's bond markets. Chapter 5 discusses China's bond markets overall and focuses on government bonds. Another discussion of the repo market, already covered in Chapter 2, is also given.

Chapter 6 looks at convertible bonds. Asian corporations prefer convertibles to corporate bonds, and we decided to put additional emphasis on this sector. Convertible and corporate bond markets may be in their infancy in China, but this sector is likely to become quite important in the future.

---

[1] China's international bonds are not discussed in this book.

For example, China's corporate bond issuance increased to RMB65.4 billion during 2005 from RMB32.2 billion in 2004. The State Council, which is the equivalent of China's Cabinet, authorized 43 firms to issue RMB60.8 billion worth of corporate bonds during 2005.[2]

Finally, we should mention the relevance of the new fixed-income derivatives that were introduced during 2005.

[2]*Source*: National Development and Reform Commission.

CHAPTER 5

China's Bond Market

Le Jiachun
Senior Editor, "Shanghai Securities News"

China's bond markets have been developing for more than 20 years. They have become the largest of all the financial markets in China. Bonds are not only one of the most important investment instruments for the Chinese family, but also a financial factor to promote China's economic growth. When international investors marvel at the rapid growth of the Chinese economy (the annual real growth rate of GDP amounts to 9.7%), particularly after China relaxed its capital controls and launched the qualified foreign institutional investor (QFII) scheme, how to invest in China's bond market has become a hot topic, increasingly attracting investors' attention.

The aim of this Chapter is to provide international investors with the basics on China's bond markets. In particular, we discuss what comprises the Chinese bond market, how the market is organized and managed, how investments are made, how market information is acquired, and who the market participants are.

5.1 STRUCTURE OF CHINA'S BOND MARKET

In this section, we first describe the basic structure of the current Chinese bond market. Then we look at its constituents. Next we discuss the market instruments and market players. Finally, we consider how the market developed in the past.

5.1.1 CONSTITUENTS

Like the mature bond markets in the United States and Europe, China's bond market can be divided into a *primary market* and a *secondary market*. The typical model of the basic structure of China's bond market is shown in Figure 5.1.

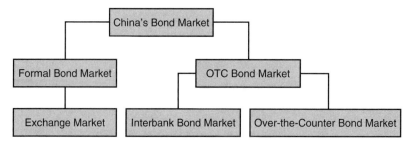

FIGURE 5.1   The Structure of the Bond Market in China

Exchange-Traded Bond Market

The exchange-traded bond market involves bonds traded inside the exchanges, which have a centralized and fixed trading place and trading time, rigorous organization and management rules, a competitive tendering scheme, and efficient trading systems. At present, there are two bond exchanges in China—the Shanghai Stock Exchange and the Shenzhen Stock Exchange—established by the end of 1990. They are membership institutions.

Currently, the instruments traded in the exchanges are mainly T-bonds and corporate bonds (including convertible bonds), which are listed there. T-bond trading plays the major role. From October 1993 to May 1995, China permitted the trading of T-bond futures. Trading flourished and was quite volatile at that time. Given the speculative character of the market, bond futures trading was terminated after the "3-27" event.[1] Thereafter, trading was basically in spot bonds and the bond repo market. Repo transactions are divided into two categories: the collateral *classic* repo transaction and the *buy–sell* transaction. The volume of repo trading has already exceeded that of spot T-bonds.

Interbank Bond Market

The so-called "off-exchange market" refers to the bond market outside of the exchanges. The interbank bond market has become the largest one among China's OTC bond markets. In 1997, the People's Bank of China declared that commercial banks were forbidden to trade spot bonds and repo in the exchanges, but they were permitted to use their bonds deposited at the China Government Securities Depository Trust Clearing Co. Ltd. (CDC), such as T-bonds, Central Bank bonds, and financial policy bonds, to do

---

[1]See Chapters 7 and 8.

trading on the spot and repo markets through the National Interbank Funding Center's trading system. The interbank bond market has developed ever since. The instruments in this market include T-bonds, financial bonds, short-term Central Bank bills, and corporate bonds. Trading is also in the form of spot and repo.

The Bank OTC Market

Actually the current bank OTC market is an extension of the interbank bond market to personal investors, that is, a kind of retail OTC bond market. During the period 1987–1991, the local OTC bond markets were the main bond trading places in China, with physical bonds traded mostly. Afterwards, because of the establishment and fast development of the exchanges, the growth of the OTC bond markets slowed. In 2002, China started to support the bank OTC market. Bond trading and related bond custody and settlement are carried on within the banks' branches. Currently, the bank OTC market is mostly made up of spot T-bond subscribing and trading.

Consequently, China's bond market now consists of the three submarkets described earlier. A multilevel market structure has been set up, with the *interbank bond market* playing the central role and the *exchanges* and *bank OTC market* acting as supplements.

5.1.2   BASIC INSTRUMENTS IN THE BOND MARKET

In this section, we discuss the classification of the instruments in the Chinese bond markets. This classification is not based on the definition of the bond, but is organized so as to help clarify how the market participants use these instruments. The classification is shown in Figure 5.2.

Presently, China's domestic bond market instruments include T-bonds, financial bonds, corporate bonds, and Central Bank bonds. Among the several basic instruments in China's domestic bond market, the T-bond is still the main instrument. T-bonds can be subdivided into certificate T-bonds, bearer-form T-bonds, and book-entry T-bonds.

Certificate T-bonds are like the savings bonds in the United States. They can't be traded on the market, but they can be discounted before maturity at the original seller, such as a bank or securities company. The *bearer-form T-bond* is the physical T-bond purchased in the exchanges or at bank counters. It can be traded at the bank's listed price. *Book-entry T-bonds* are electronic T-bonds. The issuance, trading, and payoff of book-entry T-bonds is done electronically. It is traded in the exchanges and OTC bond markets. Nowadays, China's T-bond

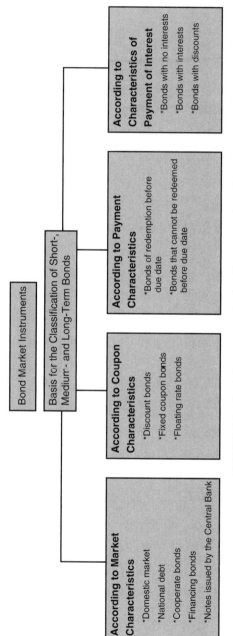

FIGURE 5.2 Basic Instruments in the Chinese Bond Market

is mostly issued in the form of a certificate T-bond or book-entry T-bond. Generally speaking, the long-term and medium-term T-bonds dominate the current Chinese T-bond market. Most T-bonds have a fixed coupon; only a few of them bear floating coupons. T-bonds can also be divided into zero-coupon bonds and straight coupon bonds.

Financing bonds are issued by policy banks. At present financing bonds include the *policy bonds* issued by financial policy banks and financing bonds issued by commercial banks. The latter are the subordinate bonds issued by commercial banks after 2004. At present securities companies have also started to issue bonds. Currently, the maturity of financing bonds is medium term or short term. These bonds also come in fixed or floating rate. In 2004, the amount of financial bond issued in the interbank bond market was about 509.68 billion yuan. In China's bond markets, financing bonds are second in volume to T-bonds.

Corporate bonds are issued by enterprises. Currently, there are two types of corporate bonds in China, *ordinary corporate bonds* and *convertible corporate bonds*. Ordinary corporate bonds have three kinds of maturity pattern: short term, medium term, and long term. In terms of interest rate, corporate bonds can be divided mainly into fixed-rate bonds and floating-rate bonds. In addition, there are callable bonds and noncallable bonds. By the end of 2004, the deposit balance of corporate bonds at the CDC amounted to RMB123.25 billion yuan, RMB39.651 billion yuan of which is traded in the Shanghai Stock Exchange, convertible bonds included. From May 2005, for the purpose of widening the direct financing channel for corporations, the short-term financing bills were introduced in the interbank bond market. By the end of September 2005, short-term financing bills amounted to RMB532 million yuan.

The *Central Bank bill* is a short-term debt certificate issued to commercial banks. These banks help the management of commercial bank excess reserves. Essentially, this is a Central Bank bond. Generally, the Central Bank bond should be short term, from 3 months to 1 year. It is always issued at a discount. With the continual increase of China's foreign exchange reserves, the Central Bank expanded the use of Central Bank bills in order to regulate the monetary base. In 2004, the amount of Central Bank bills issued by the People's Bank of China reached RMB1,507.2 billion yuan. The Central Bank bill has become the most actively traded bond type in the interbank market.

Analysis of the shares of the basic instruments in China's bond market in 2004 shows T-bonds with a 46.82% share, financing bonds with a 28.10% share, Central Bank bills with a 22.67% share, and corporate bonds with a 2.38% share, based on the deposit balance at the CDC. From this we can see that T-bonds play the major role in China's bond market, supplemented by financing bonds and corporate bonds.

5.1.3 BOND MARKET INVESTORS

In this section we consider who the main participants in this market are. Like the mature bond markets in the United States and other developed countries, the participants in the Chinese bond market include individual investors and institutional investors. Commercial banks, insurance companies, and securities investment funds are the major institutional investors. In China's bond markets, the number of individual investors far exceed that of institutional investors. But the latter dominate the market in trading scale and volume. Therefore, institutional investors are the major players in China's current primary and subordinate bond markets.

Based on funding source, we can divide institutional investors into the following categories.

- *Banks:* These are the four state-owned commercial banks, the joint-stock banks, the foreign banks, and other commercial banks. These banks are the major investors in the interbank bond market. Banks were authorized to reenter the exchanges recently.
- *Insurance companies:* According to statistics provided by the China Insurance Regulatory Commission, the annual investment in T-bonds made by insurance companies reached RMB150 billion yuan by the end of 2004. Insurance companies can play in both the exchanges and the interbank bond market.
- *Nonbank financial institutions:* This refers to the nonbank institutional investors, such as trust companies and financial companies.
- *Securities companies:* There are more than 100 securities companies in China, and they are the main players in the exchanges.
- *Funds:* There are more than 100 funds in China. They are required to invest at least 20% of their funds in bonds. By the end of 2004, the seven bond funds had invested more than RMB63.2 billion yuan in bonds. Funds are also the main institutional investors in the exchanges.
- *Nonfinancial institutions:* These are mainly enterprises and other institutional investors. There are about 340,000 nonfinancial institutions in the exchanges, but only 170 in the interbank bond market.
- *The foreign institutional investors:* The Qualified Foreign Institutional Investors (QFII) were authorized to invest in exchange market since 2003 and the Asian Bond Fund2 (ABF2) to invest in the interbank bond market in May 2005.

TABLE 5.1 Type of Investors in 2004

	Custody (primary)			Custody (secondary)		
	Interbank market			OTC		
	At the end of 2004	At the end of 2003	Increase/ Decrease (%)	At the end of 2004	At the end of 2003	Increase/ Decrease (%)
Total	5354	4135	29.48	890934	57512	
Special Settlement Party	10	3	233.33	0	0	0
Commercial Banks	229	198	15.66	0	0	0
Credit Cooperatives	667	575	16.00	0	0	0
Financial Institutions (except banks)	117	97	20.62	0	0	0
Securities Cooperative	95	87	9.20	0	0	0
Insurance Institutions	63	38	65.79	0	0	0
Funds	361	192	88.02	0	0	0
Nonfinancial Institutions	2755	1889	45.84	532	335	0
Private Investors	1056	1056	0	890402	57177	0
Others	1	1	0	0	0	0

Source: China Bond Net.

What then is the structure of the Chinese bond markets? By the end of 2004, the account numbers in the exchanges exceeded 72,114,300, about 3–5% of which participate in the bond trading. Among them, securities companies, listed companies, fund companies, and other institutional investors add up to more than 340,000. Moreover, based on the number of primary deposits and secondary deposits in the CDC, we can calculate the *number* and *type* of the investors on the current interbank and bank OTC bond markets in China. Table 5.1 displays the results.

To sum up, individual investors in the exchanges, can't be neglected in terms of numbers, but in fact nonbank financial institutions play the dominant role. Commercial banks are the leading investors in the interbank market. In the bank OTC market, individual investors and nonbank financial institutions are the main participants. Institutional investors are the main participants not only in the primary market but also in the secondary market, with great pricing power. It's not difficult to see that the participants in China's bond market are diversified.

Next we discuss how this market has been operating.

5.1.4 How the Bond Market Operates

Like the bond market in developed countries, China also hopes to gradually open up the domestic bond market to foreign issuers. In October 10, 2005, Asian Development Bank and International Finance Corporation launched renminbi bonds (Panda Bond) in the Chinese domestic market. China's bond market still relies on the domestic bond market, whose instruments issued and traded include T-bonds, financial bonds, Central Bank bills, and corporate bonds.

The domestic bond market is subdivided into a primary market and a secondary market. The primary market is where the government, banks, and companies issue bonds to the public to raise funds. The secondary market is where bond trading takes place—the exchanges, the interbank bond market, and the OTC bank market.

Primary Bond Market

In China, the major participants in the primary bond market are the Ministry of Finance, the Central Bank, commercial banks, other financial institutions, and enterprises. For a better understanding how the Chinese bond market operates, we offer the following example (see Figure 5.3). It demonstrates the general procedures for issuing a bond today.

Example
1. *Choose the main underwriter and negotiate the underwriting costs.* The Huaneng Group chose Great Wall Securities Ltd. as its main underwriter, and both parties agreed on the underwriting costs.
2. *Confirm the scale of the issue and finish the bond pricing.* In this case, Huaneng Group planned to issue renminbi bonds to raise 4 billion yuan,

---

Corporate Bonds Issued by China Huaneng Corporation in 2003

* Selected the leading issuing institutions and reached agreement on the commission of setting bonds;
* Set the scale and price of bond issuing;
* Established organizations to sell bonds;
* Finished first-phase preparations of issuing;
* Exchanged in the primary market.

FIGURE 5.3   Corporate Bonds Issued by China Huaneng Corporation in 2003

at par value. The 10-year fixed coupon rate is 4.6% payable annually. The nominal interest of the 10-year floating-rate bond equals the sum of the basis interest rate and the basis difference. The basis interest rate is quoted as the 1-year certificate of deposit interest.

3. *Form the underwriting syndicate.* The main underwriter selects the members of the syndicate and assigns the underwriting volume.
4. *Complete preparation of the issue,* including communications, advertisements, and road shows.
5. *Offer the bond on the primary market.*

The issuance procedures for T-bonds, financing bonds, and corporate bonds are similar. Generally speaking, bonds are issued via public auction or underwriting. Currently, auctions are more popular (such as the Dutch or American type).

Nowadays, more than half of the certificate T-bonds and book-entry T-bonds are issued at local bank branches and the counters of securities companies. Most book-entry T-bonds are issued through the exchanges, the interbank market, and the bank's OTC market. Corporate bonds (including convertible bonds) are mostly issued in the exchanges. In 2004, however, corporate bonds were issued on the interbank market for the first time. In contrast, financing bonds and Central Bank bills are issued on the interbank market. These places make up the primary market for Chinese bonds.

Now consider how investors subscribe for bonds. First, investors open a security trading account at a qualified securities company or traders consigned to trade for investors. Second, investors need electronic accounts at the bank OTC market in order to subscribe for T-bonds. The subscribed bonds on the *exchanges* will be registered in the security account by the China Securities Depository and Clearing Company (CSDCC). The subscribed bonds on the *interbank market* show up on the investors' primary and secondary deposit accounts in the CDC. Such bonds are generally deposited by the CDC and subdeposited by the bank handling the transaction. Once the subscription is completed, investors can designate a securities company or traders to trade in the market for them.

The rapid development of Chinese bond market issuance cannot be separated from the regulation and management of this market. To support a more orderly issuing market, a series of regulations was introduced. For example, the Shanghai and Shenzhen stock exchanges issued *The Rules of Issuing and Trading Corporate Bonds* in May 2002 and *The Rules of Issuing and Trading Convertible Bonds* in November 2002. The People's Bank of China released *The Regulations of Bond Issuing on the Interbank Market* in 2002 and *Temporary Provisions for Bonds Issued by Policy Banks* in November 1998. These regulations significantly encouraged the growth of the Chinese bond issuance.

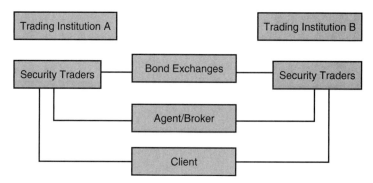

FIGURE 5.4   Typical Bond Trades

Secondary Bond Market

New bonds can be traded on the secondary market once issued. How does the secondary market operate? Figure 5.4 displays a simplified framework showing the typical trading structure of the Chinese bond market. (1) Traders such as banks and securities companies are always dealers. Some traders are also market makers. They are able to set the trading price (the ask price and the bid price), provide clients with market information, and pass on the trading price. At present, the interbank bond market has instituted a market-maker scheme. (2) Agents and brokers act only as investment agents for clients in order to earn commissions, and they do not participate in the market themselves.

In the exchanges, the agent or broker is always a securities company that is also a member of the exchanges. How do investors trade in exchanges? First, investors have to open an account at the CSDCC. Second, they need to negotiate with the designated securities company and open an account. After these steps, investors can ask the securities company to buy or sell bonds, which is completed through the computerized system in the exchanges. For example, trader 1 and trader 2 take investors' orders and fulfill the orders through their representatives inside the exchanges. That is to say, by public tendering, the electronic system in the exchanges will match the price and quantity of the bid and offer from the two parties.

When the transaction is completed, it has to be followed by clearing, settlement, ownership transfer, and deposit. Currently, CSDCC takes charge of the bond clearing, settlement, ownership transfer, and deposit.[2]

---

[2]See the analysis of the Chinese depository and clearing system in the next subsection.

In the exchanges, bond transactions include spot bond and repo trading. Spot bonds include 45 kinds of T-bonds, 37 kinds of corporate bonds, and 34 types of convertible bonds. Bond repo includes 16 types of T-bond and 3 types of corporate bonds. Trading occurs Monday to Friday, from 9:30 to 11:30 a.m. and from 1:00 to 3:00 p.m. every business day.

On the interbank market, institutional investors are the major players, since individual investors are not permitted to trade in this market. The procedure for institutional investors to subscribe and trade on this market is the same as for the exchanges. That is to say, one opens an account at the CDC first and entrusts a qualified broker to trade. However, rather than public tendering, the interbank market adopted the price-inquiry method. The two parties communicate by the system, telephone, e-mail, fax, or other ways. For example, after getting an order from the institutional investor, trader 1 and trader 2 give offers, inquire in standard format, and confirm the deal through the interbank transaction system. After the trading, bond custody, clearing, and ownership transfer are all set by the system in the CDC. As with the exchanges, the interbank market includes spot bond and repo trading. More and more traders are becoming parties in these transactions, especially since 2004, when the market-maker scheme was introduced. Today this market has become the biggest OTC bond market in China. The trading day in this market is from Monday to Friday, from 9:30 to 11:30 a.m. and from 1:00 to 3:00 p.m. every business day, legal public holidays excluded.

In contrast, OTC bond trading is rather simple. Investors only trade with banks. The instruments in this market are the certificate T-bonds and book-entry T-bonds. Certificate T-bonds cannot be traded in the secondary market, but they can be discounted before maturity, whereas book-entry T-bonds can be traded. The business day for the bank OTC market is from Monday to Friday, legal public holidays excluded. By the end of 2004, the number of bank branches had reached tens of thousands. At the same time, bond accounts increased to 888,100, 99.75% of which belong to individual investors. The turnover is RMB5.611 billion yuan (among them 1.121 billion yuan are net buying).[3]

---

[3] Currently, relevant regulations of China's bond market include: (1) Exchanges: "*The Detailed Rules of T-Bond Repo Trading*" (Nov. 2004), "*The Detailed Rules of Bond Trading in the Exchanges*" (Nov. 2004), "*The Regulations of Registration and Clearing for Bonds of Securities Companies*" (Dec. 2003), "*Temporary Provisions for Bond Management in Securities Companies*" (Oct. 2004), "*Rules for Calculating Ratios of Typical Bonds*" (Nov. 2004), etc. (2) Interbank Bond Market: "*Rules for Trading in the Interbank Bond Market*" (Feb. 2002), "*Regulations for Repo Trading in the Interbank Bond Market*" (May 2004), and "*Temporary Provisions for Enterprise Bonds Invested by Insurance Companies*" (June 2003). (3) Bank OTC market: "*Trading Rules for Book-entry T-Bond at the Commercial Bank Counter*" (2002).

The Bond Market Depository and Settlement System

Both bond issuance and bond trading involve bond custody, settlement, and clearing. Consequently, understanding how the bond depository and clearing system operates is key to the study of China's bond market. Figure 5.5 shows a sketch of the depository and clearing system in the Chinese bond market.

As shown in Figure 5.5, the exchanges adopted a secondary depository scheme. The CSDCC opens an account in the CDC. Investors in the exchanges (individual investors excluded) open depository accounts in the CSDCC, and the latter is responsible for the registration and deposit of the traded bond. Bonds trading has to obey the rule "first deposit, then trade." Before a bond is sold, it must be deposited in the CSDCC, which is under the CDC. The exchanges implement automatic matching and net cash clearing. When the deal is completed, the bond delivery is done with "T + 1" and the payment is made to the investors' account at the securities companies.

The interbank market operates on a single-level depository scheme. That is, the institutional investors open depository accounts at the CDC directly. The CDC classifies the accounts into A, B, and C based on the characteristics and operational area of the investors in order to practice a centralized administration. Trading is complete at the inquired price, and settlement is made in a single transaction. The bond delivery and the payment are separated. The CDC takes charge of investors' bond accounts and clears in real time, while money clearing is done through the payment system of the People's Bank of China or the bank where the account is opened. Bond clearing and payment are done with "T + 0" or "T + 1" settlement.

Bank's OTC market adopted a secondary depository like exchanges. That's to say, bonds are deposited at CDC first and then at the secondary depository at the four largest state-owned commercial banks. The latter are responsible for the registration and deposit of the traded bonds. The CDC will record the changes between the banks self-supported accounts and agent accounts on the base of the trading data from the agent banks. The bond clearing and money clearing in bank's OTC market are the same as in the interbank bond market.

Thus the depository systems of the three bond markets in China are founded on the bookkeeping system of the CDC. China has already set up its own relatively advanced bond depository and clearing system.

5.1.5 AN OUTLOOK ON CHINA'S BOND MARKET

China's bond market has been developing since the mid-1980s. With the expansion of the primary and secondary markets, the number of instruments has been growing. For example, the buy–sell repo transaction is similar to introducing a

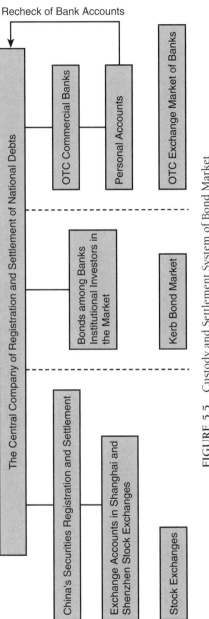

FIGURE 5.5 Custody and Settlement System of Bond Market

149

bond-shorting scheme. At the same time, the quantity and structure of investors is becoming more numerous and diverse. Additionally, trading rules have improved, and modern settlement methods have been introduced. These factors boosted the development of China's bond market, even making it exceed the stock market. The importance of the bond market grows.

However, there are also problems with this rapid growth, for instance, an unsound term structure, dispersion of the primary market, and a shortage of bonds. As part of an emerging economy, the Chinese bond markets still have room to grow.

Bond issuance is expected to expand further. T-bond issuance will stabilize, along with the fading of an expansionary fiscal policy, but the issue volume and size of other types of bonds will increase greatly. The stock of Central Bank bills will keep increasing, because they offset the effect of increased foreign exchange reserves on the monetary base. They also provide an instrument with high liquidity and safety. The issuance of financial bonds will also increase. Because of the reform in China's banking system, banks' subordinate bonds will rise significantly, and policy banks' financial bonds will keep increasing. The issuance of financial bonds may in fact exceed that of T-bonds. In the past, corporate bonds accounted for only a small fraction of total bond stock. On the premise that direct financing will be encouraged, corporate bonds will prosper in the future.

Another point worth noting is that China is considering an experiment in asset securitization. The administrative rule for Credit Asset Securitizaton Pilot Operations was publicized on April 20, 2005. Two pilots include National Development Banks' ABS (Asset-Backed Securities) and China Construction Banks' MBS (Mortgage-Backed Securities). The first instrument chosen for asset securitization is from the mortgage sector. China's RMB7,000 billion mortgage stock is huge, and this may lead to significant issuance of mortgage-backed securities (MBS).

Instruments that can be used for interest rate risk management are also coming into existence. At the moment it is difficult for China's bond market players to hedge market risk with the current T-bond spot and repo trading. Therefore, the Ministry of Finance, the People's Bank of China, and the China Securities Regulatory Commission (CSRC) approved introducing buy–sell repo transactions in 2004, which set up a mechanism for shorting bonds in China. Buy–sell transactions not only enable investors to hedge one-sided long-position risk, but they offer great liquidity to the market. Market makers were introduced as well in order to enhance the liquidity of the bond market.

Other reforms and measures continue to be taken. For example, cross-market bonds, which can be traded in exchanges and the interbank market, were introduced. These can narrow the spread between different markets on the same bond, thus lowering the risks and increasing liquidity. Finally, after the administrative rule for the forward bond transactions in the National Interbank Bond market was publicized on May 11, 2005 the first forward transaction was conducted on June 15, 2005.

The infrastructure of the bond market has been improving steadily. Presently, because bond types, market participants, and trading mechanisms vary, the infrastructure of custody, settlement, and clearing lags behind that of other markets. There is also significant market separation. These reduce bond liquidity, increase transaction costs, and lower efficiency. When the infrastructure of China's bond market improves further, this situation is likely to change. We can expect a diversified and united national bond market in China in the future.

More importantly, China's regulated interest rate system hinders the development of the bond market and highlights the investment risk. With a further liberalization of interest rates, bond issuance and trading will become more market oriented. Also, the issuance and trading price will reflect interest rate movements more accurately. On July 21, 2005, China gave up the fixed exchange rate and moved into a managed floating exchange regime based on market supply and demand with reference to a basket of currencies. These changes will affect the Chinese bond market.

Besides the broad picture just described, a steady and fast economic growth will rebuild family wealth and social wealth, thus stimulating bond demand. In the long run, these factors will firmly support the fast development of China's bond market.

5.1.6 SUMMARY

The preceding analysis offers the fundamental framework and the future path of China's bond market. The following summary should be helpful.

- China's bond market is composed of three parts: the exchange-traded market, the interbank market, and the bank OTC market. The exchange-traded is inside the exchanges; the interbank bond market is a wholesale OTC market; the bank OTC market, a retail OTC market, is an extension of the interbank bond market. At present, the interbank bond market plays the central role, assisted by the exchanges, with the bank OTC market as a complement. The multilevel bond market is coming into being in China. In scale, the interbank market is the largest, the exchanges second, and the bank OTC market third.
- The basic instruments in China's bond market are the T-bond, the financing bond, the corporate bond, and the Central Bank bill. In a number

of shares, T-bonds come first and financial bonds second, with corporate bonds and others serving only as a complement.

- The major players in this market include individual investors and institutional investors. Individual investors dominate in number, but institutional investors are the major participants in bond issuance and trading. The latter are more important because they lead the development of this market.

- By analyzing the primary and secondary markets, as well as the depository and settlement system, we get a better understanding about how China's bond market works.

- The bond-issuing procedure goes as follows: The bond issuer selects the major underwriter and negotiates about underwriting costs → determines issue scale and prices the securities → sets up underwriting syndication → makes preparations before bond issuing → sells bonds in the primary market. Bonds are issued through bank branches and securities companies, the interbank bond market, the exchanges, and the bank OTC market.

- Currently, T-bond spot and repo are the main types traded in the market. The bank OTC market deals only with T-bond spot trading, while both T-bond spot and repo trading are available in the interbank bond market and the exchanges.

- Under the present depository and settlement system, the exchanges and the bank OTC market follow the secondary depository scheme, while the interbank market follows a primary depository scheme. Issuance and trading in China's bond market are carried out by the bookkeeping system in the CDC.

As an emerging market, China's bond market possesses a great potential.

5.2   STATISTICS AND FIGURES

With knowledge of the structure and operation of China's bond markets, we can now turn to the market scale and related statistics and look at some specific aspects of Chinese bond markets.

5.2.1   FLUCTUATIONS IN THE SECONDARY MARKET

A comparison of the variation of the China bond index and that of the Shanghai exchange public bond market index and the China interbank bond market index can indicate the performance of China's bond market in 2004, enabling us to

Index Total

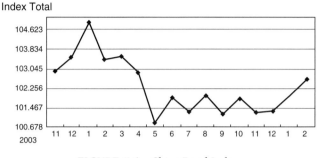

FIGURE 5.6   China Bond Index
Source: China Bond Net

gain insight into how the market was moving. Figure 5.6 shows the fluctuations in China's bond market during the period November 2003–February 2005. The base period of Chinese bond index was set from December 31, 2001 with the base point of 100. The sample includes bonds issued in China whose issue volume exceeded RMB5 billion yuan and whose maturity exceeded 1 year, weighted by the issue size, modified according to the liquidity. In doing this, emphasis is put on the interbank bond market. Thus the data reflect the general trends of China's bond prices.

As we can see from the figure, the long-term low-interest-rate policy of China has strongly influenced the Chinese bond index. Consequently, Chinese bonds experienced a bull market since 2002. However, the end of deflationary forces at the end of 2003 became a turning point and led to another round of high economic growth. By 2004, the Chinese Consumer Price Index (CPI) started to increase faster; the rate exceeded 5% in June, July, and August. At that time, however, the U.S. Federal Reserve started to raise interest rates. This obviously put pressure on the renminbi interest rate. With strengthened expectations of a rise in interest rates, bond prices became more volatile. With this pressure on interest rates to rise, bond prices remained low from May to October 2004. The People's Bank of China raised the interest rates by 0.27% on September 28, 2004, and the bond market suffered further. Then the CPI started to decline at the end of 2004, which frustrated those players who were expecting rising interest rates. As can be seen from the total bond index for January and February 2005, the Chinese bond market started to recover.

Figure 5.7 shows the overall bond index for both the interbank and exchange markets in the two biggest bond markets of China. As the figure indicates, comparatively speaking the fluctuations in the interbank bond market were mild, while the exchange market was suffering from more pronounced fluctuations. The reason for this phenomenon is that the main institutional investors of the

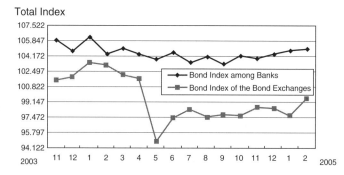

FIGURE 5.7   Comparing the Bond Indices: Interbank and Bond Exchanges.
Source: China Bond Net.

interbank market are commercial banks. At present, Chinese commercial banks
hold about RMB2,700 billion of bonds, almost half of total interbank deposits.
This shows that, as assets, bonds have become one of the main investment tools
for commercial banks. Half of most actively traded bonds in the interbank market are financing bonds and Central Bank bills, in addition to T-bonds. Since
the interbank market is less sensitive to the capital invested, the bond index for
the interbank market looks more stable.

Comparatively speaking, the most actively traded bond in the exchanges
is the T-bond. Low-coupon T-bonds issued previously (particularly medium-
term and long-term T-bonds) have slumped in price. With the expectation of
rising interest rates, the bond index in exchanges fell. The major players in the
exchanges are institutional investors. This is another source of volatility for the
exchange bond index. These investors often take part in repo trading with their
own funds or with funds from their clients. Shrinking of the bear stock market
also affects the volatility of the bond index.

Compared with the exchange market, the interbank market is of larger scale
in trading volume but has less price volatility. The trading in the exchange
market is more active. Nevertheless, the interbank market is still the main market dominating the changes in China's bond market. Generally, the exchange
market is influenced by interbank market conditions, which can also be seen
in Figure 5.7.

5.2.2   THE SCALE OF THE SECONDARY BOND MARKET

We can also gain an idea of the current scale of the Chinese bond market
by looking at bond issuance during recent years. Table 5.2 shows Chinese

TABLE 5.2 Bond Issuance in China from 1996–2004

Year	National Debt			Financing Bonds			Cooperate Bonds			Central Bank Bonds	
	Issued value	Realized value	Remained value at the end of the term	Issued value	Realized value	Remained value at the end of the term	Issued value	Realized value	Remained value at the end of the term	Issued value	Remained value at the end of the term
1996	1847.77	786.64	4361.43	1055.60	254.50	2509.59	268.92	317.80	597.73		
1997	2411.79	1264.29	5508.93	1431.50	312.30	3628.80	255.23	219.81	521.02		
1998	3808.77	2060.86	7765.70	1950.23	320.40	5121.13	147.89	105.25	676.93		
1999	4015.00	1238.70	10542.00	1800.89	473.20	6447.48	158.20	56.50	778.63		
2000	4657.00	2179.00	13020.00	1645.00	709.20	7383.28	83.00	0.00	861.63		
2001	4884.00	2286.00	15618.00	2590.00	1438.80	8534.48	147.00	0.00	925.63		
2002	5934.30	2216.20	19336.10	3075.00	1555.70	10054.10	325.00				
2003	6283.00			4520.00			358.00			7226.80	3376.80
2004	6924.00			5009.00			327.00			15072.00	9742.00

Unit: Hundred million RMB
Source: The People's Bank of China.

TABLE 5.3   A Summary of Interbank Bond Trading 2001–2004

	Total			
	Subtotal of bond exchanges	Spot	Repurchase	
	Exchange volume (Hundred million RMB)	Exchange volume (Hundred million RMB)	Exchange volume (Hundred million RMB)	Weighted average interest rate (%)
2001 Total	40973.29	840.00	40133.29	
2002 Total	106297.21	4412.00	101885.21	2.07
2003 Total	148003.42	30800.00	117203.42	2.23
2004 Total	127849.02	28196.45	99652.57	2.23

Source: The People's Bank of China.

bond issuance from 1996 to 2004. Tables 5.3 and 5.4 show the trading in the Chinese bond market from 2001 to 2004. Putting all three tables together, we can see the current total size of the Chinese bond market.

According to Table 5.2, there is a rising trend in issuance in the Chinese bond market from year to year, with T-bond issuance up the fastest. Compared with 1996, the scale of T-bond issuance almost doubled in 2004, reaching about RMB692.4 billion yuan. Financial bond issuance also increased very fast, with an annual increase of about 30%. It is quite possible that such trends will continue in the future, and they may overrun the scale of T-bond issuance one day. In contrast, the growth of corporate bond issuance was rather low.

The People's Bank of China issued Central Bank bills in April 2003. This instrument experienced a rapid increase in issuance and became the third biggest fixed-income instrument. Total bond issuance during 2004 exceeded RMB1 trillion yuan. If asset securitization can be successfully launched, issuance may even be over RMB2–3 trillion yuan a year. By the end of 2004, bonds deposited in China's bond market were RMB5.16 trillion.

Tables 5.3 and 5.4 both show the total trading scale of the Chinese bond market as a whole. Because of the relatively small trading volume of the bank OTC market, we consider only the interbank market and the exchanges. In the year 2004, for instance, bond spot transactions amounted to RMB316.292 billion yuan, while repo trading was RMB14.374 trillion yuan. The total amount reached RMB14.690 trillion yuan. Comparing the exchange market and the interbank bond market, we can see that trading in the latter has far exceeded

TABLE 5.4 A Summary of Bond Trading in the Exchanges 2001–2004

	Total					
	Total of national debt exchanges		Spot		Repurchase	
	Volume of transaction (Hundred million RMB)	Transactions	Volume of transaction (Hundred million RMB)	Transactions	Volume of transaction (Hundred million RMB)	Transactions
2001 Total	20303.21	200286.59	4815.58	45340.01	15487.63	154946.58
2002 Total	33128.32	328128.44	8708.66	84023.94	24419.66	244104.50
2003 Total	58755.96	587148.29	5756.10	57224.54	52999.86	529923.75
2004 Total	47053.09	472739.13	2966.47	31837.35	44086.62	440901.78

Source: The People's Bank of China.

that of the former. After the 2004 launch of buy–sell repo transactions, trading volume in China's bond market continued to increase rapidly in 2005.

5.3   REGULATION AND SUPERVISION

With the emergence and development of China's bond market, its regulatory framework has gradually improved, in accord with the different stages and patterns experienced by the Chinese bond markets. We think China's bond market has undergone three different stages, including the early OTC physical bond trading market, the exchange bond market, and the interbank bond market. Regulation and supervision efforts are in accord with these developments.

Before 1987, China's stock market was in a period of growth during which the bond market framework had not really taken form and no unified regulatory system had been established. In 1981, China began to issue Treasury bonds (T-bonds). The Ministry of Finance issued the T-bond in accordance with *Regulations on Treasury Bonds of the People's Republic of China* issued by the State Council. The T-bonds were issued mainly for administrative financing purposes. There was no free market at that time, so only in a small part of the country, such as Shanghai and Shenzhen, did local government establish local codes to regulate bond trading. Meanwhile, the National Development and Reform Commission was also involved in the regulation and supervision of the securities market, including the bond market.

The exchange bond market was set up in 1990, symbolizing the primary establishment of China's unified bond market system. Then the People's Bank of China (PBC) became the regulatory authority of the bond market. The PBC also participated in the management of T-bonds issued by the Ministry of Finance, though it was still in charge of financial bonds. The PBC regulated and supervised the entire bond market through its branches in Shanghai, Shenzhen, and, some other cities and, together with the local governments, formulated business rules summarized in the *Procedures of Shanghai Municipality on the Administration of the Securities Exchanges* and *Interim Procedures of Shenzhen Municipality on the Administration of the Issuance and Exchange of Securities*. Afterwards, rules on bond trading were enacted by the exchange bond market. With this, China had pretty much established the regulatory system in the bond market.

After the rapid growth of China's bond market, laws and rules related to bond issuance and trading began to take form, such as *Regulations on the Management of Enterprise Bonds* (1993), *Interim Procedures on the Administration of Securities Exchanges* (1993), and *Company Law of the People's Republic of China* (1994). In 1992, the *Securities Law* was enacted.

In line with the rapid development of China's securities market, when the exchange bond market was dominant, the China Securities Regulatory Commission (CSRC) was set up in 1992. It symbolized the ultimate institution of the regulatory system for the bond markets. At that time, the PBC was responsible only for supervising securities firms, examining and approving financial bonds, and helping other governmental entities to examine and approve corporate bonds so as to maintain the sound development of the bond market. The practical side of this market regulation and supervision was carried out by the CSRC, and thus this institution became the principal regulatory body of China's bond market. However, the Ministry of Finance was still responsible for the issuance of T-bonds and issued rules such as *Interim Procedures of the Management of the Treasury Bond Depository of the People's Republic of China* (1997) to promote the issuance of and transaction in T-bonds.

However, along with the establishment of China's interbank bond market in 1997, the PBC resumed regulating the bond market, especially the interbank market as well as the bank OTC market. Since then, the regulatory system of China's bond market has evolved into a new pattern of coregulation by both the PBC and the CSRC. This regulatory system has been in effect until the present. With the rapid development of the interbank bond market, the Central Bank had played a more and more important role in terms of its regulation function and had an increasing influence on the bond market.

Currently, the basic regulatory system of China's bond market is that the PBC is in charge, with the assistance of the CSRC. The Central Bank is responsible for the regulation and supervision on the interbank and bank OTC bond markets, while the CSRC is in charge of the exchange bond market. The Ministry of Finance is still the major regulatory institution for T-bond issuance, so it also participates in regulation and supervision on the bond market. For example, in order to centralize the management of T-bond deposits, the Ministry of Finance has authorized the "Central Securities Clearing Company," a company under the direct control of the PBC, to manage all T-bond deposits. This institution has great influence on regulating T-bond issuance and preventing transaction risks. Now nearly all T-bond deposits in China are under the control of the Central Securities Clearing Company.

A more complete legal infrastructure has come into existence with the development of the regulatory system of China's bond market. More laws and rules are issued including *Procedures on the Administration of Issuance and Transfer of Enterprise Bonds* (1998), *Interim Procedures on the Administration of Convertible Enterprise Bonds* (1997), *Interim Procedures on the Administration of Securities Investment Fund* (1997), and, more importantly, *Securities Law* (1998). Besides, all the bond markets have successively established the business rules related to spot trading and repo.

Hence, China's bond market has come a long way to build its regulatory system with more complete laws and rules on regulating the market. Meanwhile, the regulatory ability as well as the regulatory performance of the PBC and the CSRC has improved greatly. Problems in the bond market are discovered early and solved promptly through the branches of these two institutions.

With the continual opening up of China's capital markets, the bond market will inevitably face new challenges to its regulation and supervision. For instance, foreign governments or companies are now allowed to issue their bonds in China's bond market, and the number of the foreign investors, such as QFIIs, is increasing rapidly. In addition, new trading instruments in the bond market are being developed continually. These will undoubtedly require new regulatory steps.[4]

5.4   TRADING IN CHINA'S BOND MARKET

Spot trading and repo trading are the two basic transactions in the Chinese bond markets. *Spot trading* involves purchasing and selling bonds in the way agreed in the spot market, carrying out the delivery of bonds and cash within a certain period of time so as to transfer the ownership of the bonds permanently. *Repo trading* is when a bond holder makes a deal with a buyer that the holder will repurchase the original bonds at an agreed price at a certain time in the future. The holder will pay the involved interest at an agreed interest rate (or price). At present, only institutional investors are allowed to engage in repo trading, while individual investors are forbidden to participate. In this section, we discuss how to make use of these two means of trading in China's bond market.

5.4.1   SPOT TRANSACTIONS

As mentioned earlier, China's bond market is made up of three parts: the exchange market, the interbank market bond, and the bank OTC market. As a result, there is slight difference between on-exchange and off-exchange spot transactions.

---

[4]The following Websites can be accessed directly to search for information related to regulation and supervision of China's bond market: People's Bank of China (www.pbc.gov.cn), Ministry of Finance (www.mof.gov.cn), China Securities Regulatory Commission (www.CSRC.gov.cn), Shanghai Securities Exchange (www.sse.com.cn), Shenzhen Securities Exchange (www.sse.org.cn), www.Chinaclear.com.cn, as well as China Bond Website (www.Chinabond.com.cn).

On the exchange market, the spot transactions include T-bonds and corporate bonds. We take T-bond spot transactions as an example and illustrate how the spot transaction is carried out on the exchange market. Transactions in the exchanges involve opening accounts, entrusting, dealing, settlement and delivery, and transfer. Investors purchase and sell the T-bonds that have been listed in the stock exchanges, and they can carry on T-bond spot transactions through appointed brokers. Trading fees include the commission paid to the brokers, which is no more than 0.1% of the trading turnover, and the commission fee for the spot transaction (RMB1–3 yuan) paid to the exchanges.

Currently, spot bond transactions in the exchanges follow the rule of "clean price transaction." *Clean price* is the price of the bond after deducting the accrued interest calculated according to the coupon rate of bonds. As usual, the *dirty price* equals clean price plus accrued interest. According to the principle of continuous auction, during spot trading, buyers and sellers quote and make the deal according to the T-bonds' clean price, but the settlement price is still the dirty price. The quotation system as well as the quotations released by the exchanges show the clean price and accrued interests simultaneously. The spot transaction takes one lot (equal to RMB1,000 yuan par value) or its round multiple number as its trading unit. The spot transaction is carried out "T + 0," which means that the purchase and the sale of bonds can be done during the same day.

Example

The closing price of listed T-bond A is quoted RMB145.99 yuan on day T, which includes RMB6.51 yuan of accrued interest. The accrued interest is calculated according to the following formula:

$$\text{Accrued interest} = \text{coupon rate}/365 \times \text{number of accrued days}$$

If we take the quotation of the T-bond's clean price, the closing price of T-bond A should be figured as follows:

$$\begin{aligned} \text{Clean price} &= \text{RMB145.99 yuan (full price)} \\ &- \text{RMB6.51 yuan (accrued interest)} = \text{RMB139.48 yuan.} \end{aligned}$$

When investors purchase and sell bonds, they should take RMB139.48 yuan as the reference price of the transaction. But notice that the settlement price is still the dirty price, that is, RMB145.99 yuan.

Presently, bond trading follows the principle of "deposit first, transact later." Bonds must be entrusted to the CSDCC before being sold. Once the bond transaction is completed, the changes are recorded in the investors' securities accounts, and the settlement and transfer is carried out according

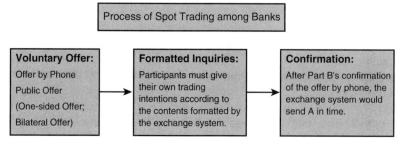

FIGURE 5.8   Steps in Exchanges

to "T + 1." Hence, both the CSDCC and the appointed securities company share the responsibility for depositing investors' T-bonds. When the T-bond is due and the interest is to be paid, investors can go directly to the appointed securities companies. At present, except for convertible bonds, spot T-bond and corporate bond transactions in the exchanges are mainly conducted this way.[5]

Spot bond transactions in the interbank bond market are more convenient. Interbank spot trading uses the inquiry mechanism, including an initial quotation, a format inquiry, and a confirmation. As illustrated in Figure 5.8, participants' initial quotation consists of open quotation and conversational quotation.

Conversational quotation is the quotation made by the market participants directly to their counterparty. The deal is done when the quote is accepted by the counterparty. *Open quotation* is the quotation made by market participants to the market. The quotation cannot be directly confirmed. And open quotation is further divided into two categories: unilateral quotation and bilateral quotation.

Institutional investors can entrust brokers to carry out spot bond transactions in the interbank bond market. Brokers will quote and inquire the price according to the dealers' code, trade partners, and elements such as transaction direction, bond type, bond code, trading price, and accrued interest. After the bond transaction has been agreed on, both parties type up the transaction notification, a contract to make sure the bond transaction has been done, and both parties conduct the clearing and bond settlement according to the notification. The settlement follows the rule of "T + 0" or "T + 1," and participants can

---

[5]Relevant trading information is available from the Shanghai Stock Exchange (www.sse.com.cn) and the Shenzhen Stock Exchange (www.sse.org.cn).

decide the date according to their preferences. This way, the spot transaction of the participants is completed.[6]

Currently, the bank OTC bond market conducts mainly book-entry spot transactions. Investors need to set up accounts as well as bond depository accounts in the bank in charge of the transaction and conduct OTC transactions through the OTC system of the bank. In the bank OTC transaction, the "clean price" convention is used as well. Within the range of the bid/ask spread of the particular bond, the bank in charge of the transaction will confirm the bilateral quotation of the OTC transaction. Investors can conduct spot T-bond transactions according to this quotation. OTC bond transactions take RMB100 yuan as the quotation and transaction unit and RMB1 yuan as capital settlement unit with two decimals. There is no transaction fee. Generally speaking, all OTC transactions are done on the spot. The trade is settled in real time.[7]

In this section we described how investors can conduct spot bond transactions in China's three main bond markets. In the following section we discuss how to conduct bond repo transactions.

5.4.2   THE BOND REPO[8]

Currently, repo trading can be carried out only in the exchange bond market and in the interbank bond market. There are two types of repo trading: collateral repo transactions and buy–sell transactions. Only institutional investors are allowed to carry out these transactions. We will analyze the bond repo transaction in the exchange and interbank bond markets.

The Collateral Repo Transaction

The collateral repo transaction refers to the short-term funding needs of the participants, with bonds used as the collateral. The "lender"[9] gives the bond to the "borrower" as collateral to get the cash, and agrees to return the cash to the counterparty at an agreed repo rate at a future date, whereas the counterparty will return the bond to the "lender" upon receipt of cash and repo interest. T-bond repo is the main form of bond repo in the exchange bond market,

---

[6]Relevant transaction information is available from China Bond Net (www.chinabond.com.cn).

[7]Related transaction information is available from China Bond Net (www.chinabond.com.cn).

[8]See also Chapter 2.

[9]In repo markets, by convention the lender is the party that lends the bond, not the cash.

while corporate bond repo represents only a small portion of the transactions. So we still focus on the analysis of T-bond repurchase.

Currently, there are about eight types of T-bonds for repo, varying from 1 day to 182 days. The repo is calculated by lot (RMB1,000 yuan) and the volume must be 100 lots at least or integral multiples thereof, for each transaction, with a ceiling of 10,000 lots. The quotation of the T-bond repo is based on the annual interest rate received or paid for every RMB100 yuan. Thus, the annual repo yield can be calculated by the following formula:

$$\text{Annual repurchase yield} = [(\text{Repurchase price} - 100)/100] \\ \times (\text{Number of days in a year}/ \\ \text{Number of days of repurchase}) \times 100\%$$

$$\text{Repurchase price} = 100 + \text{annual yield} \times 100 \\ \times \text{Number of days of repurchase}/360(365)^{10}$$

The annual repo rate is determined through online auction, with the same matching mechanism as that of the bond spot transaction. The collateral T-bond in the repo is called the *standard bond*, that is, the standardized T-bond used in the collateral repo transaction. The exchange converts all the listed T-bond trading items into the standard bond according to the yield and the market price of the listed T-bond so as to figure out the T-bond balance in the dealers' securities accounts. The standard bond is adjusted by the exchange quarterly.

The repo transaction follows the principle of "one transaction, two settlements." According to this, after the securities dealer declares and claims the deal for the client or himself, the exchange and the CSDCC will carry out the automated clearing by computer twice, at the closing date and at the expiry date, respectively. For the buyer and seller, the transaction cost of the funding and securities lending are to be settled, and relevant commissions as well as the processing fees will be paid at the closing date. At the expiry date, the payment will be processed directly between the two parties based on the purchase price calculated by the yield when the deal was concluded. The clearing date of the bond repo transaction follows the "T + 1" rule, and the transaction fee is 0.0025–0.075% of commissions and 5% commission charges.

Let us now see how the institutional investors carry out the T-bond repo. According to the procedures, the clients need to go through the transaction formalities for their securities account and then report to the transaction system for the repurchase registration by rule. Based on this report, the exchange and

---

[10]Or Repurchase price = Principal + Interest.

the CSDCC will convert the actual balance of the T-bond in this securities account into the standard bond after the closing date, and then make a record in the main standard bond account for the repurchase and settlement entrusted to the securities dealers; then the securities dealers can do the T-bond repurchase for their clients with the standard bond immediately.

In order to better understand the bond repurchase, let's take the following case as an example.

Example

Suppose Institution A has idle capital of RMB5 million yuan and would like to earn the repo rate through repo trading, while Institution B is trying to fund a purchase. So the latter will lend the bonds it holds and the former will pay RMB5 million yuan and agree to repurchase the bond at a price 3% (annual rate) higher in 18 days. As a result, the repurchase price for Institution A will be RMB5 million yuan × 3% × 18/365 as interest, plus RMB5 million yuan as principal. This equals RMB5,007,356 yuan.

It is easier to understand repo trading in the interbank bond market once repo trading in the exchange bond market is understood. As a matter of fact, in the interbank market the rules and procedures for repo trading are similar to those for spot bond trading in the interbank bond market. Repo trading follows the same three steps of initial quotation, format inquiry, and transaction confirmation. Before trading, the buyer and the seller need to register the pledged bonds with the CDC.

Bond settlement and capital clearing are also conducted according to "T + 0" or "T + 1" convention, under the principle of "one transaction and two settlements." Here, the closing date is when the two parties reach the repo agreement. The initial delivery date is the date the pledged bonds are registered. Then the borrower transfers the funds to the account appointed by the lender. The final delivery date is when the lender transfers the funds back to the account appointed by the party of borrower and thus terminates the repo.

The settlements can be divided into the initial settlement and the maturity settlement, and the amount of the maturity cash involved is equal to the amount of the initial capital × (1 + repo rate × the term/365). Currently, there are eight types of T-bond for repo, varying from 1 day to 1 year, and the trading units of the bond repo and settlement are RMB10,000 yuan and RMB1 yuan, respectively.

The foregoing analysis introduced the collateral repo transaction in the exchange market as well as in the interbank market. It is important to note that the collateral repo transaction does *not* allow selling short, and the exchanges will punish securities dealers for lack of the ownership of bond or the settlement cash. Moreover, the interbank market has a rule that the ratio of the financing to the collateralized bonds in the repo transaction cannot exceed the limits prescribed by the PBC.[11]

The Buy–Sell Transaction

In the second half of 2004, the Ministry of Finance, the PBC, and the CSRC announced *The Circular on Carrying out Buy–Sell Transactions*. This formally introduced the buy–sell transaction to the exchange market and the interbank market. At present this kind of transaction deals only with T-bonds.

What is the buy–sell transaction? It is a trading instrument—when the bond holder (the repurchase party) sells the bond to the buyer (the reverse repurchase party), both parties agree that the repurchase party will repurchase the same amount of these bonds from the reverse repurchase party at a future date at a fixed price.

On the exchange bond market, the parameters of the buy–sell transaction, such as the price, the trading unit, the transaction costs, and the bid matching principle, are generally similar to those for collateral repo transactions. One difference is that the buy–sell transaction does not require the bond to be collateralized. Instead, according to exchange regulations, the buy–sell transaction of T-bonds has to follow the custom margin requirement. That is, both the bond holder and the buyer should pay a margin on the day when the deal is executed. The margin should be supervised by the CSDCC. Before the transaction is due and the deal is liquidated, neither of the two parties can make use of the margined funds.

The margin for each buy–sell transaction should equal the product of the primary settlement price, the trade size, and the bond's margin ratio. As for the margin ratio, it is set by the exchange according to the historical price fluctuations of the T-bond with the same maturity. This ratio can change due to the situation in the market.

Another difference from the collateral repo transaction is that the buy–sell transaction may be conducted as bulk trading if the single trading volume is more than or as many as 10 thousand lots, as long as the total unexpired transaction volume of the bond does not exceed 20% of the outstanding stock. The investor is not allowed to cancel the deal before the transaction is over and the trade is liquidated. The margin is returned at the expiration. If one party fails, its margin will be passed on to the other party. If both parties breach the contract, the margins will go to the Securities Settlement Risk Control Fund.

The buy–sell settlement is conducted according to the rule of "one transaction, two settlements." At first, the CSDCC will sort out the exact

[11]For additional information, please check the following Websites: Shanghai Securities Exchange (www.sse.com.cn), Shenzhen Securities Exchange (www.sse.org.cn), China Bond Net (www.chinabond.com.cn).

amount of capital that each party ought to pay or receive; and then it will figure out the primary settlement price and the repurchase settlement price. The primary settlement price is the sum of the closing price (clean price) of the T-bond on the previous trading day and its accrued interest on the day. The repurchase settlement price is the sum of the repurchase price (clean price) and the maturity accrued interest.

On the interbank market, there are also corresponding regulations for buy–sell transactions on T-bonds. While conducting a buy–sell transaction, market participants have to sign a master agreement, including the articles that ensure enforcement of the contract. When completing the transaction, participants should make sure they have sufficient amounts of bonds and cash. The balance of bonds market participants hold for repurchasing must be less than 20% of its total turnover. And the total balance should be less than 200% of its total self-supported bond turnover mandated to the CDC. However, buy–sell repo conventions regarding quotation, settlement, and matching mechanism are the same as those for collateral repo on the inter-bank market.

Just as on the exchanges, the buy–sell repo also follows the convention of clean-price trading and dirty-price settlement. During the transaction, the parties are not allowed to exchange the bond or to complete the deal by cash before the expiration. However, the interbank market is more flexible. For instance, during the buy–sell repo both parties can take the other's credit into consideration and negotiate the margin, which could be in terms of cash or bond. If the margin is in the form of bonds, during the whole deal the bond should be blocked at the depository account. The expiration of the buy–sell transaction is decided by both parties, but it cannot be longer than 91 days, and both parties cannot prolong it by any means. The first clean price, the final clean price, and the repurchase trading volume are also fixed by both parties, while the sum of the final clean price and the accrued interest during the deal should be larger than the clean price of the first payment. All these rules seem more suited to large-scale institutional investors, such as commercial banks.

Thus the buy-sell transaction of T-bonds is a trading strategy for "selling short T-bonds." During the trade, margin requirements are in place to control risk. Furthermore, this kind of transaction helps to hedge the risk of taking only long positions in the collateral repo. This started the mechanism of trading short in China's bond market, which was considered a very important move to promote the liquidity of the market and a prelude to bond derivative trading.

5.4.3 Other Elements Influencing Bond Trading

If one wants to invest in China's bond market, it is important to understand China's macroeconomic fluctuations apart from the trading procedures of the underlying bonds. This is due to the close relationship between bond prices and interest rates. Macroeconomic policies will influence the interest rate; furthermore, they will also influence China's bond market.

After China eliminated the danger of deflation in 2003, its economy entered a new period of growth. But this also brought the danger of overheating in some sectors. For example, in 2004 China's GDP rose 9.5% from the preceding year, and its consumer price index went up 3.9%, 2.7% more than the previous year. During 2006, growth was expected, of around 11%, although the inflation was tamer, around 2%. This is important because with inflation expectations of higher interest rates rise. Meanwhile in America, the Federal Reserve raised interest rates 25 basis points since June 2004, and by the end of 2006 America's interest rates had reached a higher level at 5.25%, higher than China's 2.75%.

In order to prevent the macroeconomy from overheating in 2004, China implemented macroeconomic measures by tightening monetary policy. Since the end of 2003, China's Central Bank has raised the required reserve ratio several times, and at the end of September 2004 the interest rate went up. Influenced by this, China's bond market fell. However, as the economy stabilized during 2005, bond market sentiment improved.

Because the bond market lacks derivative instruments, the risk caused by the anticipation of rate changes still exists. Therefore, the principal difficulty of investing in China's bond market is to judge and analyze the trend of interest rates in the future.

5.5   CONCLUSIONS

In this chapter, we reviewed the development and structure of China's bond market. As an emerging market, the present state of China's bond market is much smaller than that of the developed countries, such as the United States. But the rapid growth of China's economy, further financial reform, and the high rate of household savings will highly stimulate China's bond market. Chinese bond markets may end up growing even faster than what is anticipated.

REFERENCES

The History of China's Securities (1978–1998), Ma Qingquan (CITIC Publishing House, August 2003).

The Theory and Practice of China's T-Bond, Gao Jian (Economic Science Press, April 1995).

Almanac of China's Securities and Futures, China Securities Regulatory Commission (Baijia Publishing House, April 2003).

An Introduction to the Bond Markets, Reuters (Beijing University Press, August 2001).

A Brief History of China's Securities Market, Zheng Zhenlong et al. (China Economy Publishing House, 2000).

Almanac of China's Finance and Banking, Chinese Finance Association (China Financial Publishing House, 2003).

CHAPTER 6

China's Convertible Bond Market

Liu Qiang

University of Electronic Science and Technology of China,
Chengdu, Sichuan, People's Republic of China

6.1 INTRODUCTION

On January 31, 2005, nine days before the Chinese Lunar New Year, the Shanghai Stock Exchange Composite Index closed below the psychologically important support level of 1,200 points. This was the lowest in the preceding five years, and many in the Chinese media called it a Black Monday.

Against this continuous downward slide, a relatively small market fared quite well and had been attracting investors' attention: the convertible bond market. Owing to the debt cushion of convertible bonds, their prices drop much less dramatically, which usually becomes a favorite in an extended bear market.

In this Chapter, we introduce to you the convertible bond market in China by covering the following topics: the history of the market, relevant regulations, statistics on issuances, characteristics of issuances, convertible holders, and market players.

6.2   DEVELOPMENT OF THE MARKET

Less than two years after the Shanghai Stock Exchange (ShSE[1]) opened for business, the China Baoan Group issued the Baoan Convertible (125009),[2] on December 1, 1992, which began to trade on the Shenzhen Stock Exchange (SzSE) on February 10 of the following year. This callable bond was structured simply with an annual coupon rate of 3% and a 3-year maturity. Its par of one Chinese yuan (CNY)[3] made it somewhat special. Even though there were earlier convertible debt issuances, Baoan Convertible is the first and for the next three years it was the only convertible bond on the A share market.[4]

The next convertible bond would come to the market almost six years later. To formalize the convertible bond market, the Chinese central government announced its first policy on convertible bonds, *Preliminary Regulations on Convertible Bonds*, on March 25, 1997. Qualified issuers, issuing procedures, and trading-related issues are defined in it, for example. Only (A share) listed firms and state-owned key enterprises that were profitable in the preceding three years could obtain the necessary governmental approval to issue convertible bonds. The minimum issuing amount is 100 million CNY. The maturity has to be between 3 and 5 years. When the total unconverted amount goes below 30 million CNY, a convertible bond will be delisted from the exchange. It is interesting to note that state-owned key enterprises could issue convertible bonds before having their shares listed.

Nanning Chemical Industry issued the first convertible bond under the new government policy on August 3, 1998. The provisions of this bond are much richer than those of the Baoan Convertible. The bond had a step-up coupon, was putable, and would be forced to convert under certain conditions before maturity and without any condition at maturity. Since the issuing firm was not traded on the A share market at that time, the bond simply did not specify a conversion price. This issue turned out to be very popular with investors. As a result, less than 0.2% of registered buyers actually

---

[1]SSE is unfortunately the acronym for both the Shanghai Stock Exchange and the Shenzhen Stock Exchange. To distinguish them, we use ShSE and SzSE instead.

[2]A convertible bond is named here by the Pinyin of the first two Chinese characters of its exchange-assigned name. The six-digit number in parentheses is its exchange-designated symbol.

[3]Yuan is the unit of renminbi, the currency issued by the Chinese government. The symbol RMB is equivalent to CNY.

[4]Both the ShSE and the SzSE list A and B shares, both of which are denominated in CNY. A shares are issued to domestic stockholders and traded in CNY, while B shares are issued to international investors (and later certain qualified domestic investors) and in US or HK dollars. This chapter discusses convertible bonds on the A share market.

got the bond. Nanhua Convertible (100001), with a par of CNY100, opened spectacularly at more than CNY230 on the Shanghai Stock Exchange on September 2.[5]

The market was quiet, with four more convertible bonds issued through 2002. During this time, the China Securities Regulatory Commission (CSRC) issued a series of policies regarding convertible bonds. Among those was the *Rules for Issuing Convertible Bonds by Listed Companies* (CSRC Directive No. 2, April 26, 2001), which extends the *Preliminary Regulations on Convertible Bonds*. It specifies the par of convertible bonds to be 100 CNY and the minimum trading unit to be 10 bonds, for example. These two policies were amended further by *On Streamlining the Process of Issuing Convertible Bonds by Listed Companies* (CSRC Rule of Issuing [2001] No. 115, December 25, 2001). At the same time, the Shanghai and Shenzhen stock exchanges also published trading rules for convertible bonds. Those measures made the issuing process and trading of convertible bonds regular and formal and prepared the market for healthy growth.

Institutional investors gave the convertible bond market another important boost. QFIIs, or qualified foreign institutional investors, were allowed to enter the A share market in early 2003 and became a prominent force immediately in the trading of convertible bonds. On April 2, 2004, Xingye Convertible Bond Hybrid Securities Investment Fund (163001), the first mutual fund investing primarily in convertible bonds in China, was established. In August 2004, insurance companies and insurance asset management firms were allowed to invest in convertible bonds by the China Insurance Regulatory Commission.

There were five convertible bond issuances in 2002, 16 in 2003, and 12 in 2004. Zhaohang Convertible (110036), issued on November 10, 2004 by China Merchants Bank, was a big event in a prolonged bear market. It was the largest convertible bond issued up to that time, with 6.5 billion CNY, and attracted more than 260 billion capital, of which 97.75% came from institutional investors.[6] As of January 31, 2005, 32 convertible bonds were being traded on the A share market.[7]

The convertible bond market was expected to grow rapidly in 2005 and beyond.

---

[5]Data and provisions for most convertible bonds mentioned in this and succeeding sections come primarily from the *Research on Convertible Bond* Website (xi-aogi.nease.net/cbond/cbond.htm).

[6]Xiaomeng Shao, *260 Billion Capital after the Zhaohang Convertible*, www.cs.com.cn, Nov. 15, 2004.

[7]Trading statistics from ShSE and SzSE.

6.3   THE DATA

The statistics on annual issuance through 2004 are shown in Table 6.1. Note the upward trend in both the number of issues and the total capital raised each year from 1998 on, ignoring the abnormal year of 2001. It is significant that in 2004, convertible bonds accounted for a quarter of the total capital raised on the A share market. These numbers may appear tiny, but they compare favorably with those of more mature markets, such as the U.S. market. For example, only $3,408 million convertible bonds were issued in the United States in 1984,[8] when the U.S. market was more than 100 years old.

Of the 39 convertible bonds, four had expired before January 31, 2005, while three were delisted because of early conversion. As a result, there were 32 active convertible bonds; these are shown in Table 6.2.

Let's now take a close look at the convertible bonds on the A share market as of January 31, 2005. The minimum issue is Shanying Convertible (100567), 250 million CNY, the median 881.5 million CNY, and the maximum Zhaohang Convertible (110036), 6,500 million CNY. All issuers were well established, non-growth oriented, and from traditional sectors. Specifically, there were one travel service company, two banks, 21 manufacturers, five utilities, and three conglomerates. All the bonds had a par of 100 CNY, as required by the regulations.

Except for four with a maturity of 3 years, all other convertible bonds matured in 5 years. Still, all were in fact short-term bonds. This is quite unique, compared with those in other markets, such as the U.S. market, where long-term bonds are common. Remember that according to the regulations, the maturity has to be between 3 and 5 years.

The credit ratings of convertible issues were higher on average than those in the United States as well. For example, among the 16 bonds that had a rating as shown by the Shanghai Stock Exchange, 12 were AAA rated, one AAA−,

TABLE 6.1   Convertible Bond Issuances, by Year

	1992	1998	1999	2000	2002	2003	2004	Total
Number of bonds issued	1	2	1	2	5	16	12	39
Capital raised (million CNY)	500	350	1,500	2,850	4,150	18,550	20,903	48,803

[8]Richard S. Wilson, *Corporate Senior Securities: Analysis and Evaluation of Bonds, Convertibles and Preferreds*, Probus Publishing Company, Chicago, 1987.

TABLE 6.2 A List of Traded Convertible Bonds as of January 31, 2005

Symbol	Name	Issuer	Issue date	Market
125898	Angang	Angang New Steel Co., Ltd.	3/14/2000	SzSE
100220	Yangguang	Jiangsu Sunshine Co., Ltd.	4/18/2002	ShSE
100087	Shuiyun	Nanjing Water Transport Industry Co., Ltd.	8/13/2002	ShSE
126301	Sichou No. 2	Wu Jiang Silk Co., Ltd.	10/16/2002	SzSE
125729	Yanjing	Beijing Yanjing Brewery Co., Ltd.	10/16/2002	SzSE
100016	Minsheng	China Minsheng Banking Corporation, Ltd.	2/27/2003	ShSE
100177	Yage	Youngor Group Co., Ltd.	4/03/2003	ShSE
125930	Fengyuan	Anhui BBCA Biochemical Co., Ltd.	4/24/2003	SzSE
125630	Tongdu	Anhui Tongdu Copper Co., Ltd.	5/21/2003	SzSE
100726	Huadian	Huadian Energy Co., Ltd.	6/03/2003	ShSE
100567	Shanying	Anhui Shanying Paper Industry Co., Ltd.	6/16/2003	ShSE
100236	Guiguan	Guangxi Guiguan Electric Power Co., Ltd.	6/30/2003	ShSE
100795	Guodian	GD Power Development Co., Ltd.	7/18/2003	ShSE
100117	Xigang	Xining Special Steel Co., Ltd.	8/11/2003	ShSE
125936	Huaxi	Jiangsu Huaxicun Co., Ltd.	9/01/2003	SzSE
100096	Yunhua	Yunnan Yuntianhua Co., Ltd.	9/10/2003	ShSE
100196	Fuxing	Shanghai Fosun Industrial Co., Ltd.	10/28/2003	ShSE
110001	Hangang	Handan Iron & Steel Co., Ltd.	11/26/2003	ShSE
125959	Shougang	Beijing Shougang Co., Ltd.	12/16/2003	SzSE
125069	Qiaocheng	Shenzhen Overseas Chinese Towin Industry Development Co., Ltd.	12/31/2003	SzSE
110418	Jianghuai	Anhui Jianghuai Automobile Co., Ltd.	4/15/2004	ShSE
110037	Gehua	Beijing Gehua CATV Network Co., Ltd.	5/12/2004	ShSE
110317	Yinggang	Yingkou Port Liability Co., Ltd.	5/20/2004	ShSE
110874	Chuangye	Tianjin Capital Environmental Protection Co., Ltd.	7/01/2004	ShSE
125932	Hualing	Hunan Hualing Steel Tube & Wire Co., Ltd.	7/16/2004	SzSE
125937	Jinniu	Hebei Jinniu Energy & Resources Co., Ltd.	8/11/2004	SzSE
125822	Haihua	Shandong Haihua Co., Ltd.	9/07/2004	SzSE
125488	Chenming	Shandong Chenming Paper Holdings, Ltd.	9/15/2004	SzSE
126002	Wanke No. 2	China Vanke Co., Ltd.	9/24/2004	SzSE
110219	Nanshan	Shandong Nanshan Industrial Co., Ltd.	10/19/2004	ShSE
110010	Ganglian	Inner Mongolian Baotou Steel Union Co., Ltd.	11/10/2004	ShSE
110036	Zhaohang	China Merchants Bank Co., Ltd.	11/10/2004	ShSE

two AA+, and one AA. In other words, all issues were investment grade. In the U.S. market, for example, convertible bonds are usually a cheap and convenient method for raising capital for new or growth companies with lower credit ratings that otherwise might be hard or too costly to obtain by other means. The situation in China is apparently different. The regulations dictate that only companies that have been profitable in the preceding three years in a row can issue convertible bonds. As a result, the higher credit rating as well as the shorter maturity in principle make those bonds in China less risky than their U.S. counterparts.

The coupon provisions of those convertibles were quite rich. Except for nine bonds with fixed annual coupon rates, all the rest had annual coupons that were stepped up each year. According to the regulations, however, coupon rates are not allowed to be higher than the interest rate paid by banks for saving accounts with the same maturity.

Five bonds were not allowed to convert within one year of the issue date, even though the regulations stipulate that conversion is to be permitted six months after issuing. Once again, this is different from those in other markets, where the holder can in principle convert a bond anytime without restrictions. The initial conversion premiums were quite low, with 15 bonds at a symbolic level of 0.1%, which means that buyers obtained the embedded options for free. The highest three premiums were 5% (Wanke No. 2), 7% (Yangguang), and 10% (Yanjing), respectively. All bonds except one (Zhaohang Convertible) had conditional provisions to lower the conversion price, or, in other words, complicated refix clauses. Even Zhaohang Convertible did not rule out the possibility of refix completely; it only stated that the conversion price would not be adjusted for the first three years. Note that refix clauses, even simple ones, are used rarely in the United States.

The conversion price was to be lowered conditional on m out of n closes ($m < n$; except for one 10 out of 30, the rest are 20 out of 30) for 18 bonds. Among those, the refixing was only to be done the first time the condition was met each year for five bonds. Thirteen bonds would be refixed for n closes, where n can be 5, 10, 20, or 30; two of those refixings were only to be done the first time each year. Huadian (100726) also had an automatic conditional refixing clause for three specific days (half a year, one and a half years, or two and a half years after issue date).

Let's look at Ganglian (110010), issued on the same day as Zhaohang, as an example. In any consecutive 30 trading days, if the arithmetic average of 20 close prices of the stock was lower than 90% of the standing conversion price at that time, the board of directors must lower that conversion price by more than 10% within five trading days, on the condition that the adjusted conversion price was to be higher than the net assets per share. The number of refixings was not limited. Note that it is conceivable that the price could be lower again and again in a down-trending market; it would be a challenge to price such a convertible bond, though, since its conversion price is in a sense a random variable.

Furthermore, 25 bonds were cash-dividend-protected. In other words, their conversion prices would be lowered accordingly when the underlying common stocks paid dividends. Therefore, convertible holders actually receive cash dividends in addition to coupons. This is again markedly different from the provisions of their U.S. counterparts, which in general are not dividend-protected.

Apparently, many of the conversion provisions were designed to encourage conversion of those bonds to stocks. Table 6.3 shows conversion statistics from the Shanghai Stock Exchange as of January 31, 2005. Six issuances already had more than 50% of their bonds converted, while Minsheng (100016), with more than three years to go, had a whopping conversion rate of 92.28%.

Except for Yunhua (100096), which was not callable, all other bonds had complex call provisions. Among those, 15 were soft-call-protected for six months after issuance, 11 for one year, and five for two or more years. Further, the provisions varied from issue to issue. Twenty-three bonds were callable conditional on n closes ($n = 20$, 25, or 30); nine bonds out of those could only be called the first time the condition was met. Nine bonds had a call provision for m out of n closes (20 out of 30 or 30 out of 40), three issuers were only

TABLE 6.3 Cumulative Percentages of Conversion for Convertible Bonds Traded on the ShSE as of Janaury 31, 2005

Symbol	Name	Cumulative percent of converted (%)	Trading date
100016	Minsheng	92.28	1/10/2005
100220	Yangguang	79.77	1/28/2005
100087	Shuiyun	69.59	6/10/2004
100117	Xigang	52.22	12/17/2004
100096	Yunhua	52.12	1/27/2005
100177	Yage	51.65	11/02/2004
100196	Fuxing	33.19	10/12/2004
100567	Shanying	16.49	1/20/2005
100795	Guodian	8.71	11/22/2004
100726	Huadian	4.25	10/14/2004
110001	Hangang	0.90	12/07/2004

Source: Shanghai Stock Exchange.

allowed to call the first time the provision was satisfied. In addition, one bond had multiple call prices, three had multiple trigger prices, two were callable on maturity, and Huadian was (hard-) callable over the three trading days just before the fourth year of issue.

For example, Zhaohang Convertible was not callable within six months of issuance. Thereafter, its issuer could call the bond if Zhaohang Stock (600036) closed at more than 125% of the then-standing conversion price for 20 consecutive trading days the first time each year. The call price was 103% of par (including accrued interest). On the other hand, Shanying (100567) had a classic 20-out-of-30 provisional call, with a twist. Its trigger price was 140% of the conversion price for the third year, 130% for the fourth year, and 120% for the fifth year. It is interesting to note that provisional calls of U.S. convertible bonds are usually 20 out of 30, with a fixed trigger price and a fixed call price; further, when the bond is called, a debt holder has the option to convert the bond within 30 days.

All the convertible bonds in Table 6.2 were putable. The terms of puts were quite rich as well. First, all were provisional puts, with conditions of either n closes ($n = 15$, 20, 25, or 30, with 20 being the most common) or m out of n closes (20 out of 30 was most common, though we see also 15 out of 20 and 30 out of 40). Second, 11 bonds were only putable when the conditions were met the first time each year. Third, the putable periods ranged from the last six months to the whole life of a bond (while none was putable within the first six months). Huadian (100726), an exception, also allowed a debt holder to put the bond in two specific periods, each with a length of three trading days. Fourth, the majority had a simple put term, namely, a single trigger price and a single put price. One bond (Guodian, 100795), however, had three trigger prices, while three bonds had multiple put prices. Furthermore, four bonds were also putable just before or at maturity.

Consider Zhaohang Convertible, which was putable within one year before maturity. If Zhaohang Stock (600036) closed at less than 75% of the then-standing conversion price for 20 consecutive trading days, a debt holder had the right to sell the bond back to Zhaohang at a price of 108.5% of par (including accrued interests). Again, it is worth mentioning that put terms are usually quite simple and unconditional (for example, putable on three specific days with fixed put prices) for U.S. convertible bonds.

Let's now summarize the dominant features of those convertible bonds. They were issued at a par of 100 CNY, matured in 3 or 5 years, were investment-grade bonds, had step-up coupons, and had complicated refix, call, and put provisions. These features are not commonly seen in their U.S. counterparts, and they pose a serious challenge for theoretical fair pricing (which we do not cover in this chapter).

6.4   CONVERTIBLE HOLDERS AND MARKET PLAYERS

At least 21 of the 32 traded convertible bonds were issued with favorable provisions for existing A shareholders to obtain those bonds at issuance. As a result, it is conceivable that the existing shareholders were an important factor on the primary market. Of course, existing shareholders could be either individual or institutional investors.

Without doubt, institutional investors other than the existing shareholders were another influential force on the primary market, however. For example, as newly allowed convertible investors, four insurance companies submitted bids for Jinniu (125937) for the first time in August 2004, while eight companies bid for Haihua (125822) about one month later.

Let's look at Zhaohang Convertible (110036) again as an example. The 6.5 billion CNY issue attracted 256.5 billion subscriptions from institutional investors, while individual investors bid a total of 5.9 billion. Eventually, current shareholders bought 75.43% of the issue. Institutional investors, including almost all kinds of institutional capital such as insurance companies, securities companies,[9] big enterprises, QFIIs, and mutual funds, took away 24.02% of the issue (see footnote 6). The eight biggest institutional buyers included five insurance companies, one trust company, one securities company, and one big corporation.

Mutual funds, QFIIs, and Social Security funds hold a significant amount of the traded convertible bonds. Tables 6.4, 6.5, and 6.6, which report the top 10 bond holders, were taken from the Data Center of the China Fund Network, as of September 30, 2004.[10] Mutual funds (see Table 6.4) held 21 convertible bonds with a total of 4,006 million CNY, which accounts for 21.7% of the total unconverted amount of those 21 traded convertible bonds. Note that six funds owned 53.4% of Minsheng (100016).

Even though qualified foreign institutional investors (QFIIs) had a history of less than two years on the market, they had become a vital player. As of September 30, their portfolio had 15 convertible bonds totaling 1,242 million CNY, or 11.9% of the total unconverted of those 15 bonds. That is almost one-third of the amount held by mutual funds. Only three QFIIs were actually involved (Table 6.5), but they were among the top 10 biggest holders 21 times. Citigroup Global Markets was by far the largest convertible buyer, holding 814 million (or almost a quarter of the total amount Citigroup was allowed to invest in the A share market), UBS ranked second, with 389 million, and the

[9]Roughly investment banks in the United States.

[10]www.chinafund.cn.

TABLE 6.4 Convertible Bonds Held by Mutual Funds

Symbol	Name	Amount (million CNY)	Percentage of total unconverted (%)
100016	Minsheng	164.8	53.37
100096	Yunhua	151.7	39.66
100117	Xigang	17.2	7.33
100177	Yage	86.0	14.68
100196	Fuxing	189.6	29.86
100567	Shanying	40.5	19.11
100726	Huadian	272.8	35.61
100795	Guodian	303.4	16.52
110037	Gehua	244.1	19.53
110317	Yinggang	173.5	24.79
110874	Chuangye	310.8	25.9
125069	Qiaocheng	169.6	42.41
125488	Chenming	429.3	21.47
125729	Yanjing	213.6	32.4
125822	Haihua	200.5	20.05
125930	Fengyuan	107.9	24.82
125936	Huaxi	51.0	12.81
125937	Jinniu	161.2	23.04
125959	Shougang	324.0	16.2
126002	Wanke No. 2	223.7	11.24
126301	Sichou No. 2	170.7	21.55

Source: China Fund Network.

rest went to Morgan Stanley International. The highest percentage of a single issue was 33.0% of Shanying (100567), held by Citigroup Global Markets.

Social Security funds (Table 6.6) also invested in convertible bonds, though at a much smaller scale. Eight funds held seven bonds, with 218 million CNY, or 3.2% of the total unconverted amount of the seven.

Mutual funds, QFIIs, and Social Security funds as a group owned 29.6% of the total unconverted amount of 21 convertible bonds as of September 30. The actual percentage would be higher, since only the top 10 holders for each convertible bond were totaled here. Furthermore, the percentage could be much higher still if other institutional investors were counted as well.

By the end of 2004, 24 QFIIs had obtained permits from the State Administration of Foreign Exchange to enter the A share markets. Their total convertible holdings reached 3,300 million CNY, almost triple the amount of just one

TABLE 6.5 Convertible Bonds Held by QFIIs

Symbol	Name	QFII bond holder	Amount (million CNY)	Percentage of unconverted (%)	Holder's ranking
100567	Shanying	Citigroup Global Markets	70.00	33.00	1
125936	Huaxi	Citigroup Global Markets	100.80	25.33	1
100117	Xigang	Citigroup Global Markets	35.40	15.11	2
100196	Fuxing	Citigroup Global Markets	93.20	14.68	1
125930	Fengyuan	Citigroup Global Markets	61.90	14.23	1
126301	Sichou No. 2	Citigroup Global Markets	93.70	11.84	2
100726	Huadian	Citigroup Global Markets	61.60	8.04	1
110317	Yinggang	Citigroup Global Markets	45.60	6.51	2
125959	Shougang	Citigroup Global Markets	121.60	6.08	3
125729	Yanjing	Citigroup Global Markets	29.90	4.53	6
125822	Haihua	Citigroup Global Markets	38.20	3.82	3
100016	Minsheng	Citigroup Global Markets	9.70	3.12	9
125937	Jinniu	Citigroup Global Markets	20.00	2.86	6
110874	Chuangye	Citigroup Global Markets	32.40	2.70	7
100196	Fuxing	Morgan Stanley International	14.70	2.32	8
100567	Shanying	Morgan Stanley International	4.70	2.22	7
125936	Huaxi	Morgan Stanley International	7.20	1.82	6
110317	Yinggang	Morgan Stanley International	11.70	1.67	9
100567	Shanying	UBS Limited	34.90	16.45	2
100117	Xigang	UBS Limited	36.60	15.64	1
125930	Fengyuan	UBS Limited	35.40	8.15	5
125936	Huaxi	UBS Limited	29.20	7.34	4
126301	Sichou No. 2	UBS Limited	55.60	7.02	5
125729	Yanjing	UBS Limited	33.60	5.10	4
100196	Fuxing	UBS Limited	31.20	4.92	5
100096	Yunhua	UBS Limited	17.90	4.67	7
125959	Shougang	UBS Limited	68.10	3.40	5
110874	Chuangye	UBS Limited	29.80	2.48	8
125937	Jinniu	UBS Limited	17.00	2.43	9

Source: China Fund Network.

TABLE 6.6   Convertible Bonds Held by Social Security Funds

Symbol	Name	Amount (million CNY)	Percentage of unconverted (%)
125930	Fengyuan	24.6	5.66
100096	Yunhua	16.7	4.38
100177	Yage	47.2	9.1
125822	Haihua	30.5	3.05
125488	Chenming	46.7	2.33
110874	Chuangye	26.9	2.24
110037	Gehua	25.2	2.02

Source: China Fund Network.

quarter earlier and was 20% of their 16.2 billion total invested in A share stocks, mutual funds, convertible bonds, and government debts.[11]

Other institutional investors had similar moves. According to the annual reports of 56 securities companies, 24 firms increased their proprietary convertible holdings by 24.4% to 1,182 million CNY from a year earlier, even though over the same period they actually decreased their total proprietary holdings by about 20%.[12] Insurance companies also appeared to have dramatically increased their convertible holdings by the end of 2004.[13]

Bond funds, however, had to reduce their convertible holdings, which performed relatively poorly compared to the debt markets because of the down stock market in the fourth quarter of 2004. Of course, the total size of the 16 bond funds decreased as well. Still, convertible bonds had the biggest share, compared with those of government debts and financial bonds,[14] in typical bond funds. Further, the number of convertible bonds among the biggest 10 holdings actually increased from two to three in the third quarter: Chenming (125488), Guodian (100795), and Qiaocheng (125069).[15] Another analysis of 13 bond

---

[11] "Xuejun Yang, *QFIIs Invested 7,100 Million in A Shares and 2,200 Million in Mutual Funds by January 19*, Securities Daily, January 24, 2005.

[12] Shanghai Securities News, *Securities Companies Reduced Their Proprietary Security Holdings by 20%*, www.cs.com.cn, January 26, 2005.

[13] Peng Wan, *Insurance companies and QFIIs Favor Convertibles, and Institutional Investors Continue to Increase Their Convertible Holdings*, Securities Times, February 23, 2005.

[14] Bonds issued by financial institutions, such as banks, securities companies, and insurance firms.

[15] Feng Zhao, *Weak Convertible Bonds Dragged Bond Funds Down*, Shanghai Securities News, February 2, 2005.

funds concluded that as a group, those funds invested 26.5%, 37.4%, and 45.6% in convertible bonds in the second, third, and fourth quarters of 2004, respectively.[16] This dramatic increase of relative holdings in convertible bonds is quite impressive, to say the least.

6.5   CONVERTIBLE BONDS VERSUS STOCK OR CORPORATE DEBTS

China now has stock (A and B shares), corporate and government debt, and convertible bond markets. Let's briefly compare the stock, corporate debt, and convertible bond markets.

Compared with the A share market, the convertible market was quite small. As Tables 6.7 and 6.8 show, the total market value of tradable volume of A share stocks was 30 times that of convertible bonds. On the other hand, the market value of corporate bonds (including financial bonds) was only 1.8 times that of convertibles. Further, there was only one more corporate bond listing than convertible listings. Hence, the convertible market was not that small in the later comparison. Note that the B share market was not big either. It was only slightly larger than the corporate bond market.

On the secondary market, institutional investors play an important role as well. Since mutual funds, QFIIs, and insurance companies tend to be long-term investors, the liquidity of convertible bonds was expected to be relatively low. Looking at the turnover as a percentage of the tradable volume (a liquidity measure in a certain sense), however, we found that the liquidity of convertibles (0.46%) was higher than that of either B shares or corporate bonds but slightly

TABLE 6.7   ShSE Market Statistics as of January 31, 2005 (unit: million CNY)

	A shares	B shares	Corporate bonds	Convertible bonds
Number of listings	827	54	24	19
Market value	2,419,785	29,444	54,314	28,167
Market value of tradable volume	666,354	29,444	54,314	21,533
Turnover in value[a]	5,288	38	21	105

[a]The turnover in value here is the daily average for January.
Source: Shanghai Stock Exchange.

[16]Limin Kong, *Holding Relatively Less Debts, Bond Funds Missed a Bull Market*, Securities Times, February 24, 2005.

TABLE 6.8   SzSE Market Statistics as of January 31, 2005 (unit: million CNY)

	A shares	B shares	Corporate bonds	Convertible bonds
Number of listings	522	56	9	13
Market value	991,722	46,810	18,867	13,119
Market value of tradable volume	370,560	40,418	8,622	13,119
Turnover in value	2,878	75	0.39	54

Source: Shanghai Stock Exchange.

lower than that of A shares (0.79%). Finally, since short selling of stocks is not allowed on the domestic markets, traditional convertible arbitrage is not applicable. That might be a cause of the low liquidity of the convertible market as well.

6.6   CONCLUSIONS

When this chapter was originally written, the convertible bond market was expected to grow rapidly in the coming years. Unfortunately, that prediction turned out to be incorrect for 2005, which would instead go down in history as another abnormal year in the development of this market.

From October 2004 to April 2005, about 16 companies considered issuing convertible bonds. None have come into the market so far, however. To make way for the so-called share reform[17] that started in early May 2005, the primary markets in China were put on hold.

The convertible market is actually smaller now. Two bonds, Angang and Yangguang, had matured before the share reform. Due to the rough stock market over the summer of 2005 (the ShSE Composite Index on June 6 reached its lowest point within the previous eight years), Hualing Convertible (125932) had to lower its conversion price on May 17 and faced huge pressure from investors. On July 29, Chuangye (110874) reduced its conversion price by 20%. On July 18 and August 2, Fengyuan (125930) twice lowered its conversion price within 15 days.

The share reform affected the convertible bond market adversely. Among the eight companies with outstanding convertibles that are done with or in the

---

[17]Share reform is the process of making tradable shares that are not allowed to trade on the market. Note that tradable A shares in Tables 6.7 and 6.8 account for only 30% of the total market value of the shares issued. The existence and huge number of those nontradable shares are believed to be a major cause of the continuing decline in the market in the past five years.

process of reform, five bonds were forced to convert earlier (so that investors can receive favorable treatment for holding stocks); Jinniu, Fengyuan, Tongdu, Minsheng, and Jianghuai thus far have been delisted from the exchanges because of conversion of their majority holdings. As a result, only 25 convertible bonds were on the market now.

Investors are quite pessimistic about the convertible bond market for the time being. It is reasonable to believe, however, that this important market will enter a new phase of healthy development once share reform is over.

PART III

China's Equity Markets

Recently, two major factors have been influencing China's equity markets. The first is the state-owned share reform. The second is the preparation of the major international IPOs for the big-four banks in China.

First is the issue of state-owned shares. A large majority of listed companies in Chinese equity markets were transformed from state-owned firms by floating a portion of their shares on the stock exchanges. But toward the end of 2005 more than 65% of the capitalization of these two exchanges was not tradable. These nontradable *state-owned* shares were more than 90% owned directly by government-controlled institutions. Clearly, this issue had a severe impact on investor behavior. Investors had little power in board and shareholder meetings, and the market was constantly under the fear of a sudden state-owned share sell-off.

IPO and M&A activity comprise the second major dimension of the current state of Chinese equity markets. China's capital markets were dominated by two multibillion-dollar bank listing during 2006. The Bank of China and the Industrial and Commercial Bank of China IPOs attracted strong interest. But high economic growth and state-owned share reform are also leading to medium-sized IPOs and a great deal of M&A activity. In fact, according to

Reuters, China was Asia's biggest market for M&A in 2006, excluding Japan, with deal volume rising 25% to $91.6 billion.[1]

On the other hand, nontradable share's becoming tradable had important implications for the M&A market. State-owned share reform could potentially force state-owned enterprises to privatize or sell off subsidiaries. This would provide opportunities for foreign firms to fully control mainland companies.

In this Part we discuss China's markets from a different angle. China has its own culture and in many ways its own way of doing things. Chinese financial markets will naturally be influenced by these. This book does not touch on this "original" dimension. For the most part, we try to stay within the same context as in developed financial markets. This Part is an exception. It provides a picture of Chinese financial markets as seen by the small investor and speculators, in a "Chinese way."

We believe that we can afford to take such a detour, because the objective parameters of China's stock markets were discussed in Chapter 1 and relevant data were provided there. Chapter 13 is another objective discussion of the related funds industry.

This section has two Chapters. Chapter 7 is a different attempt to discuss the parameters of China's equity markets. Any duplication of the material in Chapter 1 is unavoidable if we want some continuity. Also, the interpretation is somewhat different.

Chapter 8 discusses some episodes from China's equity market history. Chinese markets have their own share of speculative bubbles, scandals, and manipulation, and we provide a discussion of some of these here.

---

[1] The deals included Bank of America's $2.5 billion investment for 9% of the Construction Bank and the Beijing-backed oil firm CNPC's $4.2 billion takeover of PetroKazakhstan Inc.

CHAPTER 7

China's Stock Market[1]

Tan Wentao
Treasury Dealer, Malayan Banking Berhad, Shanghai Branch

7.1   INTRODUCTION

We start this Chapter on a light note. Two interesting examples might help us understand the special character of the Chinese stock market. First, we note that after coming to China some Western fast-food chains, such as McDonalds and KFC, had to change their menus significantly to attract Chinese customers. This shows how the Chinese are good at absorbing foreign cultures and then modifying them in order to fit local tastes or fulfill their own purposes. A similar point can be made about the equity market.

The second example is more telling. It turns out that the color red represents *good* news in China. So in Chinese financial markets, red serves to indicate that the markets are up, while green indicates that the markets are going down. In Western society the meanings of these colors are exactly the reverse.

These two sample examples suggest that the Western mind may not fully understand certain aspects of Chinese financial markets. Unlike Western society, where financial markets came into existence due to the needs of the economy and have developed gradually in line with the economy, in China, stock markets were born suddenly when the central government needed new financing tools for state-owned companies. The stock markets were used for partial privatization. Many of the issues the Chinese stock market faces today stem from premature introduction.

[1] I would like to thank Professor Ma Qing Quan, Vice Chairman of Security Association of China (SAC), Chairman of Board of Guang Fa Funds Management and Cai Chen Wei, Credit Portfolio Manager, ABN AMRO, for helping me with data and for their comments.

This Chapter is organized as follows. The first section introduces the structure of Chinese equity markets, including market structure and investor and stock categories. Then we turn to the historic steps that occurred since the early 1990s. We next discuss regulatory issues. Then we consider ways in which the Chinese equity markets are different from their Western counterparts. This may clarify certain challenging features of the Chinese stock market. Then we consider some ongoing changes and reforms. Future possibilities are summarized in the conclusions.

7.2   STRUCTURE OF THE CHINESE STOCK MARKET

We begin with the market and investor structure and then look at the trading instruments.

China has only two national stock exchanges: the Shanghai Stock Exchange and the Shenzhen Stock Exchange. No provincial level stock exchanges exist.[2] This is unlike the United States, where, in addition to those three "national" stock exchanges (NYSE, AMEX, NASDAQ), there are many other regional exchanges, e.g., Boston, Cincinnati, and Chicago, as well as an OTC market in stocks. In this way, the United States has built a multilevel financial trading system. We start by looking at the main exchanges.

7.2.1   SHANGHAI STOCK EXCHANGE

Founded on November 26, 1990, and having started its operations on December 19 of that year, the Shanghai Stock Exchange (ShSE) is the largest marketplace for securities trading in mainland China. This is true in terms of number of listed companies, number of new IPOs per year, total market capitalization, tradable market value, securities turnover, and T-bond turnover.[3] The Shanghai Stock Exchange is a nonprofit institution governed by the China Securities Regulatory Commission (CSRC). Based on tight supervision, self-regulation, and standardization, the ShSE has made significant efforts to create a transparent, fair, safe, and efficient marketplace.

By the end of 2004, the ShSE had a total of 996 listed securities and 837 listed companies, of which 61 were new listings in 2004. Listed securities had a market capitalization of RMB2,601 billion. The market capitalization of

---

[2]This has led to the criticism that the lack of a multilevel securities market in China results in many problems establishing a multifunctional financial marketplace.

[3]All data are from http://www.sse.com.cn and factbook (2004SSE).

exchangeable shares was 731.5 billion RMB. The total number of shares of listed companies in the ShSE by the end of 2004 was 470 billion. Of this amount, only 136.7 billion shares were tradable, accounting for 29.07% of the total.

With respect to new issuance, 45.68 billion RMB was raised from stock offerings during 2004, of which 24.48 billion RMB were A share IPOs and 21.21 billion RMB were secondary offerings. The so-called B shares raised a fractional amount of only 43 million USD.

Based on an advanced, paperless, and electronic communication network similar to developed (electronic-order-driven) stock exchange, the ShSE facilitates trading at a speed of more than 16,000 transactions per second. The orders driven from the floor or member firms through computer terminals are matched automatically by the computer system according to the principle of "price and time priority." For comparison, at the Chicago Mercantile Exchange (CME), only 61% of contracts are traded electronically, while this figure is 55% at the Chicago Board of Trade in 2004.[4] In addition, The ShSE is equipped with a nationwide satellite telecommunications network capable of disseminating real-time transaction data around the country and abroad.

During 2004, the ShSE had 37.9 million investor accounts, realizing a total turnover volume of 7,692 billion RMB. Stock trading was RMB2,647 billion, with a turnover ratio of 308%[5] and RMB4,704 billion of trading in T-bonds. The daily average volumes of trading for stocks and bonds were RMB10.9 billion and RMB19.5 billion, respectively.

7.2.2 SHENZHEN STOCK EXCHANGE

Founded on December 1, 1990, the Shenzhen Stock Exchange (SzSE) is located in the coastal city of Shenzhen, very close to Hong Kong, and is the second marketplace of security trading today. Since its founding, the SzSE has grown from a regional market to a national-level securities marketplace, with listed companies and members from all over mainland China.

Sine its establishment, the SzSE has played a secondary role in China's financial sector, with raised funds of 339 billion RMB by the end of 2003. The market position of the SzSE has gradually dropped behind that of the SzSE, in terms of the number of new IPOs, the number of listed companies and securities, the turnover volume of trading, etc.[6]

---

[4]*Financial Times*, August 10, 2004.

[5]We consider tradable shares only.

[6]All data are from http://www.szse.cn.

Based on paperless custody and invisible trading seats, the SzSE facilitates an order-driven trading system without trading floor and with real-time stock quotations. It disseminates information nationwide through satellites and leased lines linked with over 3,000 member systems. All orders sent by investors via phone or the Internet are matched according to price and time priorities. Tandem computers are used for daily trading capable of handling 20 million trades.[7]

By the end of 2004, 536 companies were listed on the SzSE, with a market capitalization of 1,104 billion RMB, of which negotiable market capitalization accounted for 433.8 billion RMB. In 2004, 34.7 million investors registered on the SzSE, with a total volume of 1,642 billion RMB.

7.2.3   SETTLEMENT AND CLEARING

Created on March 30, 2001, the China Securities Custody and Clearing Corporation Limited is the only security clearinghouse in China owned by the ShSE and SzSE. The ownership structure is similar to the way the German stock exchange (Deutsche Borse) operates its Deutsche Borse Clearing. On September 20, 2001, the two subsidiary corporations Shanghai and Shenzhen Securities Custody and Clearing Corporations were established for securities settlement, clearing, and custody in their marketplaces, respectively, ensuring the transfer of cash and securities simultaneously and the monitoring of daily trading.

A book-entry delivery system has been implemented. The settlement period for RMB-traded products is T + 1 and that for B shares is T + 3.

7.2.4   INVESTOR STRUCTURE

As described previously, the Chinese financial sector operates within a segmented financial system. Thus, the banking and insurance sectors are strictly separated from the securities sector, with "Chinese walls" between them. Laws forbid banks to run any business related to securities, except for custody of mutual funds for QFIIs (qualified foreign institutional investors). Nor can banks lend funds to their clients for securities business. Insurance companies are permitted to invest in equity markets only indirectly, in the form of asset management operated by mutual funds.

---

[7]However, thus far the historical record was 4.5 million trades.

There are four major investor categories in China's equity market:

1. Domestic individual investors
2. Intermediaries and financial service providers, including brokers, integrated securities companies, investment banks, and trust companies
3. Domestic institutional investors
4. Foreign participants

We review these next.

Domestic Individual Investors

Since the commencement of the Chinese equity market, domestic individual investors have been the main participants. By the end of 2004, the total investor accounts in the ShSE totaled 37.87 million, of which individual accounts made up 37.75 million (99%), while institutional accounts totaled only 0.12 million, a very tiny proportion. The situation is the same in the SzSE, which had 34.52 million individual investors and 0.15 million institutional investor accounts. Even if many individual accounts actually are controlled by institutional investors, the number of institutions is still tiny as compared to the number of individuals. Nevertheless, those individuals cannot influence the market's direction because their power is diversified.

However, the situation has been changing due to a strategy of institutional investor expansion promoted by the CSRC since 1999. Pension funds, fund management firms, and insurance capital were encouraged to invest in stocks mainly through developing mutual funds. Since then, those institutional investors have gradually become the main power influencing the market in terms of turnover volume capital, investment strategy, etc.[8]

Table 7.1 depicts the changes in the ShSE and SzSE from 1991 to 2004. It can be seen from these tables that after the number of investors substantially expanded from 1996 to 1999, the rate of increase slowed down.

TABLE 7.1   Investor Accounts in ShSE and SzSE (year-end figures) in millions

Year	1991	1992	1993	1994	1995	1996	1997	1998	1999	2000	2001	2002	2003	2004
ShSE	0.11	1.11	4.24	5.75	6.85	12.1	17.1	20	22.7	29.4	34.3	35.6	36.4	37.8
SzSE	0.26	1.06	3.54	4.85	5.55	11	16.1	19.1	22	28.4	32.2	33.2	33.8	34.5

[8]All figures are from *Fact Book 2004 ShSE* and *SzSE*.

Financial Service Providers and Intermediaries

This type of participant includes pure securities brokers, integrated securities companies, and investment banks or merchant banks. The pure securities broker is able to only take securities brokerage and consultancy business to their clients, while integrated securities companies can take anything related to the securities business, including brokerage, consultancy, proprietary trading, assets management, and those intermediaries covered by investment banks. These two types of financial institutions often are called securities companies. By capitalization, the top 10 players can be ranked as follows:[9]

1. Haitong Securities Co. Ltd.
2. China Galaxy Securities Co. Ltd.
3. Shen Yin Wan Guo Securities Co. Ltd.
4. Guo Tai Jun An Securities Co. Ltd.
5. Southern Securities Co. Ltd.
6. Huaxia Securities Co. Ltd.
7. Everbright Securities Co. Ltd.
8. Xiangcai Securities Co. Ltd.
9. CITIC Securities Co. Ltd.
10. Tiantong Securities Co. Ltd.

With respect to investment banks, the joint venture of China Construction Bank (CCB) with MorganStanley and the China International Capital Corporation (CICC) ranked first in providing a wide range of investment banking services.[10]

Domestic Institutional Investors

Domestic institutional investors can be divided into four types: state-owned and privately owned enterprises, private equity funds, funds management companies, and listed companies.

State-owned and privately owned enterprises

There is no limitation for privately owned enterprises to invest in China's stock market, whereas since the second half of 1999, state-owned enterprises have also been allowed to invest in stocks, whether the initial or secondary market. Both state-owned and privately owned enterprises can invest in A shares and B shares, but it is illegal to invest in H shares listed on the Hong Kong Stock

[9]Sources are from *Fact Book 2003 ShSE*.

[10]www.cicc.com.cn or mail address: 28th floor, China World Tower 2, 1 Jian Guo Men Wai Ave., Beijing 100004, People's Republic of China; tel: (86-10) 6505-1166; fax: (86-10) 6505-1156.

Exchange, despite the many actual actions in H shares taken by domestic investors in bypassing the legal limitation.

Private equity funds

Before the speculation bubble burst in mid-2001, these investors had been major players influencing the stock market in China. Those funds operated by knowledgeable and experienced professors have absorbed a huge and wide range of capital (legal and illegal) in the market. The majority is largely state-owned capital or comes indirectly from commercial banks banned by the laws that segment the financial system. For asset managers, the structure and operating model of private equity funds is very similar to that of mutual funds and hedge funds in Western society. Usually, one large private equity fund controls several listed companies, making up an investment group, the so-called "Xi."

The secondary market prices of listed companies under the control of "Xi" are monopolized by those investment groups. There are two possible ways these funds make a profit. One straightforward way is to speculate and gain profit from the upside of the controlled companies. However, this is becoming more and more difficult because of the increasing awareness of individual investors. Another, less obvious way is for the investment group to forge the balance sheet of the listed companies, obtaining money in the form of mortgages from several commercial banks. They can then make their next M&A by using the new cash obtained from the banks. As a result, either they go out with money or are left out of the market due to the break in the chain of capital.

The most famous "Xi" are the De Long International Group (De Long Xi) and the Fu Xin Investment Group (Fu Xin Xi) as well as Kai Di Xi. Essentially, they are privately run funds, even though they pool largely state-owned capital or indirectly come from commercial banks banned by the laws that segment the financial system. For the safety of the domestic financial system, the government has still not legalized their status.

For this reason, it is quite difficult for researchers to get exact statistics on their total capital, but researchers at the Central University of Finance and Economics (2004)[11] estimated that the capital of private equity funds peaked at 760–880 billion RMB in 2001. Academics and policymakers agree on their influence and main role in the Chinese financial markets. The situation changed in mid-2001. When the speculative bubble burst, the majority of private equity funds experienced huge losses in the stock market and gradually exited the market. Their position and function have been taken over by legal asset management and fund management companies.

[11] *Source*: www.business.sohu.com (July 29, 2004).

Asset management and fund management companies

Since the Securities Act and the Securities Investment Funds Act were enacted in July 1990 and October 2003, respectively, legal fund management companies have developed with tremendous speed. Today, the consensus is that closed funds and open funds definitely exert primary influence on the securities market. By the end of 2004, there was a total of 38 fund management companies managing 54 closed funds and 107 open funds. The total amount of managed assets reached 324.6 billion RMB at that time.[12] In addition to introducing new funds, such as convertible bond funds, listed open-ended funds (LOF), in December 2004 the first Exchange-Traded Fund (ETF) was launched at the SSE. The first joint-venture fund management firm initiated by ICBC and ESFB is set up.

Listed companies

There is a special type of institutional investor. That is, many listed companies, instead of running a main business with core competition, use capital from shareholders to trade stocks in the secondary market. Two methods are used to gain investment profits by these publicly traded companies. One is that they often cooperate with private equity funds, making abnormal returns in the secondary market by trading their own stocks with black-box information. The second method involves allocating their capital in securities companies or legal fund management companies in the form of asset management to indirectly invest in the stock market. The total amount of this type of capital was huge, particularly before the speculative bubble burst. Since then, regulatory authorities have branded black-box trading as illegal manipulation of stock prices, and enforced serious punishment for such acts. The listed companies have tended to discontinue such black-box trading. And as the stock market has declined, the capital involved in the latter method has also been shrinking.

Foreign Investors

There are four approaches foreigners take to the Chinese stock market, depending on the type of investor.

1. The common individual and foreign institutional investors can only invest in B shares in mainland China and H shares in Hong Kong. The majority of foreign investors fall into this type. So strictly speaking, the Chinese stock market is still isolated from the outside world. Both foreign and domestic investors face a firewall that protects the fragile domestic financial system and securities intermediaries from outside attack.

[12] Chapter 13 provides a more detailed analysis of the funds. Refer to "Security Primary Knowledge" (2005), and "Security Investment Fund," 2005, Beijing.

2. The QFII program was implemented in November 2002. It allowed foreign institutional investors to trade in the Shanghai and Shenzhen stock exchanges in A shares, T-bills, and convertible bonds, so long as the investment size does not exceed the quotas approved by the CSRC and the State Administration Foreign Exchange (SAFE). The QFII program was thought of as a test case for opening the financial market and absorbing Western investors and their advanced knowledge and experience. Those institutions as of the end of 2004 were: UBS Limited; Nomura Securities Co, Ltd.; MorganStanley & Co. International Limited; Citigroup Global Markets Limited; Goldman, Sachs & Co.; Deutsche Bank Aktiengesellschaft; The Hongkong and Shanghai Banking Corporation Limited; ING Bank N.V.; JPMorgan Chase Bank; Credit Suisse First Boston (HK) Limited; Standard Chartered Bank (HK) Limited; Nikko Asset Management Co., Ltd.; Merrill Lynch International; Hang Seng Bank; Daiwa Securities SMBC Co. Ltd.; Lehman Brothers International (Europe); Bill & Melinda Gates Foundation; INVESCO Asset Management Limited; ABN AMRO Bank N.V.; Templeton Asset Management Ltd; Barclays Bank PLC; Dresdner Bank Aktiengesellschaft; Fortis Bank SA/NV; BNP Paribas; Power Corporation of Canada; CALYONS.A.
3. Constructing a joint venture with a domestic financial institution is an alternative way of indirectly investing in the Chinese stock market, in order to share the success of China.
4. A new and indirect own investment strategy has arisen since 2003. Foreign investors have been allowed to acquire publicly traded companies in form of buy-out non-negotiable shares. On November 1, 2002, a law regarding the transfer of state-owned shares to foreign capital came into existence. In its wake, on February 9, 2003, Malaysia Sumson bought 110 million shares of state-owned Sai Ge San Xing; a publicly traded company on the Shenzhen Stock Exchange also had 14% of the claim for this company. That was the first case, and today more and more foreign investors are involved in this way when they find undervalued state-owned enterprises listed on the stock exchange.

7.3   REGULATION

The Chinese financial system is one in which banks, securities, and insurance are separately operated by segmented financial institutions and separately regulated by different supervisory authorities. We can call it a *segmented financial system*. Under this system, the securities business is regulated by the China Security Regulatory Commission (CSRC); the China Insurance Regulatory Commission (CIRC) is in charge of regulating the insurance institutions; the China Banking Regulatory Commission (CBRC), in cooperation with the People's

Bank of China (PBC), the Central Bank, and the State Administration for Foreign Exchange (SAFE), is charged with banking regulation and implementation of monetary policy.

7.3.1   HISTORICAL BACKGROUND

With the commencement and development of securities markets in China, the establishment of a centralized market regulatory body was required. In October 1992, the State Council Securities Commission (SCSC) and the executive arm, the China Securities Regulatory Commission (CSRC), were set up, responsible for supervising and regulating the equity market. Since November 1993, the expanded futures market has been under the regulation of the SCSC and CSRC.

However, at that time, other bureaus, such as the PBC, the Shanghai and Shenzhen stock exchanges, as well as their local governments, also were regulating and supervising the markets, resulting in much confusion in terms of administrative power. So, in November 1998, the State Council decided to reform and restructure the national security regulatory system, as a part of the State Council Reform Plan. The SCSC and CSRC were merged to form one ministry, directly under the State Council, namely, the CSRC. The Shanghai and Shenzhen stock exchanges were put under its supervision. Also, it absorbed the previous regulatory power held by the PBC and the local securities regulatory department. The power and the functions of the CSRC were strengthened and a national securities regulatory system established after this reform.

7.3.2   ORGANIZATION OF THE CSRC

There are 13 functional departments or offices, three subordinate centers, and one special committee in the CSRC. It also has 10 regional offices in major cities around the country and a missionary office in each province, autonomous region, or municipality.[13] The structure of CSRC is shown in Figures 7.1 and 7.2.

7.3.3   MAJOR RESPONSIBILITIES

As a leader and supervisory agency, the CSRC has overall responsibility for supervision and regulation over national security and futures markets by drawing, carrying out, and formulating the principles, policies, rules, and

[13]From http://www.csrc.gov.cn/cn/homepage/index.jsp.

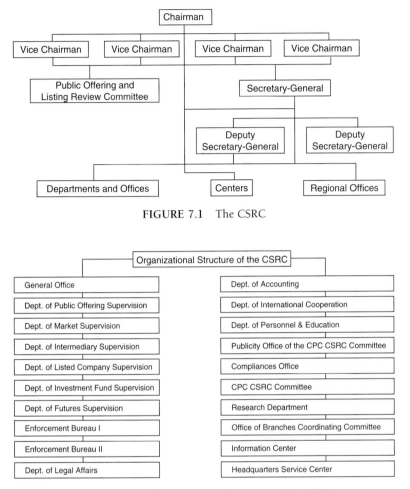

FIGURE 7.1   The CSRC

FIGURE 7.2   Organizational Structure of the CSRC

laws related to these markets. Also, with the power to investigate and penal-
ize activities that violate securities and futures laws and regulations, the
CSRC strengthens the supervision of securities and futures business, stock
and futures exchange markets, the listed companies, fund management companies investing in the securities, securities and futures investment consulting
firms, and other intermediaries involved in the securities and futures businesses.
Furthermore, it directs, coordinates, supervises, and examines affairs related
to securities and futures business in various regions and relevant departments.

Today, the CSRC is focusing on two tasks, that is, development and cleaning up of the stock market. First, as a form of market development, the CSRC endeavors to expand the stock market as a pooling of financing of Chinese companies, especially the state-owned enterprises, in order to restructure those firms' corporate governance and financial situation.

With respect to cleaning up the market, the CSRC is doing its best to make the market more efficient, transparent, and fairly rule-based. A plan of protection for small investors and stricter rules on market participants, such as listed companies, securities companies, and account holders are enforced in order to reestablish investor confidence and make the market mature fast.

Although the CSRC is playing an ever-greater role in regulating and supervising the equity market, a number of critics continue to criticize it for overregulating and interfering in the market. Because of this overregulation and overinterference, the market may lose its self-corrective function and systematic risk is thereby created. Many researchers often refer to the Chinese securities market as policy based rather than rule based or truly market oriented. However, this situation is apparently improving.

7.4   SPECIAL CHARACTERISTICS OF THE CHINESE STOCK MARKET

The Chinese stock market is rather unusual in several respects, not only because three types of stock exist simultaneously in the same marketplace, but also because there are many different types of stocks in the corporation.[14]

7.4.1   TYPES OF STOCKS

The Chinese stock market is characterized by the simultaneous existence of various types of shares, summarized briefly next.

A shares: These renminbi-denominated stocks represent the majority of traded stocks. They can be freely traded on the Shanghai and Shenzen stock exchanges for domestic investors and QFIIs. In the following discussion of the Chinese stock market, we are almost always concerned with A shares, since these comprise approximately 96% of traded stocks. By August 2004, a total of 1,326 companies with A shares publicly traded on Shanghai and Shenzen stock exchanges.

---

[14]For example, nonnegotiable state-owned shares, foreign-owned shares, and outstanding common shares.

B shares: The B share market was established in 1992 for foreign investors both in ShSE and SzSE. On February 19, 2001, this market was opened to domestic individual investors. By the end of 2004, 111 listed companies with B shares are traded on the two exchanges. But this accounts for only a tiny proportion of total market activity. In the Shanghai Exchange, the settlement is in U.S. dollars, whereas in Shenzen Exchange the settlement is in Hong Kong dollars.

H shares: Foreign investors are familiar with this type of share traded in Hong Kong. A total of 118 listed companies with H shares were traded on the Hong Kong Stock Exchange by the end of 2004. Domestic investors, individual or institutional, are not permitted to buy or sell H shares, due to foreign exchange restrictions, although this may be changing. On September 2005, insurance companies were allowed to invest in Chinese companies listed outside the mainland. In addition, 55 Chinese firms had issued 57 ADRs in NYSE, NASDAQ, and the US OTC market.

These three types of stocks coexist in the same nationwide marketplace. More importantly, 29 publicly traded companies have both A shares and H shares, while 87 companies have both A shares and B shares. Under the one price and arbitrage theory, identical corporations having the same stockholder's equity should trade at the same market price (exclusive commissions and fees). However, it turns out these companies' market prices are, in reality "gapped" after converting between RMB and USD or RMB and HKD. These types of arbitrage possibilities were seen in 2001 and 2003, respectively.

Example

Consider a collection of 10 listed companies from the population of 29 companies simultaneously issuing both A shares and H shares. Also, consider a sample of 10 companies from a population of 87 companies issuing both A shares and B shares. We would like to compare their market prices at the two stock exchanges. Table 7.2 presents the situation.[15] As can be seen, there were big price differences between A shares and B shares and between A shares and H shares at the sampled time periods. Recently, such wide price gaps have been reduced, but they may still be present at times today.

7.4.2   CAPITAL STRUCTURE

In addition to the various types of shares, Chinese corporations have a feature that may be quite difficult for outsiders to understand. Chinese corporations

---

[15]From www.sohu.com/finance Zhang W.X.

TABLE 7.2   Comparison of A Shares with H Shares and of A shares with B shares

	Stock name	A shares (RMB)			H shares (RMB)		
		Code	Jan. 2000 price	Average price for previous three years	Code	Jan. 2000 price	Average price for previous three years
1	NE Electronic	000585	4.45	6.56	0042	0.39	1.01
2	Tsingtao Brewery	600600	8.29	6.87	0168	2.45	2.35
3	BeiRen Printing	600860	6.59	5.95	0187	0.60	1.24
4	JiaoDa Hightech	600806	9.29	6.74	0300	0.44	0.82
5	GuangZhou Shipyard	600685	4.96	4.55	0317	0.50	1.25
6	Maanshan Iron	600808	2.62	2.84	0323	0.41	1.05
7	Shanghai Petro	600688	3.92	3.75	0338	1.14	1.59
8	Panda Electronics	600775	11.70	8.55	0553	1.95	1.22
9	YiZheng Chem Fibre	600871	5.24	4.57	1072	0.54	1.56
10	LuoYang Glass	600876	5.49	4.91	1108	0.44	1.05

The FX rate is 1.06 RMB against HK$.

	Stock name	A shares (RMB)			B shares (RMB)		
		Code	Jan. 2000 price	Average price for previous three years	Code	Jan. 2000 price	Average price for previous three years
1	Shanghai Tyre & Rubber	600623	7.86	10.79	900909	0.90	1.38
2	JinJiang Hotels	600754	8.39	8.19	900934	1.51	1.46
3	Shanghai Diesel Enging	600841	10.39	9.92	900920	1.54	1.30
4	LuJiaZui	600623	13.20	13.56	900932	2.46	3.07
5	Shanghai Friendship	600827	11.08	6.87	900923	1.51	1.33
6	HuaXin Cement	600801	5.99	6.12	900933	0.88	1.01
7	DaYing Co., Ltd	600844	10.76	9.83	900921	1.49	1.68
8	Phoenix Co., Ltd	600679	8.00	7.46	900916	0.90	0.81
9	ShangGong Co., Ltd	600843	9.95	8.39	900924	1.23	0.90
10	Shanghai Worldbest Co., Ltd	600094	17.46	10.24	900940	2.10	2.22

The B share price has been changed to RMB at USD/RMB=8.2 at that time.
Source: From www.sohu.com/finance Zhang W.X.

usually issue *three* types of common stock: state-owned stock known as *Guojia Gu*; legal person–owned stocks called *Faren Gu*; and *individual* stocks.

Importantly, the state-owned and legal person–owned shares cannot be traded publicly and freely in the secondary market. Instead, they may be negotiated privately between legal entities and only when counterparties obtain permission from the China Securities Regulatory Commission and state-owned Asset Administration Commission. Then this transaction becomes legal. The third type of shares, individual stocks, are similar to outstanding common stocks in the West. These can be transacted freely in the marketplace.

The Chinese stock market has two types of nontradable common stock, state-owned (Guojia Gu) and legal person–owned (Faren Gu) stock sold at book value when issued; and tradable individual common stock sold at a big premium above book value during IPOs.

Statistics from the CSRC indicate that as of August 2004, the total number of individual common stock was 253.6 billion shares, while this figure was 448.1 billion shares for nontradable stocks together with state owned and legal person owned. This means that only one-third of stock claims on corporations are in circulation and that the other two-thirds of stocks are held by state and a very few legal persons (i.e., state-owned enterprises). This is a rather unique aspect of Chinese stock markets.

Some Implications

Of course, no corporate governance norm is perfect. Although, the relatively large claims held by several large shareholders may be useful to monitor the management, the ownership structure and corporate governance norm evolving in China, create many serious problems.

First, the ownership structure is divided between investors, the state, and legal persons. This leads to conflicts among the different types of shareholders. Individual shareholders buy the underlying tradable shares at very high market prices, averaging five times the price of nontradable shares. Yet they can have barely any effect on corporate governance, because the aggregate outstanding shares account for only one-third of total shares issued.

Second, this imbalance in the stock structure results in "ownership without constraint," and small investors lack any protection.

Next we turn to the question of why and how these particular features have evolved.

7.4.3   EVOLUTION OF CORPORATE STRUCTURE IN CHINA

We begin with the same analogy discussed in the introduction. In some ways, the Chinese thought process is top-down, the reverse of the Western way of thinking. Consider two examples. When an American wants to send a letter to his Chinese friend, the correct Chinese order of writing the name is surname first, given name last, whereas the American always writes or says first the given name and then the surname. Also, with respect to the order of information in the mailing address, in China country comes first, then province or city, and last the name and number of the street. However, an American writes first the name, then the number and street, then the city, and last the country. This different thought process gives a good idea of the evolutionary paths of the stock market in China and the West.

A Comparison

The stock market in the United States is the outcome of a long historical process. After the notion of a corporation was born and gradually grew, more and more corporations arose. If there were no secondary market to allow investors to liquidate their investment and get cash, a primary market would not develop. Companies issuing shares will not typically buy back their outstanding shares, so a secondary market was needed. Given this need, before an organized exchange started, some wealthy investors met on Wall Street in New York in the shade of a Buttonwood tree to trade stocks. As the number of these investors increased and the winter approached, a building was needed to accommodate them, which was the origin of today's NYSE. Afterwards, as the number of investors continued to rise, the broken-and-dealer system arose. Meanwhile investors gradually expanded around the United States, and regional stock exchanges in Chicago, San Francisco, etc., as well as OTC markets, were established. As a result, a multilevel market mechanism was formed in the United States.

Thus we see that the evolution of the securities market in the United States was the result of a spontaneous and market-oriented process, following a bottom-up path. On the other hand, China's stock market stems form the needs of its central government. Following a top-down path, its growth is driven by government needs to achieve economic and political objectives.

At the end of the 1970s, Deng Xiaoping initiated economic reform in China, utilizing two basic strategies. First, the Chinese government encouraged the development of a private sector.[16] However, the privately owned firms were discouraged from financing their growth using capital markets or state-owned commercial banks.

The second strategy was to focus on the improvement of state-owned enterprises (SOEs). Because smaller SOEs were not regarded as very important to

---

[16]Recently this sector's output made up one-third of total industrial products.

the overall economy, the Chinese government sold these firms to their staff or outside individuals. As for the large SOEs that played an important role in the country's economy, the central government restructured their financing and governance system. This was known as the "modern enterprises regime system," and is not privatization per se.

The stock market was introduced into China in order to reach these objectives. The primary purpose of the stock markets was to shift SOE financing from bank loans to public funds. Another purpose was to improve corporate governance. The Chinese central government first established the two national stock exchanges as if they were two empty warehouses, then incorporated the large SOEs and listed them on the two exchanges. This is similar to filling the warehouses with materials. By the end of 2003, approximately 1,200 large SOEs had been incorporated, including boards of directors, boards of supervisors, and shareholder meetings, and listed on the ShSE or SzSE. Thus, the stock market was constructed essentially through the administrative power of the government. Being a top-down process without spontaneous incentive, this evolutionary process was directed by the Chinese government.

Next consider how the particular stock structure has evolved. Table 7.3 shows the transition of China's SOEs from a bureaucratic entity to a corporation, usually in a very short time, typically one year, and via three steps. Only then do the SOEs become a publicly traded company on the ShSE or SzSE.[17]

Recently this sector's output made up one-third of total industrial products. The process of incorporation goes as follows.

Step 1: A typical SOE is divided into two parts: the SOE group parent and its subsidiary. The subsidiary takes over the original SOE's productive assets and is reformed into a typical stockholder company governed by a management and board of directors and having supervisors. This part will later be the publicly traded firm. Its group parent, often restructured into a shareholding company, retains the nonproductive assets or excess staff and guarantees the debts of the original SOE, which include a large component of bad debts or nonperforming loans. In return, the parent, in the form of a shareholding firm, receives the legal-person stocks (Faren Gu), whose price, by law, is capped at 1.5 times face value (i.e., 1 yuan RMB).

Step 2: Before an SOE incorporates, its fixed assets, such as land, property, and equipment, are transferred to the government, local, or central level. Thus, depending on the capital amount and the administrative level (provincial or central), the corresponding shares are

---

[17] This section follows Deutsche Bank Research "China Special."

TABLE 7.3   The Structure of a Listed Company

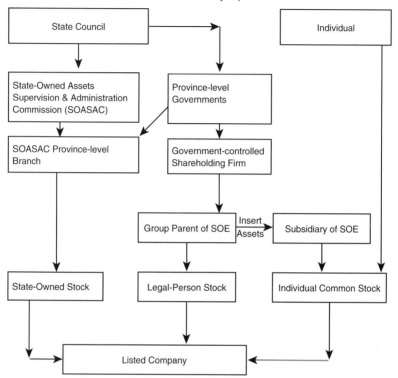

allocated to the State-Owned Assets Supervision and Administration Commission or its provincial branches. Today, these are responsible for the management of the state-owned assets. This type of share forms the so-called state-owned stocks. These are always valued at face value (i.e., 1 yuan RMB). Roughly speaking, the state-owned shares and legal-person shares priced at face value make up about two-thirds of the total capitalization of the stock market, and they are not in circulation.

Step 3: The IPO of the subsidiary is completed, and these shares become freely exchangeable in the ShSE or SzSE. These are called individual common stocks (Geren Gu). Note here that "individual" does not mean that those shares are traded by individual investors only. Both individual and institutional investors are allowed to deal in them. Shares issued through IPO account for no more than 35% of total capitalization.

Let us look at the implications of this process. First, the Chinese government essentially saw the stock market as a way of financing the large SOEs, to absorb funds from individuals and relieve the burden of bad debt or nonperforming loans (NPLs) on the central government. The private sector is unable to find financing in this market.

Second, the central government created the particular stock structure and various types of stockholder (Guojia Gu, Faren Gu, and Geren Gu as well as A, B, and H shares). Consequently, the market is divided into several segments.

Third, the rights and obligations of different shareholders are not symmetrical. This means that individual investors take more risk than the investors who own the noncirculating shares. There are, however, some twists. At first glance, the "noncirculating" shareholders take the liquidity risk because their stock may not be freely traded; but, in fact, they have already acquired excess compensation for it since they bought their shares only at very low prices, as compared to individual investors, during the SOE incorporation. Also they have passed large bad debts (NPLs) to individual investors at rather high share prices.

In addition, not only has government decided the stock structure, market components, and participants, but it also influences the IPO pricing. By law, the CSRC supervises and regulates IPOs, restricting the IPO price for SOEs at P/E ratios between 15 and 20. This means setting up a multiplier equal to between 15 and 20 for an incorporated firm's previous three year earnings? This determines the IPO price. Thought of as a desirable method of protecting state-owned assets in IPOs, this administrative pricing model has persisted until mid-2004.

7.5   SOME SPECIAL CHARACTERISTICS OF THE CHINESE STOCK MARKET

In this section we examine ways in which the Chinese stock market differs from Western markets and consider some current problems.

7.5.1   CAPITAL STRUCTURE IN THE CHINESE STOCK MARKET

As mentioned earlier, the Chinese stock market is in two segments: the predominately nontradable state-owned and legal person–owned shares versus the exchangeable but relatively small-size common shares. The nationally registered stock exchanges deal with the exchangeable common shares traded at relatively higher prices. This means that the interests of common shareholders who buy shares on the secondary market at high prices are put at a disadvantage by the shareholders of nontradable shares. We call this negative impact on the market "division of right and obligation of shares."

When this negative impact of the division in the market structure on investor confidence accumulates, China's stock market loses its financing function. At the moment, the Chinese capital market seems to have some sort of a dilemma: On the one hand, some enterprises are encouraged to raise money in the securities market, instead of obtaining loans from commercial banks.[18] On the other hand, several disappointed investors have left the market, making the market less functional in terms of raising capital.

7.6   WEAK MARKET FOUNDATIONS

Apart from the impact on the stock market stemming from the special capitalization structure, the growth in China's stock market is also hindered by the weak foundation of the market. This includes the lack of ethical norms on integrity, the lack of a credit rating system and appropriate accounting and audit systems, as well as the lack of an internal control system in the listed companies. Consequently, investors must exercise prudence.

7.6.1   ETHICAL ISSUES AND EXAMPLES

A common and serious problem with China stock market is imperfect norms on ethics and integrity. This has caused several financial scandals. Some state-owned and privately owned companies have fabricated documents or financial statements in order to obtain the certificates for IPOs on Seasoned Issues. The case of Jiang Su Qiong Hua in Shenzhen Stock Exchange on July 12, 2004 is one example.

A famous magazine in China is *Finance* (*Caijing*). The award of Asian Star for a business weekly went to this magazine in 2001 for its article entitled "Fund Black Curtain." This article investigated the trading records of 22 funds on the Shanghai Stock Exchange. Almost all of these equity funds had trading irregularities that went against the Security Act.

For example, some funds traded stock with themselves, i.e., they bought shares they were selling, pushing that stock price up by creating artificial trading information. More seriously, other funds supported the price of stock at a very high level to help speculators liquidate their investments. The *Caijing* article

---

[18]This reduces credit risk concentrated in the banking system; hence it is regarded as desirable in this respect.

resulted in something equivalent to an earthquake in China's securities markets, revealing trading irregularities.

In August 2001, *Caijing* had another famous article, called "Yin Guang Xia Trick." According to this article, the famous high-growth listed company Yin Guang Xia (000557) was suspected of manipulating its accounting reports. A later probe by the CSRC revealed a consecutive four year financial fraud, a forging of "profits" of 771 million RMB. In fact, the market price of Yin Guang Xia had gone from 8 to 70 within 4 years. After the scandal was revealed, its market price declined by 80% within one month.[19]

Next is the case of Ms. Liu Shu Wei, a researcher at China Financial University and a specialist in debt scenarios. An investigation by Ms. Liu disclosed that a listed company, Shen Tai Agriculture (600709), had forged profits of RMB500 million. Based on this story, the company had "grown" by 360% within five years, becoming an important blue chip member. It is noteworthy that these two scandals and the underlying behavior of the involved auditors severely undermined investor confidence in the transparency and fairness of the stock market.

7.6.2 ACCOUNTING AND AUDITING

The accounting and auditing systems do not adequately protect investors in Chinese shares, although the situation is improving. As assistant chairman of the People's Bank of China (PBC), the Central Bank, Mr. Li Ruo Gu,[20] has stated that a reasonable process for a firm to finance its growth in Western countries is from private "pooled" financing to local bank loans and then to the debt market, the last phase being the stock market. In China, however, financing of the large state-owned enterprises is transferred directly from commercial bank loan to the stock market. This is mostly to raise money for bad debt and, in a sense, shifting the burden to investors. Thus the phase of debt or bond markets was skipped until recently. As a result, a market-based foundation associated with the bond market, such as a jurisdictional framework, accounting rules, and a credit rating system, is not still functioning properly in China.

7.6.3 MARKET INEFFICIENCIES

Although China is changing dramatically, its stock market is still in a transitional and underdeveloped stage. Thus it is not difficult to find some irrational

---

[19] The auditor was also involved in this financial fraud.

[20] Conference of the Asian Development Bank in May 9, 2002.

and immature aspects of the market. First, there are only two national stock exchanges. Second, China's capital market reveals the same flaw in market structure as in other emerging markets; that is, the money market and bond market are relatively less developed. Third, there are few instruments and financial products other than stocks, commodity futures, and very few government bonds, and no financial futures. As a result the risk exposure investors face cannot be diversified or hedged. As discussed earlier, China's stock markets stemmed from the need for a new approach to finance the large SOEs. Improvements in the market infrastructure were until recently neglected. We can see four types of inefficiencies.

The first inefficiency is that Chinese equity markets are *policy driven*. China's stock market is influenced by administrative policy of the central government. The effects of these administrative interventions can be thought of as a big, unpredictable, and systematic risk on the market.

Let us focus on the issue of nontradable shares first. The dispute in terms of how to make the state-owned and nonexchangeable shares tradable on the secondary market has been an important systematic risk in the stock market. The history of market development suggests that at least *two* bear markets were caused by this risk and led to investor panic. In the first case, when the stock market was in expansion and the index price hit the record high of 1558 early in 1993, the central government suggested that state-owned shares should be exchangeable in the secondary market. The suggestion scared investors, which resulted in a big downturn. The index fell from 1558 to 325 within only one and half years. Then the policymakers had to take a step back and reiterate the nontradability of state-owned and legal-person-owned shares. Soon afterwards, the market climbed sharply, by 150% in only 5 days. The second time was when the market hit the record high of 2240 on June 14, 2001. The CSRC and State-Owned Assets Supervision and Administration Commission (SOASAC) required liquidation of 10% of the state-owned shares on the secondary market with current prices. This was a huge number for the market to absorb at that time, and investors again panicked. Accompanied by financial scandals, investor confidence was undermined by these events. As a result, Chinese markets began a four and a half year bear market.

Government Interference

We can find evidence of stock market inefficiency in achieving the proper allocation of resources. Here we can say that IPOs are typically controlled by central and local governments. Quotas are set and the distribution process is controlled. The initial market thus becomes an administrative environment under the control of government and serves as the pooling only for SOEs, but not for other types of firms.

There is another example of inefficiency. The IPOs and M&A in China's stock market indeed are under the influence of administrative power. For example, in China's stock market, even though a listed company may underperform, their situation will not be too bad, because local government will be responsible for the M&A of that company. The local government will organize the other participants to restructure the bad-performing company. Typically this will be its parent company. The reason local government takes this responsibility is that it is not willing to give up the claims to which it is entitled by nontradable state-owned shares. If the firm is delisted, the value of stocks will be zero. On the other hand, from the viewpoint of new participants, they just want to earn excess profits in the secondary market from the upside of the market rather than begin interested in any actual improvement of the firm's business.

In conclusion,[21] over the previous 13 years more than 1,200 listed companies raised money from the equity market. This amounts to approximately RMB800 billion. If we add in commissions, fees, and trading taxes of RMB450 billion, the figure becomes RMB1,250 billion. On the other hand, total cash dividends to investors (A shares) were only RMB70 billion for the same time period.

Asymmetrical Information

Another inefficiency in China's stock markets is the existence of information asymmetries. Usually, the managers are supposed to have better information on the firm's disclosure than outside investors. In China's stock market, it is common for the management of a listed company to have information in advance and even to create false information. This is known as *information collusion* or *information rent seeking*. As an example,[22] under the Event Study Methodology, the Cumulative Abnormal Return (CAR) can clearly be detected 20 trading days prior to any key information disclosure. Moreover, the Average Abnormal Turnover (AAT) begins to rise dramatically 15 trading days prior to any important information disclosure, reaching its highest level on the second trading day postinformation and gradually declining thereafter.

7.7   FINANCIAL DISTRESS AND BROKERAGES

Two types of market players have recently been in difficulty. Their situation had a negative impact on the growth of the market. Once type is private equity funds and the other is intermediaries, including brokerage firms.

---

[21]Mr. Zhang Wei Xing.

[22]As Dong Bei Security Co. Ltd. indicated.

Private equity funds had dominated the Chinese stock market before June 2001. From then on, however, most of them were destroyed by the downturn in the market. After the bankruptcy of De Long International, virtually all private equity funds left the marketplace. Their role in influencing direction has been replaced by mutual funds or other types of institutions, such as QFIIs or joint-venture intermediaries.

The best example of this type of player is De Long International. As discussed further in Chapter 8, at the time of the speculative bubble (from 1999 to 2001), a strategy known as *capital conduction* or *capital expansion* was quite popular. De Long International was a "successful" user of this strategy, in which, first, an original firm (called the "investment firm") colludes with the management of one of the listed companies (commonly a small or mid-capital company). The investment firm controls the listed firm by purchasing its nontradable shares, e.g., state-owned shares or legal person–owned shares, at the same time as they may buy the shares on the secondary market. This pushes the price up. When this occurs, nearly 90% of the shares in circulation typically are in their hands. Note that as long as they do not sell, the price will be stable at a high level. Afterwards, the listed company will disclose some significant information supporting that high price. If the price is accepted by the market participants, then they may collateralize these listed shares to commercial banks to obtain cash. By doing this, De Long International controlled at least three listed companies, one trust company (Jing Xing Trust), three securities companies (De Heng Security, Heng Xin Security, and Zhong Fu Security), and some financial lease firms in the form of leveraged buyout.

De Long International failed due to the broken "money chain" and to the huge debt obligations triggered on March 2004. A direct result of De Long's bankruptcy was to induce large losses on asset management in securities companies. Thus we turn next to another type of institution in financial distress—intermediary or security companies, such brokerage firms.

Since 2004, the CSRC has begun to focus on financial intermediaries, e.g., brokerage firms, because nine securities companies have been liquidated since 2003, including the biggest in China—Southern Security Co. Ltd.

It is worth examining the causes of this. The intermediaries' profits rely heavily on commission income. From Table 7.4 we see that slightly more than half of the profits are earned from commissions and fees. The Big Bang that began in 2001 and the Internet trading resulted in a sharp decline in their traditional brokerage business. In order for those intermediaries to survive this competition, they had to look for new income. There were two possibilities at that time: proprietary trading and asset management and equity repo.

TABLE 7.4 The Structure of Intermediaries' Income, 2001.

Commision Fees	51%
Interest Income	11%
Security Issuance	5%
Proprietary Trading	13%
Interbanks Account	15%
Others	5%

Source: "Research on Advanced Issued of China Security Market Development (2003)", 2004, Beijing, p. 186.

In the case of proprietary trading, the bear market led to big losses. Their asset management also suffered from this bear market, because the majority of asset management accounts were guaranteed at a certain positive rate of return, which means that asset managers took some of the price risk.

For equity repo, the intermediaries take their clients' equity as collateral, lending cash to them. However, the bear market led to defaults by their clients. Moreover, to finance the equity repo, the intermediaries borrowed money in T-bond repo or even by embezzling credit balances in other clients' brokerage accounts. The expectations that interest rates would increase reduced the price of T-bonds and made these positions untenable.

Supervisors have difficulty dealing with this issue. On the one hand, they know the State Treasury cannot afford to pay for the losses of those firms if more and more security companies fail and are liquidated. On the other hand, if government does not provide some type of guarantee, this may threaten the vulnerable banking system further. In fact, most investors regard the securities companies as some sort of commercial bank, ignoring the custody risk and credit risk they face.

Before ending this section, let us summarize the problems with the stock market. The first and the major problem with the market is division of right and obligation of share caused by the existence of nontradable shares.[23] Next is the problem of the market's foundation, which is very weak, with the lack of standards of ethical behavior, a credit rating system, accounting principles, an audit system, and internal control. The third problem stems from the policy-driven nature of China's stock market, which makes stock prices unrepresentative of firms' true values.[24] The last problem in China may be various microlevel risks, such as custody risk.

[23] This important issue is discussed in the next chapter.

[24] See "China's Financial Sector: Institutional Framework and Main Challenges, January 9, 2004," Deutsche Bank Research for China Special.

7.8 CONCLUSIONS

At the beginning of the 21st century, Chinese financial markets have become a center of attention. The rapid development of Chinese markets is truly remarkable and will, in all likelihood, continue. Yet many challenges must be overcome before needed reforms are successfully completed.

- Market-based IPOs.
- The termination of the policy-driven market. The supervisory authority will not interfere in the market. The power of the policy-driven market is becoming less and less.
- Various types of stocks will, in all likehood, disappear. That is to say, as the market opens to the outside world, more and more arbitrage investors will eliminate arbitrage opportunities.
- Market structure is changing as evidenced by the in-process reforms of nontradeable state-owned shares. The reform will and is thoroughly changing the market in terms of main players, pricing theories, corporate governance structures, and the approaches to mergers and acquisitions, as well.

REFERENCES

Stephen Green, "Enterprise Reform and Stock Market Development in Mainland China," *Deutsche Bank Research for China Special*, p. 8. March 25, 2004.

Ma Qing Quan, "China's Security Market History," 2003, CITIC Public House, Beijing.

Zhang Yu Jun, "Reform and Development of China's Stock Market in a Transitional Period," 2004, p. 112, Southwestern University of Finance and Economics Press, Chendu, China.

Zhuang Xin Yi, "Research on Advanced Issue of China Security Market Development (2003)," 2004, pp. 186, 300, China Financial Publishing House, Beijing.

"Security Market Primary Knowledge" (2005), and "Security Investment Fund," 2005, Beijing.

Zhang Yu Jun, "Reform and Development of China's Stock Market in a Transitional Period," 2004, p. 113, Southwestern University of Finance and Economics Press, Chendu.

Statistics are from "Security Market Primary Knowledge," 2005, pp. 26–28; "Security Investment Funds," 2005, pp. 15–16; China Financial and Economic Publishing House, Beijing.

Li Z. J, "China Equity Market Development Report," 2003, China Financial and Economic Publishing House, Beijing.

CHAPTER 8

A History of China's Stock Markets

Tan Wentao
Treasury Dealer, Malayan Banking Berhad Shanghai Branch

In this Chapter we examine the history of China's equity market since around 1980 and describe, step by step, how this market grew over this period. We consider four phases. Generally, in each phase we discuss changes in IPO structures, secondary market mechanisms, and the regulatory system.

8.1 GRAPHICAL OVERVIEW

In order to discuss the development of the Chinese stock market it is perhaps best to consider a graphical view of the main events and the behavior over time of the A share and B share markets.

We do this in two different ways. First we look at the actual behavior over time of the A share and B share indices. However, we also consider the underlying volatility. We calculate one-sided moving averages for the two indices. Letting x_t be the stock index series, we consider as the measure of volatility the moving standard deviation σ_t:

$$\sigma_t = \sqrt{\frac{1}{m} \sum_{i=1}^{m} (x_{t-i} - \bar{x}_t)^2}$$

These data are shown in Figures 8.1–8.4, respectively. The figures are quite telling by themselves, and they show very clearly the history of the various phases of the Chinese stock market. The details of these phases are discussed in subsequent sections.

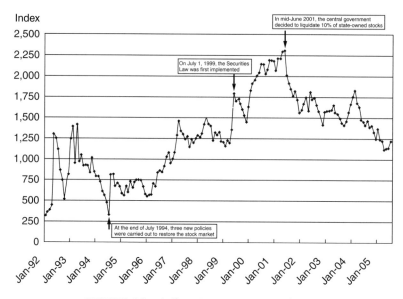

FIGURE 8.1   A Share Price over Time, Chart 1

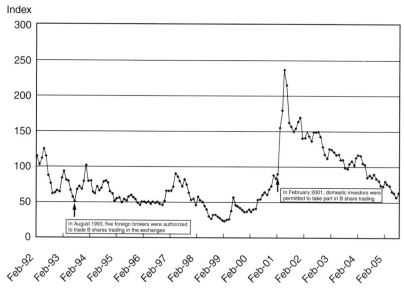

FIGURE 8.2   B Share Price over Time, Chart 2

Volatility

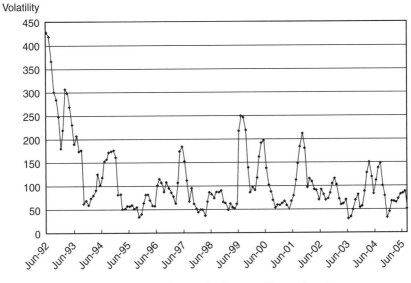

FIGURE 8.3   A Share Volatility over Time, Chart 1

Volatility

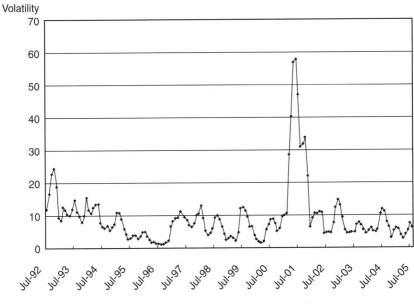

FIGURE 8.4   B Share Volatility over Time, Chart 2

8.2   FIRST PHASE: THE STOCK MARKET IS BORN

This phase covers 1979 to 1990, representing the beginning of China's economic reform proposed by the Chinese leader Deng Xiaoping. It deals with a transition from a centrally planned economy to a market-based economy. As the economic system changed, the financial and banking systems were also in transition. Chinese leaders attempted to look for new ways of investing and financing for the state-owned enterprises (SOEs). At first, the former investment strategy, the fiscal allocation to the SOEs, which depended on the central plan, was altered to the form of administrative bank loans. Afterward, as individual wealth expanded, SOEs became capable of raising money directly from a funding pool. And then, as a test bed for the Chinese government to raise money for the SOEs, the joint-stock corporation was introduced into China. From then on, the stock market's financial function became highly significant.

On November 18, 1984, China's first stock—Shanghai Fei Le (600651)—was born, in Shanghai, at a capitalization of RMB500,000 yuan. In the following six years, 14 stocks were issued, and RMB4.59 billion yuan was raised. All of these issuances were in the form of private "pooled" financing, where prices were determined by issuers, not intermediaries, since there was no financial institution to act as intermediary and there was no issuance laws or regulation at that time.

With the appearance of the primary market came a demand for a secondary market. All that was required, in principle, was a mechanism by which a holder of a particular security could find a buyer, agreeing on a price at which buyer could pay and the seller transfer his security to the buyer simultaneously. On September 26, 1986, a memorable day, China's earliest OTC market appeared, named Jing An Trust. In addition to this legal OTC market, a black market existed that took a larger trading volume than the legal one.

The People's Bank of China (PBC), China's Central Bank, and its Shanghai and Shenzhen branches were responsible for regulating and supervising the original markets.

8.3   SECOND PHASE: RAPID GROWTH

China's stock market experienced a rapid growth from 1991 to 1996, gradually forming a complete market structure in terms of trading mechanism, issuing system, regulation, etc. The most important feature during this period was that the IPO system was constructed. At that time, IPO pricing was still determined by administratively; that is, the P/E ratio multiplier was chosen to decide price.

IPO price is the product of the average P/E ratio of the most recent three years before the issuance, and the multiplier, which is between 15 and 20, is decided by CSRC according to the current market environment.

On December 19, 1990, the Shanghai Stock Exchange (ShSE)—was founded. On December 5 of the same year, modeled on the NASDAQ, the Security Trading Automatic Quotation (STAQ) system was established in Beijing. This was the first national-level OTC bond market linked by computer network. The following year, on July 3, the second stock market—the Shenzhen Stock Exchange (SzSE)—was opened. This was a prelude to growth in China's stock market. Meanwhile, a total of 14 listed companies were publicly traded on the two exchanges. These are often regarded as the "Eight Oldsters." Afterward, some local-level securities trading centers were set up, such as Wuhan, Shengyang, Tianjin, and Dalian Securities Trading Center, forming a complete multilevel trading system.

However, there were still some objections to economic reform and to the stock market from the conservative politicians at that time. These objections focused on the ideology of the centrally planned vs. market-based economy. On February 22, 1992, Deng Xiaoping put an end to these objections with his famous speech during his visit to Shenzhen. He confirmed the results of economic reform commencing in 1979 and the achievements in testing for a securities market, and he encouraged the continuing development of the securities market. A rapid expansion of China's stock market commenced, due to the elimination of further political risk.

Between 1991 and 1996, both the primary and secondary markets experienced a dramatic growth. We will now describe this growth in three areas: IPOs, changes in the secondary market, and the regulatory system.

8.3.1 EVOLUTION OF THE IPO PRICING MODEL

Before 1991, stock issuance in the primary market was implemented via private "pooled" financing. After 1991, as issuance grew, public issuance became a trend, but the pricing method was not market oriented. Instead, the fixed-pricing model was typical, for two reasons. First, fixed pricing is easy to use; second, the government wanted a discount price, making the issuance successful. Fixed pricing, also known as the P/E ratio multiplier method, is where the government chooses a reasonable P/E ratio, multiplied by the issuer's average earnings for the most recent three years. The result is the issuance price. Typically, the P/E ratio ranged between 15 and 20, and all issuers, whether good or bad, were in compliance with this multiplier. Since the issue price was deliberately discounted, it led huge numbers of funds to enter the primary market. The aggregate supply of money overwhelmed the aggregate demand for newly issued stocks. Some supplemental method had to be considered.

In 1992, Shanghai and Shenzhen issued certificates of stock purchase, resembling stock warrants, which were distributed by lottery to entitle holders of the certificates to buy IPO shares. (Unlike stock warrants, the certificates here did not set the buying price.) In Shanghai, 2.07 million certificates were issued in 1992, each worth 30 RMB yuan. The certificate holders thus acquired the right to buy new IPO shares within a year if they were chosen by lottery. By rough estimates, every certificate made a profit of at least 200,000 RMB yuan, and created the first explosion of wealth in China's stock market.

Because of this, more and more investors rushed to purchase the certificates, and amid the confusion bribes and corruption thrived. Thus in 1993, the Chinese government decided to limit issue certificates of stock purchase, plus prepayment with bank certificates of deposit for any new issuance. But this method also confounded the banking system since huge sums of cash or deposits could flow into and out of local branches frequently and rapidly. Therefore this system was soon abandoned.

In July 1994, a way to buy new issuances, invented by the SzSE, became popular, known as *subscription by network with fixed price*. With this method the underwriter, as the only seller, sells the total new issuance at the price predetermined by the underwriter and the issuer via the P/E ratio multiplier method. Investors offer the amount they are willing to buy at that price by a declaring system. Linked by computer network, this system provides one terminal to every securities company, where clients can apply. Then, lottery is used to decide which investors and the amount they can buy. An obvious flaw in this method is that the price of issuance is fixed and man-made, not chosen by the market. This could result in large excess returns when the newly issued shares are publicly traded on the secondary market. Table 8.1 depicts this big gap among IPOs in China.

What caused the large excess returns of IPOs? There are at least two reasons. One is, as we mentioned before, that by putting a ceiling on the price of new issuances, the fixed-pricing method deliberately underestimates the price, implicitly encouraging investors in the primary market, since the government longs to sell a part of their stocks. In return, the government raised money for their SOEs to offset bad debts and to throw off the burden they should have undertaken. Another reason may be that China's securities market and other financial markets are separated from the outside world, so internal money has no other investment channel than the stock market. Huge amounts of money chase the limited number of new issuances, often creating several thousands times excess subscriptions. Investors can only invest in the secondary market in hopes of making a profit. This leads to a high trading price after the

TABLE 8.1   First Trading Day Appreciation Statistics for Newly Issued Stocks
in China

	Year								
	1993	1994	1995	1996	1997	1998	1999	2000	2001
Number of listed companies	116	36	12	172	188	102	92	115	67
First trading day appreciation (%)	185.6	72	94.5	111	147.7	133	110.3	149.8	141.2

Source: Hong Yuan Securities.

new issuance becomes tradable, and large excess returns of IPOs occur. The excess returns are attractive to big players, who buy IDs and open accounts. And then they allocate money borrowed from commercial banks, where they are important clients or have special rights to obtain a loan, to the accounts they control. Once the lottery decides who has the right to purchase a new issuance, these big players are more likely to be entitled to buy stock and make excess and riskless returns since they make up a larger proportion of the total lottery. That created the second explosion of China's stock market. Tables 8.1 and 8.2 compare average first trading day returns in China with other countries.

Now consider the regulations. Before 1997, the supervisory authorities controlled the issuance numbers by quota. Each year, the State Council determined that year's quota, allocating it to every province or municipality. And then the provinces or municipalities further distributed the quota to firms seeking to be listed. Once the firms with quotas complete their corporate reforms and were audited by auditors and other asset-evaluating agencies, they can apply to the CSRC for issuance. If they obtain approval, they are put on a waiting list. In addition to the quotas used to control the number of new issuances, the CSRC matches the pace of issuance to the market environment. The better the market environment, the more new companies are listed, and vice versa.

It can clearly be seen from this description that the central government dominated the IPO process. They not only controlled the price of issuance, keeping the process of pricing from being market based, but also artificially distributed the quotas to those large SOEs. Consequently, the right to raise money went to the SOEs but not to those most eligible. The resources were reallocated inefficiently. This IPO procedure vividly illustrates some unfair and biased features of the stock market in China in the early days.

TABLE 8.2 First Trading Day Appreciation in China Versus Other Countries

Country	Number of listed companies	Period	Average first trading day appreciation (%)
France	197	1983–1992	4.2
Canada	258	1971–1992	5.4
Austria	67	1964–1996	6.5
Holland	72	1982–1991	7.2
Denmark	32	1989–1997	7.7
Finland	85	1984–1992	9.6
Belgium	28	1984–1990	10.1
Germany	170	1978–1992	10.9
Australia	266	1976–1989	11.9
England	2,133	1959–1990	12.0
Norway	68	1984–1996	12.5
Turkey	138	1990–1995	13.6
United States	13,308	1960–1996	15.8
Hong Kong	334	1980–1996	15.9
China	900	1990–2001	127.0

Source: Hong Yuan Securities.

8.3.2 SECONDARY MARKET VOLATILITY

We take the ShSE composite index (SCI) as an example. When the ShSE was established on December 19, 1991, the SCI opened at 96.04, and then the composite index rocketed to 1558 on February 16, 1993. Afterward, the expectation that state-owned shares would be publicly traded provoked a panic. The index dramatically slumped by nearly 80% to 325 on July 29, 1994.

The central government, fearing this situation, began to intervene in the market. On July 30, a plan was disclosed to rescue the market, including the promise of not trading state-owned shares on the secondary market. In the wake of this plan, the index bottomed out and sharply increased to 800 points within only five days. After this recovery, the stock market went into a recession lasting one and a half years.

Over the duration of this contraction, the securities companies and their branch offices progressed significantly. Resorting to computer and networking technology, the securities companies' branches were established nationwide; from then on, the popularity of the stock market spread from Shanghai and

Shenzhen to the whole country. The number of accounts opened in the ShSE and SzSE rose by 110% and 126% from 1994 to 1996, respectively. The huge number of investors and brokers provided a cash pool to the market and created the base for the next expansion.

After the traditional Chinese spring festival of 1996, China's policymakers proposed a continuous development plan for the stock market, after which the market composite index (SCI) bottomed out again and then rose steeply by 146% from the beginning of this year to 1258 by the end of 1996. However, the policymakers were afraid of overwhelming speculation, and they then again intervened in the stock market by promulgating several rules. Even editorials in *People's Daily* warned investors. On December 16 of that year, the ShSE and SzSE began to implement a policy by which every daily price change must be within a band of 10%. This marked the end of that bull market and the start of the next shakeout.

8.4   THIRD PHASE: ENFORCING REGULATIONS

When the Asian financial crisis started in mid-1997, Chinese officials at the highest level worried about the fragile financial system. Thus they imposed a strict regulation and supervision over the entire financial system, including banks, insurance companies, trust, the stock market, and the futures market. The segmented financial system began at that time. The time period from 1997 to 1999 represents the third phase of China's stock market. The most important feature of this period is that the framework of regulations, rules, and laws related to the securities market was established. A good example of these is the Securities Law (1998). Following are some important events influencing the stock market.

1. In March 1997, the central government decided to implement a *segmented financial system*, where the banking, insurance, trust, and securities sectors must be maintained as separate and cannot be mixed. The respective regulatory authorities are also separated and responsible for their own sectors. Under this system, all funds directly or indirectly from commercial banks have to be kept away from the stock market. And since May 1997, state-owned enterprises have not been allowed to invest in the securities market, to avoid spreading any potential crisis across the different financial sectors.

2. Since 1997, more than 100 rules and laws related to the securities sector have been enacted. This has created a basic framework of legislation for the securities market. Among these, the Securities Law (1998) and the Investment Funds Law (1997) were especially influential.

3. The futures market was strictly regulated.[1]
4. The State Council Financial Work Conference decided to close all local securities trading centers other than the ShSE and SzSE, such as Wuhan, Shengyang, and Tianjin Security Trading centers. Since then, the multiple-level securities market has been terminated in China.
5. A national universal regulatory system evolved. Before 1998, there were too many bureaus responsible for regulation and supervision of the China's securities market. Apart from the State Council Securities Commission (SCSC) and its executive branch, the China Securities Regulatory Commission (CSRC), other departments, including the People's Bank of China (PBC), the Shanghai and Shenzhen stock exchanges, the Ministry of Finance, and the State Plan Commission, were also entitled to regulate or supervise the securities market. This led to some confusion. Thus in November 1998, as a part of the State Council Reform Plan, the SCSC was closed and all regulatory power was handed over to the CSRC, which became the only authority in charge of regulating the national securities market. In its wake, the CSRC itself was also restructured, forming the organization of today. Thus, a complete national regulatory framework was established and strengthened.

Although the main theme of this period was regulatory enforcement and supervision, the CSRC and the State Council intervened in the stock market several times, attempting to keep it relatively stable and rid it of any large disturbances, seeking to protect the vulnerable financial system from the attack of international hot money. Fortunately, China was a survivor of that financial contagion due to the nonconvertability of its currency. In the stock market, they were also successful in eliminating potential threats to the domestic market. As a result, the stock market was held at a level between SCI 1030 and 1400.

With respect to IPOs during 1997 and 1998, the number of A shares continued to expand rapidly, while the B share and H share markets underwent serious shrinkage and their function of financing nearly disappeared. Both B and H shares served as the outside source of capital, which had felt the impact of financial contagion. In addition, another obvious phenomenon during this period is that SOEs dominated the listed companies on both stock exchanges. In September 1997, the CSRC proposed to define the stock market's function as raising money for SOEs to dilute the proportion of bad debt or to improve corporate governance.

---

[1] Futures markets are dealt within Chapters 1 and 9.

8.5   FOURTH PHASE: THE SPECULATIVE BUBBLE

The period from May 19, 1999 until today represents the most important time period for China's stock market, for three reasons. First, during this period the market has undergone a sharp upturn and a steep downturn. Along with it, wild speculation occurred. After the bursting of this speculative bubble, several problems with the market were revealed, which enables us to understand the essence of this period. Hence, authorities are more likely to find the appropriate methods to solve these problems.

Second, during this period, the investment strategy has moved from speculation to value discovery. This transition resulted in a profound revolution in stock price structures. This four-year downturn told investors what risks there are, including market risk, sovereign risk, custody risk, and litigation risk. Last but not least, the regulatory authorities and highest-level government officials gradually better understood the workings of the stock market.

To illustrate the details of this stage, we divide it into two subparts: generation of the bubble and its bursting.

8.5.1   THE START OF THE BUBBLE

This period is from May 19, 1999 to June 14, 2001. During these two years the SCI increased by nearly 110% from 1043 to 2240. Significant speculative capital flowed into the stock market, creating a large bubble.

In 1999, as a result of the Asian financial crisis, a serious recession started in China. Aggregate demand was insufficient to support an economic recovery from the financial crisis. In particular, a large number of SOEs faced financial distress and the banking system was confronted with a potential threat of inadequate capital ratios (Bank for International Settlement (BIS) is 8%) resulting from their huge volume of nonperforming loans (NPL). Indeed, all banking problems largely stemmed from the bad performance and bad debts of SOEs. At the same time, authorities suggested that one should resort to the capital market, which can be used as a source to raise money for SOEs under financial distress. This would incorporate the SOE into the modern corporate system. In addition, it was hoped that the upturn of the market would create a "wealth effect" and consequently stimulate spending. The policy was inclined to expand the stock market and move it upward.

On May 19, 1999, some well-informed institutional investors began to buy huge volumes of stock, causing an increase in share prices. Consequently, *People's Daily* on June 13, 1999, published the second famous editorial, in which the market environment was described as in recovery and explicitly encouraged participants to invest in the stock market. Meanwhile several rules and laws were enacted. In June 1999, state-owned firms were again permitted to participate in stock trading; since October 1999, insurance companies have been able to invest in the stock market indirectly by purchasing mutual funds; on September 23, 1999, the 15th National Party Congress issued "the decision on SOEs reform and development," in which the proposal for solving the problems of SOEs by means of the stock market is confirmed. On February 14, 2000, CSRC enacted a method for distributing newly issued shares among subscribers.

Speculative money rushed into the market, pushing the index of the SSE from the low of 1043 on May 19, 1999, to a record high of 2240 on June 13, 2001. A noteworthy point is that during this period, as opposed to the upturn in market prices, the earnings per share of most listed companies were in an obvious downturn. Despite this contradiction, a great deal of speculative money took full advantage of the investment strategy, called *backdoor listing*, associated with Mergers and Acquisitions (M&A). According to this, when a listed company is in difficulty or in financial distress, it is quite likely to be restructured by outside players or typically by its parent shareholders' firm. On the other hand, from the perspective of other players, they are also willing to restructure by M&A when the listed company is in difficulty, since the listing procedure is quite long and difficult (i.e., quote-required).

Backdoor listing is attractive to other players because not only is it a short-cut to list in the market, but also can make huge returns in the secondary market. M&A typically is fulfilled by buying the nonexchangeable state-owned shares or legal person–owned shares in private at a price much lower than those on the secondary market. Also, only one deal involving a large amount of shares is able to achieve the controlling position.

After completion of M&A, new participants in the listed company usually make abnormal returns, in two stages. First, they typically restructure the new firm by inserting some good assets or cash inflow to improve its performance and financial situation as soon as possible, even though they may be manipulating the accounting report. By doing so, they can make a profit on the secondary market when the stock price goes up. Second, they commonly make the second public offering under the excuse of financing a new project that has good prospects. This method is termed the *De Long model*, having been invented by the De Long Company.

8.5.2 END OF THE BUBBLE AND THE BEAR MARKET

On June 15, 2001, the CSRC issued a new rule that previously nonexchangeable state-owned shares were to be publicly traded on the secondary market, which meant that the highest level of central government attempted to liquidate 10% of the total state-owned shares to supplement the shortage of pension funds. This led to a downturn in the market after it had hit the record high of SCI 2240 on June 13; the market panicked.

Shortly after, on August 3, the magazine *Finance* published "Accounting trick of Yin Guang Xia," which destroyed the myth of inevitably high returns from the stock market. Meanwhile, on July 27, the PBC began to probe commercial bank funds used illegally in stock trading on the secondary market, and ordered all commercial banks to withdraw all loans to the stock market as soon as possible. This accelerated the downturn in the market. After that, the bubble burst and the market became a bear market.

8.6   CURRENT PERIOD

In the current period, apart from fluctuations in market prices, many "returning overseas PhDs" began to appear in high and key policymaker positions in the regulatory authority. Mixing their knowledge and experience of Western society with continuing lessons from today's market the upper-echelon leaders and policymakers have realized the importance of regulations and constraints. Many rules and laws on market orientation were enacted, and we can observe the large impact of these influential reforms on the market.

8.6.1   REFORMS IN IPOs

As discussed earlier, before 1992, new issuances in China were private and offered at a fixed price. This system was replaced by IPOs in 1992, and from then through April 1, 2001, the CSRC adopted quotas as a method for distributing listed company resources. The main disadvantage of quotas is the creation of rent seeking, which means the quota is valuable and corruption is inevitable. Thus on April 1, 2001, a new method, called the *approval system*, was implemented. Under this system, the quota and its associated procedure of distributing quotas were terminated. Instead, the CSRC established a new department, known as the *issuance approval commission* run by several professors and officials. This department has the responsibility for processing the applications for listing. In addition, the underwriter system is promoted as a supplement to the issuance approval system, requiring the underwriter to support the candidate *before* submitting the red envelope. Although this system does not eliminate the phenomenon of rent seeking, it still represents important progress for IPOs.

According to the Securities Law, from July 1, 1999, if the price of a new issue contains a premium over face value, the price should be determined by both sides, underwriter and issuer, and the price then must be approved by the CSRC. Practically, the CSRC first determines a usually small price range within which the underwriter and issuer decide the issue price, typically after completing a process of road show or consultancy. However, this is still not a market-based process because the market participants can only make their price decision within a very small range. In August 2004, the CSRC proposed legislation to revise the Securities Law, requiring the process of pricing to be thoroughly market based, e.g., book building or auction without limit.

8.6.2   REGULATION AND SUPERVISION

In China the direct consequences of a particular capitalization structure (majority and noncirculation of state-owned and legal person–owned shares versus minority and tradable individual shares) are the lack of protection for minority shareholders and ownership without constraints. Thus, listed companies in China usually have serious management problems, which are reflected in the following two scenarios.

First, when the majority shareholders control management and the board of directors exploits the company without constraint, the interests of minority shareholders are impaired. Statistics from an investigation in late 2002 by the CSRC indicated that nearly RMB96.7 billion (USD11.7 billion) from listed companies was embezzled by their majority shareholders. Typically there are at least three ways to strip assets from a listed company. (1) The *related-party transaction*: The management and board of directors controlled by a majority shareholder typically conduct a business operation under which the income and profits of the listed companies are transformed into gifts to firms that are private firms under the control of that majority shareholder. (2) *Direct loan or a guarantee on loan repayment for the related company*: A company related to a listed company takes a loan from a commercial bank that typically requires the listed company to guarantee this loan for its borrower. Often the borrower will never repay the loan because this deal is a trick to steal money from that listed company. When the loan is due and there is no repayment, the commercial bank requires the listed company to fulfill its guarantee. So stockholders become victims. (3) *Cash dividends*: Soon after a new issue, either IPO or secondary issue, some listed companies simply announce cash dividends in which the state-owned and legal person–owned shareholders enjoy the same cash inflow as individual investors, but the former pay substantially less than the latter for the same right.

Second, due to a lack of internal control systems and imperfect audit systems, as well as a powerful rating agency such as Moody's or S&P, the accounting reports of a listed company quite commonly are manipulated. The management usually plays a numbers game, e.g., different accounting principles, deliberate undervaluation or overvaluation. More seriously, many companies even forged their accounting reports, whereby all income and profits are fictional.

Since 2001, the CSRC has enacted more than 100 rules on corporate governance. Some of them are still being enacted and some are playing an important role in improving listed companies' performance. The following is a summary.

- Make the board of directors more independent.
- Enforce information disclosure in terms of M&A, accounting reports, and auditors.
- Encourage small investors to sue management for fraud.
- Apply tough punishment to financial shenanigans and black-box trading.
- Delist any company with bad performance.
- Promote the plans of strategic and institutional investors, including funds management, foreign institutions, and pension and insurance funds.

There is good evidence of improving governance as a result of these changes. However, regulation cannot eliminate fraud and manipulation completely. The problems with the market can only be solved by using market-based ways. In this area, the most key issue for China's stock market is the special capital structure and its consequence—inconsistent returns and risk exposure for different types of investors.

8.6.3   THE BIG BANG IN CHINA

Like May 1, 1975, in the United States and 1986 in the United Kingdom, the "big bang," that is, the elimination of the fixed commission and the adoption of the negotiable commission rate between broker and clients took place in China, on May 1, 2002, exactly 27 years after its American counterpart.

Before 2002, the stock commission rate was 0.35%, the second highest in the world. After the big bang, the capped floating commission system was implemented, but not the pure negotiable commission system. First, reduced commission fees lower the operating income from pure commission business. Thus to maintain gross profits from the core operation, securities brokers have to keep down the costs of operation. As a result, many brokers resort to Internet trading and the cash management account (CMA) resembling what Merrill

Lynch created in 1977, which is set up at commercial banks and combined with savings, securities trading, and settlement functions. Second, securities companies began to extend their core business from earning commissions to asset management and investment banking. By June 2002, the amount of client's managed assets had reached RMB58.5 billion yuan.[2]

Although these measures have fostered brokers' development, securities brokers have operated with difficulty and under financial distress since 2001. From 2002 on, the securities sector suffered universal loss in two consecutive fiscal years.[3] Not only did the big bang make competition tough and involve commercial banks indirectly in the traditional brokerage business under the CMA (because the banks possess the customer resources), but that the long-term downturn in the market produced losses from asset management, in which a certain return on investment is usually guaranteed by securities companies to their clients. If the targets are not reached, the securities company will incur a loss. This is the main reason for the bankruptcy of Southern Security Co. Ltd, one of the largest in China.

Lack of financial support is another main source of the financial distress in securities companies. Owing to the firewall between the banking and security sectors, a securities company cannot obtain funds from a commercial bank. Thus they seek alternatives. Embezzling customers' credit balances in brokerage accounts and T-bond repo are preferred ways to raise money for their business or lending to their important clients. However, the slump in bond prices due to the expectation of increases in the interest rate commencing in early 2004 caused liquidation of at least eight securities companies: Da Lian Security Co. Ltd, An Shan Security Co. Ltd, Ming Fa Security Co. Ltd, Hang Tang Security Co. Ltd, De Heng Security Co. Ltd, Heng Xin Security Co. Ltd, and Zhong Fu Security Co. Ltd.

Realizing that these serious problems with securities companies are a potential threat to financial safety, policymakers adopted the following measures.

1. Closing and liquidating some securities companies while encouraging restructuring and M&A between security sectors.
2. Under Securities Law 119, the CSRC regulates securities companies as two types: the pure broker and the integrated company.
3. On November 27, 2001, the CSRC issued a new rule permitting securities companies to make their capital ratio sufficient by increasing their capitalization.

---

[2]Figures from "Reform and Development of the Chinese Stock Market in a Transitional Period," p. 112.

[3]Figures from "Research on Advanced Issues of Chinese Securities Market Development (2003)," p. 300.

4. On June 3, 2002, the law establishing the Joint Venture Security Company was enacted. Its purpose was to reinforce the strength of domestic securities companies by introducing foreign players.

8.6.4 WOOING INSTITUTIONAL INVESTORS AND OPENING THE MARKET

Before 2000, China's stock market was dominated by individual investors, while institutional investor accounts made up only 0.4% of the open accounts in the two registered exchanges and held shares with 10.67% of total market value.[4] Thus, since the end of 1999, policymakers have promoted a series of plans named "Boosting Institutional Investors" in the hope of stimulating changes in market behavior.

- The most obvious changes have taken place among mutual funds. Since the Securities Law and Securities Investment Funds Law was enacted and came into force in July 1999 and October 2003, respectively, we have witnessed a rapid development in the mutual funds sector. By the end of 2004, a total of 54 closed- and 107 open-ended funds were run by more than 45 fund management ventures. There were RMB324.6 billion, equivalent to USD40 billion in assets managed by them.[5,6]
- On October 27, 1999, the Insurance Law approved the entry of insurance funds into the stock market in the form of asset management as a client of mutual funds. In addition, on December 20, 2001, the National Social Security Fund (ASSF) Law allowed pension funds to enter the domestic securities market directly. Also in January 2001, the Trust Law allowed trust companies to issue the trust funds to invest in the stock market.
- As Chinese policymakers realized the importance of opening the domestic market, several measures were being used to accelerate the opening process. One is that the qualified foreign institutional investor (QFII) was permitted to be involved in the domestic market since the law was enacted on November 8, 2002. Next, the CSRC encourages the establishment of joint-venture financial institutions, and on December 19, 2002, China Euro Securities Limited, the first joint-venture securities intermediary, was established. On December 27, 2002, the first joint-venture

---

[4] Figures from "Reform and Development of the Chinese Stock Market in a Transitional Period," p. 113.

[5] Refers to "Security Market Primary Knowledge," 2005, and "Security Investment Fund," 2005, Beijing.

[6] See also Chapter 13.

fund management company, China Merchants Fund Management Co. Ltd, was created. Lastly, the most important reform in opening the market is relaxing the purchase of nontradable shares by foreign investors. On November 1 and November 8, 2002 two rules related to opening nontradable shares to foreign investors were issued,[7] making it no longer impossible for foreign players to buy out domestic listed companies on the secondary market. Instead, they are allowed to control the listed companies by buying state-owned or legal person–owned shares at substantially lower prices than on the secondary market.

8.7   STATE-OWNED SHARE LIQUIDATION

Since the stock market was set up in China, the huge number of state-owned and legal person-owned shares has been the most difficult issue, with which most problems on the market are associated. Therefore policymakers, whether academic or not, are all focusing on it, because if the state-owned shares can be liquidated on the secondary market, not only is it beneficial for listed companies to clear the tangles in corporate governance, but the proceeds from selling the state-owned shares can be used to offset the huge nonperforming loans and keep the capital ratio sufficient in the banking sector. However, the key issue for liquidity is price. On June 14, 2001, policymakers decided to sell 10% of the held shares on the secondary market at the current price. Obviously the market participants could not accept this plan, contributing to a financial panic.

All investors, including individuals and institutions, objected to this plan, because when a firm is incorporated and issued an IPO, their state-owned shares are sold to the State-Owned Assets Supervision and Administration Commission at the face value of RMB1 yuan, which can be considered compensation to give up trading on the secondary market. Thus the market perceives this attempt to sell these state-owned shares at market price to be a violation of a previous promise.

On June 23, 2002, the CSRC announced the termination of this plan. The market has been in a dilemma: On the one hand, the nontradable shares are the root of bad corporate governance and contribute to most problems with the stock market, so the earlier this issue is solved, the better. On the other hand, the price at which these shares are sold to the secondary market is the

---

[7] "Notice on the Issue of Selling Listed Company State and Legal Person Shares to Foreign Investors," issued by the CSRC, Ministry of Finance and State Economic and Trade Commission, November 1, 2002. "Rule on the Restructuring of State-Owned Enterprises by Absorbing Foreign Investor," November 8, 2002.

biggest barrier to solving this issue, because the owner of these shares, the central government, is unwilling to give up the profits that they should not have earned.

8.7.1 State-Owned Share Reforms

After an enormous amount of work by both regulators and academics in mid-2005 the CSRC unveiled a series of state-owned share reform programs. On May 5, four pilot firms were selected to experiment with the liquidation of state-owned nontradable shares. In order to protect the interest holders of tradable shares, the program allows listed firms to proceed with the reform only if two-thirds of the holders of tradable shares agree on the reform proposal of the firm. All four firms chose to compensate such shareholders with bonus shares, and one of them offered cash compensation on top of bonus shares.

In order to ease market concern over possible share price declines due to market expansion, the holders of nontradable shares promised not to sell their shares in the secondary market for a certain period of time. The proposals of all four firms were approved after several rounds of negotiation between holders of tradable shares and holders of nontradable shares.

On June 21, 2005, the CSRC announced the selection of the second group of 42 firms. In order to further stabilize the market and bring greater benefits to holders of tradable shares, both the CSRC and firms promulgated several new measures. First, most firms in the second group provided holders of tradable shares with more bonus shares and cash compensation. Second, derivatives were used as a tool to offload state-owned shares. On August 22, 2005, China's first equity warrant in nearly a decade (Baoshan Iron and Steel, China's largest steelmaker) was launched on the Shanghai Stock Exchange.[8] The state-owned share reform is still moving ahead and is a crucial step for China's equity market.

Here is a chronology of state-owned share issues.[9]

November 1999:   Regulators approve the sale of a portion of state-owned shares by 10 firms.

December 1999:   Landmark sales of state shares in Guizhou Tyre and China Jialing Industry Motorcycle go badly. Prices are found too high. Investors fail to take up much of the stock on offer. Beijing suspends planned sales for the eight other firms.

---

[8] In fact, the warrant was already used in 1992. However, it was banned in 1996 by the CSRC due to excessive speculation.

[9] The data are from Reuters.

June 13, 2001:   The State Council (the cabinet) requires all state-owned firms planning IPOs as well as listed firms issuing more shares to raise the equivalent of 10% of the offering by selling state shares. The money must be given to the National Social Security Fund to help finance the public welfare system. This is the first full-scale attempt to solve the problem of state-owned shares. The aim is to allow all shares eventually to be traded on the market.

October 23, 2001:   Regulators suspend the reform as a result of a 30% slide in the benchmark index in just three months. Expectations that Beijing will eventually sell state shares haunt the market thereafter, pushing down share values whenever rumors emerge about the program.

April 29, 2005:   Beijing issues rules to revive the state-owned share reform. The approach is made more attractive to investors by requiring companies to win approval of two-thirds of public shareholders before floating state-owned shares. Also, a phased, three-year limit on the number of shares that can be sold to the market is established.

May 9, 2005:   Sany Heavy Industries Co. and Tsinghua Tongfang Co. start the reform on a trial basis.

May 10, 2005:   Four companies announce plans to give compensation, in cash and bonus shares, to public shareholders. The aim is to encourage a favorable vote by shareholders.

May 25, 2005:   China quietly suspends IPOs, to ease investor worries about the supply of new shares coming to the market.

June 1, 2005:   China's shares end at their lowest level since early 1997 on renewed worries concerning state-owned share sales.

June 20, 2005:   Regulators pick the steel mill Baoshan Iron and Steel and Three Gorges Dam operator Yangtze Electric Power to be among 43 firms subject to the reform.

August 24, 2005:   Regulators open the reform to all 1,400 listed firms.

September 12, 2005:   Forty firms, including Minsheng Banking Corp., announce they will voluntarily adopt the state-share reforms. The group of companies joining the reform scheme begins expanding quickly.

Some Recent Developments

New takeover times

China's equity markets are changing very fast. We conclude this chapter by discussing some of these changes.

On October 25, 2005, Carlyle Group, an American Private Equity Fund, announced a leveraged buyout of 85% of the claims Xu Gong Mechanism. The deal was worth by USD375 million. The target is a large state-owned company that is also the biggest shareholder of the listed company Xu Gong Tech (000425). Because this deal concerns a large state-owned company, with its listed company being acquired by an outside player in the form of an LBO, it is commonly seen as the first attempt of outside players getting into China.

Only one day later, China Oil (0857.HK), one of the largest listed Chinese companies in Hong Kong, suddenly announced a big deal in which it would buy back its three subsidiary companies for cash and privatize them. The three targets were Ji Ling Chem (000618, 00368.HK), Liao He Oil Field (000817), and Jing Zhou Oil-Chem (000763). The market consensus was that China Oil was seeking to gain from synergy and from overseas return-be listed onshore.

On October 27, 2005, China's highest legislative authority, the People's Representative Conference, approved the newly revised "Security Act" which was to come into effect on January 1, 2006. This act made several significant changes. Since then the market has entered a new phase.

Item 2 of the revised Security Act eliminated the former restriction on derivatives in the equity market, and many market professionals believe that new equity derivatives will be a bright spot in the future. The pioneers may be warrants, stock index futures, and equity-linked notes.

As we saw in Section I, China's financial industry is a segmented system, which means that the banking sector, the security sector, and the insurance sector are separate business operations that are regulated by different authorities. This system was introduced to China in 1998 to avoid the Asian financial contagion. Item 6 of the revised Security Act implies that commercial banks will be permitted to go into the equity market.

In addition, the China Construction Bank (CCB) had a successful IPOs on the Hong Kong market in the form of the circulation of all common shares. In the wake of this step, the Bank of China (BOC) and the Industry and Commercial Bank Corporation (ICBC) completed their own IPO.

Item 142 of the new services Security Act stipulates that a securities company can provide its clients with margin buying and short selling, as long as the company obtains approval from the CBRC.

Last, but not least, item 83 of the new Security Act revises the previous prescription and reopens the secondary market to state-owned enterprises.

8.8 CONCLUSIONS

Chinese stock markets had a rather volatile history. At the moment, the stock markets seem to be in a better state. Authorities have been introducing new incremental measures, which overall are quite positive. Moreover, it seemed that, in order to mature further, the Chinese equity markets had to wait for the privatization of the big four banks and further improvement in corporate governance. This is now happening.

REFERENCES

Stephen Green, "Enterprise Reform and Stock Market Development in Mainland China," Deutsche Bank Research for China Special, p. 8, March 25, 2004.

Ma Qing Quan, "China's Security Market History," 2003, CITIC Public House, Beijing.

Zhang Yu Jun, "Reform and Development of China's Stock Market in a Transitional Period," 2004, p. 112, Southwestern University of Finance and Economics Press, Chendu China.

Zhuang Xin Yi, "Research on the Advanced Issue of China Security Market Development (2003)," 2004, p. 300, China Financial Publishing House, Beijing.

Zhang Yu Jun, "Reform and Development of China's Stock Market in a Transitional Period," 2004, p. 113, Southwestern University of Finance and Economics Press, Chendu.

"Security Market Primary Knowledge," 2005, pp. 26–28; "Security Investment Funds," 2005, pp. 15–16; China Financial and Economic Publishing House, Beijing.

Li Z, J. "China Equity Market Development Report," 2003, China Financial and Economic Publishing House, Beijing.

PART IV

China's Futures and Derivatives Markets

Chinese policymakers have so far displayed a genuine interest in developing China's derivatives markets further. Still, China's derivatives markets by and large have inadequate liquidity. Where some liquidity exists, the number of instruments and the number of investors are limited.

The authorities understand very well that without proper FX and interest rate derivatives it would be inappropriate to let the renminbi float freely and at the same time to deregulate interest rates. This motivates further development of derivatives markets. Yet past scandals in this sector and the possibility of new speculative bubbles suggest caution, and restrictions on derivatives trading are being lifted slowly.

Still, the years 2005–2006 saw several important changes in the derivatives markets. Some of these developments follow.

- FX swaps are necessary instruments for a liquid FX forward market to exist. This is how market makers hedge their open positions. During 2006, serious efforts are being made to develop an FX swap market.[1]

[1] The appendix in Chapter 4 provides some information on this market.

- With the FX swap market, efforts to increase the liquidity in the FX forward market intensified.
- During 2005, China also reintroduced bond forwards. Although liquidity here is limited, this is certainly a step towards trading interest rate derivatives.
- Again during 2005, the first interest rate swaps were tested in pilot projects. Pursuing these steps further, during the year 2006 authorities started developing the foundations of the interest rate swap market by providing liquid reference rates.
- Options and warrant markets are being tested.
- Chinese authorities have also started pilot projects in asset securitization. Authorities are very well aware that asset securitization is essential in order to have an orderly mortgage sector.
- Last, but not least, the NPLs and other high-risk loan portfolios on bank balance sheets will in the future provide excellent opportunities for loan securitization. There are efforts to develop the collateralized debt obligation (CDO) sector as well.

This Part has two chapters that discuss the Chinese derivatives markets. Chapter 9 gives a straightforward discussion of the history of the relatively more liquid futures markets. Chapter 10 is a brief summary of the developments in asset securitization and the swap and option markets.

China's Futures Markets

Tan Wentao
Treasury Dealer, Malayan Banking Berhad Shanghai Branch

The years 2004–2006 were remarkable for commodity markets. Increasing demand for raw materials and energy, largely due to the dramatic growth in China's economy, pushed their prices in world financial markets to record highs. For example, the price of crude oil on NYMEX hit the 73 USD per barrel during 2006, and the price of copper on LME reached 8,000 USD per ton, the highest in 10 years.

Chinese policymakers and analysts are concerned that the country's development is overreliant on the supply of these crucial raw materials and energy. *Pricing decision center* is now a frequently mentioned term, which means China longs to have pricing power on these essential raw materials and energy on the world's futures market, instead of world prices dominating the domestic market. Hence people's interest in China's futures market has never been higher.

In this Chapter, we first give readers an overall understanding of the futures markets in three areas: regulation, marketplaces, and the main types of investors. The second section covers the history of the futures market, recalling some important events that took place in the market, in order to help understand these markets further. In the final section we focus on developments in the near future.

9.1 FUTURES EXCHANGES

This section covers market organization, the main investor types, and the regulatory structures in Chinese futures markets.[1]

---

[1] See also Chapter 1.

There are limited financial derivatives in China's futures market; until lately only commodity futures were involved. Although the Chinese government tried T-bond futures in the mid-1990s, that experiment quickly failed due to heavy speculation.

There are three national standardized futures exchanges—the Shanghai Futures Exchange (SHFE), the Da Lian Commodity Exchange (DCE), and the Zhengzhou Commodity Exchange (ZCE)—and one interbank OTC market, the Shanghai Foreign Exchange Center, which is a spot foreign exchange and bond market. The Shanghai Gold Exchange and Shanghai Diamond Exchange are two increasingly important national commodity markets, but only spot exchanges are permitted there. In addition, the Shanghai White Platinum and Silver Exchange, Guangxi Sugar Exchange Center, Hainan Rubber Exchange Center, and Jilin (Province Corn and Feusla Exchange Center) Exchange Center are OTC commodity wholesale markets, run with the same margin trading as at common futures exchanges. Because these exchange centers are invested in by State Economic and Trade Commission, and not regulated by the CSRC, their creditworthiness is lower than that of the national exchanges. We do not discuss these latter further in this Chapter. We focus on the three standardized futures markets.

9.1.1   EVOLUTION OF THE FUTURES EXCHANGES IN CHINA

China's futures exchanges, like China's futures industry as a whole, first experienced a rapid growth and very fast expansion and then shrank to today's relatively mature state.

Founded on October 12, 1990, the Zhengzhou Grain Wholesale Market, approved by the State Council, the former version of today's Zhengzhou Commodity Exchange (ZCE), is a milestone in China's futures industry. This wholesale market began with cash trading, gradually developed forward contracts, and finally was transformed into a standardized futures market—today's ZCE.

After the start of the Zhengzhou Grain Wholesale Market, China's futures industry experienced rapid expansion. The number of nationwide futures exchanges increased to more than 50, the majority of which run mostly non-transparent trading. Consequently, in 1994 the central government began to rectify the marketplace, causing a sharp decrease in the number of exchanges to 15. However, the process still did not seem well controlled. In 1998, due to the fear of east Asian crisis contagion, policymakers continued to shrink the market, and this time only three exchanges survived: the SHFE, DCE, and ZCE.

Common Characteristics

The three exchanges are homogeneous in terms of regulation, entity structure, trading, and clearing and settlement. As mentioned earlier, the three exchanges are authorized and regulated by the CSRC on the same legal basis, the "Futures Trading Management Statute," and the "Four Measures." The three exchanges run their business by quite similar sets of rules on day-to-day management. They are nonprofit self-regulated and independent, and have legal-person membership.

In every exchange, the Member Conference which comprises approximately 210 members, has only nominal power. Although the Exchange Council represents the Member Conference and is in charge of daily management, the directors of this council and all administration officials have to be appointed by the CSRC. Consequently, serious management conflicts have been common.

In addition, the three exchanges have similar trading systems and settlement and clearing. The centralized advanced computer system on the trading floor and popular remote trading terminals installed all over China facilitate the daily trading and display of information. This screen-based trading system means some orders are input by floor brokers through trading terminals located on the trading floor. However, the majority of orders are input by investors at home or at the office via Internet trading systems. The three exchanges each have their own department of settlement as a clearinghouse, while the "Big Four" state-owned commercial banks plus the Communication Bank act as custodians and settlement agents.

Competition Among the Three Exchanges

The main differences between the three exchanges come from their listed futures contract. The ZCE lists three types of futures contracts:

- Wheat, i.e., hard winter white wheat (WT) and strong gluten wheat (WS)
- Cotton, i.e., cotton no. 1 (CF)
- Green beans (mung beans)

The DCE has contracts for soybean, soy meal, and corn futures products. In the SHFE, four contracts are currently listed:

- Copper
- Aluminum
- Natural rubber
- Fuel oil

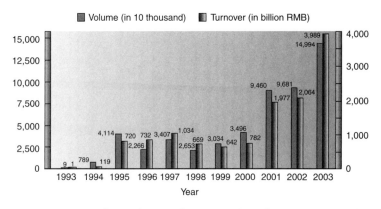

FIGURE 9.1   Trading Volume and Turnover Growth Since 1993 in DCE.

The plywood and long-grain rice contracts are being modified. Since no. 1 soybean futures[2] were launched on March 15, 2002, the DCE has gradually become the largest agricultural futures market in China and the largest marketplace for trading non–genetically modified organisms (non–GMO) soybean futures in the world.

On December 22, 2004, after the DCE started trading corn futures (on September 22, 2004), no. 2 soybean futures contracts were launched on the DCE, which involve all imported soybeans and China's homegrown soybeans. Figure 9.1[3] presents the trading volume and growth in turnover since 1993 in DCE.

The DCE and ZCE are striving to be the largest agricultural product markets in China, where agricultural product futures can be exchanged, while authorities aim at making Shanghai a financial center in Asia. The Shanghai Futures Exchange aims to establish a comprehensive futures market, including important raw materials (e.g., crude oil) futures, financial derivatives, and futures option. The exchange is also working on opening options on copper and stock index futures contracts. It looks like the SHFE will fulfill its target because, compared to its two peers, the SHFE is a more efficient and transparent market.

It is worth mentioning that among the three standardized futures exchanges, the ZCE has the somewhat lower credibility. Many scandals took place that made ZCE less transparent than the other exchanges. That is the main reason why trading is shrinking at ZCE.

---

[2]Only non-GMO soybeans are allowed to be delivered.

[3]*Source:* www.dce.com.cn.

9.2 MAIN PLAYERS

The market participants in China's futures are divided into two types: brokers and investors. *Brokers* refers to those domestic futures brokerage firms who buy seats and assign representatives to the trading floor. Up to today, all brokers have been domestic. According to the "Futures Trading Management Temporary Statute," however, these brokerage firms are only permitted to deal with futures trading for their clients in regular accounts, and they are strictly banned from conducting any proprietary trading or from trading for their clients in discretionary accounts. Additionally, brokering futures trading in the international futures markets is illegal for domestic brokers. The restriction is starting to be loosened.

Among investors, the main players in the marketplace consist of domestic and foreign investors.

9.2.1 BROKERS

The largest broker in China is the Beijing-based China International Futures Corporation (CIFCO), with a capitalization of 600 million RMB. This house controls seven subfutures companies based in Shanghai, Shenzhen, Henan, Wuhan, Shengyang, and Liaoning. Additionally, it is worth mentioning that the director of CIFCO during 2005–06, Tian yuan, is also the chairman of the China Futures Association and has a strong government background.

The second-largest broker, called (Minmetals Group), controls six futures brokerage companies, the largest one being Shenzheng Shida Futures, with a capitalization of 100 million RMB. They are specialized in metal futures trading. Table 9.1 shows the top 10 domestic brokers in terms of turnover volume.

Beginning January 14, 2003, the CSRC allowed noncredit financial institutions to merge with the futures brokerage firms in order to enhance their capitalization. As a result, there have been several mergers between securities firms and futures firms. In fact, these days behind some futures brokers we can find some securities firms, for example, Guang Dong Security Ltd. acquired Huan Qin Futures Co., Guang Fa Security Ltd. acquired Guang Fa Futures Co., Min An Security Ltd. acquired Min An Futures Co., Ping An Security Ltd. acquired Pin An Futures Co., Tai Yang Security Ltd. acquired Tai Yang Futures Co., etc. Securities companies have become important participants in the futures market.

Moreover, many listed companies are also interested in investing in futures brokerage firms. For example, in 2001 Heng Dian Group acquired Zhejiang Nanhua Futures Ltd. During the same year, Xia Men International Trade

TABLE 9.1   Top 10 Domestic Brokers as of 2004 (Futures, turnover volume by firms)
Source: *Futures Daily* newspaper and www.qhrb.com.cn.

No.	Name	Turnover (unit)	Turnover amount (RMB)
1	China International Futures Corporation (CIFCO)	13,903,797	567,434,488,445
2	Yong An Futures (YAFCO)	11,648,598	457,337,798,780
3	Shanghai-China International Futures (SHCIFCO)	9,588,060	382,155,146,535
4	Great Wall Futures (GWF)	4,465,186	321,323,205,980
5	New Central Futures (NCF)	5,322,101	307,171,835,820
6	Jing Yi Futures (JYFCO)	4,296,461	299,536,831,985
7	Jin Di Qi Huo (JDQH)	6,011,983	294,708,968,915
8	Jian Zheng Futures (JZF)	6,227,980	291,561,707,950
9	Zhong Da Futures (ZDF)	4,199,707	274,735,403,010
10	Guang Fa Futures (GFF)	5,857,669	260,701,594,795

Group increased its investment in International Trade Futures Co. and held an 80% stake in this futures company. However, because of the bursting of the speculative bubble in the stock market in 2001, most stakes in futures brokerage firms held by publicly traded companies have been transferred.

9.2.2   DOMESTIC INVESTORS

Owing to the restriction on futures trading, domestic investors consist presently of pure hedgers in state-owned firms, arbitragers, and speculators on privately owned firms and private accounts.

- State-owned companies are only permitted to hedge risk exposure to production, exports, or imports. The speculative trading is not allowed.
- All financial institutions are strictly prohibited from trading futures.
- All creditor institutions and nonbanking financial institutions are prohibited from lending funds to their customers to run a futures business.

The pure hedgers are those taking seats on the trading floor and those trading for themselves. Usually, they are large state-owned companies that deal in essential raw materials.[4] According to the laws on futures trading,

---

[4]For example, China Minmetal Group, China National Cereals, Oil and Food Stuffs Co., China Nonferrous Metals Group, China Ferrous Metals Group, China Chemical Industry Group, China Copper Industry Group, etc.

these state-owned firms are only allowed to hedge price risks in the domestic futures markets in relevant businesses, not to speculate, although often the difference between speculation and hedging is not very clear.

As for domestic arbitragers and speculators, they have a common characteristic. Individual investors with privately owned capital represent a small proportion of the market. In general, they have no power to influence the market; instead, they just provide good liquidity to the marketplace. Who are then the players that *can* influence the market?

9.2.3 FOREIGN INVESTORS

In November 2004, vice director of the Shanghai Futures Exchange stated at an international financial forum that more than 30% of the total capital in SHFE copper futures contracts belong to international funds. This proportion may be higher.

Who, then, is influential in China's futures market? "Foreign" investors from international capital markets are becoming increasingly more powerful at influencing market prices. Thus we need to discuss how they enter into trades and how much they invest in China's futures markets.

We see three ways to transfer funds in China. First, the "hot money" can proxy as international trade funds. These are freely exchangeable between China and the outside world. Second, a foreign investor can cooperate with a domestic partner by swapping funds in both domestic and offshore markets simultaneously. This mimics a euro-currency market and euro-currency deposits. Last but not least way is the "gray market." There is a sizable number of exchanges between RMB and other foreign currencies in the black market, which takes place near the border between Guangdong and Hong Kong. In today's China, due to the ever greater openness to the outside world, it is not very difficult for hot money to enter.

According to market statistics, the total capital of the futures marketplace is around RMB20 billion. If we estimate the number of foreign players as 30% of the total, then the investment of international hot money and funds may reach 6 billion RMB or more.

Compared to domestic investors, foreign investors have certain obvious strengths. Because of the greater access to more information, as well as higher operation skills, they may be able to influence market prices.

9.3 REGULATION

Futures market regulation falls to (1) the China Securities Regulatory Commission (CSRC), which exerts the power of government over the market;

(2) the China Futures Association, which takes the role of self-regulation, being responsible for the cooperation and coordination between all players and brokers; and (3) the three national futures exchanges, which supervise the daily trading, settlement, and clearing.

9.3.1 CHINA SECURITIES REGULATORY COMMISSION

At the highest level of regulation, the futures department of the CSRC is in charge of regulating the entire marketplace. Still, the daily responsibilities of supervising operations in the market belong to the suborganizations assigned by the futures department of the CSRC to local entities.[5]

9.3.2 CHINA FUTURES ASSOCIATION

Founded on December 29, 2000, and as a self-regulatory organization, the China Futures Association and many local subassociations had 188 members as of September 2003, the majority of them futures brokers nationwide. Its objectives are as follows.

- Implement rules and laws enacted by regulatory authorities over the industry.
- Bridge government objectives with those of the futures industry.
- Carry out self-regulation within the industry.
- Protect the interests and legitimate rights of its members; safeguard a fair and transparent market.
- Encourage professional training and ethical compliance.

Because the association is governed by the CSRC and its main leaders have a good relationship with the CSRC, when there are conflicts between market players and the government, it is often in agreement with the CSRC.

9.3.3 FUTURES EXCHANGES

The three national futures exchanges—Shanghai Futures Exchange, Da Lian Commodity Exchange, and Zhengzhou Commodity Exchange—carry out the daily management of and regulation over the trading and clearing

---

[5] CSRC is dealt with in Chapter 1 and Chapter 7.

and settlement. They also supervise employees in the exchanges. The highest level in the exchanges is the Member Conference, which consists of members of the exchanges, 90% of them futures brokers in China. On behalf of the Member Commission, the Council is in charge of daily management in order to maintain the markets. Although the Exchange Council is responsible for the Member Conference, the director of this council and all administration officials are nominated by the CSRC.

Because the structure of regulation in China's futures market clearly reveals the characteristics of its government background, it is not surprising that the market is under the strong control of the central government and the CSRC.

9.3.4 THE STRUCTURE OF LAWS AND RULES

There are three levels of regulations. First, as of 2005 there was no "Futures Act" issued by legislative authority. Instead, the "Futures Trading Management Temporary Statute," which was enacted by China's State Council on June 2, 1999, and which came into effect on September 1 of that year, has always been viewed as the basic law on regulation of the futures industry.

Additionally, at the middle level, four rules issued by the CSRC—"Futures Exchanges Management Measurer," "Futures Brokers Management Measure," "Senior Manager Management Measure," and "Professionals Management Measure," often called the "Four Measures,"—have been used by the CSRC to carry out its regulatory functions in the markets.

At the lowest level, since May 2000 three futures exchanges approved their sets of rules governing futures trading, settlement, and clearing. In this way a thorough framework for maintaining market operations was formed.

9.4 HISTORICAL REVIEW

9.4.1 FIRST STAGE: 1990–1994

The birth of the futures markets in China derived from the need for reforming the grain sector. Since China had begun market-oriented reforms in 1979, as an agricultural country with a population of 1.2 billion, the issue of grain has troubled policymakers. Especially after the country eliminated the protection on grain sales in 1985, the confusing situation in the production and sales of grain forced policymakers to devise an alternative in order to maintain a stable grain output. In March 1988, the Premier of China proposed in the annual government reports the idea of opening a futures market in China. In the wake of his proposal, an academic institution called the "futures market research group" was established by the State Development and Research Center, responsible for researching the possibility of futures in China and drawing up feasible plans.

Because Henan Province is the second largest agricultural province in China, the test bed of the futures market in China was chosen to be at Zhengzhou, the capital city of Henan and also the center of national railways. With the help of CBOT, in October 1989 the "futures market research group" submitted its formal report on testing the futures market at Zhengzhou. On October 12, 1990, the Zhengzhou Grain Wholesale Market to the State Council reopened, and was regarded as a milestone for the futures market in China.

Like the Zhenzhou Grain Wholesale Market, virtually all of the futures exchanges in China started from standard forward contracts. They usually were similar to their Western peers, for example, using membership in futures exchange, a margin settlement system, a centralized trading floor and time, as well as a computerized price-driven trading system.

Compared to previous spot or forward transactions in grain sales, the futures market had several strengths. First, transaction costs were reduced, because the margin settlement dramatically decreased funds pooling in the spot market. Thus many traders came to rely heavily on the futures market. Second, standardized contracts and settlement guarantees from futures exchanges provide advantages to both counterparties. Third, market-driven prices are relatively fair and transparent, effectively resulting from demand and supply. Also, futures exchanges can bring many benefits to the local economy where they are located.

- Commissions and fees created good profits and taxable income for local governments.
- Capital inflows to local banks provided them with high liquidity, which is advantageous for local development.
- Active trading volumes accelerated a prosperous economy, particularly in terms of encouraging spending on business travel, hotels, entertainment, storage, communication, and transportation.

Because of these advantages, the futures market in China initially experienced a very fast expansion from its beginnings in 1990 to the end of 1993. The statistics indicate that by the end of 1993, the number of futures exchanges expanded to 40 across the country within only three years. Fifty different types of commodities could be publicly exchanged and traded through standardized futures contracts, including corn, wheat, rice, crude oil, green beans, copper, aluminum, and steel wire. Meanwhile, the number of futures brokerage firms sharply increased to 500, where 135,500 professionals worked. By that time 27,000 financial institutions and state-owned companies were involved in the marketplace.[6]

---

[6]Data is from "Futures Daily" (September 26, 2004).

Nevertheless, as a result of this fast growth of the futures market, serious problems developed. In particular, a lack of understanding the necessity of regulation led to a rather risky marketplace. Therefore in November 1993, the State Council issued a notice called "Stop blind development of the futures market." This can be thought of as the beginning of the first rectification in China's futures market and, being consistent with the contraction in the economy,[7] was implemented by the new administration of Premier Zhu Rongji. First of all, the Chinese government closed several marginal futures exchanges. By the end of 1994, only 14 exchanges remained. The second measure was to stop futures trading in some contracts for raw materials and grain products. For example, sugar, rice, crude oil, corn, wheat, and food oil contracts were regarded by the high-level government as the main reasons for the accelerating inflation. Additionally, the regulatory authorities banned all brokers from dealing in futures business in international markets. The brokers involved either went into liquidation or transferred to domestic markets.

9.4.2 SECOND STAGE: 1995–1998

From 1995 to 1998, China's futures industry witnessed excessive speculation. Large securities companies, publicly traded firms, as well as the big state-owned enterprises took part, using borrowed funds from state-owned commercial banks or trust companies. We focus on this time period by recalling some important events that took place, not only because this period is crucial for China's futures markets, but also because this is useful to understand the relationship between China's regulatory authority and market speculators as well as the course of market evolution. First, let us examine why this period might have occurred.

After the regulatory rectification of futures took place and many exchanges were closed, the huge funds coming off those closed exchanges were looking for new investment alternatives. Meanwhile, China's equity market was experiencing a long-run bear market and the new Chinese government, the administration of Premier Zhu Rongji, was tightening fiscal policy due to inflationary pressures. Under these conditions, funds coming from both the equity markets and the closed exchanges rushed into the 14 remaining futures exchanges. In addition, these exchanges were facing a dilemma. On the one hand, due to competition with their peers, these exchanges had to maintain an active trading volume, so they needed to attract these new investors. On the other hand, the high level of regulation implied reducing clearing risks. With the trading volume and outstanding contracts becoming larger and larger,

---

[7] At that time, new macroeconomic policies aimed at reducing the serious inflation of nearly 20%.

the exchanges faced a big clearing risk, which they did not like. Therefore, clever futures exchanges discovered a good way out, that is (illegally) cooperating with large speculators to control clearing risks while keeping the daily trading active, which encouraged speculators further. Finally, many large participants in the market were big state-owned enterprises, which borrowed money from state-owned commercial banks. They thought that if they were winners in these "gambles," the result was best; otherwise, the result was still acceptable, because the lost money was not their own. Also, large players usually had more power to influence the prices and the short-term trends.

During this period there were three major markets. The first was the Shanghai and Suzhou Commodity Exchanges, where the preferred contracts were steel wire, red beans, and three-ply. The second was the Hainan Commodity Exchange, where coffee and rubber contracts were traded. And the last was the Beijing and Zhengzhou Commodity Exchanges, trading green bean contracts. But as a financial center, Shanghai with Suzhou were the leading important markets.

We now look at some cases that illustrate this period of extreme speculation. These cases also illustrate some of the characteristics of Chinese financial markets that are worth remembering.

9.4.3   TREASURY BOND FUTURES AND THE "327 EVENT"

As a rare example of *financial* derivatives in China's futures markets, the Treasury bond futures were traded during a short period between the end of 1992 and early 1995. The contract was stopped in 1995 due to the so-called "327 event."[8] The Chinese government tried to test the introduction of *financial* derivatives only during 2006.

On December 28, 1992, the Shanghai Stock Exchange introduced T-bond futures. Initially, this contract did not attract much investor interest. After 1994, with the closing of many futures exchanges and with equities sliding into a bear market, a huge amount of funds had to look for alternatives. Investors suddenly noticed the T-bond futures and their advantages in trading and settlement. The maintenance margin of only 1% and no daily price limits provided investors with more leverage for potential profits or losses.

After February 1995, many large financial institutions and speculators started entering, in large positions, using the 327 T-bond futures contracts. The so-called "327" had, as underlying, a Treasury bond issued in 1992 with a coupon rate of 9.5% p.a. with maturity in June 1995 at a face value of 100.

---

[8]327 was the code for the underlying futures contract.

However, in addition, the bond had a less well-known characteristic. It had a floating compensation depending on the realized inflation rate. As a company closely tied to the Chinese Treasury Department, one of the major players, the investment bank China Economic Development Trust and Investment Co. Ltd (CEDTI) was in a position to learn of important data (the inflation rate) prior to other market participants.

Events developed as follows. On that date, CEDTI learned that the relevant inflation figure was much higher than market expectations. So the bank pushed the futures price up to 152, forcing the shorts to pay large variation margins. In order to recover their (huge) losses, some short-side players took advantage of a weakness in the trading rules. On February 23, 1995, at 4:22 p.m., just eight minutes before the closing, the short side suddenly opened huge positions, amounting to several 10 million units contracts.[9] This pulled the price down by 3.8 to 148, within only half a minute, severely affecting the long investors' margin accounts. The day is known as the "327 T-bond scandal" in Chinese financial markets. After that event, financial derivatives were closed in China. Many Chinese government officials are still apprehensive of such an event.

9.4.4 THREE-PLY FUTURES CONTRACT AND THE "9407" EVENT

The "9407" refers to the code of one three-ply futures contract trading on the Shanghai Commodity Exchange. It represents the expiration date July 1994. With that contract, Chinese speculators for the first time realized and experienced the notion of *short squeeze*. From then on, short squeezes have become the most popular trading strategy in the marketplace. A pioneer perhaps was Shao Qiao, the most famous speculator in China between the years 1994 and 1999.

At that time, the spot price of three-ply was 40 yuan, while in the futures market the price of the 9407 contract was pushed by Shao to 50 yuan, with an outstanding position of 200,000 units. This is 10 times the physically deliverable warehouse stock of 20,000. The short side had to face the short squeeze because there was not enough underlying to deliver. However, fearing the short side's default possibility, the exchange began to interfere in the market by using some administrative measures. In the end, Vice Premier Zhou Jiahua and the Shanghai government ordered both counterparties to privately close their outstanding positions at the price of 47 yuan directly through Future Exchange Computer under the monitoring of the exchange.

---

[9]The opening margin was overdraft from the stock exchange.

Although his first experiment in squeezing the market failed, Shao had a clear view of the potential of short squeezes. According to Shao, at that time China's futures markets were isolated from the outside world and the spot market was immature. The transportation and storage sectors were weak. This increased the probability of making an abnormal return from short squeezes, because the speculators' money can be gathered more quickly and easily than the deliverable warehouse receipts. Many Chinese investors and their practices have been influenced by Shao's views.

9.4.5 STEEL WIRE FUTURES CONTRACT 9405

9504 was the code for steel wire futures contract trading at Suzhou Commodity Exchange, with April 1995 expiration. This was a very important event because it was the first time that a short squeeze had succeeded. Also, after that event, a large investment collaboration was formed in China. The coalition consisted of three big players: Shao, a representative of the Shanghai Wuzi Group; Chen Zhengzheng, a representative of the Zhejiang branch of the Industrial and Commercial Bank of China; and Shi Deyi, the biggest individual player in China at that time. Around this core were several other big individual speculators and large securities companies.[10] On the 9504 contract, Shao and his investment group put together around RMB3.5 billion in funds. On the last trading day they pushed the futures price to 3650 yuan per ton, the highest level of that year, and purchased a large amount of physical underlying totaling 498 thousand tons, equal to the warehouse capacity of the entire country. Consequently, the shorts suffered significantly from the squeeze.

9.4.6 SPECULATION ON THE THREE-PLY CONTRACT IN 1995

After the success of the speculation on the 9504 steel wire contract, during the autumn of 1995 Shao's investment coalition, faced the CEDTI investment coalition, the big winner in the 327 T-bond futures scandal, on three-ply futures that was listed on both the Shanghai Commodity Exchange and the Suzhou Commodity Exchange. Shao's coalition, jointly with Jun An Security Ltd. and South Security Ltd., two famous investment banks, again wanted to squeeze their opponents, this time the CEDTI investment coalition. Both parties gathered huge sums of around RMB10 billion and faced each other on three contracts, 9507, 9509, and 9511.

[10]For example, Jun An Security Ltd., Southern Security Ltd.

First, Shao's investment undertook nearly 120,000 boxes of warehouse receipts of three-ply on 9507 contracts from both exchanges, without any profit, and then they attempted to squeeze the short side on the 9509 and 9511 contracts. The futures price moved to 55 yuan, while the price of three-ply in the spot market was only 42 yuan. Thus a great deal of three-ply continued to be transferred into warehouses as preparation for physical delivery. The worry about increasing warehouse stocks and pressures from government led to a breakup of the collusion within Shao's investment coalition. One of the main participants in the coalition—Jun An Security Ltd.—privately closed their long positions, pushing the futures price down to 48. As a result, Shao's coalition failed in their attempt. Afterward, both securities companies, Jun An and Southern, were punished by the CSRC.

The 9511 contract created several record highs in China's futures history: the biggest daily turnover volume with 2.14 million units; the biggest outstanding position, 1.437 million units; 12 billion settlement funds with a total of 40 million turnovers on one contract.[11]

9.4.7   SUZHOU RED BEAN FUTURES: 1996

In June 1995, red bean futures contracts were introduced in the Suzhou Commodity Exchange. The contract quickly attracted the interest of investors and speculators because the relatively small production provided the long side with the excuse for a short squeeze. This great opportunity was noticed by Shao's investments coalition. Starting in October 1995 they took several long positions on 9602, 9604, and 9606 contracts at a price of 3380 yuan per ton. Taking advantage of the fact that there were limited stocks of 5200 tons in warehouses, the long side sharply increased the futures price of red bean from 3,690 yuan to 5,325 yuan per ton between December 1995 and January 8, 1996. However, the shorts blamed the long side and the exchange, accusing them of cooperating with each other and manipulating the market. On January 8, 1996, the CSRC issued a document stating that new contracts following 9606 were to be stopped and all existing outstanding contracts needed to be closed.

This administrative interference in the marketplace caused some confusion. Due to related clearing and default risks during the next few days, the price consecutively hit the daily lower limits without any turnover, and consequently about 70 settlement accounts of brokerage firms went bankrupt. But the CSRC also realized the poor results of this decision and started cooperating with the counterparties and the exchange.

---

[11] Data is from "Futures Daily" September 26, 2004.

9.4.8   HAINAN COMMODITY EXCHANGE SPECULATION

Coming off the Shanghai and Suzhou Exchanges, toward the end of the year 1996 Shao's investment coalition turned its attention to the Hainan province where Hainan Commodity Exchange has the most popular future products—*coffee and natural rubber futures.* This time they met with a tough local adversary, Zhang Shuxing, director of Hainan Zhongshang Touristry Co. Ltd., who was also the brother of the director of the Hainan Commodity Exchange.

On the F703 coffee contract both sides accumulated a great deal of out-standing positions at the price of 19,000 yuan per ton. The long side was Shao's Group. On the other side were Hainan local forces, including Hainan Zhongshang Luye Ltd. and some individual speculators from Beijing as well as, of course, the exchange. On January 24, 1997, both sides accumulated an outstanding position in an F703 contract amounting to 700,000 units, and the futures price went up to 2,300, the daily price limit. Suddenly, Hainan Commodity Exchange closed the dealing, announcing the maintenance margin was increased to 100% and all outstanding position would be closed by the exchange up to but no more than 20,000 tons, with the settlement price of 2115. Next day, Shao and his friends went to Beijing, suing the Hainan Commodity Exchange for illegal interference in the market and collusion with the short side. Under pressure from the CSRC on the exchange, Shao's coali-tion and Zhang Shuping, director of the exchange, came to a private agreement. The exchange compensated Shao with 10,000 tons of warehouse receipts for coffee and connived at monopoly with Shao's investment group on coffee con-tracts F705 and F707. Taking advantage of the physical delivery rule, which says that only 10,000 tons of coffee already transferred to warehouse receipts can be used to deliver, Shao's group, occupying the delivery position and in cooperation with the exchange, began to long the futures. They squeezed the investors in short positions without physical delivery or delivery position at the extremely high level of 34,000 yuan per ton on the last trading day in the F705 contract.

After the expiration of the F705 coffee contract, the price of natural rubber on the Tokyo Exchange dramatically dropped; the futures price of natural rubber in the R706 contract on the Hainan Commodity Exchange also was affected by Tokyo and went down sharply to 9,700 yuan per ton. Because of the different expectations in terms of future price and supply of natu-ral rubber, speculators started another fight on the R708 rubber contract around the price of 11,000 yuan per ton. Shao's coalition, with long posi-tions, again met the Hainan local force, i.e., Hainan Farms Bureau, and Beijing funds, i.e., China Chemical Industry Group. The latter gathered 100,000 tons of warehouse receipts for natural rubber and bet that Shao's group would not be able to afford so much rubber. Resorting to huge funds,

Shao's coalition led the futures price up from RMB10,750 on July 8, to 12,600 by the end of July 1997, compelling the short side to pay out huge variation margins. Nevertheless, under heavy pressure from the Hainan local force and the CSRC, the new director of the exchange decided to intervene in the marketplace with administrative measures. The exchange banned investors from opening new long positions. But new short positions were allowed. This decision, backed by the CSRC, entirely hurt Shao's coalition. The futures price on the R708 contract slumped to 11,160, and they suffered huge losses of approximately RMB500 million, which caused a default in delivery. As a result, investors with short positions also lost money because their warehouse receipts could not be delivered due to the clearing default of exchange.

The R708 event played an extremely notorious role in China's futures history. Following these events, China's regulatory authorities, including the CSRC, began to rectify the futures market practices. As a result, the market started shrinking, and this lasted more than four years. The consensus is that the R708 was a turning point for China's futures industry, which represented the end of high speculation. Also, after R708, the largest and the most famous investment coalition—Shao's investment group—was broken.

There are at least two obvious results from this time period. First, very little privately owned capital beat the state-owned firms and made abnormal profits. One example is Shi Deyi, one of the biggest players of Shao's coalition. Within three years he earned approximately RMB1 billion. Second, many state-owned firms and financial institutions were involved in the marketplaces. Usually, they borrowed funds from commercial banks to speculate in futures. Large nonperforming loans resulted.

9.5 THIRD STAGE: 1998–2001

On August 1, 1998, new rules were implemented following the Asian crisis. First, the majority of futures exchanges were closed, and only three survived: SHFE, DCE, and ZDE. On these exchanges, the previous 35 futures contracts were reduced to only six: soybeans, green beans, copper, aluminum, natural rubber, and wheat. Second, the CSRC increased the requirement for the capitalization of futures brokerage firm, from 10 million to 30 million RMB. As a result, many brokers closed their businesses, and only 190 brokerage firms remained. This was a drop of 60%. Finally, the CSRC established a unified regulatory framework. The regulatory authority issued a series of laws and rules, called the "Futures Trading Management Temporary Statute" and the "Four Management Measures."

TABLE 9.2   The Changes in Turnover Volume between 1993 and 2004 in China's Futures Market (trillion RMB)

1993	1994	1995	1996	1997	1998	1999	2000	2001	2002	2003	2004
0.552	3.16	10.06	8.41	6.12	3.69	2.23	1.61	3.01	3.949	10.84	14.69

Source: China Futures Association.

These rigorous measures contributed to a large contraction in the futures market. Many investors pulled out of futures and went into either the stock market or the real estate sector. As Table 9.2 shows, turnover volume shrank from 1998 to 2001.

9.6   FOURTH STAGE: 2002–PRESENT

Starting in 2002, China's futures market began a slow recovery, and today this process of recovery is still continuing. There have been important changes. A "Nine notices on development in capital markets," issued in February 2004 by the Congress, outlined the government's commitment to capital market development. It said that China should gradually develop futures markets with more new products. Additionally, as we can see from Figure 9.2, in 2002 the market turnover bottomed out, and then started rising by 30.9% to RMB3.948 trillion, compared to the previous year's figure. During the same year the number of market participants reached 100,000, while the turnover dramatically increased. The market environment continued to get better during 2004,

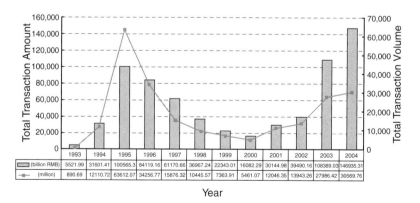

FIGURE 9.2   National Future Market Transaction Statistics (1993–2004)

when the market turnover volume reached the record high of RMB14 trillion. Some of the new products are as follows.

- Cotton futures started at the ZCE on June 1, 2004.
- Fuel oil futures started on August 25, 2004, at the SHFE.
- Corn futures were listed at the DCE on September 22, 2004.
- The sell and buy-back repo market started at the beginning of 2004.

Regarding the government's attitude, two authoritative documents are worth mentioning. The first is "Nine Notices on Development in Capital Market," issued in February 2004 by the State Council. This document said that China should gradually develop its futures market with more products. Additionally, a fundamental document, "Proposal on Drawing up the 11th five-Year Program of National Economic and Social Development" approved by Community Party in October 2005 requires that China "positively promote a stock market and a bond market and steadily develop money market, and a futures market.[12]

9.7   SOME EXISTING PROBLEMS

Although China's futures industry is in the process of its second rapid development, some problems persist. The assistant senior director of the SHFE Trading Department, Zhang Ming, said that the main differences between China and her Western peers are still in regulation and in the products, rather than in trading. The former leader of China's futures market, Shao Qiao, suggested that the lack of sophisticated participants is a major weakness hindering the development of China's futures industry.

9.7.1   WEAKNESSES IN REGULATION

The current regulatory framework was established with the purpose of regulating highly speculative investor activity. These regulatory rules and laws are unsuitable in the present market environment. Several weaknesses can be observed.

Conflicts Between Futures Exchanges and Their Members

Futures exchanges are normally nonprofit self-regulated organizations, and they are independent entities. However, this is not always the case in reality.

---

[12]"China Securities Journal" October 19, 2005.

There is an obvious contradiction in management structure. The Members Council, comprising all members, should normally be the highest power in futures exchanges. As the representative of the Members Council, the Exchange Council is responsible for daily management to serve the Member Conference. However, all directors of the Exchange Council are appointed by the CSRC, not by Member Council.

The problem is who the Exchange Council should report to, the Member Conference or the CSRC. It is not difficult to find evidence that the Exchange Council often favors the CSRC. As the director of the Shanghai subbranch of Shen Yang-China International Futures Co. Ltd., Zhuang Yanwei, indicates, the right of members have not been ensured by the Exchange Council. For example, Yanwei said that in daily operations, exchanges charge too much in fees but take minimal clearing risk, compared to the members (brokers). On the copper contract on the SHFE, the exchange charges participants 0.02% of trading volume as management fee; however, the brokers are able to charge only an additional 0.005% of trading volume to their clients. This is equal to one-fourth of the exchange's earnings. But at the same time, brokers bear the majority of the clearing risk because the exchanges just settle and clear the trading directly with brokers at the brokers' settlement account at the settlement bank, but not directly with every investor. This means that the exchanges transfer the majority of default risks to brokers.

Futures Brokers in Difficulty

In spite of the increasing improvement in the market environment, virtually all futures brokers are still under pressure in terms of their earnings. According to the *Futures Daily* newspaper,[13] during the fiscal year 2004, the average net profit of futures brokerage firms was 600,000 RMB. This is low. Under rigorous regulation, the brokers can only conduct low-profit pure-brokerage business. Consequently, this sector is not attractive to advanced and knowledgeable professionals. Moreover, due to a lack of other services providers, such as consultancy, assets management, and margin trading, the domestic brokers are in a weak position compared to their foreign peers.

Composition of Participants

Because of the strict restrictions imposed on market participants by futures laws, financial institutions such as securities companies, trust companies, and funds management companies are banned from dealing with futures. Even state-owned enterprises are only able to hedge using contracts relevant to

[13]February 1, 2005.

their spot business. So there is an unreasonable composition of participants in China's futures market. Domestic individual players account for nearly 80% of total market participants; the others are hedgers (state-owned enterprises) and professional foreign investors. Because no domestic institutional investors take part in the futures industry, the market price may end up being influenced mainly by foreign investors. Shao, for example, believes that foreign players already predominate in the market. Resorting to their advantages in funding, information, operational skills, large foreign players and their domestic representatives have in fact established the price synchronization between China's market and COMEX and LME. Shao indicates that no domestic player has enough capital to simultaneously control 180,000 tons of warehouse receipts for natural rubber in the SHFE and 500,000 tons of soybeans in the DCE, except for international funds. One result is that China is losing the pricing power on essential materials. For example, copper prices at London Metals Exchange (LME) continue to break records, and on November 12, 2005 hit USD4,135 per ton in the wake of the announcement that China State Reserve Bureau (SRB) suddenly dumped 40,000 ton copper in SHFE only within a half session of trading hours.

9.7.2   LIMITED NUMBER OF PRODUCTS

Only a few types of futures instruments can be publicly traded on the three national standardized futures exchanges. Among these, currently copper, aluminum, soybean, and sometimes natural rubber futures contracts have active turnover volumes that provide hedgers and speculators with enough liquidity. On the other hand, there are no energy futures, i.e., crude oil, and no financial derivatives.

As mentioned earlier, during 1998 Chinese policymakers decided to stop trading the majority of futures contracts, and only six types of futures product remained. From then on, Chinese policymakers have been extremely cautious toward trials of new products, particularly in the area of financial derivatives. This can be attributed to the apprehension at the highest levels of the Chinese government concerning the futures sector.

9.7.3   SOPHISTICATION OF PROFESSIONALS

Continuing shrinkage in the futures industry for several years has resulted in a severe brain drain. This sector now lacks sophisticated talent. As a result, domestic enterprises and individual investors are not fully capable of confronting international hedge funds in both domestic and overseas markets. Zhuzhou Smelting and China Aviation Oil are two vivid examples.

In 1998, Zhuzhou Smelting was short-squeezed by hedge funds on zinc contracts in LME, losing RMB1.46 billion (USD176 million). In 2004, China Aviation Oil (CAO) suffered losses of USD550 million due to speculation in crude oil option trading. These two events reveal that Chinese enterprises have not put in place up-to-date internal control systems and sufficiently well-trained risk managers.

9.8   FUTURE DEVELOPMENTS

Possible changes in China's futures sector may be driven by two motivators. One is that the competition in the pricing power for commodities is crucial to China's economy. With China's economy relying more and more on the supply of energy and important raw materials, both academics and practitioners have already realized the importance of pricing power. For example, Chang Qing, vice chairman of the China Futures Association, is quite enthusiastic in promoting increased pricing power.

Another motivator may arise from the need for financial derivatives, which started in 2006. If China wants its stock market to be attractive to additional institutional players, stock index futures and options need to be introduced. Likewise, if China wants to transform its banking sector, the interest rate and FX derivatives need to be introduced. Institutions need financial derivatives to hedge the interest rate risk and the currency risk.

In fact, Dow-Jones China Stock Index Futures has already been trading on the NYSE, and Singapore is following, which is somewhat embarrassing for the Chinese, since currently no futures contract underlying China's stock index can be traded in China's markets.

The first step in a market transaction should be the improvement on the regulation in the following twofold cases. First, futures exchanges have to be transformed from bureau-operated institutions to membership and market-oriented institutions. Second, regulatory requirement on market participants, open to outsiders, products innovations etc, have to be released.

9.8.1   IMPROVING THE COMPOSITION OF MARKET PARTICIPANTS

Some of the present regulatory restrictions are not consistent with today's market environment. Shao Qiao indicates that the restrictions on market participants need to be relaxed so that new domestic financial institutions are allowed to deal with futures, including state-owned enterprises, securities companies, investment funds, and trust funds. If such new participants are involved in the marketplace, prices may better reflect the true relationship between demand and supply. Also, if China wants to acquire some pricing power on important commodities, policymakers have to encourage and foster domestic institutional investors in the futures market. One example is to set up mutual funds investing in the futures market.

In addition, state-owned enterprises are required to improve their risk management to meet the needs for hedging price risk in the financial markets. The CAO scandal revealed that state-owned enterprises have yet to set up an effective internal control system and implement it effectively.

Today there is a trend where securities companies merge with futures brokers. This trend may continue.

9.8.2 NEW PRODUCTS

Issued on February 2004, the State Council's "Nine notices on development in capital markets" is generally viewed as a government commitment to capital market development. The notices mention research and development concerning new products relating to debt markets, equity markets, and futures markets. In the wake of this, a new mutual fund product, ETFs, were approved to trade in Shanghai Stock Exchange.

During 2004, we also witnessed a good beginning of three commodities products in the futures markets. This is the first listing of new futures products since 1997. Today there are approximately 348 items listed on the U.S. futures markets, while only 10 commodities can be traded on the Chinese markets. Moreover, financial derivatives (i.e., options and index futures) popular in the outside world still don't exist in China. These may be the next hot field of growth.

Presently, all three futures exchanges are working on commodity futures options and making their best effort to promote market acceptance. For example, the SHFE is focusing on options underlying the copper futures contract, whereas the DCE has completed the design of option contracts underlying soybean futures. The market enthusiasm on products innovation is met by the government. Currently the biggest barriers arising from legal issues have been overcome. On October 27, 2005, the revised Security Law item 2 approved by the People's Representative Conference, has relaxed many restrictions on derivatives.

According to new Security Law, Chinese policymakers seek to improve the equities market and develop a debt market. Regarding the equities market, stock index futures may be the next experiment, because with more and more financial institutional investors involved in the equities market, additional instruments are needed to hedge systematic risks. As we have seen, all mutual funds have suffered big losses during the macroeconomic cooling attempts in 2004. This was partly due to the lack of index futures and a short-selling mechanism. A market without a short-selling mechanism is risky for institutional investors.

Chinese policymakers try to develop the money market and the bond market as a supplement to equities markets. As vice governor of China's central bank, Wu Xiaoling, said on July 15, 2004, some new financial products, e.g., mortgage-backed securities (MBS), are in the process of being approved. Therefore, based on the need for hedging the interest rate risk and currency risk, fixed-income derivatives will be a promising field in the future.

9.8.3   UNIFORM SETTLEMENT AND CLEARING HOUSE

Today every futures exchange sets up a settlement department to be in charge of settlement and clearing. Similar to the equities markets, which have established a uniform clearinghouse, futures markets can also implement, in the near future, a model such as the "vertical silo" model of the German stock exchange (Deutsche Borse).

9.8.4   FUTURES INDUSTRY OPENS TO THE OUTSIDE WORLD

Earlier in the 1990s, China's futures industry was highly connected to the outside world. However, due to many scandals, the majority of which had arisen from offshore brokerage business, on March 31, 1994, Chinese regulators forced domestic brokers to terminate their offshore business. Furthermore, on June 2, 1999, the "Futures Trading Management Temporary Statute" strictly banned offshore futures business until 2001.[14]

Things have changed since 2001 and they are continuing to change. In May 2001, the CSRC issued the "State-Owned Enterprise Offshore Hedging Management Measure," stipulating that only big state-owned enterprises approved by the CSRC via an extremely strict application and approval procedure are able to hedge in offshore futures markets. Up to November 14, 2005, 31 big state-owned enterprises had acquired a license for offshore hedging.[15] In addition, on July 5, 2005, the State Council approved a new experiment of domestic

[14]*Jie Fang Daily*, July 5, 2005.

[15]*China Security Journal*, November 16, 2005, p. B6.

futures brokers taking offshore brokerage business.[16] Most recently, according to the third phase of the Mainland and Hong Kong Closer Economic Partnership Agreement (CEPA), beginning January 1, 2006, domestic futures brokers have been allowed to set up divisions in Hong Kong.[17]

This opening to the outside is bilateral rather than unilateral. Foreign players are also seeking to enter China's markets. Refco, the largest futures brokerage firm, and its Chinese peer, Jing Yi Futures Co. Ltd., are negotiating to establish a joint venture. In addition, ABN AMRO is cooperating with China Galaxy Security, the second-largest securities firm in China, to set up a new futures brokerage firm.

9.9 CONCLUSIONS

Following the serious contraction in the marketplace that resulted from the speculative period, China's futures industry today is on the path of recovery and rapid growth. Still, policymakers face a dilemma in terms of the futures market's development. On the one hand, they are afraid that the period of high speculation may recur and cause harm, given the vulnerable financial system. So they are very cautious in trying new experiments and loosening regulations. On the other hand, they are aware of the importance of the issue of pricing power in commodities, which is critical to the country's economy.

All in all, China is unlikely to make irrational changes in the futures sector before the equities market becomes efficient and fair and its banking sector completes a healthy reform.

[16] *China Security Journal*, October 25, 2005, p. B6.

[17] *China Security Journal*, November 9, 2005, p. B6.

CHAPTER 10

China's Derivatives Markets

Michelle Yuan Ménager-Xu
Regis Consulting, Shanghai, Geneva, and New York

10.1 INTRODUCTION

Along with the rapid development of other financial markets in China has come a rising demand for derivatives. In this Chapter we introduce the current state of the markets and the major new developments. This Chapter deals mostly with newly developing RMB onshore derivatives markets. Chapter 4, on foreign exchange, deals with the relatively more established FX forward and FX swap markets in China. Chapter 9, on futures markets, provides further details on the more liquid futures exchanges.

The major foreign interest in Chinese derivatives started with anticipation that the RMB would be revalued. However, for quite some time local players have traded futures, forwards, and synthetically created repos. At some point there was a very active bond futures market in Shanghai.[1] Anticipation of RMB revaluation increased the activity in offshore nondeliverable RMB forwards (NDF).

There is no doubt that Chinese derivatives markets will grow and become a very big market. This may happen slowly, sometimes in incremental, cautious steps, but RMB derivatives will be a major growth area in the future from the perspective of all market players. There are few sources dealing with RMB derivatives. The major source we can recommend is Zhang (2003). For securitization the reader can consult the analysis by Chang and Zhou (2006) and for derivatives rules the article by Liew et al. (2005). The present Chapter relies partially on the last two sources and on reports from the financial press and Reuters.

---

[1]See Chapter 9 for a discussion of the related episodes that led to the closure of this market.

10.2   THE RULES

The China Banking Regulatory Commission (CBRC) issued new derivatives rules in February 2004. This date can be considered a milestone in China's derivative markets since the rules significantly widened the scope of permissible derivatives transactions in China. The CBRC's new rules gave the *definition* of a derivative, the *approval* requirements for qualifying financial institutions, and the internal *risk management* requirements that such institutions must observe when entering into derivatives transactions.

The derivatives licences issued by the CSRC to foreign banks will cover credit, foreign exchange, and interest rate derivatives. There is some confusion as to whether this applies to equity and commodities as well. The derivatives in China include forwards, futures, swaps, and options. To this definition we can add structured products. In particular we would like to consider instruments such as CDOs as derivatives in this Chapter.[2]

On October 27, 2005, China amended the Securities Law so that *financial* derivatives could again be traded for the first time since 1995, when a scandal on bond futures produced heavy losses and prompted the authorities to stop bond futures trading.[3]

The rules allow financial institutions with derivative approvals to engage in derivative business for both hedging and profit-making purposes — a fundamental change from the previous regime, under which financial institutions were only permitted to enter into derivative transactions for hedging purposes.

Domestic policy banks have obtained derivative approvals to conduct only hedging transactions.

In addition, the hedging-only requirement remains applicable to Chinese corporations that are not financial institutions.

10.3   REGULATION

It is believed that commodities and equity derivatives potentially fall within the jurisdiction of the China Securities Regulatory Commission (CSRC), while the RMB derivatives fall under the People's Bank of China (PBC). But there is some confusion on this. A recent example is the collapse of China Aviation Oil in Singapore. This incident raised confusing questions regarding who the regulatory body was.

---

[2]However, there is some question as to whether the CBRC rules include the CDO type of instrument.

[3]The new changes permit selected firms to mix banking, insurance, and securities businesses as well.

10.4   OLD WAYS

Formal derivatives markets have just started to develop in China. Yet, typical of China, practice in financial markets often preceded formal rules. Although financial derivatives were not allowed, players still dealt in them indirectly. For instance, several domestic firms issued warrants. One example is Baoshan Iron and Steel Co. Ltd., which began issuing stock warrants in August 2005. Also, market players were using synthetic repos long before repos were formally introduced.

In fact, foreign and domestic banks could always do business with clients using "synthetic" versions of vanilla derivatives contracts. In the established practice until recently, back-to-back deals could be used to book the deals. According to this, one of the big four banks that had extensive local coverage of Chinese clients would write the deal and then would hedge the deal with a foreign bank. Such a structure would lead to credit enhancement and also reduce various operational and legal risks.[4]

Obviously, the legal foundations of such business was shaky. Consider, for example, the bankruptcy of Guangdong International Trust and Investment Corporations (GITIC) in 1998. GITIC was a major player in derivatives. After GITIC's default, Chinese courts voided its outstanding derivative contracts, saying they were not approved. GITIC had been a major player in structured products and derivatives.

The new regulations give clear guidelines on who can and who cannot trade derivatives. For example, the new rules allow foreign banks to interact with end customers directly. The previous practice was indirect, as suggested by the back-to-back deals.

10.5   NEW RULES IN FX DERIVATIVES

On September 22, 2005, China issued new rules allowing banks to run bigger foreign currency positions. This created additional flexibility for banks to hedge their FX forward positions. This should help FX risk management and the development of FX derivatives.

Under the new regulations published by the State Administration for Foreign Exchange (SAFE), banks' positions would be widened from covering transactions with *clients* to their *own* settlements on the foreign exchange market.[5]

---

[4]IFR, March 2004.

[5]According to this Reuters report, SAFE did not say by how much banks would be allowed to increase their positions or when the new rules would take effect.

Previously, banks had to settle their foreign currency positions on the official foreign exchange markets if their holdings exceeded official limits, selling more hard currency to the central bank and fueling foreign exchange reserves. Thus, designated foreign exchange banks had limits imposed on the amount of FX settlements that could be used as working capital. Amounts exceeding regulatory limits had to be squared on the interbank FX market.

The adjustment to the rules will allow banks to expand their working capital based on their FX settlement positions in transactions done on the onshore interbank FX market, including those related to the RMB against foreign currencies.

The FX settlement positions include those done for clients, the banks' proprietary business, and those through the interbank FX market.

SAFE also claimed that the amount of individual FX settlement positions allowed will need to be approved by regulators and will be partly based on the size of a bank's assets. But the overall amount allowed for banks will be increased. And the adjustment in the management of FX settlement positions will help develop yuan-linked derivatives products.

According to SAFE, Chinese banks and foreign banks that have begun yuan services can apply to the regulator within a month for approved FX settlement position limits. And those foreign banks that haven't begun RMB services can manage RMB FX settlements via special accounts.

According to these rules, domestic and foreign banks would be subject to the same treatment in holding foreign exchange positions.

10.6   FUTURES MARKETS

Currently, there are five major exchanges in the country. The Shanghai Stock Exchange, the Shenzhen Stock Exchange, the Shanghai Futures Exchange, the Dalian Commodity Exchange, and the Zhengzhou Commodity Exchange. A project to launch the Shanghai exchange jointly is planned.

The exchange would trade stock index futures, warrants, options, and interest rate futures. This project had already won approval from the State Council, China's cabinet, and could be established during 2007.

In October 2005, Beijing approved financial derivatives for the first time since they were banned following a trading scandal in treasury futures in 1995 that resulted in heavy losses to the state.

Equity warrants can now be bought and sold on China's two main stock markets. But having learned its lesson with a series of futures price-rigging scandals, the government has moved slowly in opening new financial instruments markets.

China is in particular need of forex derivatives to help its companies hedge against currency risks and improve its underdeveloped financial markets, especially since the yuan was revalued in July 2005 and placed in a managed float with reference to a basket of the globe's major currencies.

Beijing has pledged to move ahead with further financial derivative reforms, which many hope will pave the way for an eventual free float of the yuan, a stated long-term goal of the ruling Communist party.

The Shanghai Futures Exchange trades copper, aluminum, natural rubber, and fuel oil futures. The exchange was studying the launch of options on copper futures. The exchange had already completed the design of a steel futures contract and was creating a zinc futures contract.

The Dalian Commodity Exchange (DCE) trades soybean, soymeal, and corn futures. This exchange planned to create a soybean processing index. The DCE has applied to the CSRC for the launch of soy oil futures.

The Zhengzhou Commodity Exchange (ZCE) was preparing to launch white sugar, rapeseed oil, and peanut oil futures contracts. The ZCE is the world's second largest cotton futures market in terms of trading volume. It also trades wheat futures.

Finally, stock index futures is an important project of the authorities. According to the CSRC, China should start a financial derivatives pilot program by introducing equity- and stock-related derivatives before extending to other financial derivatives. To this end, China is planning a new exchange in Shanghai to trade financial derivatives.[6] There has been speculation among Chinese traders and analysts for a long time that China may establish a new financial futures exchange in Shanghai. The main task of such an exchange would be to trade stock index futures.

The stock index futures may be launched in late 2006 or early 2007. This would follow the sale of the nontrading state-owned shares. Nontradable shares account for about two-thirds of the domestic stock market's capitalization. Investor concerns related to their sale had a negative effect on the market sentiment. To this end China launched a nontradable share reform trial in April 2005 and floated selected nontradable shares. The reform then was extended to all listed companies.

10.7   INTEREST RATE DERIVATIVES

China's domestic bond market is already substantial, and there will be a natural demand for interest rate hedging from both issuers and investors as the

---

[6]*China Business News*, January 16, 2006.

interest rate system is liberalized. Client interest in interest rate swaps will grow. Interest in caps/floors and swaptions will develop somewhat later as the rates start floating freely and interest in secondary mortgage markets grows.

Interest in raising RMB funds from foreign borrowers has already resulted in some cross-currency trades. This sort of activity will no doubt increase. During 2005, JP Morgan wrote the first euro-to-renminbi cross-currency swap and swapped EUR 200m for a European corporation.

Finally, the authorities allowed the trading of bond forwards during the year 2005. However, the major effort is this area is in developing a functioning interest rate swap market, and we consider the developments here next.

10.7.1 INTEREST RATE SWAPS

During the years 2005–2006, China's onshore interest rate swap market slowly started to come into existence, although the development was slow. On the other hand, it would not be surprising to see a great deal of interest in renminbi interest rate swaps within a few years. The PBC is liberalizing the interest rate framework, and as time passes this should increase client demand for swaps. However, interest rate volatility is still low, and in the near term demand for swaps should be limited.

China's banking regulators see the sequences of reforms here as going from interest rate liberalization to FX reform. Because it precedes FX reform the regulators introduced several measures in this sector during 2005–2006. The PBC set a mechanism to periodically adjust its rediscount rate, which had been fixed at 3.24% since March 2004. Further reforms involve adjusting benchmark lending rates and freeing up large-lot deposit rates. The reference rates for such swaps would be based on benchmark interbank bond market rates and the one-year bank deposit rate set by the Central Bank.

China's renminbi interest rate swap market started trading formally on February 10, 2006. According to the rules announced by the Central Bank, China's commercial and state-run banks, branches of foreign banks operating in China, and policy banks were allowed to trade interest rate swaps. First, however, these institutions are required to register with the interbank market, the China Foreign Exchange Trade System (CFETS).

In order to become a renminbi swap dealer, a bank must first obtain a derivatives license. As of 2006 only five Chinese banks had applied for such a license. Also, the bank needs to build risk management capabilities and meet regulatory standards. This has to be confirmed in written reports filed with CFETS.[7]

---

[7] CFETS is a unit of the PBC.

Eighteen banks had submitted documents detailing their risk management and internal control systems for swap transaction to CFETS as of March 2006. Among these the local banks were the Bank of China, China Construction Bank, China Everbright Bank, China Minsheng Banking Corp. and the National Development Bank.

China's interest rate swap market is being set along similar lines as in the mature markets, except that the floating rate is the seven-day repo rate. For example, the first deals that were booked fixed interest rates ranging from 1.97% to 2.99% (for 10 years), and these were swapped for floating rates based on seven-day repurchase agreements to one-year yuan deposit rates.[8]

People's Bank of China (PBC) statistics show that about RMB10 billion in trades of nominal value were executed by the end of March 2006. The longest tenor traded was 10 years, with most of the activity being around five-year maturity.[9]

10.8 SECURITIZATION

In developed markets, asset-backed securities are popular investments for insurers and mutual funds looking for stable income streams. Issuers like the debt securities because they free up capital from their balance sheets. In China, on the other hand, bank loans remain the primary source for raising capital. This source is believed to have provided about 70% of raised capital during 2004–2005.

Securitization is in its infancy in China, and thus far mainly pilot projects have been initiated. China has two pilot securitization projects. The first deals with mortgage-backed securities (MBS). The second one is a pilot project on CDOs. China's first CDO was launched at the end of 2005. This is in fact a modest first step toward a market that may have significant weight in China's financial markets in the future.

A special task force of the China Securities Regulatory Commission picks securities firms from local brokerages to trade ABS securities. These brokers adopt a trust management or special financing structure to offer the asset-backed securities trading services.[10]

---

[8]As of mid-2006, this benchmark rate was pegged at 2.25%.

[9]China Everbright Bank and China Development Bank signed an initial swap agreement in October 2005 according to which the parties were to swap interest rates on the notional principal of RMB5 billion. This deal was approved by the People's Bank of China in February 2006. Under the deal, the two banks exchanged a 10-year fixed interest rate of 2.95% for a floating rate linked to the one-year yuan deposit rate, now at 2.25%.

[10]*China Securities Journal*, September 20, 2005.

10.8.1   THE FIRST ABS DEALS

China's market for corporate asset-backed securities (ABS) may hit RMB200 billion in 2007. This would presumably be accomplished through the increase of quotas. China took a step toward launching its first ABS on December 9, 2005. Two local trust firms were approved to issue the securities. The first is the China Development Bank, which is one of China's three policy banks.[11] The second is the China Construction Bank, which is not a policy bank.[12] The banks sold the ABS in the interbank market.

In China, trust companies operate like special-purpose vehicles (SPVs). In Western markets, investment banks use SPVs to issue securities. After all, ownership of the securitized assets needs to be transferred to some other entity in order for these assets to back the notes sold to investors. During a typical deal in the West, several different SPVs may be used, depending on the needs. These needs may differ, depending on taxation, regulation, cost, and efficiency issues.

In Chinese securitizations, approved banks use selected investment trust companies to entrust the securitized assets. China Credit Trust, established in 1995, is one such trust. It was initially backed by several coal companies. Citic Trust is another such entity. One issue is that under current rules, trust certificates can only be sold to corporations and individuals. This limits the size and liquidity of the deals. As other institutional investors are allowed to buy into the deals, this may change.

10.8.2   THE FIRST MBS

The first transaction from the CCB was a mortgage-backed security. It was backed by mortgages from the Standard Chartered Bank. The China Construction Bank issued four tranches of mortgage-backed securities; the CCB was selected to sell three tranches of mortgage-backed securities rated AAA, A, and BBB, for a maximum of CNY2.67 billion, CNY204 million, and CNY52.8 million for each respective category. An unrated fourth tranche was issued for a maximum of CNY90.5 million via a private placement.

The People's Bank of China approved Citic Trust to issue up to CNY3.1 billion in mortgage-backed securities that originate from the China Construction Bank.

---

[11] Policy banks issue financing bonds, make policy-related loans, and have no profit motive.

[12] The China Construction Bank was the first among the big-four Chinese banks to list in Hong Kong.

The first corporation to issue ABS securities was China Unicom. China Unicom, the country's second cell phone operator, issued RMB3.2 billion of asset-backed securities on the Shanghai bourse in September 2005.

10.8.3 THE FIRST CDO

China's bond market is the largest one in the country and one of the largest in the region. The liquidity and the foundations of the bond market will no doubt help the development of a future CDO market.

The need to spread out the credit risk in the portfolios of financial institutions is another reason that will support the CDO market.

Third, although China has chosen a slow path in implementing Basel II, eventually this pace will quicken. A CDO market will be essential in reaching Basel II standards in the long term.

Important reforms needed in this area are new *netting rules* and new *bankruptcy laws*. These rules need to be brought up to international standards before the credit derivatives market can start functioning on its own.

Other issues that need to be worked out over the course of the pilot project include concerns about tax and accounting treatments, the lack of decent historical data, and the question of true sale and asset perfection.

Chinese market participants are now showing increasing interest in credit derivatives, according to foreign dealers who have recently received licenses to trade in the onshore Chinese derivatives market.

The development of credit derivatives and in particular the CDO market is important for the Chinese economy.[13] This is partially due to China's nonperforming loan (NPL) portfolio, which is recognized by all parties as one of the major challenges facing China.

The China Development Bank was selected to issue CNY4.18 billion in CDO in three tranches.[14] The first tranche, with a maximum value of CNY2.92 billion, an AAA rating, had an average maturity of 0.67 years. The second tranche, with a maximum of CNY1.03 billion, A rating, had an average maturity of 1.15 years. The third tranche, worth CNY250.6 million, was unrated and is issued via private placement.

The China Credit Trust Co. has been approved to issue up to CNY4.3 billion worth of asset-backed securities in three tranches originating from the China Development Bank.

---

[13] In this chapter the term CDO is used in a broad sense, encompassing CLO, CBO, repackaging of distressed loans, etc.

[14] CDB's deal was in fact a CLO backed by a pool of infrastructure project loans made to the coal, electricity, oil, and telecommunications industries.

10.8.4　A Chronology Leading to CDOs

We provide below a list of events leading to the current state of the CDO market in China.[15]

1981　The issuance of government securities resumed after 23 years of inactivity.

1985　Banks were allowed to issue bonds.

1986　Official experiments began in secondary market trading of securities.

1988　Trading of government securities was allowed; secondary bond markets start to operate.

1990–92　The Shenzhen, Shanghai, and Wuhan stock/securities exchanges were set up.

1998　In an internal memo, Premier Zhu Rongji supported securitization.

2001　The Trust Law was passed by the National People's Congress.

2004　The PBC and the CBRC submitted the proposal to launch the CLO/RMBS pilots.

2005　The pilot securitization projects were approved by the State Council, China's cabinet. The PBC and the CBRC issued administrative measures, and the Ministry of Finance issued accounting rules, to support the functioning of the pilots; the CDB CLO, China's first CDO, issued a range of related rules; including investor rights notification/disclosure; and requirements of the originator, trustee, servicer, custodian, and other transaction parties.

September 2005　The first corporate ABS was launched.

December 2005　ABS securities were launched by the CDB and CCB.

Before the new derivatives regulations took effect, Chinese state banks acted as intermediaries for Chinese corporations and then used foreign banks to hedge positions accumulated through their dealings.

10.9　CONCLUSIONS

It appears that FX and interest rate derivatives markets will become liquid only when currency convertibility is truly established and yield curves start to fluctuate freely. When this happens, Chinese corporations will demand USD or EUR long-dated and then hedge these into renminbi. Similarly, as the markets develop there will be a demand to hedge renminbi interest rate risk.

---

[15] The chronology is from The CDO Market in China: Opportunities and Challenges, *Fitch Ratings*, February 2006. This is a useful report on the state of the CDO market in China.

Some problems involve unfamiliarity with exchange rates, interest rate risk, regulatory restrictions, and the inexperience of dealers. These hinder the development of derivatives markets. Some of these problems are as follows.

- Dealer sophistication to handle renminbi swaps is not satisfactory. A lack of foreign exchange expertise, at least in the nonbank sector, is a typical hurdle in the development of forwards and swaps. Among the big four banks, only one was actively making two-way prices in swaps as of 2006.

- Most markets are still very thin. For example, in spite of recent efforts, corporate clients do not show much interest in FX forwards. The demand for interest rate swaps will also be very low for many years.

- China's regulations are also an obstacle. For example, because of foreign exchange controls, currency trades are settled in accounts that are separated from domestic money market accounts. As a result, banks cannot easily borrow or lend RMB funds to hedge the risk of running a forward position. This exhibits itself as a difficulty in combining a spot FX transaction with a first leg of an FX swap, which is how banks hedge their FX forwards.

- Market participants have been concerned by uncertainty involving the issue of insolvency under PRC insolvency law. For example, because security law in China is not yet fully developed, taking collateral from a Chinese counterparty by way of either a charge or a title transfer arrangement requires detailed analysis due to uncertainties in Chinese law.

REFERENCES

Chang, C. and Zhou, J., The CDO Market in China, Opportunities and Challenges, *Fitch Credit Special Report*, February 2006.

Liew, C., Jiang, J., and Liu, B., *Derivatives Rules in China*, June 3, 2005.

Zhang, P., *Renminbi Derivatives*, 2003.

PART V

China's Mortgage, Insurance, and the Funds Industry

This final Part brings three important sectors together. Chapter 11 is adapted from a report on the Chinese mortgage market. This sector plays a crucial role in the recent performance of the Chinese economy, and we decided to include it in this book via this summary.

There is also the insurance sector, which is dealt with in Chapter 12. Foreign and domestic players have recently been very active in Chinese insurance markets. This Chapter gives a fairly comprehensive outline of this activity and introduces the main players.

Chapter 13 discusses the funds industry in China.

CHAPTER 11

China's Mortgage and Housing Market*

Wu Xuchuan
PBC, Researcher, Assistant Professor

The Chinese real estate market has been an eye-catching sector since 2003. Real estate in China distinguishes itself from other industries, mainly due to the fact that the development of the real estate market is closely related to the financial markets, especially the banking industry. Meanwhile, the mortgage market has also started evolving fast. Although these markets are not as mature as other Chinese financial markets, we devote this chapter to them. We use mainly the report issued by the People's Bank of China (PBC) in 2005. According to these statistics, the outstanding value of real estate loans in China reached 2765.06 billion RMB (equivalent to 337.2 billion USD) in the first quarter of 2005, in which mortgages represent the majority.

11.1 OVERVIEW

In 2004, although the real estate prices were increasing, the increase in land prices had slowed down. The appreciation of housing and land prices continued in 2005–06. The supply of low- to medium-priced houses and small-to-medium units was relatively low. Meanwhile, the growth of investment-oriented housing purchases was growing faster, especially with some overseas capital flowing into the real estate market in some popular regions. The progress of land development remained slow because a huge amount of land was already leased.

---

*This Chapter is derived from a report by the People's Bank of China, *Real Estate Financing in China*, Real Estate Committee of the People's Bank of China, August 2005.

In the mortgage market, the increase in mortgages was important, while the amount of real invested capital decreased in 2004. Certain real estate development loans maintained rapid growth, such as the loans for institutions like government land reserves. However, according to monthly statistics, mortgages issued have been decreasing since 2004. Thus loans to real estate developers also grew at a slower rate. Meanwhile, residential mortgages continued to grow at a high rate, with only a slight slowdown.

Overall, the residential mortgage market has the following characteristics.

- Residential mortgages are concentrated in few hot cities and regions.
- There is a very rapid growth of *surplus reserves* for individual house purchases.
- Mortgages have relatively low risks.

11.2   REAL ESTATE MARKET

The real estate industry is one of the pillars of Chinese economy. In recent years, with further urbanization and the reform of housing systems in towns and cities, many industry and credit policies have been inaugurated by the government in order to support the development of the real estate industry. The real estate industry developed quite fast. The privatization of housing has exceeded 80%, calculated on the basis of family units in towns and cities. The contribution of the real estate industry to the gross domestic product (GDP) has approached 10%.

Real estate provided the Chinese family with a new type of asset. Actually, property has become the most important asset for the individual, next to financial assets. The development of the real estate industry has fueled economic growth and promoted restructuring of the national economy.

11.3   THE SITUATION IN THE REAL ESTATE MARKET

Total investment nationwide in the real estate market in 2004 amounted to 1315.83 billion RMB, an increase of 28.1% over 2003. It is higher than the 25.8% growth of national fixed assets during the same period. During 2004, investment in real estate accounted for 18.8% of fixed-asset investment, compared to 12.7% in 1998. The investment in real estate development reached 232.4 billion RMB in the first quarter of 2005, a 26.7% growth as compared with the same period of the previous year. Meanwhile rate of growth of 14.4% was lower compared with the first quarter of 2003.

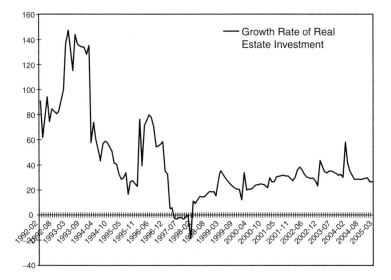

FIGURE 11.1   Growth Rate of Accumulated Investment in the Real Estate Market of China in 2005 Compared with 2004 (From China Economic Statistics Database of China Economy Net)

At the same time, the drop in newly purchased land is remarkable: In the first quarter of 2005, the accumulated land purchased by real estate developers nationwide reached 7.374 million square meters, a growth of 3.9% compared with the same period of 2004, although this rate was higher for 2004. From 1998 to 2003, the accumulated land purchased by real estate developers reached 1.29 billion square meters, with an annual average growth of 35%. And the land purchase fees amounted to 614.9 billion RMB, an annual growth of 42.6%. The land purchased grew quite fast before April 1999, the growth rate of which reached 91%. It was maintained at 45% throughout 2000–2004. However, the rate sank below 7% after June 2004.

The slowdown in new construction amounted to 140.96 million square meters in the first quarter of 2005, a growth of 9.3% and a diminishment of 13.2% in the increase as compared with the same period of the previous year.

11.3.1   IMPROVING SUPPLY–DEMAND RELATIONSHIP

There was a slowdown in the supply growth after February 2003. The accumulated growth of finished commercial real estate has been lower. Meanwhile, we observe a faster growth on the demand side. Accumulated total housing

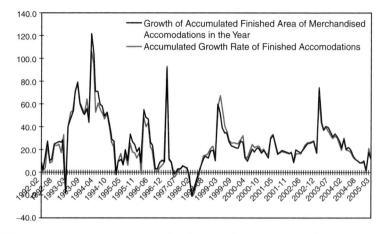

FIGURE 11.2 Growth Rate of Completed Areas of Commercial Buildings and Houses (Accumulation counted in the same periods of different years; from China Economic Statistics Database of China Economy Net)

sales totaled 380 million square meters in 2004, an increase of 13.7% as compared with 2003, in which apartments accounted for 340 million square meters, an increase of 13.9%.

The ratio of total (in square meters) of finished and sold commercial real estate decreased from 1.2:1 in 2002 to 1.03:1 in 2004. Since then, the lag between supply and demand has narrowed.

Meanwhile, accumulated housing sales improved in 2004; total unsold construction in 2004 was reduced to 123 million square meters, 3.8% lower than in 2003. At that time the total unsold construction was 128 million square meters.

Commercial housing prices nationwide remained stable, with an upward trend. And the increase was faster than in every previous year. If we set the fourth quarter of 1997 as the index base (i.e., = 100), the price index of commercial housing nationwide in the fourth quarter of 1997–2004 can be calculated. It can be concluded that the annual price increase rate in each year is faster than in the previous years.

In the first quarter of 2005, the average house sales price grew 12.5% over the same period the previous year. Transactions were 5.8% higher. The price of apartments grew 13.5%, a 7% increase. According to the report by the State Statistics Bureau, in the 35 big and medium-size cities nationwide, housing prices increased 10.5% in the first quarter, an inflation of 2.8%. Meanwhile, in eight cities the increase exceeded 10%: Shanghai 19.9%, Xiamen 16.5%, Chengdu 14.7%, Qingdao 13.7%, Hangzhou 12.4%, Jinan 11.9%, Ningbo 11.4%, and Nanjing 11.2%.

One thing to note is that the increase in housing prices is obviously higher than the increase in the CPI and rents.

11.3.2 EMERGENCE OF STRUCTURAL PROBLEMS IN THE HOUSING SUPPLY

The supply of common commercial housing in the medium and low price range is insufficient to meet demand, as indicated by the low percentage of such housing in the total supply. The final investment values of real estate development, the growth rate of townhouses and high-rise apartments is, respectively, 51.2%, 37.0%, and 39.7% in 2000, 2001, and 2002, higher than the total growth rate of investment in the overall housing market in the three consecutive years.

Looking at the finished construction sets, the growth rate for townhouses and luxury apartments in 2000, 2001, and 2002 is, respectively, 36.0%, 20.6%, and 35.4%, with the growth rate of accommodations for the same period being 9.9%, 12.8%, and 8.9%. Finished houses and luxury apartments among all finished housing rose from 2.3% in 1999 to 3.6% in 2003.

11.3.3 RAPID INCREASE IN THE PURCHASE OF HOUSING AS AN INVESTMENT TOOL

Although annual rental prices increased less than 2% since 2000, the rent revenues in most regions are still higher than the interest rates for bank deposits and personal household mortgages. Due to the fact that investment channels are hindered, especially faced with the rapid housing price increase, large quantities of social funds entered the real estate market.

In Beijing, according to research carried out by the Ministry of Construction, house purchases as an investment amounted to 17%. Soon thereafter, 28.5% of them were resold, 23.5% were rented out, and 48% were unused; owners anticipate that the price will increase in the near future. Housing purchased for investment purposes in the Yangtze River Valley was about 20% of the total.

Speculation occurred to some extent in certain cities and real estate projects. Such activities are characterized by a rapid price increase in the short term for some real estate, so some buyers are benefited by buying and reselling their properties within a short period. In some cities, the phenomenon of speculating on the "sub-new house" (no more than two years after purchase) is very pronounced. For example, in Shanghai, the transaction volume of "sub-new houses" accounted for 46.6% of the total volume of secondhand apartment transactions during 2004.

11.3.4 Foreign Investment in the Real Estate Market in Hot Areas

Lured by the rapid increase in the price of housing and the expectation of RMB revaluation, foreign funds entered popular real estate markets, such as Shanghai and Beijing, through various channels. The first is the direct establishment of foreign-funded real estate investment companies and the joint venture of domestic real estate developers. In 2004, total foreign investment in real estate developments nationwide amounted to 22.82 billion RMB, an increase of 34.2% compared with the same period the previous year.

The second channel is indirect investment, achieved via purchase of bonds issued by domestic real estate developers and the wholesaling of housing by foreign-funded real estate intermediaries, who could insure the sale of the housing.

The third channel is issuance of mortgages or loans to individuals or real estate developers by foreign-funded banks. The fourth channel is the purchase of real estate by means of the settlement of foreign currencies, after the inflow of non-citizen–owned foreign currencies. According to research carried out by the Department of Financial Markets of the PBC, from the first quarter of 2003 to the fourth quarter of 2004 the percentage of foreign investments in housing purchases in Shanghai rose from 8.3% to 23.2%. Statistics from the Shanghai Branch of the PBC also showed that the total inflow of foreign investments into the Shanghai real estate market totaled more than 22.2 billion RMB throughout January–November 2004, accounting for 12.8% of the total investment in real estate development that year, which is a growth of 13.5% as compared with the same period in 2003. Of total foreign investment, 15 billion RMB was used for real estate development, accounting for 12.8% of the yearly total investment in real estate development. Foreign investment was about 7 billion RMB, concentrated in high-end housing, such as town house and high-class apartments.

In January and February 2005, foreign funds purchased new housing in Shanghai priced higher than 11,000RMB/square meter in unit price, increased 47.6% and 73% in terms of purchasing area and amount, respectively. The purchased area and investment amount for secondhand housing in the same price range increased 2.8 times and 3.1 times, respectively.

11.3.5 Inadequacy in the Development of Leased Lands

There was also a continuing slowdown in the increase in land prices. In the first quarter of 2005, land prices in major Chinese cities grew 5.9%, a 0.2%

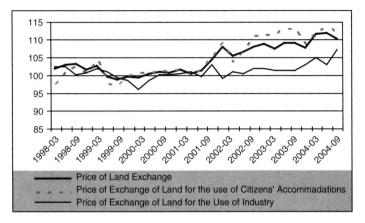

FIGURE 11.3   Quarterly Price Index of Land Exchange for 2005 (Price index for the same period of preceding year = 100) *Source*: China Economic Statistics Database of China Economy Net)

decrease in the incremental compared with the same period of the previous year. From the first quarter of 1998 to the third quarter of 2001, the transaction price of land remained relatively stable, as shown in Figure 11.3. From the fourth quarter of 2001, the transaction price of land started picking up. From the fourth quarter of 2002 until the fourth quarter of 2003, the transaction price of habital land increased more than 10% as compared with each previous quarter. Although the increase sank a bit in the first quarter of 2004, the quarterly increase since the second quarter of 2004 was again above 10%. However, this rate sunk again in the first quarter of 2005.

Although the total supply of land dropped greatly, the vitality of the leased land was augmented. In the first quarter of 2005, the total supply of land for construction use was 23,602.9 hectares, a decrease of 28% compared with the same period of the previous year, of which new land accounted for 34%, leased land 66%. The supply of habital land increased continuously. It accounted for 73% of the total land supply of real estate development in the first quarter of 2005 (5,706.9 of 7,877.9 hectares).

Although large amounts of leased land were developed by real estate developers, they did not convert timely into an effective market supply. Since 1997, the percentage of area for development use of the total area of land purchase has continued dropping. It remained 60–70% throughout 2000–2004 but sank below 50% in 2004. In the same year, the absolute area of completed land development decreased as compared with that in 2003. The gap between area of land purchased and development widened through the years, breaking 200.445 million square meters in 2004, which means that 200 million square

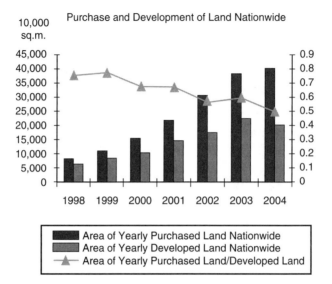

FIGURE 11.4   General Situation of Nationwide Land Development in 2004 (From China Economy Net. *Source: China Statistics Yearbook*)

meters of land was waiting for development or further development by real estate developers in 2004 alone.

Since 1999, the area of to-be-developed land has been in continual growth (except for small drop in 2001 as compared with 2000). The index was 217.826 million square meters in 2003, as can be seen from Figure 11.4.

11.4   HISTORY

The idea of commercializing housing and land property rights emerged in 1978. In September of 1980, the Beijing Construction Planning Office came into operation, which was the first of its kind nationwide, together with the Beijing City Development Company. They marked the beginning of the comprehensive development of real estate. House sales were tried in four cities in 1982, having been approved by the State Council. Land use fees were collected in Guangdong and Chongqing in 1984. The years between 1987 and 1991 form the start-up period of the real estate market in China. On November 26, 1987, the Shenzhen municipality first made a contract for leasing housing-occupied land by means of public bidding. Afterward, a plan for reforming the housing system was put forth by the Shanghai municipality. This gave rise to the first system of surplus reserves for the purpose of housing. In 1991, a plan for reform of housing in more than 24 cities and provinces was signed officially by the State Council.

11.4.1 PHASE TWO: SPECULATION (1992–1995)

The "reform of housing" was carried out in a thorough way with the promotion of surplus reserves for the purpose of housing purchased beginning in 1992. In 1993, the plan for "good housing for all citizens" was started. Beginning in 1992, the real estate industry experienced rapid growth, with the highest monthly growth reaching 146.9%. The real estate market fell into chaos in some regions for a time. In the most extreme cases, blatant bubbles occurred. However, following the macroregulation in 1993, the growth rate of the real estate industry declined sharply. The market itself did not revive for quite a long time, experiencing sluggishness for several years.

11.4.2 PHASE THREE: RELATIVELY STABLE DEVELOPMENT (1995–2002)

With the furthering of the reforms of the housing system and the promotion of individual income levels, housing has become a new focus of consumption. Since the abolition of the planned distribution of housing and the implementation of mortgage policies in 1998, investment in real estate has revived and moved into a period of relatively stable and rapid development. As a result, the real estate industry has become one of the pillar industries of the national economy.

11.4.3 PHASE FOUR: HIGHER PRICES AND MACROREGULATION MEASURES

Since the persistent increase in real estate prices beginning in 2003, the sale price of most houses in a majority of cities has exploded. Many macroregulation policies were instituted subsequently, targeted at the real estate industry.

11.5 DEVELOPMENT OF THE MORTGAGE MARKET

Since the adoption of the Reform and Opening Up Policy in 1978, real estate mortgages have experienced a rapid growth. Mortgages and consumer loans have also soared since 1998. As a result, commercial banks regarded themselves as the main avenues for adjusting their mix assets. The value of household mortgages was only 19 billion RMB at the end of 1997. That number rose to about 800 billion RMB at the end of 2002 and 1,592.23 at the end of 2004. At the end of the first quarter of 2005, this figure had reached 1,674.37 billion RMB, while the outstanding value for real estate loans at that time was 817.75 billion RMB, greatly surpassed by the outstanding value of household mortgages. The growth rate of the outstanding value of household mortgages has remained above 30%, notwithstanding the fact that it has been decreasing since 2003. The total outstanding value of mortgages grew 35.1% and 30.9% in 2004 and the first quarter of 2005, respectively, compared with the same period of the previous year. The growth rate of bank loans was only 14.4% and 13% by the same comparison method (see Figure 11.5).

However, the distribution of household mortgages is not balanced across the different regions of China, with a concentration on the east coast and scarcity in the western region. From the point of view of volume of growth, personal household mortgages on the east coast in 2004 increased to 312.91 billion RMB, 76.8% of the total national volume. The total increase in Shanghai, Guangdong, Zhejiang, Beijing, and Jiangsu was 245.24 billion RMB, 60.2% of the national volume, while the percentage of increase in personal household mortgages in the middle and western regions was only 11% and 12%, respectively. One could well conclude that household mortgages concentrate in cities and areas where the real estate industry is prosperous, and that the regional distribution of household mortgages is closely related to the regional differences in economic development.

One could also say that household mortgages, being a derived demand of life, mainly depend on individual income levels and regional economic development. The general situation for household mortgages in China could

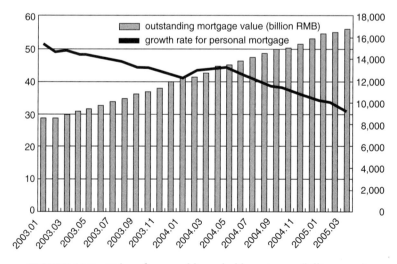

FIGURE 11.5   Value of personal household mortgages (billion yuan)

safely be summed up as rapid in development and imbalanced in regional distribution.

11.6   BASIC PARAMETERS OF THE MORTGAGE MARKET

According to research carried out by the State Statistics Bureau, total funds raised in 2004 for real estate development reached 1,716.88 billion RMB. The biggest source was the "guarantee fees and prereceived funds" reaching 739.53 million RMB, an increase of 44.4% over the same period of the previous year. It also accounted for 43.1% of the sources of investment in real estate development in 2004. The second biggest source for real estate development were funds self-raised by real estate developers, amounting to 520.76 billion RMB, an increase of 38.8%. This represented 30.3% of all sources of investment. The third biggest source is from bank loans, which in all was 315.84 billion RMB, an increase of 0.5% and representing 18.4% of total investment funds.

Actually, of all the different investment sources for real estate development, self-raised funds mainly come from the conversion of sales revenue from commercial housing, mostly home buyers' bank mortgages. If the down payment is 30% of the total house value, about 70% of all the self-raised funds of enterprises come from the bank loans. Also, around 30% "guarantee fees and prereceived funds" come from bank loans. Thus, total bank loans invested in real estate development exceed 55%.

11.6.1   HIGH GROWTH OF MORTGAGES

At the end of 2004, the outstanding value of real estate mortgages reached 2,630.63 billion RMB, an increase of 22.8% over the same period of the previous year. In 2003 and 2004, the increase in real estate mortgages tended to slow down, notwithstanding the fact that the outstanding value of real estate mortgages reached 2,765.06 billion RMB in the first quarter of 2005, a growth of 25.7% and an increase of 2.9% as compared with the end of the previous year.

The growth rate for real estate mortgages exceeds that of overall RMB loans in all financial institutions. At the end of 2003, the former was 20.1% higher than the latter. And the gap between, though narrowed in 2004, was still 11.3% higher. Mortgage growth rate was 14.9% higher than that of overall RMB loans in the first quarter of 2005.

The percentage of mortgages in the long-term loans of all financial institutions has steadily increased. At the end of March 2002, it was 27.2%.

It reached 32.1% at the end of June 2003, 34.3% in 2004, and 34.5% at the end of March 2005.

11.6.2 SLOW INCREASE IN REAL ESTATE DEVELOPERS' LOANS

Real estate developers' loans reached 781.09 billion RMB at the end of 2004 and 817.75 billion RMB at the end of the first quarter of 2005. Their growth rate remained at 40% before March 2004. The growth rate for real estate developers has been below 20% since the fourth quarter of 2004. The growth rate reached 17.3% at the end of 2004 and 15% in the first quarter of 2005. This was close to the growth rate of RMB loans, which indicates that the former were coming under control (see Figure 11.6).

Real estate developers' mortgages, which totaled 817.75 billion RMB at the end of the first quarter of 2005, include the following: (1) 460.18 billion RMB of habitable housing; developers' mortgages accounted for 56.3%, of which 17.9% was 146.83 billion RMB for the use of development mortgages of low-cost housing; (2) 160.54 billion RMB of liquid mortgages for real estate developers accounted for 19.6%; (3) 158.64 billion RMB of real estate development loans accounted for 19.4%, of which 95.02 billion RMB of loans for governmental land reserve institutions took up 11.6% of all real estate developers' loans;

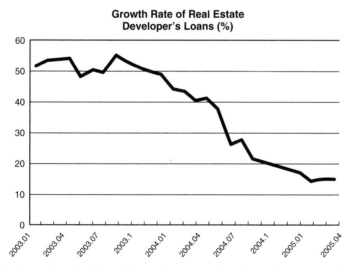

FIGURE 11.6 Growth Rate of Loans Issued to Real Estate Developers (From the statistics department of the PBC)

(4) 38.39 billion RMB of commercial housing development loans accounted for 4.7%.

11.6.3   PERSONAL MORTGAGES

The outstanding value of personal mortgages has experienced a sharp growth since 2002, reaching 1,592.23 billion RMB and 1,674.37 billion RMB at the end of the first quarter of 2004 and 2005, respectively. The growth rate was 35.1% and 30.9%, respectively. The growth rate of personal mortgages still exceeds 30%, although it has gradually dropped since 2003.

The size of personal mortgages in China is smaller than that of Western developed nations, which means that China still has room for further development. The mortgage/GDP ratio reached 11.7% by the end of 2004. In 2001, this ratio was 39% in EU countries, 60% in the UK, 47% in Germany, and 74% in the Netherlands.

From the past experience in China, we can see that since 1998 banks have been encouraged to issue mortgages to consumers. Some banks issued full sum mortgages. Several governmental notices were made to standardize the percentage of personal mortgages: the Notice to Normalize the Household Financing Business, June 19, 2003 (PBC Notice No. 195 [2001]) and the Notice to Further

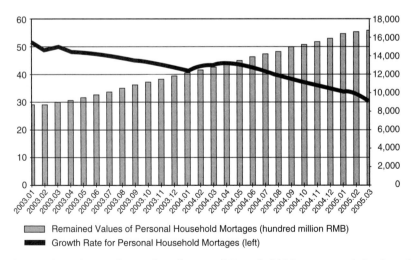

FIGURE 11.7   Outstanding Value of Personal Household Mortgages and the Growth Rate as Compared with the Same Period of the Previous Year (From the statistics department of the PBC)

Strengthen the Management of Real Estate Credit Businesses, June 13, 2003 (PBC Notice No. 121 [2003]).

These policies have set the minimum down payment amount. Mortgages can no longer exceed 80% of total house value. The percentage could be lower for people who buy two or more sets of apartments. The percentage has gradually dropped since 2002. However, it was still as high as 63% in the first quarter of 2005.

11.6.4   CONCENTRATION OF PERSONAL HOUSEHOLD MORTGAGES IN CERTAIN POPULAR AREAS

The distribution of the growth in personal mortgages is very uneven across the different regions in China: the growth of the eastern region is close to that of the whole country; that of the middle part of the country is a bit higher; and that of the western region is relatively lower. The increased value of personal mortgages was 312.91 billion RMB in the eastern region, contributing 76.8% of the national volume. The five municipalities and provinces in that region—Shanghai, Guangdong, Zhejiang, Beijing, and Jiangsu—had an increase of 245.24 billion RMB, accounting for 60.2% of the national volume. The outstanding value of these mortgages in the eastern region stood at 76.1% of the national volume, of which 59.9% belongs to the foregoing five municipalities and provinces. Therefore it can be clearly concluded that personal mortgages are concentrated in these popular areas.

The mortgage growth rate in these popular regions is also relatively high. For example, in Jiangsu in 2004 the growth rate was 50.5%, in Zhejiang 45.1%, Shanghai 42.4%, Tianjin 39.9%, Shandong 39.4%, and Beijing 30.5%. There is also a high growth rate in some provinces in the middle and western regions. For example, the growth rate in Anhui was 62.6%, in Hubei 59.5%, Jiangxi 58.8%, Hunan 49.8%, Guangxi 44.9%, and Chongqing and Yunnan both over 39%.

11.6.5   HIGH GROWTH OF POLICY-ENCOURAGED MORTGAGES

It is important to note that the existence of certain policies that encourage the fast-growing mortgage market. Such policy-encouraged mortgages mainly include personal household mortgages in the surplus reserves. At the end of 2004, the total volume of policy-encouraged household mortgages amounted to 249.30 billion RMB, of which personal household mortgages in the surplus reserves took up 84.1%, which was 209.62 billion RMB; in the first quarter of 2005, the former reached 265.01 billion RMB and the latter 222.35 billion RMB. The value of personal household mortgages in surplus reserves grew 42.5% and 38.8% at the end of 2004 and in the first quarter of 2005, respectively, compared with the same period of the previous year.

11.6.6 SURPLUS RESERVE SYSTEM OF RESIDENTIAL HOUSING

Surplus reserve of housing refers to the long-term reserves for purchasing housing services that are put aside by both employees and employers. It is designed to be used by the employees to purchase, build, rebuild, and furnish their own dwellings. The management of the surplus reserve system of housing is overseen by the Committee for the Management of the Surplus Reserve System. It is operated by the Management Center of the Surplus Reserve System, according to the principle of saving in special bank accounts and supervision by fiscal departments.

The interest rate for saving and lending in this surplus reserve system is set by the PBC and examined by the administration for construction in the State Council, who would approve them later. The Committee for the Management of the Surplus Reserve System is established as the decision-making institution of this system. It is composed of the local governments of the municipalities, counties, states, and unions, under the rule of provinces and the government of the autonomous regions. The Management Center of the Surplus Reserve System is also set up there.

By the end of 2004, the total value of the surplus reserve amounted to 489.35 billion RMB nationwide. The actual number of employees who have contributed is 61.385 million, which is 58.4% of the total workforce. The outstanding value of the personal surplus reserve of housing reached 209.62 billion RMB at the end of 2004, accounting for 42.8% of all outstanding value of surplus reserve. Aside from personal mortgages and the purchase of government bonds, there still remained 208.63 billion RMB nationwide, accounting for 42.6% of the remaining value of surplus reserve.

On March 17, 2005, the PBC decided to float 0.18% as the interest rate of surplus reserve for personal household loans. This rise includes the following: interest rates for mortgages of under five years (including five years) rose from 3.78% to 3.96%; those of longer than five years rose from 4.34% to 4.41%. The interest rate of surplus reserve for personal household loans is still more than 1% lower than that for personal household mortgages after the adjustment, comparing the same length of terms.

The main problems in the operation of the surplus reserve of housing are the following. First, it is difficult to apply for loans from the surplus reserve due to its limited size. This means that it cannot greatly assist in home purchase for workers with middle or low income. Second, the distribution of the benefit from the operation of the surplus reserve needs further clarifications.

11.6.7 POTENTIAL RISKS OF MORTGAGES

On the whole, the quality of real estate development loans of the four big state-owned commercial banks is relatively good. The NPL rate of the Bank of China (BC), the Industrial and Commercial Bank of China (ICBC), and the China Construction Bank (CCB) is 3–5%, while that of the Agriculture Bank of China (ABC) is a bit higher. The average NPL rate of the four banks is below 5%, as can be seen in Table 11.1.

The quality of the different real estate developers' loans, however, differ greatly. The NPL rate of the ABC and the BC is 16% and 12%, respectively, which are relatively high. In comparison, that of the ICBC and the CCB is lower, remaining at about 7%. The average NPL rate of real estate developers' loan is 10–11%.

The quality of home loans is relatively better, with an NPL rate of about 1.5%. The NPL rate of the ICBC, BC, and CCB is below 2%, and that of the ABC is a bit above 2%.

At the end of the first quarter of 2005, the quality of real estate mortgages was better than that at the end of 2004, thanks to the improved quality of real estate developers' loans. The NPL rate of the former is 0.1 lower than that of the latter. The NPL rate of the ICBC remained unchanged, whereas that of the other three banks has lowered.

Certain risks exist in real estate mortgages. On the one hand, the NPL rate of real estate developers' loans is relatively higher; on the other hand, although the NPL rate of home purchase has been low, risks of mortgage payback may occur, because the repayment ability of home purchasers could be affected, along with the gradual implementation of tax policies in the future and the promotion in the managerial fees of property management companies.

11.7 REASONS CONTRIBUTING TO THE RAPID DEVELOPMENT OF MORTGAGES

There are many reasons for the rapid development of personal household mortgages in China. First, the implementation of housing system reform, along with the increase in income level, promoted a third wave of consumption upgrading among Chinese citizens. Therefore, the strong market demand for houses has determined the strong demand for mortgages.

TABLE 11.1 NPL Status of the Four State-Owned Commercial Banks

Item	Remained value of real estate loans in 2004 (billion RMB)			NPL rate of real estate loans in 2004 (%)			Remained value of real estate loans at the end of Q1 in 2005 (billion RMB)			NPL rate of real estate loans at the end of Q1 in 2005 (%)		
	Total	Real estate developers' loan	Personal house purchase loans	Total	Real estate developers' loan	Personal house purchase loans	Total	Real estate developers' loan	Personal house purchase loans	Total	Real estate developers' loan	Personal house purchase loans
ICBC	581.03	168.50	4,124.0	3.0	7.4	1.2	599.80	176.40	423.30	3.0	7.1	1.3
ABC	409.91	172.34	2,375.7	8.1	16.6	2.1	425.85	182.60	243.25	7.9	16.2	2.0
BC	378.37	101.77	2,766.0	4.8	12.8	1.8	398.36	102.29	296.07	4.4	12.3	1.7
CCB	570.89	227.80	3,430.9	3.7	7.3	1.2	593.74	240.20	353.54	3.5	6.9	1.2
Total	1,940.2	670.41	12,696.6	4.6	10.5	1.5	2,017.74	701.49	1,316.15	4.5	10.1	1.5

Note: All loans are classified in the standard five levels. NPL covers three levels of loans: secondary, doubtful, and loss.

In 1998, the Chinese government terminated the system for distributing housing as social welfare policy, which had been in force for decades. At the same time, the central government shifted the distribution of housing toward a market-oriented and currency-measured system, which required citizens to realize home purchase directly from the real estate market.

First, the effective demand for commercial housing has expanded rapidly, a direct result of the rapid economic growth from the 20 years of reform and opening policy. Income level increased, as did the standard of living, and social welfare improved. Thus, people began to seek to upgrade their lives, and demand for such increased accordingly. From studies carried out on the regional distribution of household mortgages in China, it is clear that mortgages are highly related to the average income level in a certain region. Personal income has also formed a substantial basis for the rapid development of the mortgage market.

Second, since 1997 the PBC has taken many actions to encourage commercial banks to issue mortgages. In that year, the PBC promulgated *The Decrees for Issuing Personal Household Mortgages*, encouraging citizens in both towns and cities to purchase common housing built by surplus reserves. In 1998, the PBC further issued *The Notice for Increasing the Investment of Household Mortgages and Supporting Construction and Consumption of Home Building*, which declared the construction of housing a new growth point of the national economy. All commercial banks had to adjust their mix of loans in order to support the construction and consumption of housing (real estate).

Furthermore, they can issue household mortgages in accordance with the asset–debt ratio, which determines how much mortgage they could issue, once the debtor has qualified. To insure the investment for household mortgages when the loan scale is canceled, a proportion of new mortgages to total new loans issued each year should be kept at 15% and the proportion of household consumption mortgages to household mortgages should be increased in a piecemeal fashion.

On the creditor's side, all state-owned commercial banks and the Bank of Communications could be entrusted with deposits and mortgages of households, a great advance as compared with only three banks in the past, namely, the Industrial and Commercial Bank of China, the Agricultural Bank of China, and the China Construction Bank. At the same time, all commercial banks are allowed to issue personal mortgages, targeted at all the common commercial housing in all towns and cities.

Third, the mortgage characteristics—of low risk and relatively stable return—also have encouraged the commercial banks to render the mortgage as an essential measure to restructure its assets. According to the statistics of the PBC, the NPL rate of personal household mortgages in the four national banks is about 1.5%; those of the ICBC, BC, and CCB are all below 2%, and that of the ABC is a bit above 2%. But all are far below the average NPL rate of banks, which is 15%. The default rate for personal household loans has hitherto been the lowest among all the credit assets of banks, which helps explain the fierce competition among commercial banks to obtain household mortgages as their premium assets.

Fourth, the issuing of household mortgages is also convenient in terms of regulation and monitoring. Although China has not hitherto adopted *Basel's New Capital Accord*, the China Banking Regulatory Commission (CBRC) has already ironed out a set of standards for capital regulation that suits China's national condition. In regulating the risk-weighted capital adequacy rate for commercial banks in China, the CBRC, in its Decree of Capital Adequacy issued in 2004, stipulated that the capital adequacy ratio (CAR) of commercial banks should be above 8% and the core capital rate above 4%. It has also recommended the weights of risks in each category of asset for calculating the CAR: personal household mortgages are 50%, other creditors' rights for enterprises and privates are 100%.

The increase in the reserves of the banking system of China, its ratio to the value of bank loans, has exceeded 36%, which means there still remains a large amount of surplus capital needing to be utilized within the banking system of China. This phenomenon in recent years has been a joint result of the internal demand for asset restructuring within the banks. And the regulatory measures on the risk-weighted capital adequacy rate has also played an important role. Actually, according to some studies, the regulation on the risk-weighted capital adequacy rate has directly affected loan issuance in commercial banks.

Although in 2004, the government started to tighten monetary policy, household mortgages continued their rapid growth, mainly due to the relatively low weight of risks. Meanwhile, commercial banks can also issue mortgages to expand their credit asset line and evade the constraints of capital adequacy made by the watchdogs.

Last, the government's tightening of policy also has made commercial banks shift their concentration to mortgages. After a set of tightening macropolicies were implemented in 2004, price fluctuations occurred in certain industries, such as steel and electrolytic aluminum, thus bringing higher credit risks for these business loans from the banks' angle. Meanwhile, the real estate market has grown rapidly and housing prices kept increasing. Together with the low risk of household mortgages, banks found a way to use the surplus capital created by the decrease in industry loans in steel, cement, and electrolytic aluminum. Consequently, the percentage of household mortgages in the total volume of loans in commercial banks increased, instead of decreasing, after the implementation of tight macroregulation in 2004, notwithstanding the fact that the growth rate of the total volume of loans itself is diminishing.

Since 1997, the percentage of household mortgages among newly issued loans of commercial banks has continually trended upward, reaching even 25% in June 2004. Accordingly, the outstanding value for household mortgages of commercial banks surpassed 1.5 trillion RMB in the third quarter of 2004, which was 10% of the total value of bank loans.

11.8   RISKS IN THE CURRENT REAL ESTATE MARKET

There are several critical risks in the current state of the Chinese real estate markets. We discuss them next.

11.8.1   OVERHEATED MARKETS IN CERTAIN REGIONS

Overheated real estate prices occurred in some regions during 2004–05. According to a report of the PBC Shanghai branch, within the inner ring area of Shanghai the price of newly built houses increased 27% in 2004. Other studies also showed that it is worth paying attention to the secondhand market and the high-end housing market bubble in Shanghai.

The overpriced real estate market could easily produce a real estate bubble. Once the bubble bursts, houses as collateral would suffer a great reduction in value and banks would suffer losses. Thus, commercial banks in Shanghai and other regions recently started increasing the level of down payments, some even rising to 50%, in order to prevent the risks from collateral depreciation.

11.8.2   HIGHLY INDEBTED REAL ESTATE DEVELOPERS

The main financing source for real estate developers are bank loans, since they usually have very little self-raised funds. According to the statistics, among real estate developers' various sources of funding, more than 70% came from bank loans. Take Beijing as an example. The average asset–liability ratio of real estate developers in Beijing was 81.2% from 2000 to 2002. With the increasingly cutthroat competition in the real estate market, the strengthened regulatory measures, as well as the enhancement of the basic standards for development loans, the chain of capital for these real estate developers could break at any time. Such problems would bring great risk to the whole real estate market should they occur.

11.8.3 ETHICAL RISKS

Phony mortgages have become the main source of risk in the mortgage market. *Phony mortgages* refers to when real estate developers pass their own employees or other relations off as customers to the bank. According to the Consumption and Credit Department of the ICBC, 80% of all the nonperforming assets among the bank's personal household mortgages are caused by phony mortgages.

Developers have used these phony mortgages as an alternative channel of financing. Prior to March 17, 2005, the mortgage rate was lower than that of real estate development loans. Moreover, because it is rather easy to obtain approval, real estate developers have made phony mortgages another financing channel by which they could lower their financial costs and relieve their cash flow difficulties. Some developers pay back the bank loans after they get the money from the sale of the housing. However, some developers even abscond with this money, seeing no possibility of selling all of the housing.

11.8.4 OPERATIONAL RISKS

Operational risks occur mainly for the following reasons. First, the risk-consciousness of bank staff is weak. The procedure for examining and approving a loan is highly variable, and little attention is paid to the verification and legality of the materials.

Second, the management of collateral is not standardized. There is also a lack of cooperation among different functional departments. Moreover, the procedure is not carried out according to relevant rules. Too much credence is given to the estimation of collateral by intermediate institutions, resulting in their depreciation and ineffectiveness.

Third, the management of some branch banks in issuing mortgages is chaotic, with incomprehensiveness and discontinuity in the customer mortgage files and relevant risk-alert measures.

11.8.5 CREDIT RISKS IN LAND DEVELOPMENT LOANS

The outstanding value of land reserve loans in China was 82.84 billion RMB at the end of 2004; the comprehensive volume of credit endowment was larger. Bank development loans face risks in the following four ways.

The asset–liability ratio of the land reserve center is relatively high. Although the land reserve institutions are set up by government funding, they are weak in confronting risks in some regions because the government has invested very little capital reserves and this money cannot get timely in place. Thus these institutions become too dependent on bank funds.

Banks have difficulty carrying out effective supervision over these institutions. These institutions mostly adopt two separate channels for receiving and paying. The money from leased land is deposited in special fiscal accounts, which the banks find hard to supervise. In the case of tight fiscal situations in local governments, land reserve institutions could easily become the financing channels for the government.

There have been no effective warranty measures for banks when issuing loans to land reserve institutions. Currently, the measures mainly include warranty by government and collateral of land use rights, which has problems of legality. As the Warrant Law provides, government or units with public benefit aims could not provide warrants. Land reserve institutions are only deputy institutions representing part of the administrative powers, but not actually the land users, so they have no right of land use over the reserved lands. Thus, the method of land collateral is not well implemented for banks.

Among the operational risks of land reserve institutions is the large uncertainties in land value pricing. For example, prices can drop greatly, affected by policy changes. Also, if default occurs in the auction of the land and deeds of successful bidders, bank credit risks could be affected because income from the leasing of the land is lower than the original price of the land.

11.8.6 Legal Risks

New laws will probably limit the execution of loan collateral. The Supreme Court issued *The Decree by the Supreme Court to Seal up, Detain, and Freeze the Assets in the Civil Execution of the People's Court* on October 26, 2004, declaring that it would come into force on January 1, 2005. The sixth clause of the decree provided that "the people's court could seal up, but not auction, sell off, or pay as a debt, the houses that are necessary for living of the signor and the relations he or she raises or fosters," which means that even if the purchasers of the housing cannot repay, banks cannot sell off their houses to collect the loans. The decree has augmented the risks of mortgages for commercial banks.

11.9   CONCLUSIONS: THE FUTURE

Although the mortgage market in China has experienced rapid growth in recent years, its history is rather short. Given the experiences in developed countries, real estate mortgages represent a large percentage of the credit asset loans of banks. Take the United States as an example. The percentage has been increasing since the 1980s; it reached 20% in the 10 biggest banks in the nation; it is as high as 40% in the 101st to the 1,000th banks. By comparison, the mortgage percentage in the commercial banks of China is still low.

In the first quarter of 2005, the outstanding value of real estate mortgages in China was 2,765.06 billion RMB, making up 13.31% of the outstanding credit value of home and foreign currencies in all financial institutions. The percentage was far below that of other developed countries, including the United States.

Another report of the PBC showed that the scale of personal household mortgages of Chinese citizens is small as compared with that of Western developed nations, which implies large room for further development in the Chinese mortgage market. By end of 2004, mortgages were 11.7% of GDP, while that ratio reached an average of 39% in 2001 in the EU, with UK 60%, Germany 47%, and the Netherlands 74%. The future growth of personal household mortgages is promising.

With respect to future developments, we think the following innovations can be made. First, various methods of mortgage payment should be proposed. Nowadays, the payback methods are rather unitary, which only include payment by equal capital and interest and payment by equal capital.

Second, in payment by equal capital and interest, the monthly payment is determined, though this monthly payment contains mainly interest and not much initial capital is paid back. In payment by equal capital, the monthly capital paid back by the debtor is fixed. However, because the interest occurs together with the loans since the beginning of the term, the payment then could be rather large in the earlier stage of the term, but it will diminish later. In other words, such payment gives debtors higher pressure at the beginning; thus, younger people usually don't like it. That can explain why, in the overseas market, although payment by equal capital is a traditional method, it is not very popular anymore. Other methods occurred, such as escalating payment. This is based on the assumption that the monthly payment would increase as time goes by. It is welcomed by young people who have just started their career.

Third, besides the new mortgage methods, more varieties of mortgage interest structure should be created. The current interest rate for mortgages in China is the adjustable interest rate, where the interest rate is calculated for different periods. For example, for those mortgages whose term is longer than one year, new interest rate policies would be implemented according to their different positions in the interest rate hierarchy from the next year. Such a method has totally shifted the risk of interest rate risk to the borrowers. If the mortgage rate increases, the debtors' repayment burden will also be larger. Then the debtor tends to pay back earlier, thus affecting cash flow in the commercial bank.

In the United States, commercial banks also issue large amounts of *adjustable-rate mortgages (ARMs)*. The PBC claimed in its *China Real Estate and Finance Report*, which was issued on August 15, 2004, that "consideration should be given to allowing commercial banks to issue personal household mortgages of fixed interest rates." Recently, some commercial banks declared their interest in issuing such mortgages.

The issuing of mortgages requires banks with strong risk management abilities. As the mortgage rate increases, debtors will certainly not pay back in advance, but the cost of the liabilities will be higher for commercial banks. Thus their profits would diminish accordingly, and, in some extreme cases, even losses would occur. In the 1960s and 1970s, U.S. savings and loan associations, which specialize in mortgages, went bankrupt one after another under the pressure of escalating interest rates in the market, because they had issued a large amount of *fixed-rate mortgages (FRMs)*. In times of rising interest rates, debtors with such mortgages are not prone to repay; in times of decreasing interest rates, however, debtors would choose to refinance or to repay in advance directly with their previous savings. Thus, it is not a good idea for commercial banks to prevent debtors from repaying in advance.

Fifth, there are experts who have proposed that banks use both fixed and adjustable rates to calculate a structured rate for mortgages. For example, in times of escalating interest rates, mortgages at fixed interest rates should be adopted; otherwise, the variable rate should be adopted. However, if the secondary market of derivatives for the hedging of interest rate risks and household mortgages cannot be fully developed, then neither mortgages at fixed interest rates nor those at combined rates would be welcomed.

Last but not least is that the secondary market for mortgages needs further development. For the time being in China, there is only the primary market for mortgages. This means that commercial banks have to keep creditors' rights once the mortgages are issued. Due to the long duration of mortgages in general, especially when the mortgage market grows fast, cash flow problems have developed for commercial banks. Although the rapid growth of the mortgage market can be constructive in many ways, it also faces commercial banks with greater liquidity risks.

In 2005–06, authorities started a secondary market for mortgages, a market for the exchange and circulation of issued mortgages. The secondary market would provide new financing channels for the mortgage borrowers. By enabling the bank to make the sellers of mortgages play the role of media, the secondary market would turn the long-term mortgage assets into cash assets.

The main measure for this development is to securitize the mortgage market. On April 20, 2005, the Bank Regulating Committee promulgated *The Decree of the Securitization of Credit Assets*, which allowed financial institutions in China to trust their credit assets to qualified trustees, who issue beneficiary securities to investment institutions in the form of asset-backed securities. The commercial banks' securitization of real estate credits will shift not only the corresponding liquidity risks, but also the relevant credit risks, interest rate risks, and the risk brought about by repayment in advance.

An important issue relating to the meaning of private property should be mentioned. In China, the buyer of a home does not own the property. He rents it from the government. In other cases, the ownership is in terms of right to live in the property. In the former case, the property can be purchased with borrowed funds. In the latter case, the "buyer" needs to pay cash. Foreigners are not, in general, allowed to buy such property. Finally, please note that in this chapter we did not discuss real estate taxation issues, which may pose a risk to property owners.

APPENDIX

LAND POLICIES AS A MEASURE OF REGULATING REAL ESTATE DEVELOPMENT

On May 19, 2002, the Ministry of Land and Resources issued its No. 11 document, *The Decree of Public Bidding and Auctioning of the Land Use Rights of State-Owned Land*, requiring that from July 1, 2002, land for business operation such as commerce, tourism, entertainment and commercial accommodations must be publicly exchanged by means of public bidding, auction, or public listing. The implementation of all these three methods made real estate developers accelerate their land reserves, based on the expectation that land prices would increase.

On March 31, 2004, the Ministry of Lands and Resources and the Ministry of Supervision jointly issued *The Notice for the Execution of Laws and Supervision During the Further Implementation of the Policies of Public Bidding, Auction, and Public Listing of Land Use Rights of Land for Business Operations* (the 71st decree), which seriously executed the deeds of privately selling land for business operation by means of negotiation after March 31, 2004. These deeds were done as a result of historical problems.

On April 29, 2004, the General Office of the State Council issued *The Urgent Notice About the Serious Rectification of Land Market Management*, planning to rectify the market in the next half year. It planned to stop the examination and approval of the conversion of agriculture land to nonagriculture use during rectification and to stop any amendment in plans related to adjustments of basic agriculture reservation fields. For the newly approved cities (districts) converted from counties and towns converted from villages, all kinds of plans related to land use were to be terminated.

On June 6, 2004, the State Council issued *The Notice of the Control of the Size of Removal in Towns and Cities and the Management of Removal*, declaring strict control of the removal areas of housing. For regions struggling with conflicts in the removal plan, any further removal would be prohibited, except for a few key construction projects, such as the important social development project, the rebuilding of structures in danger, the construction of low-cost housing and housing with relatively cheap rent.

These measures have terminated the negotiated land lease methods that had been in use for many years. According to statistics of the Ministry of Lands and Resources, the total area of leased land reached 124,000 hectares and 194,000 hectares in 2002 and 2003, respectively, representing an increase of 37% and 56%, respectively. The total area of leased land in 2004 amounted to 179,000 hectares, a decrease of 7.7% from 2003.

REAL ESTATE CREDIT POLICY

The PBC has actively adopted credit policies to stimulate the development of the real estate industry. In 1998, it issued several decrees, such as *The Decree of the Management of Policy-Encouraged Housing Credits*, *The Decree of the Management of Housing Mortgages Operated by Commercial Banks*, and *The Decree of the Management of Personal Housing Mortgages*. With them, housing mortgages from commercial banks and from savings and loan businesses were basically established.

Since 1998, the PBC has announced a series of credit policies encouraging the construction and consumption of housing to increase domestic demand and promote economic growth, including *The Notice of Enlarging the Involving of the Housing Credit Investment to the Support of the Construction and Purchase of Housing*, *The Guiding Principles of Improving Financial Services and Supporting National Economic Development*, and *The Decree of the Management of Personal Household Mortgages*. As required by those documents, all commercial banks must adjust their mix of loans and actively back the construction of housing. In 1999, the PBC issued *The Guiding Principles of Promoting Personal Credit for Consumption*, encouraging commercial banks to provide all-around premium financial services. In September of the same year, the PBC prolonged the maturity of personal household mortgages from 20 years to 30 years.

To ensure the healthy development of the real estate credit market, the PBC issued *The Notice to Normalize the Household Financing Business* on June 19, 2003 (PBC Notice No. 195 [2001]) and *The Notice to Further Strengthen the Management of Real Estate Credit Businesses* on June 13, 2003 (PBC Notice No. 121 [2003]). In March 2005, the PBC made market-oriented adjustments to the pricing mechanism of interest rates for personal household mortgages.

These measures produced satisfactory effects and effectively backed the development of the real estate industry while at the same time strengthening the evasion of risks in the market. The value of real estate mortgages was only 310.623 billion RMB in 1998 and 2,630.63 billion RMB in 2004, an average growth rate of 42.8% over six years. Personal household mortgages in 1998 totaled only 42.62 billion RMB, which increased to 1,600.23 billion RMB in 2004, an average annual growth rate of 83.0%; real estate development loans in 1998 totaled only 268.01 billion RMB, which increased to 781.09 billion RMB in 2004, an average annual growth rate of 20%. The value of real estate mortgages represented only 3.6% of the value of RMB loans of all financial institutions at the end of 1998 and accounted for 14.8% at the end of 2004.

CHAPTER 12

China's Insurance Market

Guan Lin
FSA, FSAC, China Insurance Regulation Commission (CIRC)
Michelle Yuan Ménager-Xu
Regis Consulting, Shanghai, Geneva, and New York

12.1 INTRODUCTION

The Chinese insurance market has been developing very fast since 1993, and continued this trend during 2004–2006. This Chapter describes the history and current situation of the Chinese insurance market and its future prospect.

12.1.1 PRE-1949: STARTING PERIOD

Modern insurance practices were introduced into China in the middle of the 19th century. In 1846, two British insurance companies were established in Shanghai, with the Chinese names Yong Fu and Da Dong Fang. Domestic Chinese insurance companies began to emerge later. In 1887, the Chinese insurance company Ren Ji He was founded, in Shanghai, offering mostly shipping and marine insurance. In 1911, the Chinese life insurance company Hua An He Quan was founded, in Shanghai. This was the first domestic Chinese life insurance company.

Modern insurance emerged in only a few big cities in China and were far away from most Chinese people at that time. The old Chinese government regulated the insurance market very little. China's domestic insurance companies did not play an important role in the market then, having only 25% market share and more than 600 offices and branches. In contrast, foreign companies enjoyed 75% market share with around 60 companies. Foreign insurance companies dominated the Chinese market during this period.

12.1.2   1949 TO LATE 1970S: PERIOD OF STATE OPERATIONS

In 1949, the People's Republic of China was founded, and Chinese society entered a new era of development. The new Chinese government enacted several measures regarding the insurance market. The government set up a state-run national insurance company, the People's Insurance Company of China (PICC) on October 20, 1949. Then the government began restricting foreign insurance companies. All foreign insurance companies had exited the Chinese insurance market by 1952. Meanwhile, the government reformed and merged the Chinese private insurance companies. Finally, PICC became the sole practitioner of insurance in Mainland China. PICC had a brisk and all-around development, whether in property insurance or life insurance, in domestic business or overseas business, in urban areas or rural areas.

In 1958, PICC terminated all domestic insurance businesses by government order, because almost everything by then was under the coverage of the government. Although overseas business continued, the once-high-powered domestic insurance business plummeted.

12.1.3   LATE 1970S TO 1995: A REVIVAL

In the late 1970s, the Chinese government began its Reform and Open policy. The Chinese economy started booming. Chinese insurance also recovered vitality.

PICC resumed insurance business in the domestic market in 1980 and from then on experienced quick growth (see Table 12.1). Its main business was property insurance. PICC also provided agricultural insurance, marine insurance, export credit insurance, and reinsurance. PICC rewrote life insurance in 1982.

Along with the development of the insurance market, the Chinese government permitted new players to enter the insurance market. In 1987, the Bank of Communications of China set up an insurance department, the predecessor of the China Pacific Insurance Company later established in Shanghai. In 1988, the Ping An Insurance Company was established in the She Kou Industrial Zone of the Shenzhen Special Economic Zone, the first shareholding insurance company in China. It developed into the China Ping An Insurance Company in 1992.

Not only domestic players, but also foreign insurers came into the Chinese insurance market in the early 1990s. AIA, one life insurance company of AIG, got the first insurance license from the Chinese government and set up a

TABLE 12.1   PICC's Growth During 1980–1990

	1980	1985	1990
Premium	0.28 billion	3.265 billion	1,557.6 billion
No. of employees	4,710	43,437	84,750
No. of offices	810	2,420	4,000

Source: Almanac of China Insurance 1981–1997.

branch in Shanghai in 1992. AIA provided life insurance and introduced the individual agent marketing method. This directly stimulated the development of Chinese insurance, especially Chinese life insurance.

During this period, there were mainly three national insurers competing in the Chinese market: PICC, China Pacific, and China Ping An. Thus some people also call this period the *three-pillar stage*.

12.1.4   SINCE 1995: THE BOOM

Something very important happened in 1995. The Insurance Law of the People's Republic of China was issued on June 30 and took effect on October 1. This was the first specialized law for insurance. It prescribed the basic standards of the insurance industry, insurance policy, and insurance regulation. It also prescribed the principle of business separation, which required that (1) insurance business be strictly separated from banking and securities business, (2) life insurance business and property insurance business be separated, and (3) an insurance company be either a life insurance company or a property insurance company, not both. This principle had a great influence on the insurance market and on market players.

In 1996, according to the principle of business separation prescribed by the Insurance Law of China, PICC was restructured into a group company with three subsidiaries, later named PICC Property, PICC Life, and PICC Re. They were all independent entities and later reformed into new PICC, China Life Insurance Company, and China Reinsurance Company.

Another important event in 1996 was that three new nationwide insurance companies were set up. Hua Tai Property Insurance Co. Ltd., Tai Kang Life Insurance Company, and New China Life Insurance Company. Meanwhile, the Chinese government granted licenses to two regional domestic property insurance companies. Moreover, Chinese insurance extended the open scope of the life insurance market in 1996. Manulife got a license and set up the first life insurance Sino–foreign joint venture, Zhong Hong, in Shanghai. At the end of 1996, there were eight nationwide insurance companies and thirteen regional companies (five Chinese companies, one Chinese–foreign joint venture, and seven branch companies of foreign insurers). By this time, it is safe to assert, the insurance market of China had taken shape and was entering a phase of intense competition.

In 1998, the Chinese government established the specialized insurance regulatory ministry China Insurance Regulatory Commission (CIRC), which took over regulation from the People's Bank of China (PBC). This changed the situation in which insurance was only a minute part of the Chinese financial system receiving less policy attention. It was a milestone in Chinese insurance regulation and accelerated insurance development greatly.

In 2001, China formally joined the WTO. Based on the Chinese government's promises, China would open the market for life insurance, non-life insurance, reinsurance, and insurance brokerage gradually and would cancel almost all limitations on the admittance and business scope in the following three to five years. The Chinese insurance market was becoming more and more a part of the world insurance market.

In 2003, an important achievement happened in the restructuring of state-owned insurance companies, which was regarded as the key step to increasing Chinese national insurance companies' competitive ability. PICC, China Life, and China Re completed the process of reorganization. PICC was restructured as PICC Holding Company, which promoted and held the PICC property. China Life was restructured as China Life (Group) Company and China Life Insurance Stock Limited Company. The former continued operating the policies issued before 1999, while the latter took over policies after 1999 and operated new business. China Re was renamed China Reinsurance (Group) Company, which established three subsidiaries, China P&C Reinsurance, China Life Reinsurance, and China Continent Property Insurance Company Limited.

Moreover, PICC (Holding) and China Life (Group) established their own asset management companies. It was a big breakthrough in the insurance asset and investment management system.

Before the three insurance groups reorganized, Pacific Insurance (Group) Company and Ping An Insurance (Group) had restructured, in 2001 and 2002, respectively. Ping An Insurance (Group) Company even purchased a Chinese regional bank in 2004. Chinese insurance companies have made steps in the direction of comprehensive and diversified international insurance.

Moreover, in 2003, PICC Property became the first Mainland Chinese insurance company to be listed on the Hong Kong Stock Exchange (HKSE) (ref. no. 2328), with a market value of HK$4,226 million. On December 17, 2003, China Life Insurance Co., Ltd. got its stocks listed on the New York Stock Exchange (No. LFC) and traded on the HKSE (No. 2628). The overseas financing scale of China Life Insurance reached $3.5 billion, hitting the top fund-raising volume in the global capital market in 2003. Ping An Insurance (Group) Company Limited was also successfully listed on the HKSE in 2004. These developments show that Chinese insurance companies were trying to join the world market system.

12.1.5 SUMMARY OF HISTORICAL DEVELOPMENT

We can understand more on the development of Chinese insurance with the growth of the Chinese economy and society through examining Table 12.2.

12.2 CURRENT PARAMETERS

Chinese insurance kept developing in high speed in 2005–2006. The premium revenue in Chinese insurance market was 493.13 billion RMB, increasing by 11.3% compared with the previous year. The insurance density was 2.7 in 2005 and the insurance penetration was 376.81 yuan RMB, increasing by around 13.5% from 2004.

12.2.1 LIFE INSURANCE AS THE MAIN TYPE OF CHINESE INSURANCE

Of total premiums in 2005, property insurance business produced 370.01 billion RMB, life insurance business produced 324.69 billion RMB, health insurance business produced 31.18 billion RMB, and causal and accident insurance business produced 14.14 billion RMB, registering a growth of 13.03%, 14.57%, 14.07%, 15.02%, and 20.27% over the previous year 2004, respectively, see Figure 12.1.

Life insurance did not grow as quickly as property insurance; this was the first time since life insurance total premiums exceeded property insurance premiums in 1996. The reason was that companies adjusted the life insurance business structure. Sales of products with a short term, a single premium, and a large savings portion shrank, while long-term products with annualized premiums were promoted. This affected the earned premium but increased future revenues. Still, life insurance still accounted for around two-thirds of the total market.

TABLE 12.2   Insurance Density and Insurance Depth of China (1980–1995) and Premium Revenues from 1980 to 2004/5

Items\Year	Premium income (RMB100M)	(GDP)	Total population (m)	GDP per capital (yuan)	Insurance density (yuan/person)	Insurance depth (% of GDP)
1980	4.6	4517.8	9.87	458	0.47	0.10%
1981	7.8	4862.4	10.00	486	0.78	0.16%
1982	10.3	5294.7	10.17	521	1.01	0.19%
1983	13.2	5934.5	10.30	576	1.28	0.22%
1984	20.0	7171.0	10.44	687	1.92	0.28%
1985	33.1	8964.4	10.59	846	3.13	0.37%
1986	45.8	10,202.2	10.75	949	4.26	0.45%
1987	71.1	11,962.5	10.93	1094	6.51	0.59%
1988	109.5	14,928.3	11.10	1345	9.86	0.73%
1989	142.4	16,909.2	11.27	1500	12.64	0.84%
1990	177.9	18,547.9	11.43	1623	15.56	0.96%
1991	235.6	21,617.8	11.58	1867	20.35	1.09%
1992	367.9	26,638.1	11.72	2273	31.39	1.38%
1993	499.6	34,634.4	11.85	2923	42.16	1.44%
1994	600.0	46,759.4	12.01	3893	49.00	1.28%
1995	683.0	58,478.1	12.11	4829	56.39	1.17%
1996	800.7	67,884.6	12.17	5576	65.77	1.18%
1997	1087.4	74,462.6	12.30	6054	88.41	1.46%
1998	1247.3	78,345.2	12.42	6308	100.43	1.59%
1999	1393.2	82,067.5	12.53	6551	111.21	1.70%
2000	1595.9	89,468.1	12.63	7086	126.40	1.78%
2001	2112.3	97,314.8	12.72	7651	166.07	2.17%
2002	3053.1	105,172.3	12.85	8214	237.60	3.00%
2003	3880.4	116,694.0	12.92	9073	287.44	3.33%
2004	4318.1	136,515.0	13.00	10,502	332.19	3.16%

Sources: Almanac of China Insurance 1981–1997, Yearbook of China Insurance (1998, 1999, 2000, 2001, 2002, 2003, 2004).

12.2.2   FEW BIG COMPANIES STILL DOMINATE THE CHINESE INSURANCE MARKET

In 2004, all the property insurance companies produced 112.45 billion RMB in premiums from property insurance, short-term health, and accident insurance business. The growth rate reached 25.86%. Figure 12.2 gives out the market

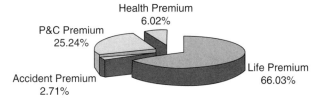

FIGURE 12.1   Distribution of Premium Revenues Between P&C, Life, Health, and Accident Insurance in 2004

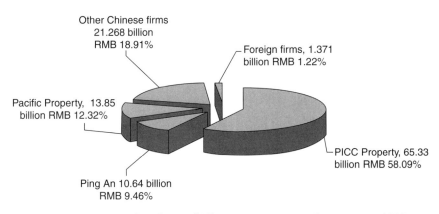

FIGURE 12.2   Market Shares of All Property Insurance Companies in 2004

share of all property insurance companies in 2004, we can see that of total premiums, the three biggest companies held 79.87%, including PICC Property's share of 58.09% with 65.33 billion RMB in premiums, Pacific Property's share of 12.32% with 13.89 billion RMB in premiums, Ping An Property's share of 9.46% with 10.64 RMB billion in premiums.

In 2004, all the life insurance companies produced 319.36 billion RMB in premiums from life, health, and accident insurance business. The growth rate reached 6.92% of the total premiums, the three biggest companies held 83.15%, including China Life Stock Ltd.'s share of 55.17% with 176.18 billion RMB in premiums, Ping An Life's share of 17.18% with 54.88 billion RMB in premiums, and Pacific Life's share of 10.8% with 34.49 RMB billion RMB in premiums. All the Chinese domestic life insurance companies realized premiums of 310.92 billion RMB, increasing by 6.17% and sharing 97.36% of the total, while foreign insurance companies realized premiums of 8.43 billion RMB, increasing by as much as 37.74% and sharing 2.64% of the total.

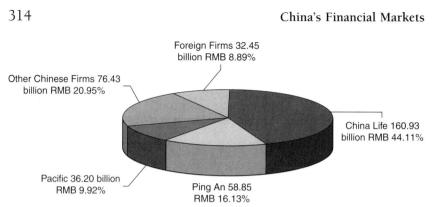

FIGURE 12.3   Market Shares of Life Insurance Companies in 2005

PICC Property, China Life, Ping An, and Pacific were the companies with the longest histories and the largest national branch networks. Most other companies were new and only operated business in limited regions. This was a sound reason why the top three companies could share such a high percentage in China. The big companies' shares had been decreasing steadily for 10 years and this trend would continue as new companies developed. But most admit that the Chinese insurance market still needed time to develop into a more mature market with a balanced structure. Market shares of insurance companies is shown in Figure 12.3.

12.2.3   CHINESE DOMESTIC INSURANCE COMPANIES VERSUS FOREIGN INSURANCE COMPANIES

We can also conclude, from Tables 12.2 and 12.3 that the domestic Chinese insurance companies dominated the market. Foreign insurance companies realized 9.8 billion RMB in premium revenues in 2004 and shared only 2.3% of the total. Among property insurance companies, foreign companies realized 1.37 billion RMB in premiums and shared 1.22% of the market while domestic Chinese companies owned 111.08 billion RMB and 98.78%. Among life insurance companies, foreign companies realized 8.43 billion RMB in premiums and shared 2.64% of the market, while domestic Chinese companies owned 310.92 billion RMB and 97.3%.

On the other hand, we must note that foreign insurance companies developed very fast in 2004. Total premiums of foreign companies increased by 45.7% over the previous year, a much higher-than-average growth rate of 11.3%. Foreign property insurance companies realized premium growth of 52.08%, and foreign life insurance companies realized growth of 37.74%, both much higher than the domestic Chinese partners, whose growth rates were 25.6% and 2.64%, respectively. The high acceleration also pushed up their market share a lot as compared with 1.7% in 2003.

Foreign companies' small market share may partly have been caused by the policy that limited foreign companies to certain cities before. In the opened cities, foreign companies' shares were not bad. For example, in Shanghai and Guangzhou, their market shares were already as big as 15.3% and 8.2%, respectively. When the policy expired at the end of 2004, foreign companies' share would be expected to continue to increase.

The total assets held by insurance companies at the end of 2004 came to 1.185 trillion RMB, 273.07 billion RMB, and 29.93% larger than at the beginning of that year. This was also the first time that total Chinese insurance assets exceeded 1 trillion. Together, foreign companies held 29.37 billion RMB in assets, or 2.48% of the total.

12.2.4   REGIONAL IMBALANCES

Generally speaking, Chinese insurance developed better in the eastern regions than in the western regions. This was consistent with the Chinese economic and social situations, in which eastern costal regions were much more developed than western inland regions. In 2004, the top five provinces that produced the most total premiums among China's 31 provinces, municipalities, and autonomous regions were all located in the eastern coastal region. (Taiwan's premium was not counted.) The top five were Jiangsu Province, Guangdong Province, Shandong Province, Shanghai City, and Zhejiang Province, with 41.97, 34.37, 31.82, 30.33, and 29.03 billion RMB in premiums, respectively. These five regions produced 167.52 billion RMB in premiums in total, which equaled 38.79% of total premiums from all around China in 2004. Meanwhile, the premiums of the 12 western inland provinces totaled 67.23 billion RMB, which equaled only 15.57% of the total.

12.2.5   FULLY OPENED CHINESE INSURANCE MARKET

December 11, 2004 was the three-year anniversary of China's entry into the WTO. It was also the deadline for the Chinese government to open its insurance market completely. In accordance with these agreements about insurance, the Chinese government canceled the limits on business area and business scope. Foreign branches and sino-foreign joint ventures could set up branches, and operate all around China through joint ventures, without limit if qualified to set up. And the joint ventures could provide every kind of insurance service to Chinese or foreign citizens, including health insurance, group insurance, pensions, and annuities. Foreign property insurance companies could set up branches directly and operate without limit to area or scope.

Thus foreign insurance companies could enter the Chinese market more easily and freely. Four new foreign companies started operation in the Chinese market in 2004. And many joint ventures prepared to operate pension, group insurance, and health insurance business. These new players and new business operation modes may change not only the business competition but also the Chinese insurance market environment. We can expect great growth and significant change in the Chinese market in the next few years.

12.3   MARKET PLAYERS

According to Chinese law and regulations, insurance companies in China can be fully state owned, limited, or stocked limited. Most domestic insurance companies were stocked-limited companies. PICC (Holding), China Life (Group), China Re (Group), China Export Credit, and China United Property were fully state-owned companies. And most Sino–foreign joint ventures were limited companies, because they usually had only two promoters. We must also mention that in 2004 CIRC approved mutual agricultural insurance companies to operate. This was based on *The Insurance Law*, whereby agricultural insurance could follow a governmental special agricultural policy. It was a big breakthrough on insurance company form in China.

Insurance companies operating in China were allowed to have foreign financial institutions as shareholders and to be regulated as a foreign company or a domestic one, based on the total share proportion held by foreign institutions. If the proportion was less than 25%, the insurance company would be treated as a domestic Chinese insurance company; otherwise it was treated as a foreign insurance company. But a Chinese insurance company would be exempt from this regulation when it was listed on a foreign stock exchange, which means that a Chinese insurance company can have more than 25% shares (less than 50%) held by foreign public investors through a foreign stock exchange.

As of the end of 2004, there were five insurance group or holding companies and 68 insurance companies in the Chinese market. Thirty-two of them were Chinese insurance companies and 37 were foreign companies, including joint ventures and foreign insurance branches. Among the domestic companies, 18 companies operated property insurance, 11 companies operated life insurance, and 2 companies operated reinsurance. Among the foreign companies, 13 companies operated property insurance, 21 companies operated life insurance, and 3 companies operated reinsurance.

Eight new domestic companies and four foreign companies started operation in the Chinese market in 2004. Moreover, 2 insurance group companies,

22 domestic companies, and 3 foreign companies were approved to be in preparation by CIRC in 2004.

Specialized insurance companies were approved by CIRC in 2004. The first specialized agricultural insurance company, the first specialized auto insurance company, and the first specialized pension company came into operation. Five specialized health insurance companies came into preparation.

At the end of 2005 almost all kinds of insurance companies were in the Chinese insurance market. Considering insurance intermediary companies and insurance investment companies as well, we can summarize market player categories in Chinese as follows:

- Life insurance companies, providing life, accident, health, and annuity insurance.
- Property insurance companies, providing auto, marine, property, liability, and agricultural insurance. After the modification of *The Insurance Law* in 2003, property insurance companies could provide short-term health insurance and accident insurance.
- Specialized insurance companies, such as health insurance companies, pension companies, auto insurance companies, and agricultural insurance companies.

  - Health insurance companies, providing medical, hospital, disability, disease, and long-term care insurance.
  - Pension companies, providing enterprise annuities and pensions.
  - Agricultural insurance companies, mainly providing agricultural insurance, with other property insurance as well.
  - Auto insurance companies, mainly providing auto insurance, with other property insurance as well.

- Reinsurance companies, providing P&C, life, health, and reinsurance business.
- Insurance intermediary companies, including brokers, agency companies, and insurance loss adjusters.
- Insurance investment management companies, managing the insurance companies' investment.

12.3.1 LIFE INSURANCE COMPANIES

There were 32 life insurance companies operating in the Chinese market in total as of the end of 2004, including two specialized pension companies (see Table 12.3).[1]

---

[1] All AIA branches were counted as one company.

TABLE 12.3   Chinese Life Insurance Companies

Index	Company name	Operating region	Registered capital (100 million)
1	China Life Insurance (Group)	Nationwide	
2	China Life Insurance Co., Ltd.	Nationwide	200
3	China Ping An Life Insurance Co., Ltd.	Nationwide	24.67 (Group)
4	China Pacific Insurance Co., Ltd.	Nationwide	43 (Group)
5	New China Life Insurance Co., Ltd.	Nationwide	12
6	Taikang Life Insurance Co., Ltd.	Nationwide	8
7	Taiping Life Insurance Co., Ltd.	Nationwide	10
8	Minsheng Life Insurance Co., Ltd.	Nationwide	8.73
9	Sino Life Insurance Company Ltd.	Nationwide	13.58
10	Ping An Pension Co., Ltd.	Nationwide	
11	Taiping Pension Co., Ltd.	Nationwide	
12	Zhonghong Life Insurance Co., Ltd.	Shanghai,Guangzhou, Beijing	5
13	Pacific-Antai Life insurance Company Limited	Shanghai, Guangzhou	5
14	Allianz Dazhong Insurance Co., Ltd.	Shanghai	2
15	AXA-Minmetals Assurance Company Limited	Shanghai, Guangzhou	5
16	CITIC–Prudential Life Insurance Company Ltd.	Shanghai, Beijing	5
17	China Life–CMG Life Assurance Company Ltd.	Shanghai	2
18	John Hancock Tianan Life Insurance Company	Shanghai	2
19	Generali China Life Insurance Co., Ltd.	Guangzhou, Beijing	5
20	Sun Life Everbright Life Insurance Co., Ltd.	Tianjin,Beijing	5
21	ING Capital Life Insurance Company Limited	Dalian	5
22	Haier New York Life Insurance Company Ltd.	Shanghai	2
23	AVIVA-COFCO Life Insurance Co., Ltd.	Guangzhou	5
24	CMG-CIGNA Insurance Company	Shanghai	2
25	Nissay-SVA Life Insurance Co., Ltd.	Shanghai	3
26	AEGON-CNOOC Life Insurance Company Ltd.	Shanghai	2
27	Heng An Standard Life Insurance Company Limited	Tianjin	13.02
28	Skandia-bsam Co., Ltd.	Beijing	2
29	Sino-US Metlife Life Insurance Company Ltd.	Beijing, ChongQing	5
30	Sino-France Life Insurance Company Ltd.	Beijing	2
31	Cathay Life insurance Comapny Ltd.	Shanghai	2
32	AIA branches	Shanghai, Guangzhou, Shenzhen, Beijing, Suzhou, Foshan, Jiangmen, Dongguan	

12.3.2   PROPERTY INSURANCE COMPANIES

There were 31 total property insurance companies operating in the Chinese market as of the end of 2004, including some auto insurance companies and agricultural insurance companies (see Table 12.4).[2]

12.4   REINSURANCE COMPANIES

There were five reinsurance companies operating in the Chinese market in total as of the end of 2004 (see Table 12.5).

12.5   BROKERS AND AGENCIES

There were 1,317 insurance intermediary companies at the end of 2004, including 920 agency companies, 199 brokers, and 181 insurance loss adjusters. And there were more than 110,000 sideline institutes providing agency business.

There were six firms that had foreign shares. Details are shown in Table 12.6.

There were four insurance investment management companies in charge of investment operation and asset management for the insurance companies within the same insurance group: China Life Investment Management Company, PICC Investment Management Company, China Reinsurance Investment Management Company, and HuaTai Investment Management Company. The first two opened in 2003 and the latter two at the end of 2004. Another investment management company was in preparation at the end of 2004.

12.5.1   LIFE INSURANCE PRODUCTS

Chinese insurance product genres also expanded very fast, as an obvious symbol of insurance development. In 2004, almost all insurance product genres were in the Chinese market. Two main factors resulted in this situation. First, rapid economic development increased people's demand for more insurance

---

[2]Group and holding were counted in, because they did not directly operate business. All branches from the same companies were counted once.

TABLE 12.4   Non-Life Insurance Companies

		Established
1	PICC Property and Casualty Company, Ltd.	2003.6
	PICC Holding Company	1949.1
2	China Pacific Property Insurance Co., Ltd.	2001.4
	China Pacific Insurance (Group) Co., Ltd.	1991.4
3	Ping An Insurance Company of China, Ltd.	.2002.10
	Ping An Insurance (Group) Company of China, Ltd.	1988.3
4	Huatai Insurance Company of China, Ltd.	1996.8
5	Tianan Insurance Company Limited of China	1994.1
6	Da Zhong Insurance Company, Ltd.	1995.1
7	Sinosafe General Insurance Company, Ltd.	1996.1
8	Yong An Property Insurance Company, Ltd.	1996.8
9	China United Property Insurance Company	1986.7
10	Tai Ping Insurance Company, Ltd.	2001.12
11	China Continent Property & Casualty Insurance Company, Ltd.	2003.9
12	Alltrust Insurance Company of China, Limited	2004.9
13	Shanghai AnXin Agricultural, Insurance Co., Ltd.	2004.9.10
14	AnBang Property & Casualty Insurance Co., Ltd.	2004.9.30
15	AnHua Agricultural Insurance Co., Ltd.	2004.12
16	Sunlight Agricultural Mutual Insurance Company	2004.12
17	TianPing Auto Insurance Co., Ltd.	2004.12
18	China Export & Credit Insurance Corporation	2001.1
19		
20	The Tokio Marine and Fire Insurance Co., Ltd., Shanghai Branch	1994.7
21	American International Underwriters Insurance Co., Branches of Shanghai	1992.9
	American International Underwriters Insurance Co., Branches of Guangzhou	1995.9
	American International Underwriters Insurance Co., Branches of Shenzhen	1999.9
	American International Underwriters Insurance Co., Branches of Foshan	1999.9
22	Royal & Sun Alliance PLC-Shanghai Branch	1998.9
23	Winterthur Insurance Ltd., Shanghai Branch	1997.5
24	The Ming An Insurance Co(Chian) Ltd., Shanghai Branch	1981.12
	The Ming An Insurance Co(Chian) Ltd., Haikou Branch	1988.1
25	Federal Insurance Company, Shanghai Branch	2000.8
26	Mitsui Sumitomo Insurance Co., Ltd., Shanghai Branch	2001.4
27	Samsung Fire & Marine Insurance Co., Ltd., Shanghai Branch	2001.4
28	Bank of China Insurance Co., Ltd.	2001.1
29	Allianz Insurance Company Guangzhou Branch	2002.12
30	Sompo Japan Insurance (China) Co., Ltd.	2003.5
31	Liberty Mutual Insurance Company, Chongqing Branch	2003.11
32	Groupma S.A., Chengdu Branch	2004.8.30

Source: Sompo Japan Insurance Inc

TABLE 12.5   Reinsurance Companies

No.	Name	Date established time	Form	Capital
1	China Life Reinsurance Com.	2003.12.2	Shareholder	8
2	China Property Reinsurance Com.	2003.12.2	Shareholder	8
3	unich Reinsurance Company, Beijing Branch	2003.6	Branch	300 m
4	Swiss Reinsurance Company, Beijing Branch	2003.9	Branch	300 m
5	Cologne Reinsurance Company plc, Shanghai Branch	2004.5.25	Branch	300 m

TABLE 12.6   Brokers

Name of firm	Established	Foreign stakes
Marsh Insurance and Risk Management Consultants, Ltd.	1993	100%
Huatai Insurance Brokers Co., Ltd.	Mar. 1993	25%
Aon-COFCO Insurance Brokers Co., Ltd.	Oct. 2003	50%
Willis Pudong Insurance Brokers Co., Ltd.	Aug. 2001 (Aug. 2004, j.u.)	50%
Pierre Leong Adjusters Co., Ltd.	Sept. 2002	100%
GAB Robins China, Ltd.	Feb. 2004	100%

services, which triggered product innovation. Second, open policy accelerated the speed of innovation. Foreign insurance companies often introduced their successful products to other areas in the Chinese market. Chinese insurance companies also paid a lot of attention to learning from other developed markets, such as those of the United States and Europe or from areas with a similar culture such as Taiwan and Hong Kong. The Chinese insurance market, in just the past 10 years, completed what took more than 50 years of product development to be completed in other areas. Of course, Chinese insurance companies must adjust these imported product genres to fit the Chinese market environment, and this might take a much longer time.

On the other hand, product innovation also promoted insurance operation and company competence. The tide of life insurance product innovation around the end of the last century was especially regarded as the main momentum of

Chinese life insurance's second boom, if individual agent marketing is treated as the first.

In 2004, CIRC reformed life insurance regulation. Most product genres no longer need to be approved before sales according to the new regulations. Relaxing product regulation gave more freedom to life insurance companies on product innovation.

Before 1999, life insurance products in the Chinese market simply followed traditional insurance styles, mainly on two points: (1) the fixed pricing factors, including interest rate, which meant the value of the insurance policy was guaranteed by insurance companies; (2) the mixture of guarantee liability and value aggregation that led to scanty transparency.

During that time, the assumed interest rate of insurance policies was extremely high. In 1988, the assumed interest rate of life insurance topped 8.8% and was 7.5% by 1997, even for such long-term life insurance as whole life insurance products. But in 1996, the People's Bank of China decreased the rate seven consecutive times, when the five-year term rate plunged to 2.88% in 1999 from 13.68% in 1996 and the one-year term rate was slashed from 10.98% to 2.25%. Correspondingly, return on investment of insurance companies fell, even a lot lower than the assumed interest rate of insurance policies, so margin deficits occurred to high-assumed-interest-rate life insurance products.

On June 10, 1999, in case of more margin losses, CIRC set a ceiling of 2.5% for the assumed interest rate of new life insurance products. The decline in assumed interest rate degraded the possibility of new margin losses but, on the other hand, double-hiked the premiums of life insurance and blocked the way to market expansion. It was hard for traditional life insurance products to survive. Then a new tide of innovation began.

In October 1999, Ping An Insurance Company provoked others to provide a unit-linked insurance product, a European product genre similar to U.S. universal variable products, with an unbundled insurance function and investment function. Policy value was nonguaranteed and reflected the new money yield rate. Policyholders undertook all the investment profits and risks.

In March 2000, AIA Shanghai, China Life, and Zhong Hong Life Insurance companies began to release participating insurance that had nonguaranteed dividend as an adjustment for policy value.

In August 2000, Pacific Insurance issued universal life insurance in Beijing and Shanghai. This product guaranteed certain benefits, provided a flexible premium-paying structure, related insured amount, and cash value partly with return on investment.

All theses new products included some nonguaranteed value partly or totally, depending on the actual investment, which was the feature distinguishing it from the traditional products. Participating insurance, unit-linked insurance, and universal life insurance products were classified into a new group, called a new-pattern life insurance product in China.

New-pattern life insurance products mitigated or rooted out the interest risk totally assumed by insurance companies, more adjustable to the fluctuation of market interest rates. Meanwhile, the new product brought about added value due to the market investment for policyholders, like something that deserved investing, appealing to policyholders. Moreover, new-pattern products forced the Chinese life insurance companies to improve operation and management in all areas, for instance, IT system, information disclosure, marketing, and investment.

The new-pattern life insurance products were well received and surged in the market, and soon they became the mainstream in the life insurance area. In 2002, they captured overall revenue of 122.51 billion RMB, accounting for 53.86% of all premiums. The new-pattern life insurance product has definitely become a highlight and a hot issue in underwriting.

Later, misleading emerged as a problem on new-pattern life insurance products. Many were sold as investment products to customers who just wanted to make money without assuming investment risk. Because the investment market did not perform as well as expected in the past few years, many new-pattern life insurance products, especially unit-linked life insurance products, did not meet policyholders' expectation. Many policyholders even tried to surrender their policy. This impaired the goodness of new-pattern life insurance products. Insurance companies then adjusted their product portfolio, paid more attention to the protective function of life insurance products, developed a balance of traditional products and new-pattern products, and improved sales conduct management. Life insurance products moved into a more rational and mature development orbit.

In 2004, new-pattern life insurance products realized premiums of 185.2 billion RMB, increasing by 1.16% over 2003, while traditional products realized premiums of 137.58 billion RMB, increasing by 12.08%. New-pattern products shared 57.4% of the total premiums from life insurance companies.

Among the new-pattern life products in 2004, participating products were provided by almost all of the life insurance companies and realized premiums of 176.05 billion RMB, which accounted for 95% of the total premiums from new-pattern products. Unit-linked products were provided by 12 life insurance companies, realizing premiums of 5.29 billion RMB, a decrease of 12.4%. Universal products were provided by six life insurance companies, realizing premiums of 3.8 billion RMB, an increase by as much as 91.3%. Ping An and AIA began to provide universal products recently, and these grew very quickly, together occupying 76.9% of the universal life insurance market.

The total number of new life insurance products in 2004 was 245, with traditional life product, participating product, unit-linked product, and universal product showing the numbers 146, 69, 17, and 12, respectively. Moreover, there were two unit-with-profit (UWP) products introduced into the Chinese market by Standard Life from the United Kingdom. The new product genre had a guaranteed interest rate, gave an expected dividend scale, and provided a retrospective dividend. It also priced the value with a unit number and a unit value.

Summing up, traditional life products and participating life products dominated the life insurance market in 2004. Universal life resumed high-speed development. And UWP as a new product genre came into the market.

The foregoing popular products had one feature in common: They provided at least some guaranteed policy value. This might be because Chinese customers still preferred some guaranteed return and retained some risk-averse psychology when choosing life insurance products. Life insurance products must fit the customers' psychology and the whole market circumstance, including investment market circumstance.

12.5.2 HEALTH INSURANCE PRODUCTS

Health insurance products included medical insurance products, disease insurance products, and disability income products, according to CIRC's classification criteria. Medical insurance products provided medical reimbursement, disease insurance product provided some predetermined compensation amount in the case of certain diseases, and disability income products provided a certain amount of money with a certain frequency during the time the insured was disabled or in the hospital.

In 2005, health insurance products realized total premiums of 31.19 billion RMB, accounting for 6.3% of total premiums. There were 440 new health insurance products released from life insurance companies, much more than the 259 in 2003. And property insurance companies also provided short-term health insurance products.

In the Chinese health insurance market, disease insurance products and hospital income products were popular. These products just provided predetermined compensation amounts, which were not related to the actual medical costs in the hospital. Because Chinese medical insurance was almost always based on a fee-for-service reimbursement mode, insurance companies had little control over hospital medical costs. Under current circumstances, medical insurance faced a high moral risk and had a very high loss ratio. Thus, many insurance companies preferred such predetermined amount products as disease insurance and hospital income insurance products.

Insurance companies also provided supplemental medical group insurance products that linked up with basic social medical insurance provided by the government. These products often insured the amount beyond the ceiling limit of basic social insurance. Insurance companies sometimes covered all the people with basic social insurance in a city or district, which quickly became huge in size of both insured people and premiums. That was the main attraction of this product to the insurance companies. But it was still very difficult to control the medical costs and the moral risk. High loss ratio was the biggest challenge for this product.

Managing medical costs was the key to expanding the scope of the health insurance product and improving business quality. Many insurance companies were researching the managed care method from the United States. Reform of the medical system and construction of a total medical protection system would be the most important external factor to health insurance development.

Moreover, a few insurance companies started to try administration services in the health insurance area as a third-party administrator (TPA). Because the current law did not stipulate this service clearly, many companies designed these TPA contracts to be similar to group medical insurance products, without any actual risk insured. TPA service could be an important new service genre in the health insurance area in the future.

12.5.3   PROPERTY INSURANCE PRODUCTS

Property insurance companies provided many kinds of products, covering auto, household, enterprise, transportation, credit, and liability insurance, in addition to short-term health and causal insurance products. In 2004, more than 1,400 products got approved or filed.

Auto insurance was one of the most important property insurance products. In 2005, auto insurance products realized premiums of 85.79 billion yuan RMB, increasing by 14.24% over 2004. Auto premiums accounted for 69.68% of total property premiums. More than 60 new auto insurance products were approved by CIRC in 2004. Auto insurance mainly included auto loss insurance and auto liability insurance. Auto liability insurance was mandatory in China, and most insurance companies designed mandatory auto liability products under the guidance of CIRC.

In recent years, some property insurance companies have begun to develop new-pattern property products, following the life insurance companies. These new-pattern property products contained an investment account with value reflecting the investment yield, and the pure property premium was deducted from this account. In 2004, 11 more new-pattern property products came from three companies into market, including 10 unit-liked products and 1 savings-like product. More time is needed to determine whether these products can become successful or popular.

12.6   MARKETING CHANNELS

Before the 1990s, Chinese insurance was almost exclusively property insurance and relied on the direct sales method. Insurance company staff went to the enterprises and other clients to sell insurance products. When AIA came to Shanghai in 1992, the individual agency marketing method for individual life products was introduced into China. Life insurance took off and grew swiftly based on the individual agent marketing channel, and individual agents became a prime marketing channel in the Chinese insurance market.

Not only did the individual agent method grow up very quickly, but some institutions began providing agents as a sideline business, which soon developed into an important channel. As auto insurance began expanding, auto dealers became a more important channel, especially for property insurance, because they were selling most new car insurance. Banks started to sell life insurance products as agents at the end of the 1990s, and this developed in a very short time into a very important channel for life insurance. The bank channel has produced almost one-third of total life insurance premiums in recent years.

Chinese insurance was developing more and more marketing channels. One insurance company usually utilized several channels at the same time, with different business lines focusing on different channels. Recently, some life insurance companies have been trying to integrate the channels in order to achieve higher marketing efficiency.

Figure 12.4 presents the distribution of premiums among the marketing channels in 2004.

12.6.1   AGENT CHANNEL

The word *agent* here means individual agents or salespeople directly connected with an insurance company. Most agents worked exclusively for one insurance company. They did not belong to an independent agency.

The agent channel is currently the most important channel, especially for life insurance. In 2004, life insurance captured 147.16 billion RMB in premiums through the agent channel, which equaled 54.45% of total life insurance premiums.

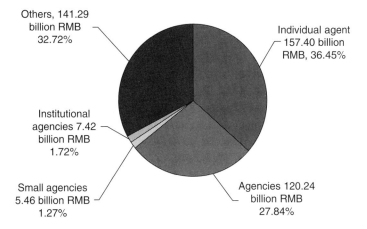

Others, 141.29 billion RMB 32.72%

Individual agent 157.40 billion RMB, 36.45%

Institutional agencies 7.42 billion RMB 1.72%

Small agencies 5.46 billion RMB 1.27%

Agencies 120.24 billion RMB 27.84%

FIGURE 12.4 Premium Distribution Among the Various Marketing Channels, 2004

As of December 31, 2004, the total number of agents was 1.34 million, 5% higher than the previous year. And on average, each agent produced 117,142 RMB in premiums in 2004. The number of agents and amount of premiums produced per agent in the top 10 provinces, ranked by premium from each agent channel, is given in Table 12.7.

Many agents were just lower-level salespeople. They were not well trained, faced heavy pressure from premium requirements, and cared most about their commission. The agent lapse rate was very high. Improvement and better management were needed in the agent channel. In 2004, some insurance companies began trying to cultivate high-quality, better-educated agents. For example, the Sino–MetLife Insurance Company recruited agents with a college background, trained them intensively, and provided a decent base salary in order to reach the better-educated customer market.

12.6.2 BANK AND OTHER SIDELINE INSTITUTIONAL AGENTS

Many institutions help insurance companies sell insurance using their own customer resources. This sideline institutional agent channel become more and more significant in China. In 2004, there were 114,935 institutions with a sideline agency license earning 4.61 billion RMB in commissions. Banks, post offices, and auto dealers were the most prominent representatives in this channel. In 2004, there were 76,437 bank branches, 12,927 post offices, and 11,640 auto dealers registered as a sideline institutional agents, earning 1.99, 0.36, and 0.93 billion RMB in commissions, respectively.

TABLE 12.7   Number of Agents and Amount of Premiums Produced by Agents, Dec. 31, 2004

Ranking	Area	Average premium per person (yuan/person)	Number of salesmen (persons)	Premium from agent(000,00 yuan)
1	Jiang Su	126,736	137,500	1,742,624
2	Guang Dong	197,260	64,357	1,269,506
3	Zhe Jiang	170,197	67,061	1,141,355
4	Shanghai	284,807	37,125	1,057,348
5	He Bei	110,561	89,146	985,604
6	Hu Bei	152,564	58,579	893,704
7	He Nan	69,663	124,398	866,600
8	Hu Nan	121,874	55,879	681,020
9	Si Chaun	106,426	62,623	666,472
10	Beijing	137,751	46,516	640,763

Banks had become one of the most vital channels, selling mostly life insurance products as agents of the life insurance companies. In 2004, the bank channel produced 79.48 billion RMB in insurance premiums, which equaled 24.85% of total life insurance premiums. Most products sold via the bank channel were participating endowments with a term of 5 or 10 years. These insurance products had a very strong savings characteristic and were similar to bank deposit products, but with longer term and a little higher interest rate. Thus a bank's customers could easily sign up for these insurance products, and the banks could become a very good marketing channel.

12.6.3   INSURANCE INTERMEDIARY COMPANIES

The insurance intermediary channel includes mainly agency companies and brokers. In 2004, agency companies produced 5.463 billion RMB in premiums, or 1.27% of total premiums. Of these, 3.732 billion RMB were property insurance premiums and 1.731 billion RMB were life insurance premiums, which represented 3.5% of total P&C premiums and 0.5% of total life insurance premiums.

Agency companies earned 533 million RMB in commissions in 2004, which included 441 million and 92.3 million RMB in commissions from P&C and life insurance, respectively.

In 2004, brokers produced 7.42 billion RMB in premiums, or 1.72% of total premiums. Of these, 3.89 billion RMB were P&C premiums and 3.378 billion RMB were life insurance premiums, which represented 3.57% of total P&C

premiums and 1.05% of total life insurance premiums. Brokers also produced 149 million RMB in reinsurance premiums and consulting fees.

Brokers earned 581.76 million RMB in commissions and 111.71 million RMB in consulting fees in 2004. Total revenue increased by 56% over the previous year. When separating the revenues by business line, property insurance commissions, life insurance commissions, reinsurance commissions, and consulting fees were 567.55 million, 62.62 million, 5.73 million, and 57.57 million RMB, respectively.

Neither agency companies nor brokers channel played an important role in the Chinese market, producing less than 3% of total premiums together. The main reason might be that insurance intermediatery companies were still young and needed more time to become professional at marketing, not just relying on a relationship with clients. Another characteristic was that P&C insurance utilized this channel more than life insurance. This might be because insurance companies employed a large number of individual agents themselves.

12.6.4   DIRECT MARKETING CHANNEL

Direct sales to groups once was the only channel utilized by Chinese insurance companies. The direct marketing channel remained an important marketing channel, especially for property insurance and group life insurance.

Property insurance business laid particular stress on enterprise customers in China. The usual marketing method was to negotiate with enterprises, directly. Thus direct marketing was an important channel for property insurance business. Maintaining good relationships with important customers was the key in this channel.

Group life insurance traditionally relied on direct marketing. Like property insurance, insurance company staff maintained good relationships with such groups as enterprises, companies, and government bureaus and introduced group life, group health, group accident, and pension products. In 2004, direct marketing staff produced group insurance premiums of 65.6 billion RMB, increasing by 35.4% over the previous year, and captured 20.51% of total life insurance premiums.

Recently, new channels have begun to appear in China. Life insurance companies especially were trying new direct marketing channels. For example, CMB-CIGNA mainly utilized the telemarketing channel, AIA Shanghai once tried broadcast marketing, and Rui Tai (Skandia's joint venture in China) used securities brokers. Moreover, quite a few Chinese insurance companies were selling simple products on the Internet. We can expect more new direct marketing channels to emerge in the near future as individuals show more diversified demands for insurance.

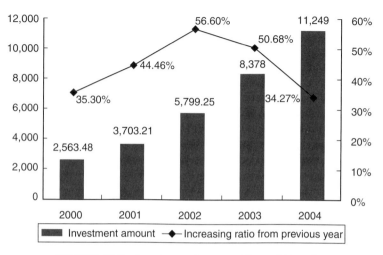

FIGURE 12.5   Investment Assets and Rate of Growth

12.7   INVESTMENT MANAGEMENT

The total assets held or managed by insurance companies have increased a lot, along with revenues since the mid-1990s. As of the end of 2005, total assets had reached 1529.87 billion yuan RMB, increasing by 27.64% over the previous year. In 2004, life insurance companies' assets were 986.94 billion RMB, property insurance companies' assets 144.08 billion RMB, and reinsurance companies' assets 25.39 billion RMB, increasing by 29.69%, 24.12%, and 14.88%, respectively.

Insurance companies' investment assets also kept the accelerating trend in 2004. They rose to 1,124.98 billion RMB at the end of 2004 and increased by 34.27%. Insurance companies' investment amount has been increasing at the average annual rate of 44.29% since 2000. We can see this trend in Figure 12.5.

Of the total amount at the end of 2004, investments in deposit were 287.13 billion RMB, in Treasury bonds 265.17 billion RMB, in financial debt 115.68 billion RMB, and in securities mutual funds 57.5 billion RMB. We can see the proportions of these main investment assets in Figure 12.6.

There are two main points about investment in 2004 worth exploring. First, the distribution of investment assets became more balanced. Previously, investment channels had been strictly limited, and only a few investment products had been available in Chinese financial markets; deposits had always been the most dominant investment asset, well over half of the total in the past. In 2004, the proportion of deposits decreased to below 50%, and bonds increased to 39.11%. Diversified investments mean less risk for the insurance industry.

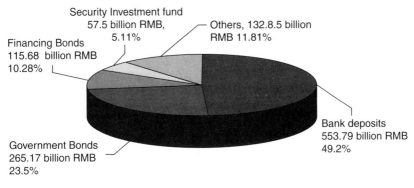

FIGURE 12.6   Distribution of Investment Assets, 2004

The investment asset structure was becoming better in 2004. Second, the insurance investment assets played a more important role in Chinese financial markets. At the end of 2004, insurance companies held 9.4% of issued Treasury bonds, 8.5% of issued finance bonds, 42% of issued enterprise bonds, and 22.06% of issued securities funds. And insurance companies held more than 70% of issued negotiation deposits as well.

12.7.1   New Asset Management Style

Asset management of insurance companies became more and more professional in 2004. In the past, Chinese insurance companies had managed the assets by themselves. This style might have been fit for an investment environment with few investment channels. Insurance companies were not permitted to outsource to general asset management companies. Along with more channels being opened to insurance companies and more assets being needed for dynamic management, some insurance companies tried to set up special subsidiary asset management companies in order to improve efficiency and the yield rate. It was a breakthrough in asset management style when the PICC Asset Management Company and China Life Asset Management Company opened at the end of 2003.

In 2004, CIRC promulgated the *Regulation on Insurance Asset Management Companies*. This not only set out criteria on insurance management companies, but also affirmed this new mode by which insurance assets could be managed by special insurance asset management companies. Insurance asset management companies must be initiated by an insurance company or an insurance group (holding), and at least 70% of its total shares should be held by domestic insurance companies. The insurance asset management company could manage the assets as trustee for the insurance companies that were its shareholders or as another subsidiary of its shareholders. Insurance asset management companies earned management fees from the insurance companies.

At the end of 2004, in accordance with regulation, CIRC approved two more insurance asset management companies: Hua Tai Insurance Asset Management Company and China Re Insurance Asset Management Company. A few others were in the process of applying. We can expect the number of insurance asset management companies to reach six to eight in the Chinese market.

12.7.2 NEW INVESTMENT CHANNELS

New investment channels became available in 2004, which spurred insurance company investment a lot. In China, investment channels for insurance assets were strictly regulated. The *Law of Insurance*, as modified in 2003, limited the investment channels to bank deposits, Treasury bonds, financial debt, and other channels permitted by the State Department. The strict regulation aimed at avoiding asset risk for insurance companies before the insurance industry had matured enough to manage high risk. But it also objectively limited the room for asset–liability matching at the same time. Later, the Chinese government permitted insurance companies to invest negotiation deposits, interbank loans, and securities mutual funds.

In 2004, the Chinese government continued widening the scope of investment. The following new channels became a reality.

- *Overseas investment*: On August 9, 2004, CIRC and the People's Bank of China (PBC, China's Central Bank) together promulgated the *Provisional Regulation on Overseas Investment of Insurance Foreign Currency*. It first permitted Chinese insurance companies to invest foreign currency in overseas markets, under strict regulation. Foreign currency had to be owned by the company itself, not exchanged from RMB. This was still very useful for the companies that had capital in foreign currency, for example, Sino–foreign joint ventures. PICC, China Life Stocked Ltd., and Ping An financed billions of USD and HKD through IPOs and could also invest that foreign currency in overseas investment markets. Insurance companies had to choose bonds as the main overseas investment asset.
- *Stock investment*: On October 24, 2004, CIRC and the China Securities Regulatory Commission (CSRC) together promulgated the *Provisional Regulation on Insurance Institutional Investors Investing in Stocks*. It permitted insurance companies to invest in stocks directly, whereas in the past, insurance companies could enter the stock market only indirectly

through mutual funds. Insurance companies can participate in both the primary stock market and the secondary market. The proportion invested in stocks was strictly regulated.

- *Convertible bonds and secondary bonds*: In July 2004, CIRC permitted insurance companies to buy convertible bonds. CIRC also permitted insurance companies to invest in secondary bonds and secondary liabilities issued by banks. Later, insurance companies were approved to buy secondary bonds issued by other insurance companies. These investments were treated as financial debt investments, and their proportion was counted into the total bond investment proportion, which had to be within the allowable maximum limits.

For foreign insurance companies, RMB negotiation deposits were opened as an available investment channel in 2004.

Though insurance companies were still looking forward to more investment options, such as infrastructure construction, the main investment channels were available to the insurance industry after 2004. The widened scope of investment gave more options to insurance asset investment and was very good for asset–liability matching (ALM). Of course, the scope of investment would not resolve all problems; the entire Chinese investment environment and insurance companies' ALM ability were more important. For Chinese insurance companies, how to improve their ALM ability was becoming more and more significant, once the policy obstacle to limiting investment had been removed.

12.8 CHALLENGES

The Chinese insurance industry had been developing very rapidly and continually since the mid-1990s. It was still young and not as mature as other developed markets with more than 100 years of history. So it was inevitable that something still needs to be improved in the Chinese insurance industry.

First, the credit system should be improved. Utmost truth was the basic principle of insurance. But the Chinese credit system was under construction, and there was no perfect credit system in the insurance market. So some cases violating the truth principle occurred in the Chinese insurance market. Many of these cases were related to misleading, which impaired the credit of the Chinese insurance industry. A few insurance companies' individual agents exaggerated the investment function or insurance liability of insurance products, in order to induce customers to buy the policies generating higher commissions. These often meant that customers bought products with too high on expectation and little understanding. When claiming or surrendering, customers suddenly found they could get nothing or much less than promised. Several insurance branches even connived at the individual agents' misleading, just for more premiums to complete the revenue goals of the home office. On the other side, some insured tried to cheat insurance companies for underwriting or claims, especially in the health insurance market. Creative medical invoicing for more reimbursement was not unusual. In some sense, customers and insurance companies did not trust each other. Therefore, the lack of a credit system was a big challenge to Chinese insurance's long-term development.

Second, Chinese insurance companies should improve their management further. Insurance companies should pursue long-term and stable development. Chinese insurance companies were not so experienced at operating modern insurance. The interest margin deficit in the second half of the 1990s is an obvious example. From this lesson, Chinese insurance companies, especially life insurance companies, made a lot of progress on company operation, actuarial control, and business management. But there was still a long way to go. Insurance companies must change the operational strategy of caring only about premium amount, learn to control risk, and produce a reasonable profit. Meanwhile, insurance companies should follow the solvency principle and manage capital professionally. Insurance companies should also set up a mature system of corporate management and internal control.

Third, insurance companies should try their best to meet the demands of people and society. With Chinese economic development and societal advancement, more and more insurance demand emerged in China. People needed more pensions, health insurance, and property insurance; enterprises needed more employee benefit plans and liability insurance; the government needed the insurance industry to help construct a medical protection system. The current insurance industry has not totally achieved these goals. This leads to some disadvantages. One is to limit insurance's impact on the whole society. The second is to lose market share to banks, funds, and the like, especially in such common markets as pensions. The third is to let government rely more on social insurance and to compress commercial insurance's space. The fourth is to miss the opportunity to improve if these demands are neglected.

12.9   FUTURE PROSPECTS

In 2004, the Chinese government clearly indicated its desire to construct a harmonious society following ideas of scientific development. The insurance industry would and could play a more important role in society's upgrading. Meanwhile, China fully opened the insurance market, and many big companies went out for IPOs. The Chinese insurance market was joining the international market. This could intensify competition and improve Chinese insurance companies' competence. Moreover, CIRC strengthened solvency regulation and market conduct regulation, coming down on misleading, and promoted insurance innovation. These should lay a more solid foundation for future development.

Looking forward to the further development of the Chinese insurance industry, we can expect the following.

- *Continuing rapid development.* Sound economic development will push continued insurance development. And more potential insurance markets could grow into real opportunities with increasing insurance demand, especially in the large western regions.
- *More players coming into the market.* Many newly approved insurance companies in preparation in 2004 and 2005 will begin to practice. And more foreign insurance companies will set up branches in cities around China. More players means a more balanced market structure, and the market share of the top three will surely decrease.
- *More products and new services appearing in the market.* Competition and more players will let many insurance companies occupy more of a niche market and provide fit products and services for that special market. And newly established specialized insurance companies, such as health insurance companies, auto insurance companies, pension companies, and agricultural insurance companies, must provide special products and service.
- *Marketing channels getting refined.* Individual agents, banks, and group direct marketing should remain the three pillars in the future, but more transformations and refining will happen. Companies should manage individual agents more strictly and segment into different levels for different products and different market fractions, such as special agents for rural markets. Insurance companies will continue trying to establish tighter relationships with banks to decrease commissions and upgrade bank insurance products. More direct marketing methods will be adopted by more insurance companies as well.
- *Investment management becoming more professional.* Most investment channels had been opened to insurance, so insurance companies will pay more attention to ALM and to improving investment management. Investment strategy will become more rational, focusing not only on new money yield, but on long-term return and matching liability.

REFERENCES

Almanac of China Insurance (1981–1997).
Yearbook of Chinese Insurance (1998, 1999, 2000, 2001, 2002, 2003).
Report of Chinese Life Insurance Development (2004).

12.10 APPENDIX: CONTACT INFORMATION FOR RELEVANT INSTITUTIONS

Name	Address	Website	Telephone	Fax	E-mail
CSRC	Focus Place, 19 Jin Rong Street, Xicheng District, Beijing 100032, China	www.csrc.gov.cn	8610–88061000	8610–66210206	csrcweb@publicf.bta.net.cn; intl@csrc.gov.cn
CSDCC	F22–23 Investment Plaza, 27 Jin Rong Street Xicheng District, Beijing 100032, China	www.Chinaclear.com.cn	8610–66210988	8610–66210938	webmaster@Chinaclear.com.cn
SAC	10/F Building B, Tongtai Plaza, 33 Jin Rong Street, Xicheng District, Beijing 100032, China	www.sac.net.cn	8610–88061927	8610–88061121	sac@public.bta.net.cn
CFA	7th Floor, Taiyang Securities Building, No. 34, Fu Wai Da Jie Street, Xicheng District, Beijing 100037, China	www.cfaChina.org	8610–68573109	8610–68571529	cfa@cfaChina.org
Shanghai Stock Exchange	528 Pudongnan Road, Pudong, Shanghai 200120, China	www.sse.com.cn	8621–68808888	8621–68804868	webmaster@secure.see.com.cn
Shenzhen Stock Exchange	5045 Shennan East Road, Shenzhen 518010, China	www.szse.cn	86755–82083333	86755–82083947	cis@szse.cn
Shanghai Futures Exchange	500 Pudian Road, Pudong New Zone, Shanghai 200122, China	www.shfe.com.cn	8621–68400000	8621–68401198	info@shfe.com.cn
Dalian Commodity Exchange	No. 18, Huizhan Road, Dalian 116023, China	www.dce.com.cn	86411–84808888	86411–84808880	dce@mail.dce.com.cn
Zhengzhou Commodity Exchange	69 Weilai Avenue, Zhengzhou 450008, China	www.czse.com.cn	86371–5610069	86371–5613068	zhanglei@czce.com.cn
CIRC	No. 15, Jin Rong Street, 100032, China	www.cirl.gov.cn	8610–66286688		circ.gov.cn

CHAPTER 13

Investment Funds in China

Mu Xianjie
Chief Investment Officer in Golden China Asset Management Company, Shanghai

13.1 HISTORY AND INTRODUCTION

China's investment fund industry is a relative newcomer in comparison to its counterparts in most developed countries, such as the United States and the United Kingdom. But the US$40 billion fund management industry has already experienced various ups and downs.

China's funds industry can trace its roots back to the early 1990s. In October 1991, the first investment fund of China, Nan Shan Risk Investment Fund, was founded by the China Southern Securities Company with a capital of US$9.66 million. The Shenzhen Investment Fund Management Company, the first specialized fund management company in China, was established with a registered capital of US$6.04 million in November 1992. One year later, Shandong Zibo Township Investment Fund was listed on the Shanghai Stock Exchange. It is the first listed close-end fund, with a size of USD12.1 million and a maturity of 8 years.

On November 14, 1997, the China Securities Regulatory Commission (CSRC), the watchdog of the securities and futures markets, issued the "Management Regulation on Securities Investment Funds." This marked the beginning of a new era for the Chinese investment fund industry.

Chinese funds are now invested in the money market, the stock market, and alternative investments.

13.1.1 MONEY MARKET

Investing in the money market is an investment with a low risk. Depositing the funds in the money market for a short period bears interest and provides for liquidity needs. It can bring high returns in periods of high interest and low inflation. In the money market, funds choose the following securities in most cases.

Government bonds. The funds can invest in negotiable securities directly and indirectly guaranteed by the government, including Treasury bonds, government public debts, and other bonds issued by government organs. Such investments are very safe.

Bank acceptance bills and bank time deposit receipts. Such investments have little risk and low returns, but they can ensure the liquidity of the fund assets.

Corporate bonds. Such investments are made to get current returns, and interest is higher than that from government bonds for the same period. Moreover, the floor-limit purchase of such bonds by investors is also higher than that of government bonds, but the risk is also greater.

13.1.2 STOCK MARKET

Just since the early 1990s, China's stock market has developed into Asia's third biggest market, with more than 1,300 listed companies, 4 trillion yuan (US$483 billion) of market capitalization and more than 70 million stock traders.[1] It has been estimated that the market might even become the world's second largest, after the United States, within a decade. The size of Chinese equity market is shown in Figure 13.1.

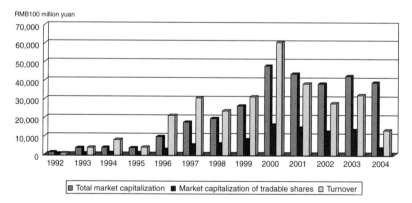

FIGURE 13.1 Comparison of Market Capitalization, Market Capitalization of Tradable Shares, and Turnover (1992–2004)

[1]See Chapters 1 and 7.

The Chinese capital market is not yet mature. Weak fundamentals of the listed companies and systematic flaws in the market have not changed much. Investors are still calling for more transparency, fairness, and chances to get returns in the market. The dominant form of fund investment is in common stocks. The aim of such investment is primarily to seek capital profit and long-term capital increment.

13.1.3 ALTERNATIVE INVESTMENTS

Apart from investment in the money and stock markets, funds can also be invested in futures, real estate, and venture capital. China's futures market, set up in 1990, experienced a rapid expansion into the mid-1990s, when loopholes in the regulatory scheme led to irregularities such as fraud and heavy speculation.[2]

China's total futures trading in 2004 was valued at 14 trillion yuan (US$1.7 trillion), up 45% year-on-year, compared with the previous record of 1.005 billion yuan (US$121.37 million) in 1995 (see Table 13.1). According to the latest figures released by the China Securities Regulatory Commission,

TABLE 13.1 Summary of Futures Trading (1993–2004)

Year	Annual turnover (RMB100 million yuan)	Annual trading volume (10,000 lots)	Annual delivery value (RMB100 million yuan)	Annual delivery volume (10,000 lots)
1993	5,521.99	890.69	—	—
1994	31,601.41	12,110.72	—	—
1995	100,565.30	63,612.07	181.52	83.09
1996	84,119.16	34,256.77	174.13	78.33
1997	61,170.66	15,876.32	93.75	38.18
1998	36,967.24	10,445.57	48.04	20.56
1999	22,343.01	7,363.91	109.41	16.12
2000	16,082.29	5,461.07	65.11	8.40
2001	30,144.98	12,046.35	57.54	64.85
2002	39,490.28	13,943.37	101.44	141.16
2003	108,386.90	27,986.42	127.46	29.10
2004	147,500.30	30,566.76	88.40	65.60

Trading volume involves bilateral calculation, while delivery volume uses unilateral calculation.

[2]See also Chapter 9.

as of the end of 2004 customers' total margin in the futures markets is estimated at more than 20 billion yuan (US$2.41 billion). China's futures market is basically a narrow-banded commodities market. It is still far from certain when China might embrace financial derivative futures such as stock index, bond, and currency futures. According to some estimates, 15–20% of funds in LME are Chinese cross-market arbitrage funds.

The Chinese Mainland's property development market started to come into existence, which makes it more attractive to Chinese investment funds. According to the National Bureau of Statistics, by the end of November 2004, China's housing price had risen 12.5% year-on-year, up 0.8 percentage points from 11.7% in October. The growth rate is even higher in 35 major cities. From December 1, 2002, the developers' own capital stood at 30% of their total investment, 10 percentage points higher than before, while the threshold was further increased to 35% last year. As banks tightened their controls on property development loans, developers had to find new financing channels. Such restrictions on loans seemed to deal a blow to some small property enterprises but offered opportunities to investment funds.

After strenuous efforts in recent years, the legal and political environment for China's venture capital (VC) industry has improved, but the progress still fails to fully meet the requirements for the industry's development. VC was dominated by state-owned companies or organizations. Enterprises and governments were the major sources of capital. Limited partnership and VC units in large companies, two popular forms internationally, still could not be applied in China. With the depression of the VC sector since 2000, the focus of investments shifted to the later stage of a company's development. More than 611 million yuan (US$79.83 million) of investments went to the electronics and information industries, while biotechnology, medicine, and the medical equipment sector attracted 210 million yuan (US$25.36 million).

13.2   SECURITIES INVESTMENT FUNDS

Individual investors have dominated China's securities market since its inception. As of December 31, 2004, a total of 71.06 million securities investment accounts had been opened at the CSDCC. There were 69.45 million A share investor accounts, of which 69.12 million were individual investor accounts and only 330,000 institutional investor accounts, representing 99.52% and 0.48% of the total A share investor accounts, respectively (see Table 13.2).

Here *common institutional investors* refers to legal entities other than securities companies, securities investment funds, QFII, and Social Security funds. In recent years, the CSRC has made further efforts to bolster the growth of

TABLE 13.2   Composition of A Share Securities Investment Accounts as of December 31, 2004

	Shanghai Stock Exchange	Shenzhen Stock Exchange	Total
Total accounts	35,482,669	33,976,031	69,458,700
Common institutional investors	114,850	104,765	219,615
Individual	35,294,885	33,831,584	69,126,469
Securities companies	72,575	39,419	112,094
Securities investment funds	214	201	415
QFII	21	21	42
Social security funds	24	41	65

institutional investors in order to balance out the investors' structure. In recent years, China's fund industry has increased its importance in building the idea of rational investment, guiding the development of a well-ordered market, and functioning as active investors of listed companies.

A Chinese funds management company is a nonbank financial institution that, established with the status of an independent legal person in accordance with laws and regulations, relies on its expertise and experience; respects the regulations of the administrative body and the articles of incorporation or stipulations of the indenture in trust of the fund company; operates the funds in the name of the fund to make investments in all fields open to investment; and seeks to keep increasing the value of the fund assets under its management and to ensure income for holders of the fund shares.

With the promulgation of the *Interim Measures on the Administration of Securities Investment Funds* in October 1997, China's securities investment fund industry began developing faster. In 1998, five contractual closed-end funds were launched. In 2001, the first contractual open-end fund was launched. Since then, the number of funds has grown and the funds have expanded their product mix, such as stock funds, bond funds, index funds, capital guaranteed funds, and money market funds. On June 1, 2002, the CSRC issued *Rules on the Establishment of Fund Management Companies with Foreign-Owned Shares*.

At the end of 2003, there were only 34 fund management companies (including eight Sino–foreign joint ventures) managing 54 closed-end and 56 open-end securities investment funds, with total net assets of RMB169.9 billion yuan under management. However, as of December 2004 there were 45 fund management companies (including eight Sino–foreign joint ventures) managing 170 securities investment funds, with total net assets of RMB330.8 billion yuan under management.

Fund management companies in the market have been scrambling for a larger piece of the pie with the launch of new products such as index funds, guaranteed funds, and money market funds. New fund products, such as Exchange Traded Funds (ETF), also began to trade in China.

Selling Securities Investment Funds

Initially, Chinese residents stood in line to buy mutual funds. But as the number of mutual funds grew, the situation changed. Now fund companies will have to work hard to promote their products and earn investors' trust.

Mutual funds, namely securities investment funds, now mainly depend on the banking system to sell its products. For decades, Chinese residents' assets were largely in the form of bank savings. Bank loans in January 2005 reached 18.11 trillion yuan (2.18 trillion US dollars), rising 14.2 percent year-on-year, but the growth rate was down 5.9% compared with the same period the previous year.

Retailers have become mutual funds' target customers. Although banks may lose some of their depositors to fund managers, they are not overly concerned about the competition. More are using the fund boom as an opportunity to increase their intermediary service income, acting as custodians and sales agents for the funds. The state Big Four—Bank of China, China Construction Bank, Industrial and Commercial Bank of China, and Agricultural Bank of China—are the main marketing channels for mutual funds. Regional commercial banks also play some role in the market. But their marketing ability could not match that of the Big Four.

Besides banks, securities brokerage firms play an important role in the marketing of securities investment funds. This is because almost every fund management company has a brokerage house as one of its shareholders. They cooperate closely in the sale of securities investment funds. A brokerage house will endeavor to sell funds for its subsidiary securities investment funds.

Recently professional marketing companies for securities investment funds started to appear in China. In 2004, Beijing Tian Xiang Investment consulting obtained a license from Chinese regulators to act as agent for securities investment funds. A similar kind of company was permitted to set up early in 2005 in Shanghai.

Fund management companies also market their own products directly to some institutional investors, such as insurance companies and pensions. See Tables 13.3 and 13.4.

A Profile: China Southern Fund Management Co., Ltd.

In March 1998, with the approval of the China Securities Regulatory Commission (CSRC), the China Southern Fund Management Company (CSFMC),

TABLE 13.3 Summary of Securities Investment Fund Issuance (1998–2004)

Year	Number of funds	Number of open-ended funds	Total units of funds (100 million)	Net value (RMB100 million yuan)	Ratio of net value to market capitalization of tradable shares (%)
1998	5	0	100	104	1.81
1999	22	0	505	575	7.00
2000	34	0	562	847	5.27
2001	51	3	804	809	5.59
2002	71	17	1,319	1,186	9.50
2003	110	56	1,615	1,699	12.90
2004	170	116	3,305	3,308	37

TABLE 13.4 Assets Under Management for the Leading 10 Firms as of December 31, 2004

Rank	Name	Number of funds	Assets under management (billion)
1	China Southern	9	3.5855
2	Huaan	8	2.7426
3	China Asset	11	2.4825
4	Boshi	9	2.4595
5	Harvest	8	1.8611
6	E-fund	8	1.5258
7	China Merchant	5	1.4181
8	Fortis Haitong	2	1.4135
9	Dacheng	9	1.1590
10	Changsheng	9	1.1590

the first regularized fund management company, was officially established, with a registered capital of RMB100 million. Its establishment marks the beginning of China's new fund industry.

In 1998, CSFMC issued the first regularized closed-end equity fund, the Kai Yuan Fund, which started a new era in the fund industry. In September 2001, the company launched its first open-end fund, China Southern Sustaining Growth Fund, leading the domestic fund industry into a new developmental stage. By virtue of its courageous innovations, the fund has been outstanding for years in the fund industry. In September 2002, CSFMC launched

TABLE 13.5   Typical Funds Under Management

Name	Kai Yuan equity fund	Baoyuan bond fund
Type	Closed-end	Open-end
Size	2 billion shares	3,488,938,200 shares (initial inception)

the first open-end bond fund of China, the China Southern Bao Yuan Bond Fund. In December of the same year, CSFMC also came in first in the national appraisal of Social Security fund managers, carving out a new field of development for the company. By 2004, the company was managing four closed-end funds and five open-end funds, and it has more than RMB30 billion assets under management. It is one of the largest fund management companies in terms of assets under management in China. See Table 13.5.

Kai Yuan is a closed-end, contractual fund. Since the company's 1998 establishment, CSFMC has cumulatively distributed over RMB3 billion in dividends to investors. Kai Yuan Fund has achieved a cumulative NAV growth rate of 86.46% over the 5 years between 1998 and 2003 and distributed RMB1.698 billion to its investors at RMB8.49 every 10 shares. On average, the annual compound growth rate of Kai Yuan Fund is 14.85%.

Sino–Foreign Joint Ventures

Foreign fund management companies are vying for a chance to gain access to China's fund industry, lured by the country's 7–8% economic growth and its US$1.3 trillion savings pool. ABN AMRO XIANGCAI was set up in July 2002. It is the first joint venture in the fund management industry.

Currently, however, foreign firms can only access the Mainland market through two channels: buying a stake in an existing fund management company, and forming a new joint venture with an existing financial services entity.

Joint ventures are thus the main vehicle for foreigners to enter China's fund management industry. A foreign partner can now hold up to 33% of a fund management firm. Beginning in 2005, they were expected to be able to raise that stake to a maximum of 49%.

While foreigners expect easy access to funding and distribution channels and quick knowledge of China's capital markets, their partners in China want them to help enhance investment management techniques and expertise soon. Given the vast market potential, foreign firms will continue to extend their reach into Mainland markets. See Table 13.6.

TABLE 13.6   Joint Ventures in the Fund Management Industry
(as of December 31, 2004)

Rank	Name	Date established
1	ABN AMRO XIANGCAI	July 2002
2	Fortune SGAM	January 2003
2	GTJA Allianz	March 2003
3	Fortis Haitong	April 2003
4	Invesco Greatwall	June 2003
5	SYWG BNP Paris	December 2003
6	Everbright Prameria	March 2004
7	China International Fund Management	April 2004
8	BOC International Investment	June 2004
9	Guohai Franklin Templeton	September 2004
10	AIG Huatai	November 2004

13.2.1   LOCATION OF FUND MANAGEMENT COMPANIES

As the largest commercial and financial center of China, Shanghai is the most popular location for securities investment funds. Shanghai has up-to-date infrastructure, various financial institutions, as well as abundant qualified professionals and other advantages. The municipal government of Shanghai is also encouraging, including providing direct subsidies to attract more securities investment funds to relocate to Shanghai. Because of its special geographical location, Shenzhen is the second optimal choice for the investment fund industry. Other Chinese cities are much less attractive for fund management companies. See Table 13.7.

TABLE 13.7   Number of Securities Investment Fund Management Companies by Geographical Location (as of December 31, 2004)

Shanghai	Shenzhen	Beijing	Zhuhai	Tianjin	Chongqing	Nanning	Guangzhou
19	17	3	2	1	1	1	1

13.2.2 RECENT DEVELOPMENTS

Mutual Funds Set Up by Commercial Banks

On February 20, 2004, Chinese regulators agreed to let selected commercial banks set up or acquire fund management companies, widening access to the industry as part of their efforts to promote development of the nation's capital markets. Banks would be allowed to sell stocks, bonds, and money market funds on a trial basis. Allowing banks to enter the fund management industry will bolster profits eroded by a loss of loan business.

The government is also encouraging more institutional capital to flow into the stock market after the Shanghai and Shenzhen composite indexes fell to more than five-year lows in January 2004. The Shanghai benchmark slumped 25% in 2003, while the Shenzhen index was down 30%.

Regulators issued joint rules, effective February 20, 2004, after the State Council, or Cabinet, gave approval in principle in September 2003 for banks to set up fund units. Several banks applied to set up fund companies. Chinese Commercial banks were urged to form fund management ventures with foreign investors to improve the management and efficiency of the new units.

According to the regulations, joint ventures with foreign fund management institutions, domestic insurers, and Social Security fund are especially encouraged. A commercial bank can establish a maximum of two fund management firms.

China's commercial banks were given the opportunity to manage funds only after the June 2004 implementation of a law governing securities brokerages' investment in fund management companies, and the amendment to the country's law on commercial banks, which came into force in February 2004. Prior to that, Chinese commercial banks were prohibited from investing in nonbanking financial sectors. As a result, their revenues were relying too heavily on deposits and loans.

Allowing Chinese commercial banks, with their combined saving deposits of 11 trillion yuan (US$1.33 trillion), to operate a fund management business provides the opportunity for the Chinese central government to deal with the country's low direct financing ratio. The nation's high level of indirect financing poses great risks to the country's banking system, according to the Central Bank's third-quarter monetary report in 2004. The entrance of commercial banks will intensify competition in the fund management sector.

Players

There are currently only two types of players in this sector—domestic fund management firms and joint ventures, in which foreign investors have been able to hold a stake of up to 49% since November 2004. Compared with them, commercial banks generally have the great advantage of a massive customer base across the country, allowing them to provide better access to potential investors. They also enjoy better credibility, which the mass of individual investors views as the most important quality.

However, commercial banks face their own challenges. As newcomers, they should relish the opportunity and establish a good reputation among investors from the very beginning. The most important thing is to give the investors handsome returns. But this is not easy in China's current investment market.

Banks, including the Industrial and Commercial Bank of China (ICBC)—the country's biggest lender—and the China Merchants Bank are lining up to be among the first batch to be approved.

Custody Services

Securities investment funds are held in the custodian's name. There are comprehensive rules on who can instruct the custodian and how money can be transferred between investment managers. As an independent organization, the master custodian plays a critical role in monitoring and safeguarding securities investment funds' assets.

According to the Provisions of the Securities Investment Fund Law of the People's Republic of China, the fund custodian has the following rights and duties.

1. Safeguard the custody assets and maintain the interests of the holders.
2. Supervise whether the investment operation of the custody assets conforms to the provisions of the laws or regulations and the Fund Covenant or the Entrustment Contract.
3. Make fund settlement for the investment operation of the custody assets.
4. Make accounting and assets valuation on the custody assets.
5. Keep account books and physical securities.

As an independent organization, the master custodian plays a critical role in monitoring and safeguarding securities investment funds' assets. On February 24, 1998, after authorization by CSRC and PBC, ICBC became the first custody bank of securities investment funds in China.

Regulators have issued 10 licenses to commercial banks as securities investment funds custodians. According to statistics of CSRC, five banks, including the Big Four and the Bank of Communications, have the largest share in the custodian business market. For example, net assets under the custody of ICBC are over 30% of total assets under the custody of all banks. Small joint-stock commercial banks still have a long way to go in the market.

13.2.3   PENSION FUNDS

China's national Social Security system runs the majority of pension funds. Outside the national foundation, many Social Security funds still belong to local government. Local Social Security funds, which are still banned from the stock market, are mainly used to cover current Social Security expenditures.

The National Council for the Social Security Fund (NCSSF) operates a strategic reserve fund controlled by the central government to support the Social Security demand that will come when the aging population reaches its peak.

The National Council for the Social Security Fund was launched in November 2000. China's National Social Security Fund, which totaled 132.5 billion yuan (US$16 billion) at the end of 2003, is a strategic reserve fund controlled by the central government to support future Social Security demands as the nation's population gets older, while the welfare funds overseen by the Ministry of Labor and Social Security are mainly used to cover *current* Social Security expenditures. Its sources include funds acquired from reducing state shareholding, stock ownership assets, funds from the central budget, funds raised by other means approved by the State Council, and investment returns. See Table 13.8.

The national Social Security fund is administered by the National Social Security Fund Executive Council and is operated on market principles in accordance with the procedures and requirements prescribed by the "Interim

TABLE 13.8   Securities Investment Fund Custodians (as of December 31, 2004)

Rank	Custodian	Number of funds	Shares (billion)	Net assets (billion yuan)
1	Industrial and Commercial Bank of China	40	114.702	112.819
2	China Construction Bank	26	50.413	50.197
3	Agricultural Bank of China	26	40.276	39.192
4	Bank of Communications	28	39.892	39.41
5	Bank of China	26	51.566	50.127
6	China Everbright Bank	5	6.802	6.42
7	China Merchants Bank	6	25.04	24.307
8	Shanghai Pudong Development Bank	4	2.19	2.165
9	China Mingsheng Bank	0	0	0
10	CITIC Industrial Bank	0	0	0

Measures for the Management of the Investment of the National Social Security Fund." The National Social Security fund provides an important financial reserve for the implementation of old-age insurance and other Social Security programs. By the end of 2003, it had accumulated over 130 billion yuan. Nearly one-tenth of China's state assets, which stand at more than 12 trillion yuan (US$1.4 trillion), will be transferred to the insufficiently funded Social Security System within five years.

In 2001, the Chinese government lifted the stock-investment ban on the National Council for the Social Security Fund as a last resort to cover the increasing number of urban people who were retiring. The government set a 40% asset-allocation cap on the amount that the fund could invest in stocks and a 10% cap for bonds.

China's central Social Security fund formally entered the stock market in June 2003 after prolonged debate among fund owners, academics, and market professionals. The fund's capital has been used for the launch of follow-on and rights issues of four listed companies on the domestic A share markets. For the Social Security fund, of paramount concern was a balance between risks and returns. With predictable long-term liabilities, pension funds are not normally invested in high-risk equities. The Social Security fund used to have nearly all its funds in banks and the bond market, with little investment in the stock market. The income could scarcely meet the growing demand for welfare funding. Fund owners said they believe the stock market can garner satisfactory returns for pensioners in the long run.

The council is the administrator of the pension fund, which was worth 130 billion yuan at the end of 2003. In December 2002, the council chose six domestic fund management companies to be fund managers and help it conduct securities investments. It authorized all together 14 billion yuan (US$1.7 billion) worth of assets for the companies. In October 2004, the council added E-fund, China merchants, Guotai and China International Capital to the list of fund managers. According to NCSSF statistics, the foundation reported a 2.71% return rate in 2003, which was higher than the average return rate on Treasury bonds and interest rates of one-year fixed deposits.

Apart from the National Social Security Fund, the new force expected to enter the capital market is the pension funds of personal accounts of individuals covered by the state pension system and the occupational pension, which is paid by enterprises voluntarily for their employees.

The occupational fund, as a supplementary part of the basic pension system and commercial insurance, is the voluntary, private pension system run by some employers. The Ministry of Labor and Social Security released a temporary regulation on occupational pensions, which took effect in May 2004. It said the employers can authorize some qualified institutions to manage the pension and conduct investments. Some parallel rules on the detailed standards of choosing fund managers and principles during such investments have also been approved by insurance, securities, and banking authorities and are expected to come out soon. They will also further clarify requirements on risk control and information disclosure during asset handling, as well as market entry and withdrawal channels, helping build a comprehensive legal framework in the sector.

Occupational pensions first emerged in China in 2000. The scale, limited due to policy obscurity, has been estimated at about 27 billion yuan (US$362.4 million) by 2002. However, it has become a new favorite among securities houses, asset management companies, insurers, and even trust companies in China, all of whom have seen opportunities in the business.

Banks are also enthusiastic to become agents and further develop the business. Shenzhen-based China Merchants Bank, for example, signed a cooperative agreement with American International Group (AIG) in 2005 to jointly develop occupational pension management in China.

Experts have estimated China's occupational pension to expand by 100 billion yuan (US$12 billion) each year when the market mechanism is fully launched and more tax incentives and other policy supports are provided.

13.2.4 INSURANCE COMPANIES

On February 15, 2005, three financial market watchdogs jointly published a set of guidelines to clear the way for insurance companies investing in the domestic stock market.[3] The guidelines, jointly issued by the China Insurance Regulatory Commission (CIRC), the China Securities Regulatory Commission, and the China Banking Regulatory Commission, specified technical details—such as seats at bourses, assets custody, and settlement—for insurance companies' entry into the stock market. The guidelines also apply to foreign insurance companies operating in China. CIRC said in an announcement that issuance of the guidelines is a "substantial breakthrough" for insurance companies investing in shares. Insurance companies investing in the stock market will then enter the stage of practical operation. There are still many unanswered questions, such as which insurers will be the first ones to be approved to trade stocks and when they will do so.

---

[3]See Chapter 12 for details of the insurance sector in China.

Up to 5% of total assets will be allowed to be invested in the stock market. In theory, this means funds worth 59.3 billion yuan (US$7.2 billion) will flow into the stock markets in Shanghai and Shenzhen, worth 3.7 trillion yuan (US$445 billion) at the end of 2004.

The right to trade stocks will mean an important investment instrument for China's underwriters, which are garnering huge premiums but are also facing obligations to their customers that are expected to peak in years ahead. Before the announcement of the rules, insurance companies were only allowed to invest in banking deposits and bonds and invest no more than 15% of their assets in securities investment funds. Nearly half of their 1 trillion yuan (US$120 billion) of total assets at the end of May 2004 ended up in bank deposits, while only 65.2 billion yuan (US$7.9 billion) was invested in securities investment funds, statistics indicated.

The narrow investment scope has impeded the growth of the country's insurance industry, which has expanded by an average 30% since the mid-1980s, and it hampers insurance firms' repayment capacity.

China's life insurance companies face a huge burden of negative-spread policies written in years of high interest rates in the early and mid-1990s, making investment yields crucial to their ability to settle claims.

Let us look at some special cases.

- Huatai Insurance Company of China, Ltd. had directly bought domestic shares, the first investment from US$7.2 billion of insurers' assets set to be pumped into the beleaguered stock markets. Huatai, founded in 1996 with a paid-in capital of 1.33 billion yuan, is partly owned by Bermuda-based property underwriter ACE, Ltd. Huatai became the first Chinese insurer to trade directly on China's domestic stock market by building up some positions. Previously, insurers had to use domestic mutual funds to invest in stocks, driving up costs.
- Rival China Life Insurance Co., Ltd., the country's largest insurer, is expected to enter the market after having obtained trading seats on the Shanghai and Shenzhen bourses.
- Insurers had been given the green light to set up between six and eight asset management companies (AMCs)—vehicles for insurers to trade directly in stocks—by the end of 2005. China Life Asset Management Co., Ltd. secured its exchange trading seats early in 2005. The company is China's largest insurance asset management company and one of the largest institutional investors in China. It had more than 400 billion yuan in assets under management by the end of May 2004. See Table 13.9.

That means the bulk of China's insurance money poised for stock investment will soon enter the markets.

TABLE 13.9 Main Life Insurance
Companies in China

Rank	Company
1	China Life
2	China Ping An Life
3	China Pacific Life
4	AIA
4	New China Life
5	Tai Kang Life
6	Tai Ping Life
7	Manulife-Sinochem Life
8	Allianz-Dazhong Life
9	Min sheng Life
10	AXA-Minmetals Life

13.2.5 QFII SCHEME

On December 1, 2002, the *Provisional Measures on Administration of Domestic Securities Investments of Qualified Foreign Institutional Investors* (QFII) was put in place jointly by the CSRC and the People's Bank of China. Qualified foreign institutional investors are defined in this regulation as overseas fund management institutions, insurance companies, securities companies, and other asset management institutions that have been approved by the China Securities Regulatory Commission (hereinafter referred to as CSRC) to invest in China's securities market and granted investment quota by the State Administration for Foreign Exchange (SAFE). See Table 13.10. The top 10 QFIIs are shown in Table 13.11.

This was the landmark date for rules allowing qualified overseas investors to purchase A shares listed on the Shanghai and Shenzhen stock exchanges. Previously A shares, listed Treasury bonds, listed convertible bonds, and corporate bonds were open only to Chinese Mainland investors.[4] Provisional Measures for the Administration of Domestic Securities Investments of Qualified Foreign Institutional Investors (the provisional measures), unveiled by the CSRC and the People's Bank of China (PBC), supplemented by the Provisional Regulations on Foreign Exchange Administration of Domestic Securities

---

[4]A shares account for most of the Chinese Mainland's free-floating stock market capitalization in more than 1,300 firms. In addition, A shares are often considered more representative of the Mainland's economy than many overseas-listed Chinese firms.

TABLE 13.10   List of QFIIs in China (as of October 31, 2005)

	Name of QFII	License issued	Custodian
1	UBS Limited	05/23/2003	Citibank
2	Nomura Securities Co., Ltd.	05/23/2003	Citibank
3	MorganStanley and Co. International Limited	06/05/2003	HSBC
4	Citigroup Global Markets Limited	06/05/2003	Standard Chartered
5	Goldman, Sachs and Co.	07/04/2003	HSBC
6	Deutsche Bank Aktiengesellschaft	07/03/2003	Citibank
7	The Hong Kong and Shanghai Banking Corporation	08/04/2003	CCB
8	ING Bank N.V.	09/10/2003	Standard Chartered
9	JP Morgan Chase Bank	09/30/2003	HSBC
10	Credit Suisse First Boston (Hong Kong) Limited	10/24/2003	ICBC
11	Standard Chartered Bank (Hong Kong) Limited	12/11/2003	Bank of China
12	Nikko Asset Management Co., Ltd.	12/11/2003	Bank of Communications
13	Merrill Lynch International	04/30/2004	HSBC
14	Hang Seng Bank	05/10/2004	China Construction Bank
15	Daiwa Securities SMBC Co., Ltd.	05/10/2004	ICBC
16	Lehman Brothers International (Europe)	07/06/2004	Agricultural Bank of China
17	Bill and Melinda Gates Foundation	07/19/2004	HSBC
18	INVESCO Asset Management Limited	08/04/2004	Bank of China
19	ABN AMRO Bank N.V.	09/02/2004	HSBC
20	Société Générale	09/02/2004	HSBC
21	Templeton Asset Management, Ltd.	09/14/2004	HSBC
22	Barclays Bank PLC	09/15/2004	Standard Chartered
23	Dresdner Bank Aktiengesellschaft	09/27/2004	ICBC
24	Fortis Bank SA/NV	09/29/2004	Bank of China
25	BNP Paribas	09/29/2004	Agricultural Bank of China
26	Power Corporation of Canada	10/15/2004	China Construction Bank
27	CALYONS. A.	10/15/2004	HSBC
28	Goldman Sachs Asset Management Intl.	—	—
29	Government of Singapore Investment Corporation	—	—
30	Martin Currie Investment Management, Ltd.	—	—

TABLE 13.11   Top 10 QFIIs in China (as of December 31, 2004)

Rank	Name	Quota approved
1	UBS Limited	US$800 million
2	Citigroup Global Markets Limited	US$550 million
3	HSBC	US$400 million
3	MorganStanley and International Limited	US$400 million
3	Deutsche Bank	US$400 million
3	Fortis Bank	US$400 million
4	Credit Suisse First Boston	US$300 million
4	Merrill Lynch International	US$300 million
5	Nikko Asset Management Co., Ltd.	US$250 million
6	Goldman Sachs Asset Management International	US$200 million

Investments of Qualified Foreign Institutional Investors (the provisional regulations), issued by SAFE in November 2002, outlined the framework for the QFII scheme.

South Korea and Taiwan District have implemented similar schemes and benefited a lot. The QFII scheme in China has been designed to improve corporate governance in the market, for domestically listed companies will hopefully be motivated to reorganize themselves so as to attract investments from authorized overseas institutions. Furthermore, the QFII scheme is expected to facilitate the introduction of overseas capital and expertise into China's securities market while minimizing disruptions that might arise from increased capital inflow.

The QFII scheme is a transitional arrangement designed to introduce overseas portfolio investments into China before the renminbi becomes freely convertible. Through the QFII scheme, authorized overseas institutions are permitted to invest in the Chinese Mainland's capital market by opening special renminbi accounts with approved custodians. In addition, for trading purposes, overseas institutions must open securities and renminbi settlement accounts. Through these accounts, qualified investors can receive foreign currencies and convert them to renminbi to invest in China's stock market. There is a limit for a specific period in relation to the amount of foreign capital that can be converted into renminbi, and authorized overseas institutions must appoint domestically registered securities companies to conduct their trades.

Five Chinese Mainland banks—the Bank of China, Industrial and Commercial Bank of China, Agricultural Bank of China, China Construction Bank, and Bank of Communications—and the Shanghai branches of three overseas-invested banks have received approval to be custodians under the QFII scheme. The three banks are HSBC, Citibank, and Standard Chartered Bank.

In the provisional measures, only four kinds of institutions—overseas fund management companies, insurers, securities firms, and commercial banks—are allowed to participate in the QFII scheme. However, pursuant to a CSRC circular issued on March 19, 2003, referred to as the *March Circular*, the net has been widened to encompass overseas trust companies and government investment institutions.

Whereas the provisional measures and regulations allowed qualified investors to participate in the QFII scheme to buy renminbi-denominated A shares and government and corporate bonds, the March circular stipulated that investors could also invest in new share issues, rights issues, additional share issues, convertible bonds, and open- and close-end funds without investment-ratio limitations.

Following the rules relating to the Establishment of Foreign-Funded Securities and Fund Management Companies in China, introduction of the QFII scheme was expected to attract significant interest from global investment companies. On balance, the remittance restrictions and investment limitations outlined previously might prove unattractive to many fund managers, in particular those managing open-end funds. The relative lack of transparency in business and legal affairs on the Chinese Mainland also continues to hamper investor sentiment. The lack of research and credible analysis of A shares, the exclusion from major indices reflecting performance and inconsistency in key aspects of governmental policy in China continue to represent significant challenges.

Since the Provisional Measures on the Administration of Domestic Securities Investments of Qualified Foreign Institutional Investors came into effect, several related rules were also released to help put the measures into practice.

Although the QFII welcomed the opening-up policies of the Chinese capital market after the file was released, only several have made any substantial moves to begin investment.

Essentially, the readiness of qualified institutional investors to enter the capital market is decided by their present investment strategies. Such strategies differ markedly according to where the investors are from. Most institutional investors from Europe prefer to invest in funds. Entering China's capital market as a QFII must be studied and approved by their boards of directors, which will take time.

London-based Barclays Bank is likely to pursue a model it established in South Korea. Under this model, it will cooperate with local partners in developing new financial product derivatives and share the benefits.

U.S. investors, however, usually don't invest or formulate joint ventures with local financial institutions. They prefer to focus on cooperating and controlling projects they like. Many U.S. investment banks have their eyes on purchasing corporate shares in state-owned enterprises.

The Chinese stock market is a small part of the global market investment Japanese companies make, feeling that there are many more opportunities in the U.S. stock market. Japanese investors are still unfamiliar with the A share market in China and need some time to become better acquainted.

Foreign insurance companies who have won licences to run business in China and foreign institutional investors who are planning or have established joint-venture fund management companies and securities houses have little interest in winning QFII status. However, virtually all institutions have said that the filing offers an opportunity for investment and that they are seriously pondering their next step to make good use of the proposal.

Their reluctance may be due to two issues. First, foreign institutional investors lack an in-depth understanding of the listed companies. Rumors about inefficient management, lack of transparency, and false financial statements do not encourage good relations. Therefore few foreign institutions research the A share market. Their impressions are heavily influenced by their judgment concerning the B share market and the H share market in Hong Kong.

The second reason is that most QFIIs did not aggressively invest in the A share market after winning the status because they find it is only an opportunity for investment instead of a chance to garner profits from the investment. Behind the effort of winning QFII status is profit. In managing the assets and wealth for individuals or other investors, their major source of income is fees for such financial management. If they cannot earn revenue higher than the management fees for their customers, they would rather stay away from the market.

In the eyes of QFIIs, the average price/earnings ratio for A share stocks, which stands between 30 and 40, shows that the stocks are already overpriced. There is not much room for the price to go higher, which writes off the possibility of profiting from stock price hikes. Furthermore, the listed companies on the A share market seldom pay out dividends; institutional investors can't make money from holding stocks either.

As a result, QFIIs prefer to watch the developing market and wait for a better chance for profit-making. As of the end of December 2004, 27 overseas financial institutions had obtained QFII licenses with a total investment quota of USD3 billion, and 11 banks (including four overseas banks) had been licensed as the QFIIs' custodians.

According to statistics of the CSRC, as of the end of 2004 QFIIs had allocated 16.2 billion yuan in securities, which accounts for 66% of QFIIs' total assets. QFIIs invested 7.1% billion yuan in A shares, about 44% of their securities assets, 2.2 billion yuan were put into securities investment funds, which accounts for 13% of their securities assets, 3.3 billion yuan were invested in convertible bonds, equal to 20% of their securities assets; 3.7 billion yuan, or 23% of the securities assets, were in the form of government bonds.

By introducing foreign investors into the domestic securities market, the QFII scheme will help round out the investor structure of China's securities market. The regulators also expect that QFIIs will bring in the investment strategies and philosophies of developed financial markets and lead to more effective allocation of resources.

Foreign institutional investors—who were eager to qualify to invest in the Mainland's securities market—are not having as much of an initial impact as anticipated or hoped. The QFIIs, however, are unlikely to use up all their investment quotas immediately, because the pace and volume of investments are directly related to the performance of the securities market as well as the short- to long-term macroeconomic outlook.

A few pioneers have made initial forays into the A share and bond markets, which had earlier been inaccessible to foreigners.

Liquidity is also an important criterion for international funds when picking stocks—the QFIIs' preferences are similar to these of domestic institutions that seek long-term and value-oriented investments, said an official with China Merchants Antai Fund Management.

The broad aim of allowing QFIIs is to intensify value-oriented investment, but they are not exactly breaking new ground, with more and more domestic institutions already moving in the same direction from earlier.

But how much funds will flow in still depends on the performance of the market and the quality of the listed companies.

13.3   TRUST FUNDS

In China, *trust* refers to the act in which the trustor, based on the confidence in the trustee, entrusts certain property rights it owns to the trustee and the trustee manages or disposes of the property rights in its own name in accordance with the intentions of the trustor and for the benefit of the beneficiary or for specific purposes. See Table 13.12 for the top 10 trust companies in China.

China's first trust company was founded in 1979, when the country adopted the reform and opening-up policies. The number of trust companies reached a peak of 1,000 in 1988 but then dropped to 329 in 1999. In fact, Chinese trust companies witnessed rapid growth in the 1990s, but mismanagement and irregularities finally led to a painful industrywide consolidation and the sensational closure of the bankrupt Guangdong International Trust and Investment Company. In 1998, the company, due to irregularities and poor management decisions, was China's largest state-owned enterprise to declare bankruptcy. It lost close to US$2 billion.

TABLE 13.12 Top 10 Trust Companies in China

Rank	Name
1	CITIC Trust and Investment Co., Ltd.
2	Chung Mei Trust and Investment Co., Ltd.
3	Shanghai International Trust and Investment Co., Ltd.
4	Beijing International Trust and Investment Co., Ltd.
5	Fortune Trust and Investment Co., Ltd.
6	China Foreign Economy and Trade Trust and Investment Co., Ltd.
7	Northern International Trust and Investment Co., Ltd.
8	Anhui Guoyuan Trust and Investment Co., Ltd.
9	Zhongtai Trust and Investment Co., Ltd.
10	Shangdong International Trust and Investment Co., Ltd.

As a major part of the consolidation, trust firms were required to boost their capital bases and trim nonperforming assets resulting from their securities business, which they are not allowed to do now.

An overhaul that started in the late 1990s is still taking place in the sector. It has already cut the number of firms from 329 in the industry's heady days to the current figure of 59. Some casualty companies have switched to other businesses, and others have been closed or merged. According to the People's Bank of China, by the end of December 2003, 57 trust companies had completed reregistration with the regulators. They manage 163.5 billion yuan trust assets. In 2003, the net profit of the trust industry was about 1.6 billion yuan.

China's first trust law was put into effect in October 2002, ending the long-standing practice of trust businesses having no legal guarantee for development for 20 years. The law, which covers the rights and duties of trustors and trustees, has led to a series of changes in China's trust businesses. The first trust company to pass the cleanup test was registered in October 2002. With regulatory environment getting warmer as the restructuring deepens, trust companies have gathered pace in launching new projects, many of which are real estate trusts or financial trusts.

China's first trust industry association was set up in 2004 to enhance the development of the once-trouble-laden sector. Establishment of an industry association has long been desired by trust companies. The move is an essential step for China as it nurtures the fledgling industry and helps it to grow on a smooth track.

Because most trust projects in China are currently based on infrastructure and real estate projects, trust companies are seeking greater room for improvement to trust products. The Beijing International Trust and

Investment Co., for example, launched four trusts for public investors in 2004, including a bond investment trust that has an estimated annual return of 4–8%, company sources said. In 2004, Beijing-based China Credit Trust Co., Ltd. also issued three real estate trusts and a bank asset trust to the public and was expected to distribute another 100 million yuan (US$12 million) real estate trust.

The new trust project, with a term of two years and an expected 4.9% annual return for buyers, is expected to raise 100 million yuan (US$12 million) to finance the Flower City real estate project in southwestern Beijing.

Meanwhile, lured by the market potential in China, foreign companies are also heading to the trust business. The State Council is said to be reviewing applications from China National Cereals, Oils and Foodstuffs Import and Export Corporation, one of the biggest trade companies in China, to set up a joint venture trust and an investment company with a trust company in the United States and a financial institution in Hong Kong.

A Profile: Chung Mei Trust and Investment Co.

Chung Mei is a nationwide nonbanking financial institution, set up on November 20, 1995, with a registered capital of 400 million yuan, including 15 million U.S. dollars in foreign currency. The business license covers the following activities.

Trust savings deposit and crediting, trust investment; entrusted savings deposit and crediting; lending and investment of equity capital; securities; leasehold business for financing purposes; proxy; surety and witness business; economic consulting; other financial operations approved by the PBC.

Trust savings deposit and crediting, trust investment in foreign currencies; entrusted savings deposit, crediting, lending, and investment in foreign currencies; interbank borrowing in foreign currencies; borrowing and lending in foreign currencies; investment in foreign currencies; surety in foreign currencies; investigation on credibility; consulting services and witness business.

Since its establishment, Chung Mei has developed steadily and actively, both in an increased scale of assets and a growth of economic return, and had formulated a set of sound and efficient internal management systems. By the end of 2000, the total assets of the company amounted to 5.28 billion RMB yuan and the profit accumulated reached 8.36 million RMB yuan.

In 1999, the company implemented the unified arrangement of the Central Party Committee and the State Council for the disconnection of enterprises from governmental institutions, and it completed the work assets clarification and organizational restructuring.

13.4   PRIVATE FUNDS

Private funds are initiated by an individual or an investment company and are raised privately by a few rich investors. But the purchase and redemption of these private funds is often made through private negotiations. Such funds target investors whose financial needs cannot be satisfied by existing publicly raised funds. Therefore, they are filling the spectrum of the country's fund management industry.

More than 600 billion yuan (US$72.5 billion) of private investment funds is believed to be circulating in securities trading in China, an academic report claims. The paper, released by the Central University of Finance and Economics, is based on investigations into the scale and impact of private investment funds in 10 Chinese cities. Accordingly, such privately raised investment funds produce about 30–35% of the transactions in China's stock market and have become an important force for investors in the bourses.

In Beijing, Shanghai, and Shenzhen, more than 3,600 companies are engaged in the private funds business, according to a report by the People's Bank of China. The report estimated these companies control about 700 billion yuan (US$84.6 billion) of capital. Most of the money is ploughed into the stock market, where the value of all circulating shares is about 1,600 billion yuan (US$193.3 billion).

China's private investment funds have doubled the 300-billion-yuan (US$36.3 billion) size of the country's publicly traded mutual funds, according to their research paper. In 2001, when private investment funds became a hot topic among regulators, the size of these funds was about 100 billion yuan (US$12.1 billion), according to statistics from the People's Bank of China. By the end of 2003, China's privately raised investment funds had increased to about 620 billion yuan (US$75 billion), according to a research paper by Li and his colleagues. But Xia Bin, director of the Research Institute of Finance of the State Council's Development and Research Centre, estimates that the figure has exceeded 700 billion yuan (US$84.6 billion). Private investment fund trading now accounts for about 30% of all trading activities in the country's domestic A share market.

Almost 90% of private fund management companies have been unable to acquire licenses to conduct financial businesses. These private investment funds have often registered as financial consultancy firms or investment consultancy firms without the licenses required to manage funds. Many managers of these private investment funds call themselves market analysts. They use the service of securities analysis as bait to attract clients and then ask them to invest in their privately raised funds, which basically invest in the country's volatile stock market.

13.4.1   CASE STUDY: DE LONG

As a private business, De Long was founded in 1986 in Urumchi, northwest China's Xinjiang Uygur Autonomous Region. In early 2000, De Long was registered in Pudong New Area, Shanghai, with a registered capital of 500 million yuan. After several years of operation, De Long forged a core competency in capital operation and industry consolidation. It grew into a business superempire of 57,700 employees in a total of 177 subsidiaries, including six listed companies in China's A share market.

However, rather than relying on its own abundant cash flow, De Long's usual model of acquiring new firms was to borrow money from banks using the original company as a guarantee. These guarantees made the company vulnerable when facing financial pressure. Complicated capital maneuvers and deep involvement in stock speculation finally led to a breakdown of its funding chain. It is reported that the overall debt may be more than 20 billion yuan.

The conglomerate is on the brink of collapse due to a drain of funds, for in 2004 the government introduced restrictive measures to strengthen its supervision over the stock market and tighten credit lines to ensure healthy economic growth.

China Huarong Asset Management Corp. has made substantial moves to reconstruct De Long. Huarong was set up in 2000 to take over the bulk of delinquent assets from the Industrial and Commercial Bank of China, the country's largest state-owned bank, and has since been resolving such assets. It is the first time that a concrete reshuffling announcement has been made by Huarong about De Long-related firms since the bailout, a rare step by the state to sort out a private firm's affairs. Huarong has been designated to help handle the massive debt and funding problems of De Long, its affiliates, and its subsidiaries. Although it has never revealed the details of the reshuffling, the restructuring methods are supposed to be market-oriented, Huarong sources said. It is hard to predict the exact restructuring trend of the De Long firms by Huarong.

13.5   REGULATIONS

China has segregated regulatory schemes for the banking, securities, and insurance industries. Before, the three were not allowed to interfere in each other's business. The fact that some financial conglomerates that hold independent subsidiaries in banking, insurance, and securities businesses, already exist in China does not mean that the regulatory schemes for the three have been unified. Such subsidiaries, though put under one holding company, are separated from each other's business and supervised by three regulatory bodies and follow different laws and regulations. This is different from the concept that a single entity can do banking, securities, and insurance at the same time and be supervised by the same watchdog.

In a memorandum of work coordination between CBRC, China Securities Regulatory Commission, and China Insurance Regulatory Commission, it is said that the supervision of financial holding companies will be based on the core business of such companies. For example, CIRC will supervise those whose core business is insurance, and CSRC will watch over those focusing on securities. A joint meeting mechanism should be established among the CBRC, the CSRC, and the CIRC.

On December 12, 2001, the CSRC repromulgated the *Measures on the Administration of Stock Exchanges*, setting forth detailed provisions for the founding and dissolution of stock exchanges, functions of stock exchanges, and stock exchanges' responsibility in supervising securities trading, and securities registration and clearinghouses. Specific rules were also put in place regarding the management and supervision of the exchanges themselves.

The *Measures on the Administration of Futures Exchanges*, which defines the functions and responsibilities of futures exchanges, was amended by the CSRC and came into effect on July 1, 2002.

According to the *Securities Law* and *Measures on the Administration of Stock Exchanges*, stock exchanges in China are nonprofit and self-regulating legal entities. The exchanges provide the forum for the centralized trading of securities and enforce applicable laws and regulations. At present, there are two stock exchanges in China: the Shanghai Stock Exchange and the Shenzhen Stock Exchange. Both are supervised by the CSRC.

According to the *Provisional Rules on the Administration of Futures Trading* and the *Measures on the Administration of Futures Exchanges*, futures exchanges in China are self-regulating legal entities that perform functions as stipulated in their articles of association. At present, there are three futures exchanges in China: the Shanghai Futures Exchange (SHFE), Zhengzhou Commodity Exchange (ZCE), and Dalian Commodity Exchange (DCE). All of them are under the CSRC's supervision.

The Securities Law, Securities Investment Funds Law, and Criminal Law expressly provide for the civil, administrative, and criminal liabilities of a party guilty of securities and futures offenses and crimes. These include fraudulent practices, insider dealings, and market manipulations.

A crucial complement to prudential regulation and supervision is regulatory enforcement. Without it, policy and institutional credibility weakens, moral risk grows, and manageable systemic deficiencies fester unchecked, creating the conditions for a crisis. The main challenge in enforcement is to insulate it as much as possible from political interference. Regardless of the mechanism chosen, achieving the outcome of strict regulatory enforcement is critical.

13.5.1 REGULATIONS REGARDING SECURITIES INVESTMENT FUNDS

The Department of Investment Fund Supervision under the CSRC is directly responsible for the supervision of securities investment funds and funds management companies in the securities market. The Department of Investment Fund Supervision was set up in September 1998. It has the following main functions.

1. Formulate rules for the supervision of securities investment funds.
2. Approve the launch of securities investment fund and fund management companies.
3. Supervise the operation of fund management companies.
4. Grant the status of securities investment funds custodian together with other authorities and supervise the funds custody business.
5. Approve and supervise QFIIs.
6. Approve the establishment of representatives or branches of foreign asset management companies.

On October 28, 2003, the Securities Investment Funds Law was adopted in China. The law stipulates the provisions regarding fund managers, custodians, the placement and trading of funds, subscription and redemption of funds, operation of funds, information disclosure, modification and termination of contracts, termination and liquidation of funds, supervision and administration of funds, and legal liabilities.

Previously, the Chinese government had relied on a series of administrative regulations, most notably the *Provisional Measures on the Administration of Securities Investment Funds* promulgated in 1999, to regulate this vibrant business.

The Securities Investment Fund Law applies only to securities investment funds that are publicly offered and sold. Funds established through private placements as well as the business of private wealth management will be regulated under separate rules to be formulated by the State Council pursuant to the basic principles set forth in the Investment Fund Law.

13.6 TYPES OF FUNDS

Securities Investment funds in China are not separate legal persons, but they are created based on contractual relationships among a fund management company, a fund custodian, and investors. The Investment Fund Law focuses specifically on the regulation of fund management companies and fund custodians, the issuance and public trading of fund units, and the protection of investors in funds.

The Investment Fund Law provides for two types of funds: closed-end funds and open-end funds. *Closed-end funds* refer to funds that are divided into a fixed number of units that may be traded but may not be redeemed during the existence of the fund. *Open-end funds* refer to funds that may be purchased and redeemed at any time pursuant to the terms of the fund contract (resulting in a constant fluctuation in the total number of units).

13.6.1   Fund Management Companies and Fund Custodians

Under the Investment Fund Law, only fund management companies approved by China's securities regulatory authority, the CSRC, may establish and manage investment funds. A fund management company must meet certain criteria, including the following.

- The company must have registered capital of renminbi 100 million (approximately US\$12 million) or more.
- The principal shareholder(s) of the company must be in the business of securities management, securities investment consulting, trust asset management, or other financial asset management.
- Each principal shareholder must have registered capital of no less than renminbi 300 million (approximately US\$36 million).

Certain restrictions are imposed on fund management companies to control conflicts of interest. For example, a fund management company must show fairness when managing different funds under its management and may not commingle in the same investment its own assets and the funds under its management.

Commercial banks that are licensed by CSRC may act as *fund custodians*. Fund custodians are responsible for safeguarding fund assets, opening and maintaining bank accounts, executing the investment instructions of fund managers, and handling transaction settlement and clearance. Fund custodians also assume the task of monitoring the investment activities of fund managers. For example, a custodian must refuse to execute a fund manager's investment instructions that violate the law or the terms of a fund contract and must report such instances to the CSRC.

The Investment Fund Law prohibits a fund management company and a fund custodian from owning equity interests in each other.

13.6.2   ESTABLISHMENT AND TRADING OF FUNDS

To establish a fund, a fund management company must apply to the CSRC for approval. If approved, the fund management company may start selling fund units to the public. To achieve a valid public offering for a closed-end fund, the fund management company must sell more than 80% of the total number of the units approved by the CSRC. For an open-end fund, the fund management company must sell more than the minimum number of units (as approved by the CSRC) to a minimum number of buyers (as stipulated by the CSRC). If the public offering meets these requirements, the fund management company must then register the fund with CSRC, on which the fund contract becomes effective. If the public offering fails, however, the fund management company must refund all the money deposited by the subscribers (together with interest) and bear all the costs and expenses incurred in the offering.

Closed-end funds may be publicly listed if certain statutory conditions are satisfied. These conditions include a total offering of no less than renminbi 200 million and a minimum of 1,000 total unit holders. In contrast, liquidity is provided to open-end fund investors through redemption instead of trading. Open-end funds are required to hold an adequate amount of cash and Treasury bonds to meet the redemption requirements of unit holders. It is unclear in the Investment Fund Law whether fund managers of open-end funds may seek short-term financing from commercial banks to meet liquidity demands, but an official at CSRC's legal department told Perkins Coie that such borrowing is prohibited.

13.6.3   RESTRICTIONS, DISCLOSURE, AND SHAREHOLDER PROTECTION

Under the Investment Fund Law, funds may invest only in listed stocks, bonds, and other securities products designated by the CSRC. The Investment Fund Law prohibits the use of fund assets for certain types of investments or business activities, including the following.

- Underwriting securities, extending loans, or buying other funds (except as otherwise provided by the State Council).
- Making equity investments in the management company or custodian of the fund.
- Buying securities issued by a controlling shareholder of the fund management company or of the fund custodian or by other companies that share a material interest with the fund management company or the fund custodian.

- Buying, within the underwriting lockup period, securities underwritten by a controlling shareholder of the fund management company or of the fund custodian or by other companies that share a material interest with the fund management company or the fund custodian.

The public disclosure of information related to funds is also regulated. For example, public disclosures by fund management companies or fund custodians may not contain performance projections or statements guaranteeing returns or compensation for investor losses.

While the main objective of prior legislation was to increase the stability of the securities markets, the Investment Fund Law reflects a stronger emphasis on investor protection. For example, the Investment Fund Law expressly provides fund unit holders with the right to sue fund managers and/or custodians. Fund unit holders also have the authority to determine (by passing a unit holder resolution) certain matters, such as the early termination of fund contracts, the renewal of the term of fund contracts, the increase of compensation to fund managers and/or custodians, and the replacement of fund managers and/or custodians.

The Investment Fund Law is the first of its kind in China and has far-reaching implications for the future of securities investment funds and the fund management business. It also is likely to stir up further excitement within the international fund management community regarding China's fund management market. This market is still in its infancy, but it has a huge potential in view of the roughly renminbi 1 trillion of bank savings in China.

The securities Investment Funds Law went into force on June 1, 2004. In conjunction with the Funds Law, the China Securities Regulatory commission issued a series of measures, including the Measures on Administering the Sale of Securities Investment Funds (the "sale measures"), the Measures on Administering the Operations of Securities Investment Funds (the "operations measures"), and the Measures on Administering Information disclosure on Securities Investment Funds (the "disclosure measures"), all of which went into effect on July 1, 2004. The securities Investment Funds Law, together with the CSRC Measures, will regulate the transactions and players in the securities investment fund industry.

Prior to the securities Investment Funds Law going into effect, the Provisional Measures for the Adminstration of Securities Investment funds ("the 1997 measures"), promulgated by the State Council and effective on November 14, 1997, governed investment funds.

The 1997 measures and the Securities Investment Funds Law overlap in their scope of coverage. Although the Funds Law and the CSRC measures are meant to replace the previous regulator regime under the 1997 measures, they do not expressly repeal the 1997 measures. The Securities Investment Funds

Law will take priority over the 1997 measures should there be any conflict between the two statutes.

The Securities Investment Funds Law still leaves out many important issuers. For example, "securities investment fund" is not defined under the Funds Law. It only describes some of the characteristics of a securities investment fund. The Securities Investment Funds Law only governs public offering of securities investment funds.

13.6.4 PENSION FUNDS

The Ministry of Labor and Social Security and the Ministry of Finance supervise pension funds, while pension funds investment in the securities market is under direct supervision of the CSRC. Different parts of the Social Security fund should follow different management and operational principles. The basic pension, for example, will still be restricted to traditional investment spheres because of its high demand for safety, while other parts of the pension can be more flexible.

On December 13, 2001, the Ministry of Labor and Social Security and the Ministry of Finance jointly issued the "Provisional Measures on the Investments of the National Social Security Fund" (provisional measures).

The provisional measures stipulate the principles of investment, the fund managers and the custodians, etc. According to the provisional measures, the National Social Security Fund can put only 40% into securities investment funds and common stocks. At the same time, it can only invest 10% of its assets in corporate bonds.

The Ministry of Labor and Social Security has also released a temporary regulation on occupational pensions, which took effect in 2004.

Existing rules stipulate that pension fund custodians, including commercial banks and other institutions, must maintain at least 5 billion yuan in assets. They will also further clarify requirements on risk control and information disclosure during asset handling, as well as market entry and withdrawal channels, helping build a comprehensive legal framework in the sector.

13.6.5 INSURANCE COMPANIES

The China Insurance Regulatory Commission is the main regulator for insurance industry. Yet CSRC and CBRC also have regulatory authority over insurance companies with respect to investment activities in their respective fields.

In February 2005, three sets of guidelines were issued for insurance companies' investment activities in the domestic stock market. The first set of guidelines is on general matters. The other two were on practical details in risk control and custody of the underwriters' stock investment assets. These guidelines explicitly define the relationships and responsibilities of insurance asset trustor, trustee, and custodian. Therefore these guidelines completed the regulatory and operational framework for insurers' trading of shares. The insurance assets intended to be invested in the stock market should be under the custody of an independent custodian. To encourage a diversified approach to investing, the guidelines stipulated that an insurance company's investment in a single listed company should not exceed 5% of the insurer's assets available for stock investment.

Insurance companies are required to report to the commission any drastic fluctuations of their stock investment value. Specifically, insurers should report when their losses in stocks decline by 10% or more of the amount they spent to buy the stocks or when their gains exceed 20% of that amount.

Insurance companies are also prevented from controlling too many shares in a single company. The guidelines say that an insurance company is not allowed to control 5% of tradable capital stock of a single listed company.

13.6.6   QFIIs: Regulatory Issues

The CSRC, the People's Bank of China (PBC), and the State Administration for Foreign Exchange (SAFE) are jointly responsible for the supervision of QFIIs. The People's Bank of China is the Central Bank of China. The State Administration for Foreign Exchange, which is under the State Council, deals with affairs on the administration of foreign exchange in China.

CSRC and SAFE supervise and govern the securities-investing activities undertaken by QFIIs within the jurisdiction of China in accordance with the laws. Approvals from the CSRC, the People's Bank of China, and SAFE are required for custodian status.

The "Provisional Measures on Administration of Domestic Securities Investments of Qualified Foreign Institutional Investors (QFII)," which went into effect on December 1, 2002, is the main statute governing qualified foreign institutional investors' investments in China's securities market and promoting developments of China's securities market.

To qualify as an investor under the QFII scheme, the overseas institution must meet certain criteria: It must have a sound financial and credit history, must meet CSRC assets requirements, and must meet risk-control procedures established under the laws and by securities authorities in its home jurisdiction.

The asset requirements are as follows.

- Overseas fund managers must have a minimum of five years' experience in operating funds and must be managing not less than US$10 billion in assets in the most recent accounting year.
- Insurance companies and securities companies must have at least 30 years of experience, a minimum paid-up capital of US$1 billion, and securities of not less than US$10 billion under management in the most recent accounting year.
- Commercial banks must be ranked among the world's top 100 in terms of assets, and they, for the most recent accounting year, must be managing at least US$10 billion.

The applicant's employees must meet professional-qualification requirements in the applicant's home jurisdiction. The applicant must have a sound management structure and internal control system and should conduct business in accordance with relevant regulations. The applicant should not have received any substantial penalties in its home jurisdiction in the three years prior to its application.

The applicant's home jurisdiction should have sound legal and regulatory systems. Securities regulators in the applicant's home country or region must also have signed a memorandum of understanding with CSRC officials and have maintained an efficient regulatory and cooperative relationship. There are other criteria as stipulated by the CSRC based on prudent regulatory principles.

Interested overseas institutions must apply to the CSRC for a securities investment license. They must also apply to SAFE for an investment quota. The application procedure is a two-step process. The CSRC will issue a securities investment license if it is satisfied with the overseas institution's application. Upon receipt of the securities investment license, the overseas institution must submit relevant documents to SAFE to receive an investment quota. The securities investment license becomes invalid if the overseas institution fails to apply for the quota within a year of receiving the license. Under the provisional measures, the CSRC is obliged to decide within 15 working days of receiving an application if the overseas institution is approved. However, please note that the time begins only when the CSRC has acknowledged receipt of all requisite documents.

Within three months after receiving a securities investment license from the CSRC, the QFII should remit principals from outside into China and directly transfer them into RMB special accounts after full settlement of foreign exchange. The currency of the principals from the QFII should be exchangeable currency approved by SAFE, and the amount of the principal should not exceed the approved quota.

If the QFII has not fully remitted the principals within three months after receiving a foreign exchange registration certificate, the actual amount remitted will be deemed as the approved quota; thereafter the difference between the approved quota and the actual amount shall not be remitted inward prior to the obtaining of a newly approved investment quota.

The following are key limitations and restrictions for the QFII scheme: The provisional measures are subject to the "Foreign Investment Industrial Guidance Catalogue," and investments are restricted to the permitted ratio of overseas investments applicable to different industries; qualified investors are allowed to acquire up to 10% of the total stocks in a listed firm, and the total shareholding in a listed company by all qualified investors cannot exceed 20%; capital in the special renminbi account must not be used for lending or to provide security; the provisional regulations set the investment floor at US$50 million for each applicant and capped the amount at US$800 million; and fund remittance restrictions, subject to SAFE's approval, are particularly onerous.

SAFE requires that:

- Closed-end Chinese fund management companies can remit in installments their investment principal after three years. Such remittances cannot exceed 20% of the investment principal each time. Also, there should be at least a one-month interval between remittances.
- Other institutions will be subject to a one-year lockup period for remitting their investment principal. Remittances must be made in installments, every three months or more, of not more than 20% of the investment principal.

Remittances of investment principal can be made only to qualified investors. There are, however, no provisions relating to the requirements and approval procedures for remittances of investment proceeds. Such remittances can, therefore, be subject to tighter SAFE control if an imbalance emerges in the state's foreign exchange.

In addition to the restrictions outlined, fund managers should note the ongoing compliance requirements and tax considerations arising from the QFII scheme. In particular, should the qualified investor change its name or merge with another institution, it will have to reapply for a securities investment license. It remains to be seen whether there will be tax levied in China on the investment proceeds received by fund managers.

QFIIs may mandate domestically registered securities companies to manage their domestic securities investments. Each QFII can only mandate one investment institution. For domestic securities investments, the QFII should observe the following requirements: Shares held by each QFII in one listed company should not exceed 10% of total outstanding shares of the company;

total shares held by all QFIIs in one listed company should not exceed 20% of total outstanding shares of the company.

There are also some requirements for commercial banks to become custodians of QFIIs. A custodian should meet the following requirements:

- Have a specific fund custody department.
- Have paid-in capital of no less than RMB8 billion.
- Have a sufficient number of professionals who are familiar with the custody business.
- Be able to manage the entire assets of the fund safely.
- Have qualifications to conduct foreign exchange and RMB business.
- Show no material breach of foreign exchange regulations for the previous three years.

Domestic branches of foreign-invested commercial banks with more than three years of continual operation are eligible to apply for the custodian qualification. Their paid-in capital eligibility shall be based on their overseas headquarters' capital. A custodian should strictly separate its own assets from those under its custody. A custodian should set up different accounts for different QFIIs and manage those accounts separately. Each QFII can mandate only one custodian.

CSRC and SAFE annually review QFIIs' Securities Investment License and Foreign Exchange Registration Certificate. The CSRC, PBC, and SAFE may require QFIIs, custodians, securities companies, stock exchanges, and securities registration and settlement institutions to provide information on the QFIIs' domestic investment activities, and may conduct on-site inspections if necessary.

The following three articles in the provisional measures are particularly important.

Article 34: "In the event of any of the following, the QFII should file with the CSRC, PBC, and SAFE in five working days":

1. Change of custodians.
2. Change of legal representatives.
3. Change of controlling shareholders.
4. Adjustment of registered capital.
5. Litigation and other material events.
6. Imposition of substantial penalties overseas.
7. Other circumstances as stipulated by the CSRC and SAFE.

Article 35: "In the event of any of the followings, the QFII should reapply for its securities investment license":

1. Change of business name.
2. Whether acquired by or merged with other institution(s).
3. Other circumstances as stipulated by the CSRC and SAFE.

Article 36: "In the event of any of the following, the QFII should surrender its securities investment license and foreign exchange registration certificate to the CSRC and SAFE, respectively":

1. Repatriation of all its principals.
2. Transfer of its investment quota.
3. Dispersion of authorized entities, entering into bankruptcy procedures, or assets being taken over by receivers.
4. Other circumstances as stipulated by the CSRC and SAFE.

If QFIIs fail to pass the annual review of securities investment licenses and foreign exchange registration certificates, the licenses/certificates will automatically be invalid. And the QFIIs should return these licenses/certificates as required. In accordance with their respective authorities, the CSRC, PBC, and SAFE will give warnings or penalties to QFIIs, custodians, and securities companies, etc., who violate this regulation.

13.6.7 TRUST FUNDS

In March 2003, the National People's Congress approved the Decision on Reform of the Organizational Structure of the State Council, separating the supervisory responsibilities of the PBC for banking institutions, asset management companies, trust and investment companies, and other depository financial institutions. Instead, the CBRC was established to supervise the related institutions.

The Nonbank Financial Institutions Supervision Department under the CBRC is directly responsible for the supervision of trust funds. China's first trust law, adopted by the National People's Congress, the country's top legislature, in April 2002, took effect on October 1 of that year.

The law, which covers the rights and duties of trustors and trustees, has led to a series of changes in China's trust business. This law was formulated to regulate the trust relationship, normalize trust acts, protect the lawful rights and interests of the parties to a trust, and promote the healthy development of the trust business. *Trust* in this law refers to the act in which the trustor, on the basis of confidence on the trustee, entrusts certain property rights it owns to the trustee and the trustee manages or disposes of the property rights in its own name in accordance with the intentions of the trustor and for the benefit of the beneficiary or for specific purposes. This law applies to the trustor, trustee, and beneficiary (hereinafter referred to in general as parties to a trust) conducting civil, business, or public trust activities within the boundaries of the People's Republic of China.

Supervision on trust companies focuses on the establishment and implementation of trust contracts. According to regulations, trust companies are not allowed to float bonds or advertise themselves through newspapers, television, radios, or other public media. On one hand, the sector does not yet have a set of detailed rules and regulations. There are, for example, no law of trustees and no specific rules and regulations governing the responsibilities of trustees.

Further, the investment activities of trust funds must be subject to the other laws in the specific sector. For example, the CSRC will supervise its trading activities in the securities market, and relevant laws, such as the Securities Law, shall govern the investment activities.

13.6.8   REGULATORY ISSUES RELATED TO PRIVATE FUNDS

The business of private funds is similar to trust asset management. They accept capital from clients, invest, and then pay clients promised returns. One unique aspect is that private funds often have a high threshold for the amount of client capital, which rules out the vast army of small investors. Such a limited scope of customers exempts them from obligations to disclose information to the public.

Not many people in China have a clear idea about private funds, primarily because these funds serve specific patrons only and also because they are underground and not legalized yet. However, the clout of private funds in the stock market has become so powerful that the country's legislators are considering letting them surface.

Some experts argue that private funds should be brought to light and in line with the law. Chinese law does not explicitly allow individuals or unlicensed institutions to launch private funds, but with a growing number of rich people collecting a large amount of idle funds and limited legal investment channels, such funds have become popular, especially in the southern and coastal regions.

Because there are no clear rules to govern them so far, private funds tend to manipulate share prices to secure the hefty profits they promised customers. By maneuvering the astronomical amounts of money they hold, they could make the atmosphere in the market more speculative. Moreover, the legal vacuum on private funds has brought great risks to principals.

Private investment funds may be required to disclose the details of their investment portfolios to improve the industry's transparency and to protect investors' interests. Such funds may be forbidden from seeking bank loans or attracting individuals unable to deal with the risks.

The fast-growing private investment fund industry has become a potential source of instability for the country's financial sector and caused difficulty for regulators. Since 2003, some of them have launched investment projects to a limited group of clients via the network of banks, with similar structure and features to private funds. But because such products prevailed in the country, regulators also sensed the risk—some companies exaggerated the returns of the projects to attract more customers and ignored potential risks. The banking and securities watchdogs therefore banned these products early in 2004, drafting regulations to set up standards in the business before reopening the gate. A high threshold would be set up for market entry to launch such investment products to avoid risks.

13.7 PROBLEMS AND FUTURE TRENDS

The majority of investment fund management companies are state-owned enterprises. The flaws of ownership for state-owned enterprises may hinder the healthy development of the fund industry. The operational model of many investment companies is still not market-oriented. Private capital and foreign investors should be encouraged to play a more important role in the fund management industry. Fair competition in the market economy should also be encouraged.

Corporate governance and supervision also face problems. Poor corporate governance and lack of strict regulation may lead to moral risk. The most noticeable problem is that the fundholders' interests could not be fully protected. Further, fund managers' remuneration lacks a direct connection with the performance of funds. When internal control is fragile and information disclosure is insufficient, conditions are ripe for insider trading, price manipulation, and other fraud.

Regulators are often caught in a dilemma between the desire to crack down on irregularities and the wish to save the businesses with more policy support.

In 2001, the CSRC said eight of China's 10 fund management firms had engaged in abnormal trading activities, and more than 30 senior fund management personnel were sacked, demoted, or fined following the investigation. Chinese regulators have been cracking down on market irregularities, launching a widespread probe into brokerages, banks, and other institutions as well as fund management companies since then.

Cultivating a credit culture and a competitive environment is also crucial for business' healthy and sustainable development and helps to rebuild investor confidence, dampened by a slew of scandals and irregularities. Meanwhile, it is also urgent for regulators to upgrade the regulatory framework and strengthen supervision on the investment management business and relative information disclosure requirements.

A competitive storm is brewing in China's fund management sector, which could mean the end of the road for some unqualified players. The entry of new players to this sector will accelerate product innovations and the improvement of both the service and reputation of the existing fund management firms. And increased competition in terms of sales and trading from commercial banks running fund management companies means that some poor-performing securities brokerages could also go to the wall.

13.7.1 CONCLUSIONS: FUTURE OF INVESTMENT FUNDS IN CHINA

With the gradual phase-in of China's WTO commitments, China's domestic fund management industry may be among the first sectors to reflect these changes. Under the WTO agreement, China has agreed to allow foreign companies to form joint ventures with Chinese brokerage firms for the purposes of money management with immediate effect and in three years for the purposes of securities. China, with its long-term goal of forging sound and efficient capital markets, will eventually have to liberalize its capital accounts.

The Chinese government formulated a nine-point strategy early in 2004 to create a better environment for the healthy and smooth development of the securities market. The policy, issued by the State Council, is aimed at reforming and expanding China's capital market. Industry insiders are hailing the announcement as a milestone in the industry's development.

Commodity Funds

Chinese futures companies, which number around 200 or so, serve primarily as agents and are not involved in broader business dealings. Stock and fund brokerages cannot currently participate in futures transactions. The current rules of China do not permit the public IPO of commodity funds.

Up to now, individual investors have dominated futures trading. According to statistics from the CSRC, 80% or more of investors' initial margin is below 3 million yuan. As a result, the future becomes more volatile and unstable. Therefore, it is of practical importance to develop institutional investors such as commodity funds.

In 2004, the CSRC permitted three futures brokerage firms to operate managed futures business as an experiment in setting up commodity funds in the future. There are unimaginable spaces for the development of commodity funds.

Qualified Domestic Institutional Investor (QDII) Schemes

Domestic institutional investors will also be allowed to invest in the overseas capital market in the future. A system regarding qualified domestic institutional investors (QDIIs) is under study. QDIIs will be allowed to penetrate the international capital market when conditions are mature. As a first step, the CIRC promulgated a regulation in August 2004 allowing Chinese insurers with total assets of no less than 5 billion yuan (US$600 million) to invest up to 80% of their forex funds in overseas capital markets, mainly bonds and other money market instruments. The CIRC signed an agreement on regulatory cooperation with Hong Kong's insurance authorities in November 2004, which covers information sharing and exchange of visits by senior officials.

Other qualified institutional investors will gradually be permitted to invest overseas.

Hedge Funds in China

Hedge funds are fast becoming one of the most exciting asset classes in Western markets. The industry is attracting more interest and is growing in size.

The figures in hedge funds look very healthy, and the prospects are boundless. It is estimated that there are now more than 8,000 hedge funds worldwide with AUM (assets under management) of more than US$800 billion. According to a hedge fund industry group, Hedge Fund Research Inc., the industry pulled in the remarkable figure of US$22.2 billion in the first quarter of 2004 alone.

However, there are still some concerns among major market players in Asia. For China investment funds industry, hedge funds are still mysterious. In most cases, investors in China are not fully aware of the well-known and well-respected hedge funds based abroad, since hedge funds lack a large global presence.

Some pioneers have done a lot of hard work to follow the road of foreign hedge funds. In early 2004, a hedge fund named Shanghai Hedge Investment was set up. Shanghai Hedge is primarily an arbitrage fund. Another hedge fund, named Golden China Asset (GCA), was launched in March 2005. In the future, there will be more and more market players in the hedge funds industry.

13.8   CONCLUSIONS

Emerging China is changing the face of global economics and politics. As the economy of China booms, there is increasing demand for diversified investment instruments and vehicles. The large savings pool in China still leaves room for fund managers to come up with more diversified investment products to meet the growing demand.

Within decades, China's investment funds industry has experienced almost what its foreign counterparts encountered since the appearance of the investment funds industry in the world. Although it is still in its infancy in China, it has great potential for the future. The industry will embrace the investments from the private sector and from overseas.

With a series of reform plans adopted by regulators, supervision systems have been undergoing a reshuffle. The watchdogs will stick to their position as referees to ensure order and fairness during the competition.

The market will go forward on a healthy track in the future. China will benefit from cooperation with market leaders such as the United States and the United Kingdom. Foreign investors will bring advanced mechanisms and market-oriented products to China. Chinese investment funds will also play a more important role in overseas financial markets.

REFERENCES

China Banking Regulatory Commission: www.cbrc.gov.cn.

China Insurance Regulatory Commission: www.circ.gov.cn.

China Securities Regulatory Commission: www.csrc.gov.cn.

China Securities Depository and Cleaning Corporation Limited: www.chinaclear.com.

Green, S. (2003). *China's Stock Market: A Guide to Its Progress, Players and Prospects.* London: Profile Books and the Economists.

Liu Xinhua. (2003). The 2002 Funds Market: A Review and Consideration of Prospects. Working Paper, Taiyang Securities Company.

Ministry of Labor and Social Security, P.R. China: www.molss.gov.cn.

Shanghai Stock Exchange: www.sse.com.cn.

Shenzhen Stock Exchange: www.sse.org.cn.

Xiabin. (2001). *Report on China's Privately-Raised Funds*, Caijing.

Zhao Tao and Phil Malone. (2003). Closed-End Funds and Market-Efficient Hypothesis: Evidence from the Chinese Stock Markets, Working Paper, University of Mississippi.

LIST OF FIGURES

LIST OF TABLES

Index